EGO PSYCHOLOGY AND MENTAL DISORDER:
A Developmental Approach to Psychopathology

Other books by Dr. Ausubel

Ego Development and the Personality Disorders, 1952

The Psychology of Meaningful Verbal Learning:
An Introduction to School Learning, 1963

Theory and Problems of Child Development, 2nd edition
with Edmund V. Sullivan, 1970

Theory and Problems of Adolescent Development, 2nd edition,
in press

EGO PSYCHOLOGY AND MENTAL DISORDER:
A Developmental Approach to Psychopathology

David P. Ausubel, M.D., Ph.D.
Graduate School and University Center
The City University of New York;
Bronx Psychiatric Center
The Albert Einstein College of Medicine
Yeshiva University
Bronx, New York

Daniel Kirk, Ph.D.
Marist College
Poughkeepsie, New York

GRUNE & STRATTON
A Subsidiary of Harcourt Brace Jovanovich, Publishers
New York San Francisco London

Library of Congress Cataloging in Publication Data

Ausubel, David Paul.
  Ego psychology and mental disorder.

  Bibliography: p. 299
  Includes index.
  1. Psychology, Pathological.   2.   Ego (Psychology)
3.   Developmental psychology.   I.   Kirk, Daniel, joint
author.   II.   Title.
RC454.A9   616.8'9'07   77-2323
ISBN 0-8089-1004-3

Grune & Stratton, Inc.
111 Fifth Avenue
New York, New York 10003

Distributed in the United Kingdom by
Academic Press, Inc. (London) Ltd.
24/28 Oval Road, London NW 1

Library of Congress Catalog Number 77-2323
International Standard Book Number 0-8089-1004-3
Printed in the United States of America

to Carl Leff
uncle, friend, and counselor,
and
Elizabeth Kirk
with affection

CONTENTS

PREFACE

It is now 25 years since the senior author's *Ego Development and the Personality Disorders* first appeared. This book was intended as a comprehensive, non-psychoanalytic, developmental theory of mental disorder—as a naturalistic, non-instinctual theory derived from clinical experience, but congruent with available empirical evidence—psychiatric, psychological, and ethnological. At that time psychoanalysis was at its zenith of power and influence in the fields of psychiatry, clinical psychology, social work, ethnology, literature, and law. The book was thus greeted with dismay and incredulity. It seemed to make little difference that the notion of instinctual drives at the human, or even the primate level, had lost complete credibility in the scientific world,* that doctrines of preformed ideas had been completely demolished by John Locke the famous English philosopher of the seventeenth century, and that preformed and predetermined sequences of development had fallen completely into disfavor in genetics and embryology. Instead, this attempt to make personality and psychiatric theory compatible with advances in philosophy, biology, and developmental psychology was dismissed as presumptuous heresy, and either totally ignored or roundly condemned in psychiatric and psychological journals.

In the intervening 25 years, the *Zeitgeist* has changed. Disillusionment with psychoanalytic theory is now widespread—not only in the mental health professions but also in related social sciences, in the arts, and among informed intellectuals. This disillusionment has gone beyond the relatively minor doctrinal changes introduced by the neo-analysts and by psychoanalytic ego psychologists. The very basic tenets of psychoanalysis itself—the prepotency of the unconscious; the theory of psychosexual and character development; the doctrines of "infantile sexuality" and of libidinal and aggressive drives; the principle of sublimation; the theory of topographical layers of the mind; the extreme view of psychological determinism and moral unaccountability—that *Ego Development and the Personality Disorders* challenged in 1952 have been, since then, widely called into question. Many persons have even argued that psychoanalysis itself is little more than a dogmatic, unparsimonious, and ethnocentric mythology, based largely on unreliable retrospective childhood memories of a very biased sample of neurotic upper-middle-class individuals from a dying empire in Western culture and extrapolated unwarrantedly to normal persons in all cultures. Almost without excep-

---

*See Beach and Jaynes, 1954; and Ford and Beach, 1951.

tion, every adequately controlled empirical test of Freudian hypotheses of character structure and of the personality disorders, both cross-culturally and intraculturally, has yielded negative findings. (See studies cited in this book, particularly chapter 3 and 4.)

The time is thus ripe for re-introducing into the profession the same ideas that were rejected 25 years ago without a reasonably fair hearing. This time the senior author has also had the advantage of having used this framework successfully in interpreting the mental disorders of his patients in the intervening years and thus has more subjective confidence in the plausibility, validity, and explanatory power of this theory of ego psychology in the field of mental health.

This book differs from its predecessor in giving a highly telescoped account of ego development; in introducing such new topics as ego development among minority groups in our own and other cultures; and in treating middle-class delinquency. By dividing responsibility for the writing of this book, the senior author was able to focus on the theoretical aspects of ego psychology and on clinical psychiatry, while the junior author was able to provide many valuable insights from the standpoint of community psychology and personality theory.

In our opinion, one of the major difficulties with psychoanalysis is that its theorists and practitioners tend to confuse illustration with evidence. When they find their interpretation of a case challenged, they simply cite another one to "prove" the point. Untrained in psychological research methods, they fail to realize that a single case study can never support *any* theoretical system. Instead, definitive evidence in the behavioral sciences—as distinguished from useful illustration—requires a representative sample, an adequate control group or a multivariate research design, tests of statistical significance, and a research design that minimizes alternative interpretations of the data.

In contrast to psychoanalytic theorists, we have relied in this book on naturalistic data gathered from scientific, observational, experimental, and clinical studies employing suitable controls that focus on significant interpersonal variables in the individual's life experience (parents, siblings, spouse, peers, social class factors, cultural values, school, vocation, etc.). We have rejected completely all doctrines that hold human behavior to be sublimated from innate libidinal or aggressive drives or triggered by preformed or predetermined ideas. We view all ideas, drives, and reaction patterns as learned or as the products of experience. We thus see different drives as arising autonomously and continuously throughout the life cycle, as genic predispositions to various forms of activity that are sampled and found rewarding. We do not believe that all major aspects of personality development are virtually completed by the age of seven or that the major determinants of character structure are parental child-rearing practices that impinge on a phylogenetically predetermined sequence of psychosexual development.

In our view, the critical factors predisposing persons to various mental and emotional disorders are distortions that arise during critical periods of ego development. This does not mean that these factors alone are determinative, but rather that they interact with genic temperamental and coping predispositions, the individual's degree of exposure to stress, and his adaptive resources, as well as various genically determined defects in the neuroanatomical and neurophysiological substrates of behavior and personality. As in all complex behavioral and social phenomena, mental disorder is a function of multiple causality. We choose to classify mental disorders in accordance with their developmental determinants solely because we believe that such a classification has greater explanatory power than any other nosological scheme—both for therapist and patient.

Although we believe a coherent, non-eclectic theory is more helpful in understanding and treating patients in clinical psychiatry than a hodgepodge of unintegrated and often contradictory theoretical positions, we feel that therapy should be eclectic. In the first place, in the present state of the art, we cannot afford to overlook any therapeutic tool that is effective even if there is ignorance or disagreement as to why or how it works. Second, therapeutic tools that are effective may be so for reasons quite different from those advanced by their originators.

This book is intended as a text and reference work in psychiatry and abnormal psychology for professional psychiatrists, psychologists, social workers, and psychiatric nurses, as well as for students of medicine, psychiatry, school, community and clinical psychology, and nursing. It does not purport to be a *complete* textbook in clinical psychiatry; too much space is devoted to theoretical issues to describe in sufficient *detail all* the clinical syndromes discussed in descriptive textbooks of psychiatry (e.g., Klein & Davis 1969). Instead, it is addressed to practitioners and students who desire a coherent, non-eclectic, explanatory theory of abnormal psychology and psychiatry that is related to most of the relevant empirical psychiatric, psychological, and ethnological evidence; and who desire to know how this theory is dynamically and organically related in a general way to the phenomenology of the *principal* mental disorders. The phenomenology of these disorders is not presented in great detail and little attention is given to differential diagnosis or specific aspects of therapy.

Appreciation is expressed to Grune & Stratton, the publishers of the senior author's *Ego Development and the Personality Disorders* (1952); *Theory and Problems of Adolescent Development* (1954; 2nd edition in press); and *Theory and Problems of Child Development* (1958; 2nd edition 1970 with E. V. Sullivan; 3rd edition in press, with E. V. Sullivan and S. W. Ives) for permission to use excerpts from these works; to the Journal Press for permission to use excerpts from Ausubel's "Introduction to a threshold concept of primary drives" (*Journal of General Psychology,* 1956); to Holt, Rinehart and Winston, for permission to quote from Ausubel's *Maori Youth* (1965); to Random House, for permission to quote from Ausubel's *Drug addiction: Physiological, Psychological, and Sociological Aspects* (1958; 2nd edition, 1977); to the American Psychological Association for permission to use excerpts from Ausubel's "Relationships between Shame and Guilt in the Socializing Process" *(Psychological Review,* 1955), "Qualitative characteristics in the learning process associated with anxiety" (with H̄. Schiff & M. Goldman) *(Journal of Abnormal and Social Psychology,* 1953), "Relationships between psychology and psychiatry: The hidden issues" *(American Psychologist,* 1956), and "Personality disorder *is* disease" *(American Psychologist,* 1961); to the *Psychiatric Quarterly* to permit the use of excerpts from "Some comments on the nature, diagnosis, and prognosis of neurotic anxiety" (1956); to the *Catholic Educational Review* for permission to quote extensive sections from Ausubel's "Psychological factors in juvenile delinquency" (1966); to Teacher's College Press for permission to quote from D. P. Ausubel and Pearl Ausubel, "Research on ego development among segregated Negro Children" in A. H. Passow (ed.), *Education in Depressed Areas* (1963); and to the University of Toronto Press for permission to use excerpts from "Psychology's undervaluation of cognitive aspect of moral behavior", in C. Beck et al. (eds.), *Moral Education: Interdisciplinary Approaches* (1972).

We are also indebted to Pearl Ausubel for critical reading of the manuscript and for many helpful suggestions for its improvement.

DPA
DK

New York City and Poughkeepsie, N.Y.
January 1977

EGO PSYCHOLOGY AND MENTAL DISORDER:
A Developmental Approach to Psychopathology

1

Approaches to Psychopathology and Ego Psychology*

GENERAL APPROACHES TO PSYCHOPATHOLOGY

Biological

In reviewing the evidence on schizophrenia, Zubin (1975) concludes that with but few exceptions we are still ignorant about the cause of mental disorder. One such exception is general paresis, a psychosis characterized by a cerebral lesion that is caused by syphilitic infection. Despite the relative rarity of such discoveries researchers continue to attempt to localize neurological defects or mechanisms (anatomic or physiological) underlying psycho-physiological dysfunctioning to explain behavior disorders. Nevertheless, even though this type of reasoning plausibly accounts for the psychological symptoms found in *general paresis,* various toxic deleria, and other comparable conditions, it is an extremely improbable explanation of *all* instances of personality disorder. Unlike the tissues of any other organ, brain tissue possesses the unique property of making possible awareness of and adjustment to the world of sensory, social, and symbolic stimulation. Hence by virtue of this unique relationship of the nervous system to the environment, diseases of behavior and personality may reflect abnormalities in personal and social adjustment, quite apart from any structural or metabolic disturbance in the underlying neural substrate. We would conclude, therefore, that although brain pathology is probably not the most important cause of behavior disorder, it is undoubtedly responsible for the incidence of *some* psychological abnormalities *as well as* for various neurological signs and symptoms.

An adrenal cortex deficiency has been hypothesized as the cause of inadequate response to stress. Selye's (1952) analysis of the stress reaction led to the formulation of a general adaptation syndrome. Current hypotheses concerning a

*Reference notes for this chapter are on page 331.

biological basis for the affective disorders suggest that depression and mania are associated with altered availability of brain amines at functionally important receptor sites. A bright future for the catecholamine hypothesis is pictured by Schildkraut when he says "some if not all depressions are associated with an absolute or relative deficiency of catecholamines"[1] (Schildkraut, 1965, p.509).

There are several features of the affective disorders that would appear to support a biological etiology. For example, accompanying severe depression are various somatic symptoms: sleep disturbance, appetite loss, gastrointestinal dysfunctioning, fatigue, and diminished sex drive. Also the diurnal pattern of depression (worst in the morning and gradually improving over the rest of the day) suggests metabolic or endocrine dysfunction. The onset of depression is often marked by the absence of any apparent external stress thereby suggesting endogenous factors. Reviews of brain amine studies, (e.g., Shopsin, et al., 1974) have not yet confirmed Schildkraut's optimistic expectations.[2]

A single exclusive biological etiology, for example, brain amines, ignores the complexity both within and between organic structures and psychological functioning. Even in organic psychoses, psychological factors are involved in determining incidence and symptomatology so that biological and psychological causes cannot be viewed as mutually exclusive. An intact neuroanatomical and neurophysiological substrate is no guarantee against the occurrence of a behavior disorder on purely psychological grounds. Conversely, the therapeutic effects of physical treatment modalities, for example, electro-convulsive shock or chemotherapy do not exclude the presence and potency of psychogenic factors. If disruption of the neurophysiological or neuroanatomical substrate can induce behavioral symptoms, it is plausible to suppose that amelioration of the same damaged substrate can improve symptoms of solely psychological origin. Lastly, it is quite conceivable that reduced brain amine levels and inadequate response to stress are either effects rather than causes of depression or else are merely mediating factors. The cyclic and recurrent nature of depression can be equally and as plausibly explained in terms of persistent personality dispositions, unresolved problems, or repeated instances of excessive stress.

Environmental Stress

Another approach to psychopathology is to consider the incidence and prevalence of behavior disorders between and within cultures. Using symptoms as the index of psychopathology, Ihsan (1970) reviewed and summarized findings on behavioral disorders in non-Western cultures. Anthropologists in the 1930s, for example, claimed that schizophrenia was non-existent among certain culturally isolated peoples in Brazil, Africa, and India. These reports led to a cultural theory about the causation of schizophrenia in terms of Western influence. For example, Devereux (1934) hypothesized that schizophrenia may be the result of increasing cultural complexity that leads people to become disoriented and confused about their social roles. The review of more recent studies makes it evident that not only schizophrenia but also manic-depressive psychoses, psychoneuroses, and psychosomatic disorders are found universally as well (Costello, 1970). Goldhammer and Marshall (1953), who found no difference in mental hospital admission rates in this country before and after 1900, helped to discredit the cultural complexity hypotheses of psychopathology.

Studies of social causation theory, which have been reviewed by Dohrewend and Dohrewend (1969), have also emphasized intracultural class differences. A consistent finding has been that behavioral disorders (particularly schizophrenia) occur more often and are more severe among the lowest socio-economic group as compared with the higher socio-economic classes (Hollingshead & Redlich, 1958, Srole, et al., 1962). The sociological explanation for the inverse relationship between the incidence of psychological disorders and social-class status is that excessive stress inheres in eking out a daily existence. A current situational approach is the study of life events, for example, bereavement, divorce, loss of employment, etc. as the causes of behavior disorders.

The external environment, like the internal environment, if considered separately, is inadequate to explain the etiology of psychological disorders. There is no absolute correspondence between social class and type of behavior disorder; for example, drug addiction and reactive schizophrenia occur in the middle as well as the lower class. Moreover, variations in economic conditions and changes in political attitudes and priorities regarding mental disorder can raise and lower incidence and prevalence rates. In the instance of personal crisis, the more apparent the external stress is, the more credible the social hypothesis, but the latter hypothesis fails to explain how the normal exigencies of life often precipitate behavior disorders. Lastly, it could be argued that genic factors are responsible for the selective migration of the mentally ill to the most disorganized and impoverished areas (Faris & Dunham, 1939).

Genic

Considerable evidence from many sources is available to support the belief that hereditary factors cannot be dismissed in accounting for the course of psychological disorders. Kallman (1946) showed that morbidity rate in schizophrenia increases in proportion to an individual's degree of blood relation to the patient. Twin comparison studies reported in the last two decades continue to support Kallman's findings, although the concordance rates are not so high as Kallman found and are more variable[3] (Dohrewend and Dohrewend, 1969). While not so extensive as the literature on schizophrenia, other research findings suggest a genetic factor in other types of psychoses and neuroses and in personality disorders. These results have been summarized in a review by Essen-Moller (1965), which demonstrates that genetic etiology is not limited to schizophrenia.

To separate the genic from environmental influences, Heston (1966) studied the children of schizophrenic mothers placed in foster homes shortly after their birth and compared them with a control group of children of normal mothers, also placed in foster homes and matched in other characteristics. As adults, the offspring of the schizophrenic mothers showed a higher incidence of schizophrenia as well as a variety of other neurotic and personality disorders.[4] In order to rule out possible toxic conditions in the pregnant schizophrenic mothers, Wender et al. (1968) showed that adopted children whose biological fathers were schizophrenic also were more likely than the control group to manifest psychopathology. A recent and more direct genic approach is the study of chromosomal anomalies. For example, Jacobs et al. (1965) found a higher frequency count of an extra Y-chromosome among psychotic and criminal populations compared to non-institutionalized samples.[5]

The evidence cited requires qualification about the hereditary cause of any behavior disorder.[6] Genic factors set the limits and determine the initial direction of growth, but the final outcome is always a resultant of continuous interaction between genic predisposition and the environment in which it operates. Even an instant after conception takes place the morphogenic matrix that shapes the nature of the growth process is not simply the sum total of genetic elements, but rather the result of these factors plus the influence of the existing cellular structure and the maternal environment. It is not that the genes change, but that genes alone do not constitute a growth matrix except at the moment of conception. For the determination of a psychological disorder, only the present effective predisposition—which is a precipitate of all the influences that have ever impinged on an individual's growth—is the immediate, relevant variable contributed by the organism. And in many cases of behavior the effective predisposition operating at any given time may be a far cry from the original genetic predisposition (Ausubel, 1952a).

Psychogenic

A composite approach to psychopathology is the study of the effect of the family environment upon the growing child. Most personality theorists have adopted this orientation and have speculated about the kinds of child rearing and the critical periods in early development that result in predispositions to behavioral disorders. While the field of child rearing is replete with theories, there is little empirical evidence to support this view—unlike the case for other causal approaches—and even this is open to diverse interpretations (Orlansky, 1949). More recent studies also question the influence of adverse child rearing as a determinant of psychopathology. Rosenthal et al. (1975) found that genic variables were more potent in causing psychological disorders than unfavorable childhood experiences.* And Bleuler (1974) found that childhood neglect and deprivation, even of a dire type, apparently have no bearing on the development of behavior disorders.[7]

---

*These findings may be artifactual inasmuch as the intrafamilial factors investigated may have been non-crucial in nature.

If it is to be effective, the psychogenic approach, must identify developmental predispositions that are not predetermined, that are based on naturalistic causes, and that are amenable to experimental testing. Unitary, innate factors, whether biological or psychological, whose expression is automatic, inevitable, and universal, are contrary to the spirit of modern biological and social science. The proper object of study and source of data must be direct and systematic observations of personality development, both normal and abnormal, from infancy through adolescence. Finally, to provide coherence to and evaluation of such observations there must be theoretical constructs that allow for the establishment of testable hypotheses.

The approach in this text is psychogenic and hypothesizes that there are two critical stages of ego development: early childhood and preadolescence. Parental attitudes of acceptance and intrinsic valuation enable the infant to begin to satellize (a form of identification) with the parents and thereby accomplish the transition to childhood with appropriate personal and social attributes for that age. In late childhood and adolescence, on the other hand, the task is reversed and desatellization, that is, emotional and volitional independence, enables the individual to acquire the personal and social attributes appropriate to and expected of mature adults. The predispositions toward behavior disorders occur, therefore, because of non-satellization (parental rejection or extrinsic valuation) in early childhood or because of failure to desatellize (parental extremes of domination and protectiveness) in preadolescence and adolescence. To demonstrate that the theory is suitable for empirical validation, Willenson (1959) tested six hypotheses related to the effects of non-satellization, and Ausubel et al. (1954) related parental attitudes of acceptance and extrinsic valuation to such various ego-structure variables as ideas of omnipotence, acceptance of parental values, level of aspiration, etc.[8]

Multiple Causality of Psychopathology

On the basis of current theories and empirical findings, behavior disorders cannot be explained by any single cause.* The general principle that complex behavior is based on multiple causes (Anastasi, 1958) is particularly apropos for the study and understanding of psychopathology. One inherent advantage of the multiple causality approach is that it resolves the artificial either/or arguments of the nature vs. nurture and organic vs. psychogenic controversies that still appear and are popularized (Szasz, 1960). Positing multiple causality or claiming that both heredity and environment contribute to psychopathology is stating the obvious. What is not so obvious and what provides justification for a more defensible and comprehensive interaction premise is the determination of how and how much each factor contributes to a specific type of psychological disorder. In order not to mislead the reader, the relationship between heredity and environment in the behavior disorders cannot be fitted into a single equation or fixed mathematical

*Even Sigmund Freud (1974) conceded that there are probable neurological factors in the etiology of hysteria

model. For example, the relative contributions of biological and environmental factors vary for each psychopathological condition and at different age levels. The proportional contribution of each factor also varies in each culture and subculture. We can, therefore, determine only the *average* contributions for each in a given culture or subculture. Within these inherent limitations, we can then consider how the effects of the genes and the environment are meditated.

A. The effects of genes are mediated through:
 1. adaptive resources: intelligence, originality, creativity, flexibility, improvising ability, resourcefulness, problem sensitivity, emotional stability;
 2. general resistance to stress, both acute (catastrophic), and chronic (cumulative), and novel (e.g., through the adrenal cortex);
 3. predispositions to specific organ system involvement in reactions to stress (psychomotor disorders) or physiological expressions of anxiety;
 4. temperamental predispositions to:
    a. level and distribution of energy;
    b. self-assertiveness, aggressiveness, perseverance, volitional independence, venturesomeness, initiative;
    c. ego maturation variables (hedonistic needs, executive independence, frustration tolerance);
    d. manner of resolving ego development crises;
    e. introversion-extraversion;
    f. preferred specific adjustive techniques or coping mechanisms (withdrawal, denial, projection, rationalization, regression);
    g. emotional stability (Ausubel and Sullivan, 1970).
B. The effects of the environment are mediated through:
 1. cultural or subcultural sources of stress (e.g., caste, class, sex, ethnic origin) and kind—whether catastrophic, cumulative, or novel;
 2. choices of coping mechanisms approved by culture or subculture (e.g., resignation and stoicism or aggressive combatting of difficulties);
 3. familial and idiosyncratic ways of resolving ego-development crises (e.g., rejection, extrinsic valuation, extremes of domination and protection); demands, pressures, expectations, limits, discipline;
 4. available choices among values transmitted by culture and subculture (e.g., degree of achievement or amount of responsibility expected);
 5. approved cultural and subcultural ways of socializing, satisfying drives, and expressing or repressing emotions (Ausubel & Sullivan, 1970).

Based upon what a person has inherited together with his unique life, there is what Zubin (1975) calls a vulnerability to disease, for example, to schizophrenia. This reflects a balance between predisposition to disease, on the one hand, and the availability of adaptive resources, on the other, both of which are both genically and environmentally determined. An individual may have such a high degree of vulnerability that almost any one of the daily demands of living is sufficient to catapult him into a psychotic episode. Another individual may have such a low degree of vulnerability that nothing short of a horrendous catastrophe will elicit such an episode and even then only a temporary one (Zubin, 1975). As long as the stress level is below the threshold of vulnerability, the individual responds well within the limits of normality. When the stress exceeds the threshold, a behavior disorder results. Hence there is an inverse relationship between degree of vulnerability and degree of stress required to cause a disorder: the greater the vulnerability the less the required degree of stress, and vice versa. Also, the greater the degree of vulnerability, the earlier the age of onset of the disorder (less cumulative stress or insult is required to induce the disorder).

When the degree of vulnerability exceeds the threshold, then ensuing disorders may reflect organic causes (disturbances in the neuroanatomical and neurophysiological substrate); psychogenic causes (developmental predispositions); or a combination and interaction between both kinds of factors (psychosomatic and somatopsychic disorders). As indicated earlier, the organic and psychogenic are not mutually exclusive causative factors. For example, a brain amine disturbance in conjunction with unfavorable personality predispositions may cause a severe depression. Some examples of the interaction between the biological and the psychogenic are:

1. physiological effects of anxiety in the neurotic anxiety syndrome;
2. cumulative physiological effects of excessive ambition and aggression (coronary attacks, hypertension);
3. effects of anxiety (spastic colitis, peptic ulcer);
4. effects of anxiety in lowering the threshold for allergic responses (bronchial asthma);
5. effects of depression and lack of desire to live in recovery from surgical trauma and critical illness;
6. and, under the heading of somatopsychic disorders, instances where physical illness, disfigurement, or abnormal rate of maturation affects body-image, self-concept, self-esteem.

Superficial examination and preoccupation with the symptoms of the behavior disorders distracts from and impedes the attainment of an understanding of the nature of psychopathology. De Forest (1950), for example, proposed that neurotic anxiety can best be understood as a self-protective device that is highly effective in impressing others with one's helplessness and in thus gaining their sympathy and protection as well as various immunities from the rigors and pressures of competitive existence. Although certain anxiety neurotics sometimes utilize their anxiety for this purpose, it seems more credible to regard this use rather as an incidental one, to which existing personality damage can be put, than as the primary cause for the development of the anxiety. Further, considering both the low esteem in which anxiety is held in our culture and the heavy penalities inflicted on an individual suspected of being a victim of anxiety, it is extremely unlikely that anxiety is used frequently as a defense, even in an incidental fashion.

Teleological reasoning, however, is so ingrained in the biological and social sciences that it is very difficult for a psychopathologist to concede that a given behavioral symptom of reaction to stress could be anything but adjustive or compensatory. Even organic pathologists lapse into the same error in interpreting physical symptoms as compensatory responses of organs to physical lesions or physiological stress.* Although most psychopatholologists are willing to recognize neurotic anxiety as a reflection of ego damage rather than as a compensatory form of defense, the influence of the teleological approach is still discernible in present day theorizing about the nature of anxiety.

In addition to clinical confusion, emphasis on the behavioral symptom has impeded the progress of epidemiological research. According to Clausen, "with symptoms still our primary basis for classification, we are at the same stage of knowledge about mental disease that medicine occupied a century ago with reference to the 'fevers'" (Clausen, 1961, pp. 131-32). Many researchers have tended to assume that disabling symptoms indicate a self-perpetuating defect in personality. Contrary to this hypothesis, of 39 people classified as neurotic in the Stirling County Study, almost half of them, four years later were classified differently or with no psychological disorder (Leighton et al, 1963). There appears then to be considerable room for disagreement about the nature of symptomatology observed in the community studies of "true prevalence" (Dohrewend and Dohrewend, 1969).

THE CONCEPT OF ABNORMALITY

Some of the ambiguity about the nature of psychopathology is a product of the statistical concept of behavior disorders. Assuming that mental health is a unitary trait distributed normally, then abnormal behavior is located at either end of the continuum. This concept might be valid if it were concerned only with symptomatology, that is, the physiological signs of anxiety. But it is completely invalid to include similar symptoms reflective of different psychopathological mechanisms and significance on the same behavioral continuum.

The claim that outmoded classification in psychiatry is retarding the progress of the science only confounds the issue. Generally, classification mirrors the state of clarity prevailing as regards the various concepts and their interrelationships within a given science. Hence, an inadequate classification is not a cause of theoretical confusion but a reflection of it. If we still adhere to the Kraepelinian

---

*For example, many pathologists and internists still believe that polyuria is a compensatory mechanism in chronic nephritis that makes possible the excretion of nitrogenous wastes through the elimination of a greater volume of urine. Actually, there is no possibility for further excretion of such wastes after the glomerular filtrate is formed. The polyuria, therefore, is not a compensatory mechanism but the outcome of secondary tubular damage in acute glomerulo-nephritis with impairment of water resorption. The net effect is the production of a greater volume of urine with a lower specific gravity and no change in the quantity of nitrogenous wastes excreted.

descriptive nomenclature, it means that our so-called "dynamic" systems of psychopathology are lacking in sufficient clarity and self-evident plausibility to command widespread adoption for clinical or research purposes (Ausubel, 1952a). Hence in the absence of any alternative classification system the retention of the *Diagnostic and Statistical Manual* of the American Psychiatric Association is still justified.

The United States-United Kingdom Diagnostic Project (Cooper, et al., 1972) and the WHO Pilot Study of Schizophrenia (1973) demonstrate the usefulness of the *Diagnostic and Statistical Manual*. Historically the major disorder reported in England has been the affective psychoses while in the United States it has been schizophrenia. Sharpened criteria and improved interviewing of sample admissions in the two countries indicate that the differences are not in the patients but in the examiners. The World Health Study found in the nine cultures studied specific syndromes of schizophrenia. Although the nature of schizophrenia remains unknown, the WHO study attests to its reality and argues for its continued use in the study of psychopathology.[9]

Szasz (1960) contends that the notion of mental illness has outlived whatever usefulness it may have had and that it now functions merely as a convenient myth. In a response Ausubel (1961c) takes issue with Szasz's position and argues for the retention of a disease model. He disagrees specifically that only symptoms resulting from demonstrable physical lesions qualify as legitimate manifestations of disease and therefore mental symptoms cannot be considered a form of illness; that only physical symptoms allegedly objective in nature and independent of cultural-ethical norms are amenable to medical treatment; that mental symptoms are merely expressions of problems in living and hence cannot be regarded as manifestations of a pathological condition; and, lastly, that personality disorders can be most fruitfully conceptualized therefore as products of moral conflict, confusion, and aberration.

Ausubel rejects Szasz's assertion that only a physical lesion can constitute the source for a genuine manifestation of disease. Such a criterion would be arbitrary and inconsistent both with medical and with lay connotations of the term "disease," which is generally regarded in current usage as including any marked deviation—physical, mental, or behavioral—from normally desirable standards of structural and functional integrity. The evaluation of all symptoms, physical as well as mental, is dependent in large measure on subjective judgment, emotional factors, cultural-ethical norms, and personal involvement of the observer. There is also no valid reason why a particular symptom cannot both reflect a problem in living and constitute a manifestation of disease. When the threshold of vulnerability is crossed for some individuals, they respond to the problems of living with behavior that is either seriously distorted or sufficiently unadaptive to prevent normal interpersonal relations and vocational functioning. The latter outcome, gross deviation from a designated range of desirable behavioral variability, conforms to the generally understood meaning of mental illness. Lastly, even if it were true that all personality disorder is a reflection of sin and that people are accountable for their behavioral symptoms (Mowrer, 1960), it would still be unnecessary to deny that these symptoms are manifestations of disease. Illness is no less real because the victim happens to be culpable for his illness. A glutton with hypertensive heart disease undoubtedly aggravates his condition by overeating and is culpable in part for the often fatal symptoms of his disease. But what reasonable person would claim (Ausubel, 1961) that he is not ill?

APPROACHES TO EGO PSYCHOLOGY

Orthodox Freudian Approach

Freudian theorists have devised an elaborate scheme for adult characterology based upon the psychological development of infant and child (Fenichel, 1945; Freud, 1924; Freud, 1933; Jones, 1923; Lorand, 1933). The theory is based, however, on predetermined and rigid sequences of personality development that are in conflict with modern conceptions of psychology and anthropology. Orthodox psychoanalytic theory is fundamentally rooted in biological instincts and instinctual energy. It posits hypothetical stages of psychosexual development and the concomitant development of "oral", "anal", "phallic," and other character types. The individual who seems not to have satisfactorily progressed through one of these hypothetical development stages (because of over or undergratification) is automatically considered as fixated at this stage, which is then cited as the cause of his neurosis or as the underlying basis of his personality structure. The specific content and course of development of the basic drives, however, are not given innately but are determined by unique factors of culture, constitution, and personal history (Fromm, 1941, Kardiner, 1939, Orlansky, 1949). Social anthropology has abundantly proven that the specific form of expression that any drive assumes can be understood only as an outcome of the interaction of biology, idiosyncratic experience, and culture (Hilgard, 1948). Hence, theoretically, it is untenable to regard even basic drives as undergoing preformed, inevitable, and universal stages.

PSYCHOANALYTIC DOCTRINE.

As we have already noted, the orthodoxy handed down by Freud postulated an instinctual pattern of psychosexual development that unfolded in accordance with a predetermined design. This does not mean, however, that no allowance was to be made for the individual differences of childhood experience. Such differences were conceived of as constituting individual variations on a universal theme. At each stage of development, several possibilities presented themselves; an adequate degree of gratification could be achieved, following which the child passed on normally to the next stage; or else, either excessive gratification or frustration resulted in a certain amount of fixation. These vicissitudes in psychosexual development were held to be dependent on differences in parental care and discipline in relation to such factors as suckling, weaning, toilet training, and gential manipulation. And far from being trifling matters, such vicissitudes were related in point-to-point fashion to specific attributes of adult personality.

Originally the only "data" bearing on this subject were obtained from the recollections of adult neurotic subjects who had undergone psychoanalytic treatment. As noted above, however, "the reconstructions of infant experience obtained from the analytic couch do not constitute empirical findings on the infantile situation" (Orlansky, 1949). But in the last 30 years, some empirical evidence bearing on these hypotheses has become available. Orlansky (1949) has reached certain conclusions after surveying evidence that denies the impact of infant care practices on adult personality. These conclusions are consistent with those reached by a number of writers (DuBois, 1941; Fromm, 1941; Horney, 1937, 1939; Kardiner, 1945; Leighton & Kluckhohn, 1947; Murphy, 1944). They stress the fact that personality structure is so much a product of multiple causality that no single item of parental discipline is likely to be of crucial significance; that the emotional and cultural context in which a particular item of training is imbedded is more important than the specific practice itself (Murphy, 1944); that neither constitutional factors nor later childhood, adolescent, or adult experience can be ignored (Erikson, 1948; Frenkel-Brunswik, et al., 1947; Orlansky, 1949); that due account must be taken of the social factors of class, caste, sex, and peer group affiliations (L.B. Murphy, 1947; Orlansky, 1949; Sherif & Cantril, 1946), and of the possibility of "emergent qualities" developing in the course of "personal and group interactions" and social change (Sherif & Cantril, 1946).

INFANTILE "SEXUALITY"

In the course of bodily exploration the infant inevitably discovers and manipulates his genitals. Upon experiencing the pleasurable effects of this activity, he may repeat it in order to re-experience the pleasant sensations involved, or (as in the case of thumbsucking) to obtain a non-specific type of tension relief following frustration or anxiety of any origin. In some primitive cultures, as a matter of fact, it is common for mothers to stroke the naked genitals of crying, fretful infants as a means of soothing them (Leighton & Kluckhohn, 1947; Whiting & Child, 1953). The incidence of self-stimulation (at one time or another) in children under three years of age is exceedingly high (Leighton & Kluckhohn, 1947; Levy, 1928). Girls reportedly indulge much less frequently than do boys, but this difference may be misleading since the habit is appreciably more difficult to detect in girls. Toward the close of the preschoool period, as more and more children become introduced to its pleasurable properties and become aware of its availability as a tension-reducing device, the practice tends to become more widespread and persistent, especially in emotionally tense children; and in accordance with the imposition of parental and cultural taboos, indulgence tends to become more furtive (Dillon, 1934). Beginning at this age also, curiosity about sexual anatomy and differences may stimulate some children to "peek" and play genitally exhibitionistic and manipulative games with youngsters of the same or opposite sex. Although varying tremendously in extent from one culture or subculture to another (in direct proportion to adult tolerance for such experimentation), these interests and activities are still relatively sporadic and uninsistent in comparison with those of post-pubertal individuals (Kinsey, et al., 1948; Malinowski, 1927).

THE "OEDIPUS SITUATION"

Subsumed under this designation is the Freudian doctrine that during the "genital phase" of psychosexual development the parent of opposite sex is the child's principal love object. Supposedly inherent in the "phylogenetic unconscious" of the male child is a potent libidinal drive for incestuous sexual union with the mother, accompanied by hatred for the father as a sexual rival and desire for his death (Fenichel, 1945; Freud, 1930).* Giving this theory a certain measure of superficial plausibility is the fact (impressionistically established, to be sure) that within many—although not all—families in our culture the father-son relationship in early childhood appears to be marked by more hostility and less intense emotional attachment than either the mother-son or father-daughter relationships. Other explanations for these phenomena, however, are available that seem far more parsimonious and self-evidently valid.

The young boy's typically more affectionate regard for his mother can be explained satisfactorily on the grounds that in our culture she provides the major source of his emotional support. During early childhood, the father tends to play a relatively secondary and less clearly defined role than the mother in the child's upbringing. Thus, the mother's greater importance in the boy's emotional security system rather than her alleged role as a sex object is the crucial factor in determining the greater intensity of his emotional attachment to her. This interpretation is bolstered by the majority of studies in this area, which show that the mother is the preferred parent of *both* boys and girls (Gesell & Ilg, 1943; Mott, 1937; Simpson, 1935). In addition, no incontrovertible evidence exists to justify the inference that the young boy's emotional response to his mother is sexual in nature or ordinarily involves anything more than affection or desire for bodily warmth and personal closeness. In our culture, such overtly affectionate relationships between mother and son (or between daughter and either parent) are regarded as quite appropriate, whereas, even when the underlying feelings are present, expressions of affection between father and son tend to cause embarrassment for both parties. We would conclude, therefore, that if sexual considerations as such do enter into the child's preference of parent, they originate more likely with the parent, whose biological sex role is undoubted, than with the child, in whom adult-like sexuality has never been unequivocally demonstrated.

---

*The oedipus situation in the female child corresponds to that described for the male except that the respective objects of love and hatred are reversed.

Turning now to the other side of the coin, conflict between father and son can also be attributed more credibly to the former's authority role in our culture and to competition for the mother's *affectional* attention than to the boy's perception of the father as a sexual rival. If fathers have any distinctive role in our culture, it is that of disciplinary agent and moral arbiter; and traditionally, in enforcing the disciplinary code, they are sterner and more demanding in relation to sons than to daughters. True, the mother also administers punishment, but her punitive role is not only generally less harsh but is also apparently resented less; because she is concomitantly the child's principal source of emotional security, he probably regards her as more entitled to control his behavior. In support of this view that the father's actual authority role (rather than a phylogenetically determined perception of him as a sexual rival) is the principal cause of whatever hostile feelings the boy manifests toward him are the findings (1) that in father-separated families, the father is perceived both as less aggressive and more affectionate than in father-home families and in approximately the same light as he is received by girls in father-home families (Bach, 1946); and (2) that in matrilineal societies, where the mother's brothers enforce discipline instead of the father, boys tend to resent their maternal uncles in much the same way as boys do their fathers in our culture (Dennis, 1940).

Finally, mutual rivalry for the mother's affection may play a role in engendering father-son conflict. The child may perceive the father as he would an older sibling—as a competitor for the love and attention of the most important individual in his interpersonal world. The father, in turn, particularly if he is emotionally overdependent on his wife or has good reason to feel supplanted by the child in his wife's affections, may react to him with feelings of hostility that tend to be reciprocated in due time.

EROTIC SIGNIFICANCE

What is the erotic significance of the several phenomena that psychoanalytic theory groups under the heading of "infantile sexuality"? To what extent is the meaning of the oral, anal, and genital activities we have reviewed above qualitatively equivalent to that of adult sexuality? Our position here is that *adult sexuality (true eroticism) can only be conceived of as a form of self-expression in which the individual enacts and experiences himself in a biological sex role.* Prerequisite to such experience, we believe, is (1) either current hormonal facilitation or exposure to such facilitation in the past, and (2) social and self-recognition as a sexually mature person capable of desiring a sexual object as such, and of serving in this capacity himself (Ausubel, 1952a). Since these conditions cannot possibly be fulfilled prior to puberty, the "erotic" behavior of children cannot be regarded as qualitatively comparable to adult sexuality. It lacks the social significance in the total economy of personality organization, its rich feeling tones, its urgency and regularity, and its status as an absorbing interest in its own right separate from other play. Hence despite the not infrequent attempts of children to engage in intercourse (Kinsey, et al., 1948; Kinsey, et al., 1953; Whiting & Child, 1953), and the occurrence of orgasm experience in female children (Kinsey et al., 1953), both Kinsey (1948) and Malinowski (1927) conclude that a qualitative as well as a temporal break in continuity occurs frequently between preadolescent and adolescent sex activity.[10]

"Infantile sexuality," therefore, consists chiefly of erogenous *sensuality* that is both indulged in for its own sake and to relieve the tensions of frustration and anxiety. It also includes the elements of exploratory and manipulative activity, of curiosity about the anatomy and physiology of sex and reproduction, and of desire for affectional closeness with the parent, accompanied perhaps by feelings of rivalry for perceived competitors. As we shall see later, however, because the child lacks a true biological (erotic) sex role, sex differences are not intrinsically important to him. Their true significance for personality development in childhood inheres in the fact that they constitute one of the principal bases for the differential structuring of social roles and behavior.

The origin of the psychoanalytic confusion between infantile sensuality and adult sexuality is not difficult to locate. First, it is easy to be overimpressed with the obvious fact that the same bodily parts are involved in both phenomena. This superficial resemblance, however, is both irrelevant and misleading: masturbation, for example, does not have the same psychological significance for child and adult simply because both individuals stroke the same organ. Second, in adult life sensuous and sexual pleasure *are* interwoven in erotic experience (Ausubel, 1952a). Hence, since adults find it extremely difficult to exclude their cumulative experiential perspective in interpreting the behavior of children (adultomorphism), they may confidently attribute erotic significance to the oral and genital play of the latter or "remember" that the same activities had sexual meaning in their own childhood. Even the sensual pleasure connected with anal and bladder evacuation, which ordinarily is not incorporated into adult sexual expression, may be "remembered" as having had erotic significance in early childhood years. This can be explained by the close association between eliminative and genital functions as a result of anatomical proximity, the shame and pleasure that is common to both, and their linkage in folklore and folk language. Thus, by virtue of this prior association, when genital activities are eroticized in adult life retrospective distortion may operate to superimpose some sexual significance on childhood memories of anal-urethral sensuality.

Although they recognize that "infantile" and adult sexuality are not phenomenologically comparable some neo-Freudians argue nevertheless that *eroticism* or *sexuality* should be defined broadly enough to encompass both sensuality and expressions of affection as well as sexual behavior in the more literal sense. In the writers' opinion, this only results in unnecessary semantic confusion and in a lamentable loss of scientific precision. If three distinguishably different phenomena can be discriminated conceptually, what possible advantage accrues from subsuming all of them under the same single term that is commonly understood as referring to only one of the three?

A more nebulous but critical theoretical concept is the process of innate and unconscious identification. In order to resolve the "oedipal complex", the male child unconsciously and automatically through a mechanism established prior to birth, identifies properly with the father in order to channel appropriately libidinal sexual and aggressive impulses. Such a theoretical construct is indicative of a preformationistic and mechanistic model of behavior and resurrects the refuted philosophical theory of innate ideas. Although it is the predominant pattern in child-parent relationship, child identification with parents is neither innate nor inevitable, but is rather a function of a specific interaction between parent and child.

Even if the term "instinct" is interpreted liberally, it is applied in a rigid and mechanical manner. Freud considered only a few drives, difficult to sublimate, and endowed with virtually explosive intrinsic energies. The sexual instinct is treated as if it were "the" basic instinct. Motives related to ego, however, are not only modified social derivatives of instinctual sexual impulses but are also products of continuous social experience. These motives are constantly emerging under the impact of new experiences and are the outcome of positive impulses to manipulate the environment as well as of compensatory reactions to cope with frustration. It would be gratuitous to point out that society creates as many needs as it represses. As regards sublimation, it is one thing to say that one motive is substituted for another, but it is quite a different matter to contend that the energy from the one is *directly* channelled into the other.[11]

Basic to the entire structure of psychoanalytic characterology is the assumption that infantile sexuality is continuous with adult sexuality. Among primates and humans in our society and primitive society, there is, of course, abundant evidence that sex interest, curiosity, and activity prior to puberty are phenomena that occur naturally and frequently (Ford and Beach, 1951; Kinsey, 1948). Adolescent sexuality, however, does not begin where childhood sexuality ends, which means there is a qualitative difference, i.e., a discontinuity in development. Childhood sexuality consists primarily of sensual feelings from the erogenous zones, of exploratory and manipulative activity, and of curiosity about anatomy. It is more or less a part of his other play and is usually sporadic. After pubescence, the sex drive becomes an "end in it self, frequent and regular, (Kinsey, 1948). The enactment of a biological sex role, on the other hand, implies the existence of feelings and impulses in the individual that are dependent on critical levels of gonadal stimulation and upon social recognition of him as a sexually mature individual.

Freudian theory has for the most part arisen from clinical investigation of adult neurotics. Hence, its assumptions regarding personality development in infant and child must necessarily be subject to all of the errors and distortions produced by selective forgetting and the manifest impossibility of an adult retaining childhood experiences intact and untainted by interpretations derived from an adult frame of reference. The claim that Freud revised his theory continuously is not supported by his latest published work (Freud & Bullitt, 1967). For the creator of psychoanalytic theory the fundamental principles remained relatively constant.

Neo-Freudian Approaches

The obvious and inevitable revision of analytic theory and practice was the inclusion of social and cultural influences and the corresponding reduction of the impact of biologic and instinctual factors on personality development. According to Horney (1950), the negative effects of early social exchanges between parent and child produce hostility and conflicts that produce a neurotic personality. The threat of parental disapproval during infancy is ascribed by Sullivan (1940) as the source for adult behavior disorders, particularly neurotic anxiety. Fromm (1941) assesses cultural patterns in general and their impact on the individual.

It is somewhat difficult to comprehend the theoretical position of the writers cited above who have repudiated Freud's phylogenetic determinism and have recognized the role of culture and ego in producing the types of structures and mechanisms that were heretofore declared to be given innately. It seems like indulging in verbal magic to deny the prepotency of instincts, on the one hand, and to describe on the other, personality in terms of the very same "layers" and "stages" that imply acceptance of instinctual origins and predetermined sequences of development. If it is genuinely believed that concepts of conscience and self are developmental products of interaction between a unique organism and a unique social environment, what justification is there for retaining phylogenetic concepts like "superego" and "id"? Also, to retain the same basic concepts of Freud but merely to give them a social derivation is a poor compromise indeed when these concepts are inextricably bound up with a set of "simple sovereign" assumptions such as "libido" and "sublimation" (Sherif & Cantril, 1947).

Humanistic and Existential Approaches

Writers such as Rogers (1942), Maslow (1954), and Frankl (1962) represent a radical departure from orthodox and neo-Freudian views regarding ego psychology and the behavior disorders. In place of, or as an alternative to, the disturbed personality they stress the positive and optimal self-development of which the individual is capable of. The self is not considered as biologically or environmentally determined, unconsciously motivated, or unduly influenced by prior experiences. Rather the individual is viewed as in the here-and-now, responsible for and capable of striving towards a true self (Rogers)—an actualizing self (Maslow), a self that has meaning (Frankl). The problems that beset the individual are conceived of as more philosophical and on a spiritual level and, until resolved, constitute, if not a psychopathological condition, then something less than the "ideal."

The humanistic conviction that man can deliberately select and take steps to ensure the realization of whatever goals he chooses, and, hence, is ''the master of his own fate,'' would be a perfectly defensible proposition if it were related to and qualified by the actual psychological capacities of human beings. More often than not, however, it is a philosophical desideratum. This is especially detrimental to its acceptability since it is becoming increasingly more evident that the extent of developmental plasticity is no longer a question that can be settled by speculative fiat. Furthermore, it is extremely unlikely that one blanket generalization could ever suffice to cover all aspects of development. In the modern era, this issue (the extent of human plasticity) is more properly regarded as a matter for empirical determination in each particular area of development. Any realistic statement of human objectives and potentialities should, in our opinion, be formulated within the framework imposed by man's genic endowment as currently conceived in the light of all relevant data.

Psychoanalytic Theories of Ego Psychology

The psychoanalytical approach to ego psychology is represented by such writers as Hartmann (1958), Kriss (1951), Mahler (1968) and Erikson (1950). For the most part, their ego psychology is derived from and reflects orthodox Freudianism, but it focuses on ego development and autonomous ego functioning. Erikson's theory of personality development, for example, in common with that of Hartmann, Mahler, and Kris, places undue emphasis on the individuation of self to the exclusion of other significant aspects (ego maturation). It also fails to differentiate between the two major kinds of identification (i.e., satellization and non-satellization) that determine in turn basic predispositions to particular character structures and personality disorders. Their formulations overvalue unconscious ideas and motives, do not relate, in general, to research evidence, and are highly impressionistic in nature.

A Naturalistic Developmental Approach

This volume attempts to formulate a general theory of psychopathology. It starts with the thesis that the most important determinants of future personality structure are the changing aspects of the child-parent, and child-society relationship through successive stages of ego development. It focuses on such naturalistic determinants as parent *attitudes* and the child's perceptual maturity as they affect transitional or crisis stages of ego development rather than on innate ideas or on the impact of child-rearing *practices* on predetermined sequences of psychosexual development. By rigorous systematization of existing data and reformulation of existing concepts, the theory developed here intends to fill some of the gaps in current approaches to psychopathology. To illustrate the type of systematization that is being attempted, a brief listing is made of some of the deficiencies perceived in current approaches to ego psychology.

1. There is a general tendency to discuss concepts such as "security" and "anxiety" without relating them to maturational capacity for responsiveness to emotional stimuli or to subtle manifestations of parental attitudes (e.g., Adler, 1925; Freud, 1936; Plant, 1937; Rank, 1929, 1936).
2. While it is appreciated that most children go through a period of dependent identification with their parents (a situation referred to as satellization in the text), little notice is taken of the sizeable number of children who fail to undergo this stage. In like manner, for those children who do identify emotionally with their parents, little attention has been paid to the following stage of achieving emotional independence from them.[12]
3. The various attributes of infantile ego structure are not followed through developmentally in a systematic fashion from childhood to adult life or related systematically to the behavior disorders on the basis of maturational defects.
4. In discussing the child's need for dependence or independence no distinction is drawn between the volitional and the executive* aspects of the problem. It is tacitly assumed that both aspects vary concomitantly, an assumption that, as will be seen later, is a far cry from reality.
5. There has been a lamentable lack of precision in defining and using various terms descriptive of parental attitudes and practices (e.g., "indulgence," "underdomination," "overvaluation," "extrinsic valuation").

Ego development is the outcome of continuous biosocial interaction. Since the very meaning of ego implies abstraction of individuality derived from unique personal experience, ego development must primarily be a resultant of ontogenetic rather than phylogenetic factors. At the same time, there are intracultural and intercultural uniformities in process that issue from a common core of problems associated with shifts in biosocial status and from a common set of psychological capacities for perceiving self and environment.

The thesis of this book, then, is that behavior disorders are largely the outcome of unfavorable modifications in ego development that predispose the individual toward undesirable adjustments to life situations. As the biosocial status of the individual shifts, changes in ego structure are required. These alterations may or may not be in accordance with the socially approved direction of adult maturation. The changes may or may not help produce a stable and well-integrated personality resistant to behavioral distortion. The crucial task therefore is to inquire into the relationship between specific defects and distortions in ego development and the particular types of behavior disorder to which they predispose the affected individual.

*"Executive" refers to the manipulative activity involved in completing a need-satisfaction sequence, whereas "volitional" refers solely to the act of willing the satisfaction of a given need apart from any consideration as to how it is to be consummated. An infant, for example, displays marked notions of volitional independence and omnipotence, but at the same time may conceive of himself as executively impotent and dependent. In adult life there is greater correspondence between these two aspects of dependence-independence.

2

Some Key Concepts in Ego Psychology and Psychopathology*

EGO VS. PERSONALITY

Personality is a more inclusive term than ego. It includes all the behavioral predispositions characteristic of the individual at a given point in his life history. It thus embraces the peripheral, transitory, and trivial as well as the central aspects of his behavioral repertoire. The distinction between personality and ego highlights the crucial role of the ego in the individual's personality organization. His psychological world can be ordered in terms of degree of ego involvement, with concentric zones of objects, persons, values, and activities varying in distance of affective proximity to self. The more central zones are areas of concern and importance to him. He has a vital stake in them. What happens in these areas is a source of pride or shame, of feelings of success or failure. It is these central ego-implicated constituents of personality that give continuity, consistency, and generality.

EGO AS AN ORGANIZING ENTITY IN PERSONALITY

It seems perfectly legitimate to refer to an identifiable abstraction as an entity as long as one does not reify it. Yet, to say that the ego is not an entity because it is constantly in a state of flux is to set up a philosophical criterion for identity that has no psychological reality. All of nature is in a constant state of flux as well as all concepts of the mind; hence in a phenomenological sense there can be no absolute entity. To have psychological reality as an entity, a concept must be endowed only with personal identifiability and some measure of continuity. Thus, although "the subjective sense of ego varies from time to time. . . and its content keeps

*Reference notes for this chapter are on page 336.

shifting . . . this shifting scene does not mean that there is no stable and recurring structure'' (Allport, G. W., 1943, p. 474). Through the web of memory thus formed, the ego retains its phenomenological identity (Hilgard, 1949).

But once attaining this highly differentiated and abstracted form that is endowed with continuity and personal identifiability, the ego becomes an entity in a more complete sense of the term than is implied by Sherif and Cantril's use of the phrase, "constellation of attitudes" (Sherif & Cantril, 1947). The process of conceptualization has already proceeded one step beyond the stage of "constellation of attitudes" to a stage that exists at a higher level of abstraction and enjoys a certain measure of psychological substantiveness but none of the corporeal, personified, or teleological properties of the reified ego. The end result may be conceived of as a personalized common denominator rather than as a constellation of ego attitudes. This developmental non-reified ego, unlike the psychoanalytic ego, can be systematically related to naturalistic data (Willenson, 1959). It makes no untenable assumptions, instinctual or otherwise, and does not require any "unfolding of an inevitable pattern" (Hilgard, 1949). Hence, it can qualify as a respectable scientific construct. "And like any other scientific construct . . . it will be useful to the extent that it simplifies the understanding of events" (Hilgard, 1949, p. 378).

The ego, however, is more than a derivative product of experiences related to the self. It also plays a crucial role in the hierarchical ordering of experience. By serving as a "dead center of gravity," objects, persons, and events can be arranged along a gradient of affective proximity in relation to it. Thus, as Murphy (1947) points out, it is difficult to speak of a self-not-self dichotomy. More comprehensible is the notion of an ever-expanding gradient of objects in the external world organized hierarchically by an individual on the basis of intensity of ego involvement. It is this "central polarity of the self" that is responsible for such varied phenomena as narcissism, egocentrism, invariable "self rightness," and ethnocentrism (the self-evident superiority of in-group practices). For the very same reason, experience has a crucial effect on personality structure when it creates needs relative to ego status. As will be seen later, so much emphasis is placed on the experiences of rejection or overvaluation in childhood because they give rise to more or less permanent constellations of ego needs. It is these needs and the characteristic modes of self-evaluation and ego defense in a given person which give continuity to his personality structure.

Nevertheless, because we are required to invest the processes of perception and motivation with a directed self-reference, we are not simultaneously committed to the hypothesis that "the more and better selfhood a person has, the less is available for others—that no one can enhance or defend himself without encroaching upon the self-enhancement and self-defense of others" (Murphy, 1947, p. 524). This point of view is by no means universal or inevitable (Mowrer & Kluckholn, 1944; Murphy, 1947). It flourishes especially in a highly competitive society, and, as will be pointed out later, as a consequence of a certain type of ego development.

EGO VS. CONSCIENCE DEVELOPMENT

It is customary for many psychiatrists and psychologists—even those who are not psychoanalytically oriented—to use the Freudian term ''superego'' as if it were synonomous with conscience. This practice is not only exceedingly unprecise but is also highly misleading, since superego does not refer to the developmental conscience described above as a part of the ego, but to a separate, reified layer of personality derived from a specific, inevitable, and universal event in psychosexual development.

Our approach to conscience development stresses Sherif and Cantril's proposition that ''there is for the individual no psychological difference either in the genesis of or the function of 'moral' codes (which psychoanalysts separate out as the 'superego') and other norms of behavior the individual learns. The emerging developing ego is in large part composed of *all* these interiorized social values'' (Sherif & Cantril, 1947. The values subsumed under conscience are merely internalized in an ethical context and are more closely related to such factors as self-criticism, obligation, self-control and guilt feelings. Arising in developmental fashion and in no more mysterious way than the ego itself, are a group of moral values and standards that may be referred to collectively as ''conscience'' and a set of self-evaluative attitudes that may be abstracted as a ''self-critical faculty.''

LONGITUDINAL STABILITY IN PERSONALITY ORGANIZATION

Factors Making for Stability

Consistency in individual personality development can be explained by three factors: those originating from within (1) the person himself, (2) his environment, and (3) various integrative and self-perpetuating mechanisms involved in the organization of personality.

The child furnishes a cluster of genically determined temperamental predispositions (see Chapter 1) which, in accordance with their strength and resistiveness to environmental modification, help perpetuate the sameness of his response to social experience. These predispositions may even be strong enough in certain cases to persist despite considerable training and cultural pressure in the opposite direction (Shirley, 1933, 1941). In addition, different children respond differently to the same pattern of parental behavior, and thereby serve either to change or reinforce the latter. A self-assertive child, for example, reacts differently than an apathetic child to parental overdomination. The child's temperament in and of itself selectively evokes differential responses from significant persons in his environment; and to the extent that his genically conditioned traits and the reaction of parents, teachers, and associates to him are relatively consistent, an additional source of long-range continuity is provided. Everyday experience indicates that irritability or peevishness in a child "tends to arouse impatience and annoyance in others, and by so doing . . . helps to produce an environment that fosters his peevish ways" (Jersild, 1954).

The parent contributes to the continuity of the child's individuality by providing a relatively constant interpersonal environment during the important formative years in which personality is developed. This constancy, of course, is a function of the longitudinal consistency of the parent's own personality and child-rearing attitudes. Moreover, sex differences in the twin dimensions of aggression and passivity "show long term stability if that behavior is congruent with the cultural definition of the sex roles of the individual" (Kagan and Moss, 1962). The fact that boys maintain their position on the aggressive continuum and girls on passive dependency hints at possible genically determined biological determinants (Honzik, 1964). Children showing stability come from families that are homogenous, stable, and free from traumatizing vicissitudes (Murphy, 1964). It is true that sooner or later the child is directly exposed to extrafamilial values in the culture that are at variance with those of the home; but in general, by virtue of prior conditioning and differential exposure, he tends to be selectively influenced by the particular values or judgments emanating from the social class and institutional affiliations of his parents.

Perpetuation of the formative effects of early (postinfantile) experience may be attributed in part to their initially deep entrenchment. The family-biased sample of the culture exerts disproportionate influence on the child's personality development. For, the restricted nature of his early environment and the unstructured condition of his major value and attitude systems make him maximally susceptible to any form of recurrent and pervasive patterning influence that is affectively toned. Then, once established, canalization and reaction-sensitivity tend to impose further restrictions on the theoretical array of behaviors open to any individual. What would otherwise constitute just one of many potentially adequate ways of meeting a need or solving a problem becomes the only adequate way (Murphy, 1947). "Habitual modes of reaction" in turn, "sensitize" the individual "to certain aspects of his experience and dull him to others. When he enters new surroundings and meets new people, he is more ready to respond in one direction than another, and this readiness itself acts selectively to bring him more to similar kinds of experience" (Cameron, 1947, p. 30).

Once organized on a stable basis, distinctive personality structure, like any developmental equilibrium, tends to remain intact in the absence of substantial cause for change. The child does not start from scratch in each new situation, but brings with him a precipitate of all past learnings. He attempts to maintain the same orientations, habits, adjustive mechanisms, and modes of striving and interacting with others that he used before.[1] Even if change occurs in the objective properties of a situation (e.g., parental attitudes), habitual apperceptive sets may be strong enough in certain cases to force altered stimulus content into preconceived perceptual molds ("perceptual constancy").* When this kind of perceptual manipulation is precluded by major change in the environmental situation, the child attempts first to respond in terms of his existing personality organization and to utilize habitual adjustive techniques found successful in the past before venturing to reorganize his personality or to improvise basically new patterns that are no longer appropriate or acceptable at higher age levels, for example, temper tantrums, "baby talk, enuresis, motor helplessness in an eight year old."

Finally, the longitudinal continuity of individuality can be attributed to the fact that certain central dimensions of personality play a crucial integrative role in its development and organization: "as a result of characteristic ways of interacting with significant persons in the environment, more or less permanent constellations of ego needs and habitual modes of self-evaluation arise. Examples of such constellations are differential feelings of security and adequacy and needs for ego status and independence that emerge in crucial developmental sequences like satellization** or failure to undergo devaluation. These constellations give rise to propensities for characteristic modes of learning, aspiring, socialization, ego defense, and attitudes toward authority and group demands' (Ausubel, 1954).

It would be surprising indeed if the prior existence and operation of such salient aspects of individual uniqueness did not have some functional residue in personality structure. The latter, in turn, could affect directly the kind of current biosocial status an individual seeks and the basis on which he assimilates values. "Thus, for example, although an adult who satellized as a child obtains most of his current status from earned rather than from derived sources, some satellizing patterns [could] still remain operative in adult life and furnish a subsidiary source of status, e.g., satellizing-like relationships with boss, spouse, pastor, physician, membership group, etc." (Ausubel, 1957). In addition, a residue of prior satellizing experience could conceivably constitute an inner core of self-acceptance that would be independent of situational success and failure. Although this would not function as a subsidiary source of currently generated status, it could exercise a substrate influence serving to keep his ego aspirations within realistic limits and to protect him from catastrophic impairment of self-esteem.

Factors Making for Instability

The enduring characteristics of ego organization and ego attributes should not be construed to mean that, once formed, the ego is fixed and final. Neither later

---

*This "freezing" of perception despite change in stimulus content is facilitated further by the acceptance of general categorical propositions that dispose individuals to ignore the information supplied by firsthand experience. Once general categories of objects and relationships are established, the properties of currently experienced stimuli are simply inferred on the basis of their categorical membership.

**A form of dependent identification with superordinate figures as a result of which an individual acquires derived status if he is accepted and intrinsically valued by the former.

childhood, adolescent, or adult experience can be ignored (Erikson, 1948; Frenkel-Brunswik, et. al., 1947; Orlansky, 1949) nor can the possibility of "emergent qualities" developing in the course of "personal and group interactions" and social change (Sherif & Cantril, 1947). Changes in satellization for example, may take place as new opportunities are offered to the rejected nonsatellizer.

Although strongly influenced by the agreeableness of initial social contacts and by a possible genic predisposition toward "thickness" or "thinness of skin," tendencies toward introversion-extraversion are probably more reversible than originally believed. Marked changes in the social climate of the child, such as are likely to occur when he first enters unsupervised group play or the more autonomous, demanding and status-giving peer culture of adolescence (Ausubel, 1950), can bring about unexpected shifts in this dimension of personality. These shifts appear especially marked if the environmental change is favorable to the expression of original trends that have been suppressed, usually because of parents who are either over or underdominating.

INTERNAL CONSISTENCY OF PERSONALITY ORGANIZATION

Perhaps even more basic to the concept of personality than the longitudinal continuity of individuality is internal consistency at a given horizontal level. The entire concept of personality would be meaningless if it did not refer to a relatively stable and consistent organization of individually unique behavioral predispositions; otherwise, behavior could be explained completely in terms of general reaction capacities, situational determinants, and transitory motivations generated in the course of current experience.

Both contemporaneously and longitudinally, consistency in personality structure is largely a function of behavioral traits that become organized and hierarchically ordered in relation to certain gradients or core aspects that are centrally unifying. In human beings, motives, values, aspirations, and orientations toward other persons and groups—all having significant self-reference—play this crucial integrative role in personality organization and development (Ausubel, 1954; Murphy, 1947; Sherif, 1953). It constitutes in itself a self-consistent, integrated and enduring system; and further consistent development is insured by the tendency to assimilate new trait trends compatible with it and, hence with each other. As a result, generality in responding to a host of objects, persons, values, and institutions in an unending variety of concrete situations becomes possible (Sherif, 1953), and syndromes of functionally and developmentally meaningful personality traits can be identified.

In children, the evidence indicates that although a nucleus of horizontal consistency does exist, considerable tolerance for inconsistency in personality organization is also present, which probably diminishes with increasing age. Sanford, et. al. (1943) were able to identify twenty meaningfully-constituted personality syndromes in school children based upon intercorrelations among traits that averaged about .5 within each syndrome. Demonstrated relationships between interpersonal traits and differential cognitive abilities were reported by Ferguson and Maccoby (1966). General studies of children have shown relationships between category styles of analytic-reflective vs. impuslive thinking (Kagan and Henker, 1966). Bruner and Tajfel (1961) and Tajfel, Richardson, and Everstein (1964) report consistent preferences for *broad* or *narrow* categorization.[2] A component aspect of personality organization involves moral, character, and value traits. Children characterized as *humanistic* as opposed to *conventional* on moral judgments give more guilt responses on a story completion test (Hoffman, 1963; Hoffman & Saltzstein, 1960). In cases where IQ and age are controlled, delay of gratification discriminates cheaters from non-cheaters (Mischel, 1963). Moral character and value traits, however, probably provide too rigorous a test of trait generality in children.

Consistency is a measure of the compatibility of parts with the whole, and with each other. Hence, since the child's personality is relatively unformed and is changing rapidly, there is obviously less basis for consistency than in the adult. Until a crystallized and stable representation of individuality is achieved, many divergent trends are compatible within the existing total organization. Further, since the child requires some experience with a given kind of behavior before he can judge congruence with his major goal and value systems, he is apt to give many unsuitable patterns a "provisional try" before he finally rejects them. With increasing age, however, a more characteristic portrait of the individual emerges and a clearer standard of gauging compatibility becomes available. Many alternatives experimented with on a tentative basis are found wanting and sloughed off. By a process of progressive "acquisition of dislikes by individuals whose initial attitude is favorable toward everything," personality organization thus becomes increasingly more integrated and self-consistent. Even in the turbulence of adolescence such character traits as honesty, responsibility, and moral courage acquire considerably more generality than in childhood (Havighurst & Taba, 1949).

We do not wish to imply that judgments of consistency are necessarily deliberate: very frequently they are made quite incidentally. Yet with advancing age, as the child's personality takes more definite shape and as he develops a clearer conception of it and greater capacity for perceiving incompatibility, the need for preserving self-consistency gradually increases. Unlike the young child the older individual employs a conscious monitoring system which, by virtue of selective assimilation, retention, and rejection, helps maintain congruence between his personality structure and his self-concept (Ausubel, 1957); but since unbiased conscious control is often insufficient for this purpose, he also utilizes such supplementary mechanisms as perceptual and logical distortion, repression, and the isolation of discordant beliefs in logic-tight compartments. Nevertheless, even the well-integrated adult displays considerable tolerance for consciously appreciated inconsistency. The widespread belief that all inconsistency must necessarily be "unconscious" or below the threshold of awareness is one of the major psychological myths of our time.

Relatively recently it has also been recognized that some of the apparent lack of trait generality in children as well as in adults is spurious because of the failure to hold ego involvement constant. It stands to reason that trait behavior in different situations is not comparable unless degrees of self-implication is approximately equivalent. Level of aspiration in the laboratory (Harvey & Sherif, 1951), real-life tasks (Ausubel, 1953), memory tasks (Rosenzweig, 1941), and tenacity of vocational goals (Ausubel, 1953) all increase, for example, with magnitude of ego-involvement.

Lastly, some of the apparent inconsistency in children's personality structure is merely a reflection of the grossness and invalidity of existing measuring instruments. In the absence of subtle measures capable of penetrating beneath (1) normative-commonalities characterizing all children at a particular stage of development, and (2) different phenotypic expressions of the same genotypic tendency, spurious inconsistency is inevitably added to whatever already exists. Thus, to advocate dismissal of research on contemporaneous trait consistency in personality (Brim, 1960), represents an attempt at premature closure of a problem that is just beginning to show its research possibilities (Cronbach, 1957).

PERCEPTION AND EGO DEVELOPMENT

Perceptual variables play a mediating role in the interactional process underlying ego development. Before social experience (e.g., parent attitudes, cultural norms); various competencies related to self; and different ego needs, motives, and attributes can be brought together in the same interactional field, they must first be related to the ego perceptually (i.e., give rise to a clear content of awareness). The stimulus world, therefore, whether of internal or external origin, is not the proximate antecedent of behavior or development.[3] Rather, such an antecedent is the perceptual world.* Thus, although a child's role and status in the home and his parents' behavior toward him are objective social events in the real world, they affect his ego development only to the extent and in the form in which they are perceived. The importance of this proposition rests on the fact that children's person perceptions are realities that are quite different from the assessments based on observations of researchers (Dubin & Dubin, 1965). This does not imply that the perceived world *is* the real world, but that perceptual reality is both psychological reality and the actual (mediating) variable that influences behavior and development.

---

*Perceptual reality considered as a dependent variable is itself an interactional product of stimulus, cognitive maturity, and ego structure.

Insofar as perception itself undergoes systematic developmental changes during the life cycle, level of perceptual maturity must be considered a determining as well as mediating variable in ego development. Perceptual immaturity insulates the young infant from awareness of environmental threat and from the attitudinal effects of parent practices. The young child fails to assess accurately his executive dependence and the underlying motivation of parental deference because of perceptual immaturity. On the other hand, increasing perceptual maturity makes it possible for the self-concept and the ego to become abstract conceptual entities. Also, many of the more complex constituents of the ego, such as self-esteem, self-critical ability, and the ability to set consistent levels of aspiration could only exist in very rudimentary fashion in the absence of verbal symbols.

One explanation for growth in perceptual ability is that perceptual maturity is a function of cognitive capacity and sophistication, which tend, in turn, to increase with age and experience. Some aspects of perceptual maturation, however, are probably attributable to normative modifications of ego structure itself, e.g., changed perceptions of parents and peers following ego devaluation in early childhood.

There are specific characteristics of cognitive sophistication during infancy and childhood that have relevance for developmental trends in perception. They may be summarized as follows:

Widening and Increasing Complexity of Cognitive Field. Kindergarten and first-grade children, for example, tend to be relatively oblivious of events in the environment that have no immediate or personal significance for them (Russell, R., 1940).

Increasing Familiarity of the Psychological World. One of the most important consequences of repeated encounters with the same array of stimulation is an increase in the familiarity or recognizability of the stimuli in question (Draguns & Multari, 1961; Gollin, 1965).

Decreasing Dependence of Perception on the Stimulus Field. As a child's cognitive structure becomes increasingly more elaborate and systematized, the stimulus field tends correspondingly to become a decreasingly important determinant of perception (Witkin, et. al., 1962).

Acquisition of Object Permanence and Constancy. An important aspect of cognitive sophistication is learning that objects have permanent properties despite fluctuations in sensory data (Piaget, 1954; Werner & Kaplan, 1956; Wohlwill, 1963). Some other attributes of perceptual maturation are: increasing differentiation and specificity of cognition; transition from the concrete to abstract; transition from specific to general; increasing detection of distinctive features; decline in egocentricity and subjectivity, and finally increasing attentional capacities.

In addition to these cognitive factors, perceptual capacity also relates to and determines ego formation and development. Despite the objective limitations of an infant's abilities, perceptual immaturity explains, in part, how an omnipotent sense of self can develop during the first stage of ego development. Similarly, the later reversal in roles between parent and infant in early childhood, can be partly explained by improvement in perceptual ability. In spite of resistance to the changes in ego development that are imposed by parents—which may be expressed in periodic bursts of negativistic behavior—the changes do occur nevertheless, and take hold because of increased perceptual insight into parental motivations and more realistic self-appraisal.

NATURE OF DRIVES

Implicit in neonatal behavior patterns such as response to pain, hunger, and noxious stimuli is the idea that specific movements and general bodily activity fluctuate periodically because of the operation of drive states. We have assumed that because of various universally distributed genic predispositions, physiological processes, and environmental conditions, all individuals may *potentially* develop certain drives but do not necessarily acquire all the drives that they potentially could. Thus some drives develop in all human beings; others are found in all or most cultures except for certain groups or individuals; and some drives are unique to particular cultures or individuals within a culture. In any event, our position is that no drives are innate or completely independent of experience.

Drive is an inferred neurobehavioral state that accounts for transitory fluctuations in the organisms's propensity for responding to stimulation with its available repertoire of reaction tendencies. These momentary differences in reactivity may be attributed to the existence of a drive state consisting of a partly generalized but nonetheless selective lowering of response and perceptual thresholds in accordance with their relevance to or capacity for terminating the drive state that is operative. The drive is *not* a persistent afferent or humoral *stimulus* but a multiply determined neurobehavioral *state* that is coextensive with the lowering of response and perceptual thresholds. It is necessary therefore, to distinguish between drive as an altered state of reacitvity and the various determinants (including stimuli) that induce it. Drive is always a summated (net) resultant of the threshold-changing effects (both raising and lowering) of its numerous determinants. [4]

According to the ''state'' conception of drive, drives are never innate but may or may not be inevitable. If humoral conditions or afferent stimulation are only regarded as *partial* determinants of a summated drive state that is complexly determined by all kinds of external, visceral, situational, and cognitive factors, then, the generation of drives must always be considered acquired or dependent upon particular past and present experience rather than innate or invariable. The inevitability of a drive depends on how essential it is for the maintenance of life and upon the extent to which it is cortically or environmentally regulated. Since external (e.g., cultural) inhibitory conditions may sometimes be more potent than internal (hormonal) facilitating conditions, drives are not necessarily inevitable. Unlike the hunger drive, the sex drive, for example, which is not essential for the maintenance of life and which in human beings is largely regulated by situational and experiental determinants, may fail to develop in post-pubescent individuals. In this case it is more parsimonious to speak of agenesis than to invoke the concept of repression.[5]

Rather than considering new drives as derived, an emerging view is that drives constantly emerge in the course of new experience, in the further development of personality and in the acquisition of new capacities and values (Allport, 1937; Jersild, 1954; Maslow, 1954; Murphy, 1947). According to this view, the exercise of learned capacities and the pursuit of satisfying activities connected therewith are, generally speaking, wholly autonomous needs in their own right from the very beginning of their availability.

UNCONSCIOUS MOTIVATION

In psychoanalytic theory "the unconscious" forms the cornerstone of psychopathology. It is the domain of instinctual urges and the locus of repressed libidinal impulses referrable to earlier stages of psychosexual development that had become fixated for some reason at a primitive level of evolution. It is also the region to which unacceptable feelings and ideas and regressive desires of current origin are banished, if they somehow manage to enter the sacred precincts of consciousness. Through the surreptitious influence exerted by unconscious motivation, symptoms are formed that fulfill symbolically the goals of their hidden progenitors. In the absence of the unconscious, behavior disorder is unthinkable in the psychoanalytic sense.

Psychoanalytic theories of the unconscious are topographical rather than functional, implying an all-or-none differentiation, depending on regional location, between the conscious and the unconscious.[6] It does less violence to modern concepts of psychological functioning to conceive of "varying degrees in the accessibility of person's behavior to his own analysis" (Cameron, 1947, p. 129). In order of importance we may differentiate between four different varieties of inaccessibility: (1) perceptions or motives that are attended to on a subthreshold level of awareness because of their habitual, autonomous, or unobtrusive nature; (2) experiences that occur in a state of panic or behavioral disorganization with the consequent impairment of perceptual and memory functions; (3) emotional and visceral feelings or attitudes that cannot be formulated in verbal terms, and hence are recalled or reidentified with great difficulty; and (4) material that is actively repressed as a form of adjustment.

We can agree that unconscious motivation can give rise to symbolic symptom-formation, and that it often compounds the seriousness and intensity of guilt and anxiety by impeding integrative and constructive solutions.[7] But we must reiterate that these consequences of repression are not mainly responsible for the evolution of behavior disorders but merely have the status of complications. Most behavior, abnormal as well as normal, is determined by prior experience and by drive determinants that are accessible to unconsciousness. Unconscious motives are thus not the real, primary, or true causes of behavior.

Unconscious motives are not more prepotent or qualitatively different from conscious motivations. Rather, they are less subject to conscious and rational control and must thus operate more deviously, that is, in disguised and symbolic form. Hence, to be elicited, indirect measures must be taken, for example, projective techniques, free association, and hypnosis. Therefore, motives that are not conscious are less directed, integrated, and consistent than motives at the conscious level. Conscious motives may also include material or impulses that produce shame, guilt, and anxiety without having to be repressed.

For example, moral responsibility can constitute a force to inhibit a good part of the conscious hostility and culpable negligence underlying an attitude of parental rejection. In the effort to highlight "unconscious" sources of aggression, many writers seem to forget that a large portion of the cruelty and hostility entering into everyday interpersonal relationships is carried on at a conscious level and thus subject to voluntary inhibition. The pretty dichotomized picture of *homo psychoanalyticus* with a conscious stratum populated by noble, socially acceptable and self-edifying impulses and an unconscious stratum seething with phylogenetic and repressed amoral and aggressive urges is tremendously overdrawn. There is a tendency toward self-consistency and self-embellishment in the organization of conscious material, but it is never complete. Individuals can live quite comfortably with a good deal of awareness of their own inconsistency and of their own unconscionable impulses. Morally reprehensible behavior is subject to more voluntary control than the proponents of the "psychopathological" theory of delinquency are willing to admit.

Unmotivated Behavior

Contrary to Freudian theory, all behavior is not motivated, as for example, in momentary, short-term, and non-sustained learning situations. Forgetting, for the most part, is similarly attributable to cognitive rather than motivational factors (e.g., lack of original attention; lack of meaningful learning set or logically meaningful learning material; lack of stable, relevant anchoring ideas in cognitive structure). Slips of the tongue and pen are also caused mainly by cognitive competition or intrusions (e.g., similarity), fluctuation in attention, and preoccupation rather than reflective, symbolic wish-fulfillments or expressions of repressed motives.

LEVEL OF ASPIRATION

The experimental psychology of motivation (Lewin, et. al., 1944) and the social psychology of attitude formation (Sherif & Cantril, 1947) indicate that level of aspiration is related to ego development. As it is used here, ego involvement refers in one sense to the degree of self-implication in a given task or performance, that is, to what extent the outcome is a matter of concern or importance to the individual. The underlying motivation, however, is another matter. In an ego-involved task, the primary object of the activity may either be task oriented or directed toward self-enhancement (prestige motivation); in the latter case we speak of level of ego aspiration. Hence, in both instances the setting of levels of aspiration is a function of ego structure and development. In most normal situations aspirational level is flexible and reflects prior experiences of success and failure in the particular area of ego involvement. Given certain types of ego development, however, aspiration levels may become inflexible and be set unrealistically high or low.[8]

Hartog's work (1950) indicates that the level of aspiration for a specific task may be excessively lowered by persons with anxiety in order to insure future success following an initial, frustrating experience. This phenomenon is referred to as adaptive ego disinvolvement. He found that in simple paper and pencil tests, anxiety patients "showed an unduly high initial level of aspiration with the following goal levels kept intentionally low (Hartog 1950, p. 931). The results can be interpreted as evidence of the high level of ego aspiration prevailing in anxiety neurotics before they are fully aware of the nature of the task and the threat it entails, which is followed by protective ego disinvolvement once frustration is experienced.

At the other extreme, aspirations may be unrealistically high and inflexible where a compensatory need for earning high status and achievement exists because of lack of intrinsic self-esteem.[8] In addition, maintenance of high aspirations is expected in the American middle-class culture and is fostered by the ubiquitous pressures emanating from a competitive society.

Finally, self-esteem depends on more than the discrepancy between aspiration and performance level. Clinical observation in vocational guidance leads to the hypothesis that the absolute magnitude of aspiration level—regardless of discrepancy—is in itself an independent determinant of self-esteem. Instances abound where completely idle or hopelessly mediocre individuals bolster their self-esteem almost indefinitely by maintaining ridiculously high levels of aspiration that successfully block realistic and appropriate adjustment. Similarly, the attainment of modest goals does not usually lead to a cessation of striving but does tend to raise the aspiration level to a point where failure is clearly risked (Allport, 1943). If high aspirations levels per se did not tend to enhance self-esteem, these situations would not be so commonplace as they are. Thus, the original "discrepancy" formula for self-esteem proposed by William James and restated by the

Lewinian School as accounting for subjective feelings of success and failure (level of aspiration experiments) appears to oversimplify the facts. The relative weights that must be attached to the "discrepancy" and "absolute" value" variables still await determination. We suggest that a complete devaluing of aspirational level results in greater loss of self-esteem than occurs from ignoring a substantial discrepancy.

INTROVERSION AND EXTRAVERSION

Historically, these concepts are associated with problems of self and ego since they imply characteristic differences in the tendency to be concerned with self as against the outside world (Murphy, G., 1947). Actually, it seems more fruitful to use these terms to describe the varying degrees of emotional *directness* with which different persons participate in the problems of living. The extravert prefers to participate directly in his emotional relationships with objects and persons in the environment. The introvert recoils from direct emotional participation and interposes a buffer of symbols and abstractions. Since introversion implies a great deal of solitary cerebration, the illusion is created that the introvert is primarily concerned with self as such; and since extraversion customarily involves more manipulation of objects and social situations, it is assumed that the extravert's focus of interest is in the outside world and not in the self. Although this difference is almost inevitable it is more of a distinction in terms of *product* than of *process*. The introvert, for example, may be intensely interested in mechanical or social relationships without participating in them directly at all; they may merely furnish raw material for his abstractions. The extravert, on the other hand, may be intensely interested in inner psychological processes, but less from the point of view of finding abstractions than as a rich source of vivid personal experience.

The factors accounting for these differences in directness of emotional involvement are not too clear. Constitutional predispositions undoubtedly play a part. A highly hedonistic individual, for example, would hardly be content with symbolic satisfaction of his pressing visceral needs. A dominant, ascendant, and "tough-skinned" individual is not apt to be too concerned about the opinions of others or overly sensitive to rebuffs. As Gardner Murphy puts it, "extraversion may prove to consist primarily of the capacity to retain self confidence despite social onslaughts upon it" (Murphy, 1947, p. 603). Equally crucial perhaps, are environmental factors relating to ego defense or enhancement. In the personal history of the introvert, there can usually be found "early distasteful experience with reality 'in the raw,' setting up a need for 'cushioning'" (Ausubel, 1949). The parent may have differentially rewarded introverted activity. Early social rebuffs or rejection by the parent may have been traumatic enough to create powerful inhibitions in the child about directly exposing himself emotionally to environmental vicissitudes.

As a characteristic mode of reacting emotionally to life problems, introversion-extraversion is obviously an important dimension of personality structure. In addition—when acting with other psychopathological determinants—it furnishes predispositions toward adopting certain types of undesirable adjustive techniques. The introvert's proclivity and ability to withdraw from reality and adult maturation predisposes the individual primarily to "process" and secondarily to "reactive" schizophrenia. The extravert, on the other hand is more predisposed to drug addiction and reactive depression.

SELF-CRITICAL CAPACITY

An important factor affecting the individual's sense of adequacy, the probability of his being frustrated, and the level of anxiety he manifests is the state of his self-critical faculty. This refers to his tendency to evaluate with varying degrees of severity or leniency the acceptability of his behavior, the degree of status he has acquired, and the quality of his productions. This self-critical faculty also reflects in part the influence of maturational factors and various parent attitudes and, in part, the level of his self-esteem and the critical standards that prevail in his environment. Although tending to remain fairly stable and consistent in line with long-range personality trends, it still retains a certain adaptive flexibility. In persons who are secure and adequate, it tends to be more lenient and to fluctuate less than among individuals who feel insecure and inadequate.

The infant is able to entertain grandiose conceptions of his volitional power *partly* because of his very limited self-critical ability. Afterwards, improvement in this ability becomes one of the precipitating causes of the crisis of ego devaluation. Nevertheless, self-critical ability is still rudimentary as evidenced by the child's tendency to overvalue the extent of his executive competency and by the negativism due to the "gap between biological and social maturity" (Cameron, 1947) or to the conflict regarding the issue of self-help (Jersild, 1947; Murphy, 1947; Murphy, 1944).

During the succeeding years, the further development of the self-critical faculty becomes a progressively more crucial aspect of personality maturation. This growth is facilitated by parental practices that require the child to take responsibility for the consequences of his inappropriate behavior or inadequate performance.[9] Undue laxity in excusing misbehavior or in evaluating inferior performance favors the emergence of an impaired self-critical faculty. The acquisition of achievement motivation on an adult and realistic level presupposes the ability to recognize imperfections in performance; otherwise the individual feels completely satisfied with a highly inferior product, aspires to nothing better, and initiates no efforts toward improvement.

Disturbances in the development of the self-critical faculty contribute to depressed and manic states.[10] Depressive reactions are closely related to acute states of anxiety. In relation to his own abilities the anxiety neurotic generally has a well-developed self-critical faculty that tends to become even more severe as anxiety increases. Furthermore, he tends to react to frustration with a lowering of self-esteem and a disorganization of performance ability, which further increase his feeling of worthlessness. If he is using the state of disorganization as a means of frustrating the acceptance of a "half-loaf adjustment" and of justifying his executive and volitional dependence on others, he has reason to exaggerate his incompetence even further and to erect all kinds of irrelevant barriers and impossibly high standards.

Because of the anxiety neurotic's high tolerance of goal frustration, however, defeat is not accepted easily. He continues for some time to maintain his grandiose ego aspirations despite the collapsed state of his self-esteem and to look for some new basis on which he may restructure shattered ambitions. Hence arises the mixture of frantic aimless activity, acute anxiety, emotional depression, and intense fear of death, all of which are found in agitated depression.

Ordinarily, change in the expression of the self-critical faculty is effected only on a psychological plane in the course of ego defense measures or as the outcome of ego damage. However, there is evidence that such changes can be effected by bringing physical influences to bear on its anatomical substrate. The effect of opiates and prefrontal lobotomy on the thalamo-cortical tract, in depressing the self-critical faculty, and thus causing euphoria and relief of depressive states, is a case in point.

CAUSE AND EFFECT IN DEVELOPMENTAL SEQUENCES

Both Mead (1947) and Murphy, Murphy and Newcomb (1937) have criticized the uncritical psychoanalytic imputation of cause and effect relationships to developmental sequences. The former has pointed out that while a child is being subjected to a given aspect of infant care, he is *simultaneously* being exposed to many of the unique cultural values and aspects of adult personality that prevail in his society; and that it is therefore unwarranted to conclude that the latter products are *caused* by the child-training practices. "Because . . . symptoms are part of a syndrome, they are always found to be correlated and present at the same time or in a certain sequence; they are then erroneously thought to be cause and effect" (Murphy, et. al., 1937). For example, both homosexual trends and a marked tendency to distort experience unfavorable to the self are tendencies frequently found in the personality type that is characterized by "ego hypertrophy" and predisposed towards the development of paranoid trends. The first tendency is often a modified expression of the exaggerated self-love characteristic of persons with "hypertrophied egos," and the second is a device that is often employed for ego enhancement. But according to psychoanalytic teachings, repressed homosexual trends are the *cause* of paranoid delusions.

3

Dimensions of the Parent-Child Relationship in Relation to Ego Development

PRIOR TREATMENT OF PARENT-CHILD RELATIONSHIP IN RELATION TO EGO DEVELOPMENT

Although commonplace today, conceptions of personality development that emphasize the crucial role of the parent-child relationship in its broader aspects have appeared only relatively recently in the history of personality theory. The belated recognition accorded to this factor can be attributed largely to the influence of Freud. He and his followers were among the first to stress the importance of early childhood experience and parental treatment for later personality formation. However, Freudian theorists selected out of this experience only those specific child-rearing practices that impinge on the individual's alleged psychosexual development such as weaning, toilet training, etc. (Medinnus, 1967). They more or less ignored the impact of broader emotional *attitudes* (e.g., rejection, over-protection), on the salient features of ego development.

Neo-analytic writers have stressed such other factors in the parent-child relationship as: "feeling of inferiority" (Adler, 1917), "authoritarian conscience" (Fromm, 1947), "maternal overprotection" (Levy, 1943), and "identity crisis" (Erikson, 1950). Erikson designates eight stages in personality development starting in infancy and extending into adulthood. The bases precipitating each stage as well as the "crises" (e.g., autonomy vs. shame or initiative vs. guilt) lack clarity and precision. As a result, the theses proposed by both Freud and Erikson have not generated much research to support their theories (Paplia & Olds, 1975).

Non-analytic approaches to child rearing embrace a variety of speculations, a limited number of empirical studies, and an applied approach. The theoretical orientation of Gesell (1946) posits a "spontaneous maturation" hypothesis that has promoted a permissive approach to child rearing. Coopersmith's study (1967) attempted to identify the antecedents of self-esteem. He assessed the parental effects of such dimensions as acceptance, permissiveness, democratic practices, and independence. Spock's latest revision (1976) is a common-sense approach to dealing with a variety of problems of child rearing. And the Parent Effectiveness Training (P.E.T.) approach delineates techniques that parents can learn and apply to particular situations.

DISTINCTIVE ASPECTS OF OUR TREATMENT

Using Zubin's vulnerability model for behavior disorders (1975), the first critical stage in personality development is in early childhood. Developmental evidence, particularly language studies, indicate that a differentiated and conceptualized sense of identity or "I" emerges only past the age of two. The presence of sufficient ego structure at this time makes the parental attitude of hostile rejection threatening to the child's self-concept. Hence, an attitude of rejection, overt or covert, prevents the child from satellizing (identifying) with his parents. Acceptance, however, is not sufficient for satellization to occur. Although a child is accepted, it may be for the wrong reasons. In some instances a parent may see the child as an extension of himself and not as an entity with a right to its own existence. Rather, the worth of the child is based on its serving as a potential resource for satisfying the ambitions of the parent. Such an attitude of extrinsic overvaluation also leads to non-satellization. Since this attitude does not pose an immediate threat to the self-concept, and its implications are more subtle, the issue of satellization is delayed. In any event, the attitudes of rejection and extrinsic valuation lead to non-satellization and constitute one type of maturational failure.

Parental attitudes differ in intensity and their impact is contingent upon the particular stage of ego development of the child. They reflect a variety of causes that determines in turn their persistence and pervasiveness. On the one hand, attitudes that serve adjustive purposes for a parent's personality, and that originate in his own childhood, have potentially more disruptive effects than attitudes that appear because of stresses from life events or transitional stages in the child's development.

The effect of parental attitudes is constrained by the different ego needs of the child at different stages of development. For example, the child's identification with his parents, is perhaps *the* most important event during the preschool period. Kagan, for example, takes this position and expands on the meaning of identification. "Identification is, in part, the belief of a person that some attributes of a model (e.g., parents, siblings, relatives, peers, and fictional figures) are also possessed by him. A boy who realizes that he and his father share the same name, notes that they have similar facial features, and is told by relatives that they both have lively tempers, develops a belief that he is similar to his father. When this belief in similarity is accompanied by vicarious emotional experiences in the child that are appropriate to the model, we say that "the child identifies with the model" (Kagan, 1958). Satellization also includes, however, both an attitude of dependent subservience on the part of the weaker member and an attitude of benevolent protection on the part of the dominant member in the relationship. A hostile, threatening, rejecting parent cannot serve as a figure with whom a child identifies freely in order to secure vicarious ego enhancement. Identification under such conditions can at best serve the ends of expediency or reduce anxiety by allowing the threatened child to imagine himself as the possessor of the form and powers of his threatening parents. In the more normal and usual family setting in this and other cultures, therefore, the typical child upon leaving the period of his infancy will seek, given but half a chance, to establish a satellizing relationship with his parents. The strength of this desire is frequently great enough to influence the child to interpret—more favorably than objective conditions warrant—the crucial aspects of parental attitudes which make this re-formation in ego structure possible. In clinical practice one frequently encounters children who rationalize their parent's brutality as a manifestation of love.

　　A second critical stage in personality development revolves around the issue of maturity, that is, the transformation of certain aspects of childhood into their socially acceptable adult counterparts. Hence, preadolescents and adolescents are vulnerable to parental attitudes that inhibit or retard such a personality reorganization. The attainment of volitional and executive independence, and the constellation of traits that support and implement these capacities are subject to the damaging effects of parental overprotectiveness, underdomination, and over-domination. The consequences of such attitudes represent a different kind of maturational failure than the failure to satellize. They stem from the failure to desatellize.

GENERAL DETERMINANTS OF PARENT ATTITUDES

　　How do parents come to acquire the attitudes they hold in relation to their children? In general, four categories of determinants may be delineated: the wider culture; the parent's own family and childhood experience; his personality structure; and various situational variables. The first factor accounts for intercultural or subcultural (psychosocial) variability in parent attitudes, the latter three factors for idiosyncratic variability.

Determinants of Psychosocial Variability in
Parent Attitudes

The extent to which parents are disposed to be accepting, protective, dominative, etc., in dealing with their children is obviously determined in part by the ways
that prevailing cultural ideology defines appropriate norms of parent-child interaction.

The norms and values relating to parent-child interaction are therefore products of custom, tradition, ideological evolution, and historical accident; of
economic, social, political, and religious beliefs and institutions; of institutionalized modes of timing and handling shifts in the biosocial status of the
child; and the different ways of ordering marital relationships, family structure and
intrafamilial roles (Clausen, 1966; Murdock & Whiting, 1951). In our own culture
approved standards of parent behavior tend to correspond to shifts in attitudes and
practices advocated in successive editions of such widely read manuals as the
Children's Bureau Bulletin on *Infant Care* and Spock's *Baby and Child Care*
(Bronfenbrenner, 1961). Conformity to these currently approved child-rearing
fashions is more characteristic of middle-class than lower-class parents (Bronfenbrenner, 1961; Caldwell, 1964; Hoffman & Lippitt, 1960; Kohn, 1963; L.
Yarrow, 1963).

Cultural ideology influences parents' child-rearing attitudes because it serves
as a major, prestigeful frame of reference in their evolution. It has been shown, for
example, that parents' expectations of children's level of play are easily manipu-
lated by "expert" opinion (Merrill, 1946). Parents also feel a sense of obligation
to rear their children in conformity to prevailing social values, and fear both social
censure and feelings of guilt if they deviate too much from what is expected of
them. If alternative philosophies of child rearing are available, the parent is
naturally more apt to choose one that is consonant with his temperamental
preferences. His choice is also characterized respectively by varying degrees of
intellectual objectivity or subjective rationalization, of independent thinking or
uncritical acceptance of the current vogue, and of emotional or merely verbal
identification. Irrespective of the basis on which they are chosen, as long as
emotional involvement is present, such beliefs have the same impact on parent
behavior as do attitudes derived from idiosyncratic personality factors. Purely
verbal acceptance of child-rearing beliefs is not entirely without effect on parental
behavior, but obviously leads to less spontaneous impulses, as well as to impulses
that are often negated by underlying attitudes.

The aforementioned factors relating to "cultural ideology" probably account
for the cross-cultural differences observed in certain dimensions of child rearing.
Cross-cultural differences are complexly organized into clusters of child-rearing
attitudes and practices. Thus, the general observation that German mothers are
more *controlling* than American mothers (Rapp, 1961) must be qualified by the
fact that German mothers control more than American mothers in behaviors such
as table manners and toilet training, whereas the opposite obtains in sexual

behavior (Karr & Wesley, 1966). In addition, German parents rely more on love-oriented discipline (e.g., withdrawal of affection) as compared to English and American parents (Bronfenbrenner, 1969). Cultural ideology probably also accounts for such differences in parental attitudes and practices as are observed in Japanese (Matsumoto and Smith, 1961), Israeli (Rabin, 1959; Rapaport, 1958), and Russian culture (Bronfenbrenner, 1968, 1969).

SOCIAL CLASS FACTORS

Present-day investigations of social-class differences in parental attitudes suggest that more middle-class than lower-class parents have assimilated the permissive approach in interacting with children and managing child care routines. They have especially moved away from the more strict styles of care and discipline advocated in the early twenties and thirties (Bronfenbrenner, 1961).

> Generally, the research has shown that middle-class parents provide more warmth and are more likely to use reasoning, isolation, show of disappointment, or guilt-arousing appeals in disciplining the child. They are also likely to be more permissive about demands for attention from the child, sex behavior, aggression to parent, table manners, neatness and orderliness, noise, bedtimes rules, and general disobedience. Working-class parents are more likely to use ridicule, shouting, or physical punishment in disciplining the child, and to be generally more restrictive. (Becker, 1964, p. 171)

Social-class differences in child-rearing practices and attitudes have generally diminished in the past twenty years (Bronfenbrenner, 1958, 1961). In spite of these diminished differences, however, social-class differences are still apparent between the middle and lower-class stratas with regard to parent-child relationships. Middle-class mothers typically exercise much greater supervisory control and direction over their children's activities (Walters, Connor & Zunich, 1964). They extend this supervisory role outside the home by placing restrictions on the child's freedom to come and go as he pleases, to attend movies alone, to keep late hours, to choose his own associates, and to explore the life of the streets (Davis & Havighurst, 1946; Havighurst & Taba, 1949; Maas, 1951; Short, 1966). Yet, within the home, middle-class parents value curiosity, happiness, consideration, and self-control more highly than do lower-class parents (Kohn, 1963). Lower-class parental values tend to center on conformity to external prescriptions, whereas middle-class parents place greater emphasis on self-direction (Kohn, 1963).

Where social-class differences are present, it is very difficult to determine the mechanisms that mediate these differences. Social-class studies that directly link social-class status to behavioral consequences in the child are open to the criticism that the conceptual jump between class membership and behavioral differences leaves open many possible alternative explanations for any empirical relationship (Hoffman & Lippitt, 1960). Although social-class differences are negligible at the present time, the same practices probably have a different basis in each class. In the lower-class they are more a matter of custom, tradition, and folklore acquired from parents, relatives, and friends. In the middle-class they are more an expression of belief in the formal ideology of child rearing currently approved of by the "experts" (Bronfenbrenner, 1958, 1961). Kohn (1963) takes a different slant on the differences observed, arguing they are a reflection of differences in values held by parents of different classes. The values held by parents of different classes reflect in turn the different life situations that are experienced by the members of these classes. For example, middle-class occupations deal more with interpersonal relations, ideas, and symbols, whereas working-class occupations deal more with the manipulation of things (Kohn, 1963). These types of differences create different value orientations, which are reflected in the kinds of family interactions that develop (Kohn, 1963). Situational factors may also operate to account for the fact that there are no differences between social classes in the frequency of physical punishment when size of family is controlled (Clausen, 1966).

Determinants of Idiosyncratic Variability in Parent Attitudes

Since all aspects of goal and method in child rearing are not culturally standardized, much room remains for the operation of situational factors and of genically and experientially determined differences in temperament, values, and resourcefulness. But even in those areas in which cultural prescriptions do exist, idiosyncratic variability in parental attitude may still occur. First, even in a relatively homogeneous subculture, parents perceive much heterogeneity in child-rearing practices and interpret them selectively in accordance with their own preferences. Whatever the degree of objective homogeneity that does exist (Brodbeck, Nogee, De Mascio, 1956; Kohn, 1963), the more heterogeneous the cultural norm is perceived to be, the less coercive is its influence on individual attitudes. Hence, in the absence of any clear-cut normative standard of discipline, mothers tend to rely more on their own experience and predilections than to conform to the perceived view (Brodbeck et al., 1956). Second, all cultures tolerate a certain degree of deliberate non-conformity from its members, which is quite variable from one culture to another. In our own culture, the norms and ideal conceptions of what a good family should be are relatively diffuse, admitting of many alternatives and variations within different segments of the population; thus even marked deviations may draw only mild disapproval (Clausen, 1966). Generally speaking, greater individual latitude is permitted in matters of method than in matters of goal since it is often appreciated that different techniques may yield the same end result. The culture thus makes fewer demands on parents for conformity during early childhood when the achievement of goals is still distant and when children are largely restricted to their own homes. On the other hand, parents may be more inclined to follow their own prefernces when their children are older, for, by that time, the parents have acquired a greater backlog of child-rearing experience. In any case, the extent to which the individual parent is disposed to ignore social guideposts and expert opinion and follow his own notions is extremely variable (Merrill, 1946) and depends on such traits as self-sufficiency, self-confidence, independence of thought, suggestibility, critical sense, and need for public approval.

Idiosyncratic variability in parental attitudes is partly a function of family tradition since, in some ways, the family as a whole tends to evolve its own unique culture, norms, values, and role definitions (Handel, 1965). Idiosyncratic variability is also a function of parents' memories of their own childhood, and of their affective reactions to the practices of their own parents. The structure of the family may mediate unique interactions relating to size of the family and ordinal position (Clausen, 1966; Rosenberg & Sutton-Smith, 1966). For example, mothers of single-child families exhibit higher overall rates of talking to their infants than mothers in families of several children (Gewirtz & Gewirtz, 1968). The influence of situational factors such as current economic stresses and marital discord, must also be considered (Clausen, 1966). As discussed previously, the personality characteristics of the child may make it difficult to predict the outcome of certain forms of parent-child interaction. The child's unique personality characteristics may contribute to the production of unique interaction patterns with his parents (Bell, 1964, 1968).

Also important, in relation to intracultural variation in child rearing, is the fact that parent attitudes are largely a characteristic manifestation of an individual's ego structure (e.g., feelings of adequacy and security, ego aspirations, level of anxiety, volitional and executive independence, moral obligation, self-preoccupation, ability to postpone hedonistic gratification, emotional relatedness to others) and of other personality traits such as ascendence, introversion-extraversion, motherliness, hostility, and acceptance of the female role. Observed parental behavior and measured personality characteristics of parents are substantially related. "In the mother's social interaction with the child as she takes on the maternal role she . . . expresses . . . emotional needs" that are salient in the current economy of her personality organization (Behrens, 1954). The attitudes that are evoked by these needs are sometimes directly adjustive in the sense that they satisfy needs for ego enhancement (as in overvaluation) or reduce anxiety (as in overprotection). On the other hand, they may chiefly give vent to deep-seated feelings (e.g., hostility) or insulate the individual from parental obligations that interfere with the satisfaction of more pressing needs (as in rejection attributable to anxiety or narcissism).

CHARACTERISTICS OF PARENTAL ATTITUDES

Attitudes and Practices

We have already taken the position that child-rearing practices, in and of themselves, can only affect the immediate behavior of the child if they are reflective of broad, pervasive, and reasonably self-consistent attitudes on the part of parents. Although personality factors are undoubtedly prepotent in fashioning the major content of the more significant parental attitudes, cultural, familial, and situational determinants cannot be ignored. Regardless of their source, all parental attitudes affect child-rearing practices. Purely verbal and ego-peripheral beliefs, however, are associated with practices that tend to have a transitory effect on the behavior of the child rather than a more lasting influence on his personality development. The child's adjustment, as illustrated by his responses to parental socialization techniques, is thus a reflection of a cluster of maternal personality characteristics rather than of specific child-rearing practices (Bayley & Schaefer, 1960; Behrens, 1954).

Because of other non-attitudinal determinants of child-rearing practices, and because of individual differences in the meaning that identical practices have for different parents, it is not possible to infer *from the mere presence of a practice in a given parent what its attitudinal significance is*. We have to look for the latter in the parents' manner of administering a large number of specific practices in recurrent situations. This very pervasiveness of parental attitudes renders any single practice relatively insignificant as a determining factor in personality development. It is also important to realize that parental attitudes can be communicated to children in other ways than through rearing practices, and that such attitudes are both reinforced and counteracted by other socializing agents.

Consistency and Continuity

Consistency is an important aspect of parental behavior because of its undoubted effect on the behavior and personality development of the child. Inconsistency generates confusion regarding what is expected, contributes to the production of antisocial behavior and maladjustment (Becker, 1964), increases susceptibility to fear and anger, and probably retards ego maturation and socialization. Although parents naturally vary greatly in the consistency of their child-rearing attitudes (Becker, 1964; Clausen, 1966), such attitudes (like any other meaningful expression of personality) must necessarily be characterized by considerable intersituational generality. Apart from reasons inherent in the very organization of personality, a conscious need for self-consistency apparently operates in many persons. This does not preclude, of course, inconsistency stemming from situational factors, ambivalent feelings, or particular idiosyncrasies; inconsistency that the parent is unable to recognize; or genuinely high tolerance for self-perceived inconsistency.

Some direct evidence of intersituational consistency in parent attitudes has been found in studies of parent-child interaction (Lafore, 1945; Medinnus, 1967; Shirley, 1941). Such consistency can also be inferred from the fact that logically related parental behaviors intercorrelate ·meaningfully to form more inclusive attitudinal clusters (Baldwin, Kalhorn & Breese, 1945, 1949; Bayley & Schaefer,

1960b; Becker, 1964; Cline, Richards & Needham, 1963; Nichols, 1962; Sears, Maccoby & Levin, 1957). On the other hand, apparent evidence of inconsistency—that is, non-significant intercorrelations among permissiveness scores on different child-rearing practices (Sewall, Mussen & Harris, 1955; Schaefer, 1965)—is mostly phenotypic; it reflects the operation of non-attitudinal meanings associated with a given practice. Although mothers may employ seemingly contradictory practices, the attitudinal content permeating the *manner in which they are administered* may be highly uniform for both mother and child. This supposition is consistent with the finding that high positive correlations may exist between the child's adjustment and the mother's character structure and maternal role even though no significant relationships prevail between adjustment and specific child-rearing practices (Behrens, 1954).

CONTINUITY

Despite the abundance of clinical impressions (Levy, 1943; Shirley, 1941; Symonds, 1949), systematic empirical evidence of longitudinal continuity in parental attitudes is extremely sparse. Nevertheless, since a parent's child-rearing attitudes might be expected to remain about as stable as his personality, it is plausible to suppose that within certain limits of variation a given parent tends to manifest the same general kinds of child-rearing attitudes throughout his parental tenure. The determinants of longitudinal continuity in personality structure have been discussed in detail elsewhere. In addition to those factors that tend to keep personality functioning in a relatively stable way, numerous cultural expectancies regarding parental role tend to constrict intra- as well as interindividual variability in the expression of parental attitudes.

Considerable basis also exists, however, for discontinuity in parental attitudes—both in the culture and in the personality functioning of the parent. Apart from the influence of changing fads and fashions, many culturally standardized modifications and reversals in parental attitudes are expected with shifts in the biosocial status of the child; and even if basic changes do not occur in the parent's personality structure, the manifest behavioral correlates of feelings of security and adequacy, of level of anxiety and ego aspiration, and of self-preoccupation all tend to vary with vicissitudes in life history. Because of the inescapable ambivalence in his feelings, the parent is also apt to be more impressed at certain times than at others with either the satisfactions or the burdens of child rearing. As more children are added to the family, he may find one sex or temperament more or less congenial; he may also either adapt better to the responsibilities of parenthood or find them increasingly intolerable. For example, sex of the child interacts with dimensions of child-rearing; mothers of boys show more stability and continuity in the factor "loving vs. hostile" and less stability in autonomy-control when compared with mothers of girls (Bayley, 1964, Shaefer & Bayley, 1960b). In addition to the above, parents are more or less inclined to think of children as advantages during different segments of the life cycle (Pohlman,

1967). As already suggested, because of marked preference or distaste for different age-period aspects of the parental role, parents may undergo marked change in their overall attitudinal orientation toward the child. Finally, the child precipitates discontinuity by sometimes forcing parents to change their attitudes and values (Brim, 1967).

Difficulties in Measuring Parent Attitudes

Inasmuch as parents are highly ego-involved in their role, it is extremely difficult to obtain valid measures of their child-rearing attitudes. Observational and self-report techniques are partly contaminated by parents' natural hesitancy in revealing information or behavior that would give an unfavorable impression of their adequacy or intentions as parents (Hoffman & Lippitt, 1960; M. R. Yarrow, 1963). It is especially difficult to overcome this methodological problem in the case of middle-class parents, since they are particularly well informed about the kinds of attitudes and practices approved by the "experts" (Hoffman & Lippitt, 1960; Kohn, 1963; L. Yarrow, 1963). This may be one of the reasons why "approved" items on scales designed to measure parental attitudes tend to have little discriminating power (Schaefer & Bell, 1958). Distortions occurring in an interview with the mother can be partially counterbalanced by also interviewing the father and child (L. Yarrow, 1963). Retrospective reports are highly suspect (M. R. Yarrow, 1963) although there are individual differences in the accuracy of retrospective data (Wenar & Coulter, 1962). Retrospective reports of mothers also vary in accuracy across different content areas (Mednick & Schaffer, 1963). The problems with retrospective data make *observation* of parent-child interaction more attractive as a viable method of measuring parental attitudes (M. R. Yarrow, 1963).

Instruments of research on parental attitudes have been devised (e.g., Schaefer & Bell, 1958), but they have not as yet been very successful in predicting parent or child behaviors in observed settings (Becker & Krug, 1965; Brody, 1965). In general, most studies carried out on parental attitudes have considered the adult as the active agent of the interaction with the child serving as the passive recipient of these attitudes (Bell, 1968; Clausen, 1966; Medinnus, 1967). More sophisticated studies of parent-child interaction will have to develop designs that will assess interactions in a reciprocal manner (Bell, 1968). Evidence for reciprocal interactions between parent and child is indicated by the finding that scores on parental attitude are consistently higher in mothers with children who have congenital defects as compared with mothers of normal children (Bell, 1964). Finally, because self-report techniques with parents are contaminated and also because the personality development of children is influenced more proximately by the attitudes *they* perceive than by the objective properties of the latter (as reported by parents or observers), we have advocated that parental attitudes be measured by ascertaining how they are perceived by children (Ausubel et al.,

1954). This can be done either through direct, subjective inquiry or by using projective techniques. Although the former method is more transparent, it enjoys the advantages of greater denotative specificity and intersituational generality.

Maternal and Paternal Roles

The bulk of the early literature on parent-child relationships has analyzed the roles of parents without any further specification of sex (Brim, 1957). The father, especially, has been ignored by psychologists when studying the relationships between parents and children (Nash, 1965).

Although maternal and paternal roles overlap to a great extent, they are clearly differentiated in all cultural settings. The differentiation is naturally related to the social sex roles, to the concepts of masculinity and femininity, and to the division of labor prevailing in a given culture. The traditional family in Western society during earlier centuries tended to be patriarchal with the father having maximum power over both wife and children (Clausen, 1966). Although this condition still prevails in Oriental, Moslem, and Latin Catholic societies, the trends in contemporary American society are moving in the direction where both law and public opinion put definite limits on the husband relative to the wife (Clausen, 1966). Although marriage relationships in contemporary American society are characterized by joint family decisions, there is nevertheless ample evidence to indicate that the father still maintains priority and the stronger final voice (Clausen, 1966).

Although our culture is patriarchal in law, it is matricentric rather than patricentric as regards child rearing (Ostrovsky, 1959). Interestingly, as the allocation of authority is moving away from the father and is being shared reciprocally by both husband and wife, there is a corresponding increase in the father's participation in child-rearing and household tasks (Bronfenbrenner, 1961; Rogier, 1967). In general, the mother's role remains more highly structured and culturally standardized than the father's; for one thing fathers, unlike mothers, seldom compare notes about their offspring. The father's role is also derived more completely from learned concepts and interpersonal experience; it is reinforced at no time by hormonal factors or by childbearing and lactation.

As mentioned previously, American culture is somewhat diffuse in terms of its role allocation when compared with other societies. The relative power of the spouses depends on the husband's occupational status, the couple's comparative educational status, the wife's work participation, the involvement of the wife with small children, and the personalities of husband and wife (Clausen, 1966). In general, there appears to be a division of parental role functions in the family, the father exhibiting primarily instrumental functions (e.g., economic support) and the mother expressive (nurturant and affectional) functions (Clausen, 1966; Miller & Swanson, 1958; Nash, 1965; Parsons & Bales, 1955). The mother is perceived as providing most of the routine nurturant care, emotional succorance, and discipline (Droppleman & Schaefer, 1963; Emmerich, 1962; Ghosh & Sinha, 1966; Radke, 1946), and she is viewed as a more friendly and less threatening (Kagan, 1956a). For these reasons she is more frequently the preferred parent, especially in time of stress, and also occupies the central position in the child's image of the family (Clausen, 1966; Mott, 1954). This position may be somewhat challenged if the mother is employed and the father takes a greater share in the household tasks (Clausen, 1966). She is also perceived by girls as a model to be emulated in growing up (Gardner, 1947).

In the early years of the child's life, the father's role is more passive, but as children grow older they discriminate male roles on the basis of power (Emmerich, 1961). If the father has any special role in the family (apart from economic provider), it is that of chief authority figure, moral arbiter, and disciplinarian. Traditionally his discipline is more arbitrary and severe (Kagan, 1956a; Radke, 1946) than the mother's; when mutiny is brewing it is he who "lays down the law."* The father is conceptualized on the semantic differential as stronger, longer, and darker (Kagan, Hosken & Watson, 1961). Studies on boys' moral development indicate that the role played by fathers in discipline takes on greater significance with increasing age (Hoffman, 1963). If their reactions to thematic materials are truly reflective of real-life behavior, children adopt more submissive attitudes toward the father than toward the mother (Kates, 1951). This situation probably still prevails despite the trend toward a more equalitarian type of father-child relationship (Radke, 1946; Tasch, 1952). Also, insofar as their limited time permits, fathers consciously play the roles of guide, teacher, companion, and affectionate rearer; influence the mother's practices; and help establish the value structure of the home (Clausen, 1966; Hoffman, 1963; Tasch, 1952).

Extremely important in structuring the father-child relationship is the mother's attitude toward her husband and his parental role. As the major socializing influence in his life, the child takes his cue from her in responding to the father, especially when the latter is separated from the home (Nash, 1965). The perception of the father is also related to social class, children from middle-class families seeing their fathers as more powerful in the family than lower-class fathers (Hess & Torney, 1967). This situation is partially a reflection of the father's occupation; because as the male becomes more dependent, passive, and conforming in the occupational world, the wife's relative authority increases in the home (Clausen, 1966).

The father's role is also somewhat differentiated for the two sexes. He helps the girl define her biological and social sex role by treating her endearingly as a little woman (Colley, 1959). She, in turn, tends to find his personality more congenial than the mother's (Gardner, 1947). In relation to the boy, although not

---

*Mothers actually give more coercive responses than fathers to hypothetical problem situations because they bear the greater share of the responsibility in managing children's misbehavior. To act consistently with cultural expectations of femininity, however, they tend more to sugarcoat their aggressiveness (Jackson, 1956).

consciously recognizing it, the father serves as a model of masculinity and of the male sex role, including acceptable forms of exhibiting male aggression (Gardner, 1947; Mischel, 1966; Sears, Pintler & Sears, 1946). Preschool boys, characterized as generous, perceive their fathers as warm and nurturant (Rutherford & Mussen, 1968). Nevertheless, the father ordinarily subjects his son to more rigorous disciplinary control than his daughter and is much less affectionate toward him; boys accordingly tend to regard their mother's disposition as more congenial (Gardner, 1947). Middle-class fathers tend to play a more active and supervisory role but at the same time are more supportive of their sons as compared to lower-class fathers (Clausen, 1966). Finally, several studies indicate, especially in the case of boys, that when the father rather than the mother is the disciplinarian, the child is more likely to be angry, assertive, and directly aggressive, whereas maternal discipline is more related to inhibition of anger and hostility and to psychosomatic ailments (Clausen, 1966).

Ordinal Position in the Family

Parent attitudes toward and treatment of the child vary to some extent with the latter's ordinal position in the family constellation:

> Birth order, i.e., the position of an individual among his siblings, is obviously linked with family size. It is also linked with age of the parents since first-born children will tend to have younger and last-born children older parents. Moreover, the sex of siblings and their spacing may contribute substantially to the meaning of a given position. Being first, middle, or last may tend to have certain meanings and consequences, but so may being the only boy or girl in a family with several children of the opposite sex. (Clausen, 1966, p. 15)

The above conditions obviously make it difficult to draw clear conclusions about birth order effects, but some tentative findings are worthy of note. The positions of the oldest, youngest, and only child are most highly differentiated. The first child is more likely to be planned and wanted and to be the recipient of his mother's succorance for a longer period of time (Sears, Maccoby & Levin, 1957). At the same time, because of the parents' inexperience, they are more likely to be more anxious with the first child (Clausen, 1966; Warren, 1966). Although first-borns receive slightly greater warmth and affection than the second-born (Clausen, 1966), parents at the same time tend to be less relaxed and more interfering with first-born children (Hilton, 1967). Parents are less permissive with first-borns with respect to feeding and weaning, more worrisome about sickness and danger, and more nurturant at bedtime (Sears, 1950). The oldest child is often given responsibility for other siblings and is expected to "set a good example" (Bossard & Boll, 1955; Mauco & Rambaud, 1951); his early self-concept is based more on parents' appraisal, whereas later-borns' self-conceptions have a large component of peer reflection (Clausen, 1966). Because of his initial privileged status, he is more likely than later-born children to feel that a sibling is favored by one of his parents (Clausen, 1966).

The youngest child receives a considerable amount of attention since he interacts with parents and older brothers and sisters. He is most likely to be called by affectionate names (Clausen, 1966), is most frequently the "spoiled one" in the family (Bossard & Boll, 1955), is most likely to display infantile home relationships (Wile & Davis, 1941), and is most given to peculation (Wile & Davis, 1941). He also exhibits more attention-seeking behavior (Mauco & Rambaud, 1951), school difficulty, and intersibling conflict (Wile & Davis, 1941). In larger families, the mother tends to be more closely involved in both affection and authority with the youngest child, whereas the father tends to play a relatively greater authority role with the oldest child (Clausen, 1966). In keeping with his greater possibility of being "spoiled," the youngest son or daughter at any age level is less likely to be spanked than is a first-born son or daughter of the same age (Clausen, 1966). This difference between youngest and oldest children in amount of punishment increases as the size of the family increases (Clausen, 1966).

Although there are many inconclusive results in studies of birth order effects, it is safe to indicate some general, though tentative, conclusions. Measured intelligence (I.Q.) is not appreciably related to sibling order, although there is a tendency for first-borns to score slightly higher on verbal intelligence, which is consistent with the finding that they speak earlier and receive more verbal stimulation (Clausen, 1966). First-borns score slightly lower on tests of perceptual discrimination when compared with later-borns (Clausen, 1966). Oldest male children have higher achievement needs than their siblings (Altus, 1965; Bartlett & Smith, 1966; Chittenden, Foan, Zweil & Smith, 1968; Clausen, 1966; Warren, 1966). There is also some evidence that oldest children are more susceptible to normative influence while later-born children are more susceptible to informational influence (Becker, Lerner & Carroll, 1966; Clausen, 1966; Warren, 1966). These findings, however, are not unequivocal (Clausen, 1966; Warren, 1966). For example, first-born males are more readily influenced by group pressures (Clausen, 1966), yet the findings for females are inconsistent with regard to this type of influence (Carrigan & Julian, 1966; Clausen, 1966).

The positive findings on oldest children concerning susceptibility to influence may be partly attributed to their initial greater internalization of parental values (Altus, 1965; Palmer, 1966). Apart from intense anxiety situations, there appears to be no clear-cut consistency relating affiliation needs or affiliative behavior to birth order (Clausen, 1966; Warren, 1966). In anxiety-provoking situations first-borns appear to be more affiliative and conforming (Carrigan & Julian, 1966; Clausen, 1966; Schachter, 1959, 1963). In the judgment of parents and teachers, later-born siblings are more comfortable and relaxed with peers than are first-borns (Clausen, 1966). Oldest children are also less likely to involve themselves in high-risk sports (Nisbett, 1968) and are more cautious in other aspects of play

(Collard, 1968). Consistent with the greater pressures placed on oldest children, they exhibit more anxiety than later born siblings (Clausen, 1966; Zucker, Manosevitz & Lanyon, 1968). This finding is clearer in younger children and is confounded with sex differences at older ages (Sutton-Smith & Rosenberg, 1965). Finally, although oldest children have demonstrated higher adjustment scores on personality tests (Lessing & Oberlander, 1967), there are several studies that report less behavior pathology for later-born children (Clausen, 1966). Part of the apparent inconsistencies in these findings is probably due to the lack of differentiation between younger and middle siblings in these studies (Warren, 1966).

There have been many studies in the past few years showing that first-borns demonstate greater scholastic and vocational achievement (e.g., Bracileg, 1968).

IMPACT OF PARENT ATTITUDES ON PERSONALITY DEVELOPMENT

Basis of Impact

On what grounds is it postulated that during early childhood parental attitudes exert extremely important determining effects on later personality development? First, the parent is associated from the very beginning in a benevolent and altruistic light with the satisfaction of the child's visceral needs, biological survival, and emotional security; and throughout the entire period of childhood he continues to wield tremendous power in regulating the child's motivations, satisfactions, and standards, and in influencing the course and outcome of various stages of ego development (Clausen, 1968a). Since perception of persons and emotional response to their presence and absence antedate similar awareness of and reaction to inanimate objects (Tagiuri, 1969), the sense of self emerges and grows in an interpersonal context (Adams, 1967; Clausen, 1968a).

Second, early experience has a disproportionate effect on development because it enjoys the benefits of *primacy*. In the unstructured attitudinal field of children, from which most competing influences are excluded, the specific behavioral differentiations and value systems of parents soon become relatively preemptive in their patterning effects. These effects tend to perpetuate themselves by making the individual selectively reaction-sensitive to the conditions that bring them about; and once consolidation occurs, reorganization is resisted because of "perceptual constancy," the tendency to utilize existing orientations and habits before acquiring new ones, and the stability of ego-involved components of personality. Further enhancing the effects of primacy is the fact that childhood embraces many critical periods of development in which maximum susceptibility to environmental influences prevails. During these periods, when development is still not committed in a particular direction, the individual is extremely flexible; afterwards, the very fact that commitment has already occurred makes for rigidity.

Although less crucial in their contribution, several additional factors explain the importance of parental attitudes for personality development: (1) increased susceptibility to trauma because of immature interpretive and adjustive capacities; (2) the insusceptibility of preverbal learning to counteractive verbal influences, (3) the resistance of inconsistently reinforced learning to extinction, and (4) the transferability of attitudes and habits acquired in early family life to later behavior as spouse and parent (Child, 1954).

Factors Limiting the Impact of Parental Attitudes

The above statement regarding the impact of parental attitudes on personality development requires many serious qualifications. The effects of parental attitudes are dependent on their communicability to children; are variable with normative and individual differences in cognitive capacity and perceptual acuity, with the particular developmental needs that are dominant at a given stage of personality growth, and with the temperamental characteristics of the child; and are modifiable for better or worse by concurrent or subsequent experience outside the home. Thus, since parental attitudes are not the sole determinants of personality development and are frequently not even communicable to children, the widespread tendency to blame parents for *all* behavior problems is not only unwarranted but leads to unwholesome self-recriminatory and apologetic attitudes toward children.

There is some evidence of very early ability in children to distinguish certain emotions (e.g., the fact that babies cry when they are shown contorted faces) but their discriminative capacities do not go beyond this primitive level (Tagiuri, 1969). As we have already emphasized repeatedly, the infant's cognitive immaturity insulates him from all but the most overt and obvious manifestations of interpersonal attitudes. This insulation is seen in the striking lack of specificity in the stimuli capable of evoking a smile, since even scolding can elicit such a response (Tagiuri, 1969). Hence, the impact of the parent's attitudinal substrate first begins to overshadow the influence of his grosser feelings and actions when the child enters the postinfantile stage (Kagan, 1967). But even later it is highly questionable whether many covert and adequately screened attitudes that are only uncovered in the course of psychotherapy (e.g., hostility underlying apparent oversolicitude) are ever perceived—even "unconsciously"—by many children. Here much depends on individual differences in perceptual sensitivity or in empathic ability.

> Determination of whether a parent is rejecting or not cannot be answered by focusing primarily on the behaviors of the parents. Rejection is not a fixed invariant quality of behavior qua behavior. Like pleasure, pain, or beauty, rejection is in the mind of the rejectee. It is a belief held by the child; not an action by the parent. (Kagan, 1967, p. 132).

Cognitive and verbal immaturity set limits on the child's ability to make fine distinctions among feeling tones, to conceptualize and generalize his impressions, and to retain his experiences over long periods of time. Furthermore, when he is mature enough to form categorical judgments, he often tends to dismiss the manifest content of immediately perceived experience (unless it is too obtrusive to be ignored), and to infer from a culturally standardized proposition (e.g., all parents are *supposed* to love and protect their children) that his parents must obviously love him.

Constitutional factors also limit and modify the influence of parental attitudes (Becker, 1964; Bell, 1968). Because of variable, genically determined temperamental predispositions in children, the *same* parental attitude may have different effects. Apathetic and submissive children tend to become passively dependent in response to overprotection, whereas self-assertive and ascendent children are more apt to react aggressively (Meyers, 1944). Depending on their strength, such predispositions may prove very tenacious—even in the face of opposing environmental pressures (Bell, 1968). They not only *evoke* different kinds of behaviors in the parent but may also modify the latter's child-rearing attitudes (Bell, 1968; Medinnus, 1967). For example, children who are characteristically "person-oriented" reinforce social responses in parents, whereas children of "low person-orientation" tend to induce less nurturant responses in their parents (Bell, 1968).

Apart from changes in the parents' needs, personality traits, insights and current level of adjustment, other influences both within and outside the home modify and counteract the impact of early parental attitudes on the child's personality development. Balancing forces are usually at hand to soften extreme attitudes and practices. The deviant parent must first contend with the objections of his spouse, and later on with the opposition of relatives, neighbors, and friends. As the child grows older, he is increasingly exposed to the direct influence of persons other than parents—to siblings, age-mates, relatives, teachers, and other adults. Some children, who never manage to identify with their parents, find an almost satisfactory substitute in a relative, teacher, or parent of a playmate. By the same token, the beneficial influence of favorable intrafamilial experience in early childhood may be partly undone by detrimental parental attitudes in later childhood, or by crippling disease, delayed pubescence, economic hardship, racial discrimination, etc.

Unfavorable parental attitudes are also limited in their effects when they are not operative during the particular critical periods of developmental need or maximal growth for which they are especially relevant. In the presatellizing period, all that is required for adequate personality development is a certain amount of succorance, personal attention, and overt affection. The other major dimensions of the parent-child relationship that are so crucial for later stages of ego development seem relatively unimportant for the essential developmental tasks of infancy. Overdominating and overprotecting parents, parents who value their children for ulterior motives, and parents who are basically rejecting despite a veneer of affection, all seem to provide an adequate enough environment for the development of the omnipotent ego structure. During the second and third years of life, however, genuine emotional acceptance and intrinsic valuation of the child are essential for satellization; and the child accordingly becomes selectively sensitized in perceiving these aspects of parental attitude. Hence it no longer suffices for a parent to exhibit the outward manifestations of affection; evidence of an intrinsically accepting attitude in the smaller and more subtle aspects of feeling and action is required. It is at this time therefore that rejection has the most damaging effects on personality development. At a later age the child's more versatile and mature ego structure and his well-established set of defenses protect him somewhat from the trauma of rejection. At this time also there is more opportunity of forming satellizing and satellizing-like relationships to other adults and to the peer group.

Finally, the dominative, protective, motivating and critical aspects of parental attitude are most crucial during the period of desatellization; and children are accordingly most susceptible to such influences during the middle years of childhood (McGuire, 1969). Unless the parent sets appropriate expectations, standards, and limits; applies necessary coercive pressures; allows sufficient freedom for exploration, goal setting, and decision making; and shows appreciation of the child's progress in these directions, the ego status and ego maturity aspects of desatellization may be retarded.

A final limiting factor that should be considered is the *wide margin of safety* that applies to parental attitudes as to most regulatory conditions affecting human development. If the attitudes of parents are generally wholesome in relation to their children, considerable deviancy from the theoretical optimum and occasional "mistakes" are still compatible with normal personality development. In view of this fact and the probable noncommunicability of many attitudes, merciless self-recrimination about the underlying motivations and the possible irrevocable consequences of minor deviations from "accepted" practices is not only unnecessary but also robs parenthood of much joy and spontaneity.

DIMENSIONS OF PARENT ATTITUDES*

The preceding discussion of the impact of parental attitudes on personality development points up the importance for theoretical and research purposes of identifying and defining clearly as many significant variables as possible that are encompassed by the parent-child relationship. In no other way will it be possible to

---

*Our discussion of dimensions of parental attitudes will be restricted to an interpretation that is consistent with our chapter on ego development. Recent discussion of this topic may be found in Becker (1964), Schaefer (1961), and Zigler & Child (1969).

determine unambiguously the antecedents and consequences of various parental attitudes. Much of the difficulty in the past can be ascribed to confusion between popular and scientific usage, to overlapping of terms, and to lack of clarity in defining the precise aspects of the parent-child relationship. In the popular literature on child care, for example, "spoiled," "indulged," "overprotected," "underdominated" and "overvalued" are used almost interchangeably.

Early attempts at a more precise categorization of parental attitudes tended to oversimplify matters by using unidimensional (acceptance) or bidimensional (acceptance-domination) scales. With the growth of computers in the 1950s, larger samples and more complex statistical procedures have been increasingly utilized in attempting to distinguish between the multiple influences that parent attitudes have on the child's development (Becker, 1964). More explicit multiple scale approaches have emerged that initially were too unwieldly and atomistic in orientation to be useful in elucidating developmental sequences (e.g., Fels Parent Behavior Rating Scales; Champney, 1941). These multiple scales have been reduced in size by factor analysis or by interrelating variables meaningfully into naturally occurring syndromes (Baldwin, Kalhorn & Breese, 1949; Becker, 1964; Roff, 1949; Schaefer, 1961). Factorial structure of scales is dependent on the type of parent involved; thus experienced mothers, for example, reveal simpler patterns (Schaefer, 1961).

The number of factors that emerge also depends on the types of scales utilized (Schaefer, 1961). Even when statistical techniques are utilized to reduce the number of dimensions, these scales still leave much to be desired from the standpoint of making significant predictions from parent-child relationships to child behavior or to adult personality. Without differential weighting in terms of relationship to and significance for successive developmental tasks, they do not help us to understand how children in general progress from one sequential stage of personality to another or why a particular child acquires or fails to acquire the major attributes of ego structure characteristic of his age level. It is not surprising that certain dimensions of parent attitudes are thus less stable over time than developmentally more sensitive dimensions. For example, the dimension of autonomy versus control is much more variable developmentally than the dimension of love-hostility. "Differential consistency appears reasonable since the child's need for love is constant through time but the child's need for autonomy changes greatly from infancy to adolescence" (Schaefer, 1961).

Similar parent attitudes may have quite different outcomes depending on whether the individual is or is not a satellizer. Overprotection, overdomination, and rejection have very different effects in infancy, early childhood, and preadolescence. Also, phenotypically different attitudes such as rejection and extrinsic valuation are both associated with the same outcome of non-satellization. Without some conceptual scheme for systematizing the data, one ends up with a bewildering maze of discrete and uninterpretable correlations.

Another source of confusion has arisen from the widespread tendency to subsume the dominative aspects of parent behavior under overprotection, that is, to consider over and underdomination as subtypes of overprotection (Levy, 1943). Although such combinations of attitudes are frequently encountered, they are by no means inevitable. Many overprotective parents are able to maintain a proper balance of domination; contrariwise, over or underdominated children are not necessarily overprotected. The dimension of protectiveness refers to extent of parental care and solicitude. The overprotecting parent unduly prolongs infantile care, provides excessive personal contact and supervision, and seeks to furnish an environment for his child that is free of hurt, disappointment, failure, frustration, and exposure to the harsher realities of life. Its source inheres in projected anxiety: the parent mitigates his own unidentifiable anxiety by projecting threat onto the child and giving it more concrete reference. The dimension of dominance, on the other hand, refers to the relative balance of volitional self-assertiveness and deference between parent and child and is not related in origin to parent anxiety. Thus the confounding of the protective and the dominative aspects of parental attitudes is extremely unfortunate since each refers to clearly different roles and functions of parenthood. Only conceptual confusion can result when two discriminably different variables are treated as if they were coextensive. The confusion is even more regrettable when the entirely different origins and consequences of the two kinds of attitudes are considered.

It is true that overprotection and underdomination have an important point in common, namely, great reluctance in frustrating the child. In the overprotecting parent, however, it is part of the larger goal of reducing parental anxiety by sparing the child psychological and physical trauma rather than manifesting unassertiveness. If deferring to the child's will exposes the latter to physical or social danger, the overprotective parent would sooner frustrate the child's volitional independence. Thus, although the underdominating parent tends to be consistently deferential, the overprotecting parent can be yielding only in situations that either increase the child's infantile dependency or that do not contain threats of illness, injury, or failure.

It seems more fruitful and economical of effort to start, therefore, with a theoretical structure hypothesizing various stages of personality development with their component attributes and developmental tasks. By defining and categorizing parent-child relationships in terms of dimensions compatible with this structure, one can then test various hypotheses regarding the intrafamilial antecedents of various developmental outcomes by relating measurements of these dimensions to personality outcomes in children and adults. The dimensions of the parent-child relationship designated in Table 1 were formulated with this end in view. They are not the only dimensions that can possibly be identified, but they encompass the major aspects of this relationship that have relevance for the developmental tasks and processes described in Chapters 4, 5, and 6.

Although the above dimensions are separate variables, permitting in theory

Table 1

Dimensions of the Parent-Child Relationship*

Dimension (Parental Attitude or Behavior)	Child's Position on Scale	
	Upper Extreme	*Lower Extreme*
1. Emotional acceptance	Accepted	Rejected
2. Valuation of child for self or in terms of parent's ego needs	Intrinsically valued	Extrinsically valued
3. Magnitude of valuation of child's importance	Overvalued	Undervalued
4. Protectiveness (care, solicitude)	Overprotected	Underprotected
5. Dominance (self-assertiveness or deference to child's will)	Overdominated	Underdominated
6. Level of aspiration for child	Overmotivated	Undermotivated
7. Criticism of child (overt or implied)	Overcriticized	Undercriticized
8. Appreciation (recognition of child's competence)	Overappreciated	Underappreciated

*Adapted from D. P. Ausubel, Ego Development and the Personality Disorders.

an almost infinite number of combinations and permutations, the actual number of important combinations occurring in practice is sharply limited by hierarchical factors and psychological compatibility. Most important is the patterning influence of the key attitudes leading to satellization and non-satellization respectively. Satellizers are all both emotionally accepted and intrinsically valued, whereas non-satellizers are either rejected and extrinsically valued or accepted and extrinsically valued. The rejected group of non-satellizers is usually underprotected, overdominated, underappreciated, overcriticized, and undervalued. The extrinsically valued group of non-satellizers, on the other hand, is almost invariably overvalued, underdominated, overmotivated, undercriticized, and overappreciated. For all practical purposes, it is most convenient to refer to these two groups of non-satellizers as "rejected" and "overvalued" respectively. Greater variability in patterning prevails among parents of satellizing children. Except for the uniformity provided by the two prerequisite conditions, almost any combination of the remaining parental attitudes is possible.

ORIGIN OF SPECIFIC PARENTAL ATTITUDES

The attitudes that an adult displays as a parent go back in large part to his own childhood and the kind of relationship he enjoyed with his own parents. They reflect both the impact of the parent-child relationship on personality development and the influence that parents exert as models of parental role and function.

Rejection and Overvaluation

Both clinical experience and developmental logic suggest that non-satellizing children tend to have parents who themselves were non-satellizers. It is by no means true, however, that all non-satellizers have non-satellizing children. A history of rejection or extrinsic valuation in the parent's childhood predisposes him toward high ego aspirations and neurotic anxiety; and in such an individual immersed in his own ambitions and harassed by constant threat to self-esteem, self-preoccupation is easily understandable. In the case of women, it leads to reluctance to accept the feminine role in life and the compromises in prosecuting a career that motherhood necessarily entails. Under these circumstances, responsibility for the protective care and emotional succorance of a child may seem like such a formidable and burdensome duty that rejection becomes a very likely alternative. Other equally possible alternatives are attempts to achieve vicarious ego enhancement through projection of omnipotent ego aspirations onto the child (overvaluation) and efforts directed toward anxiety reduction through the mechanism of displacement, that is, perceiving the child as the object of threat (overprotection). The tendency toward self-preoccupation is also enhanced by narcissism and the inability to relate emotionally to others, which so frequently characterizes non-satellizers. These traits are more pronounced in overvalued than in rejected persons, since they proceed more from habituation to a one-way flow of affection and interest than from dread of emotional involvement for fear of repeating an experience of rejection. In some instances the hostile attitudes of a rejecting parent seem to stem at least in part from an unresolved residue of hostility toward his own parents or siblings, which in turn resulted from a situation of rejection or favoritism. By identifying with the role of his own rejecting parent, he vicariously gives vent to these feelings.

Given all of these personality predispositions toward becoming an overvaluing or rejecting parent, however, it does not necessarily follow that the non-satellizing individual will actually become one. Much depends on other personality traits as well as on various situational factors. His level of anxiety, for example, can be kept under better control if he is an able, enterprising, organized, and socially perceptive person. The more self-indulgent and viscertonic he is, the more resentful he is of any responsibilities toward others that interfere with the gratification of his own hedonistic needs. If he has a strong sense of moral obligation, he may endeavor to inhibit much of his hostility or even become oversolicitous in order to avoid guilt feelings. The unhampered expression of rejecting tendencies is also limited by the individual's sensitivity to prevailing cultural norms and to social censure. If he is concerned with appearances, he can usually find "reputable excuses for hating a child" (Symonds, 1949); and only too frequently the same narcissistic preoccupation with himself that causes him to neglect his child provides him with a thick skin in the face of public or private criticism.

The prevailing level of anxiety or hostility that becomes manifest from underlying personality trends is also affected by numerous situational factors. Latent residual hostility toward a parent is often reactivated by an unhappy marital relationship and then displaced onto the child. This is more likely to occur if the parent feels that he is being rejected by his spouse in favor of the child. A moderately positive correlation thus prevails between marital adjustment and the acceptance of children (Clausen, 1966; Porter, 1955). The entrance of an infant into the household, especially if he is ill or if his parents are confronted by vocational or financial difficulties, frequently exacerbates chronic anxiety. In any event the child's chances of being rejected are obviously increased if his sex, physique, or temperament are at variance with the parent's preferences. A docile child's reaction to rejection usually encourages a hostile or narcissistic parent to continue this treatment since the parent is not even required to placate his nuisance value. An irritable, self-assertive, and rebellious child, on the other hand, may destroy the equilibrium of an anxiety-torn parent who then utilizes the child's behavior as justification for the original rejection and the subsequent counteraggression.

The probability of developing *consistently* rejecting parental attitudes is determined in part by the individual's capacity for relating himself emotionally to others. In rejected persons this capacity, which is ever latent but inhibited by fear of rejection, has an excellent opportunity for overt expression in the form of warm, accepting parental attitudes since little threat of rejection can be anticipated from a child. Self-preoccupation here is largely a function of anxiety and can be mitigated if other personality traits and situational factors are favorable for keeping the level of anxiety under control. In overvalued individuals, on the other hand, self-preoccupation seems to be more a reflection of narcissism and incapacity for relating emotionally to others, and hence is less apt to be favorably influenced by benign environmental conditions. For similar reasons, the overvalued parent is also more disposed than the rejected parent to extend a more *passive* kind of rejection to his children. Lack of concern for the needs of others stemming from narcissism leads to neglect and indifference that arouse little guilt feelings since they reflect an habitual orientation in interpersonal relations. If current exacerbations of anxiety induce self-preoccupation in rejected parents, passive neglect and avoidance of parental responsibility are more likely to engender guilt feelings. The rejected parent thus tends to continue to care for and interact with the child—but resentfully and with evident hostility that he tries to rationalize as a form of counteragression made necessary by the latter's perverseness.

A final problem has to do with the basis of choice between rejecting and overvaluing attitudes. What differences might we anticipate between two parents, both non-satellizers with grandiose ego aspirations, one of whom finds the child a cumbersome and unwanted burden, while the other utilizes him as a principal vehicle for ego aggrandizement? Much seems to depend on the parent's capacity to perceive the dependent child as an extension of himself rather than as an entity in his own right, and to react to his triumphs as if they were his own achievements. This capacity probably reflects in part some degree of pessimism in the parent's appraisal of his chances for ego aggrandizement through his own efforts. Also, everything else being equal, the parent faced with the choice of either rejecting or overvaluing his child is more likely to choose the latter alternative as he is less hostile, embittered, and withdrawn, and is more extraverted, sociocentric and better able to relate to others.

Overprotection

We have already suggested that the principal basis of overprotecting attitudes is a form of parental anxiety in which the object of threat is displaced from parent to child. The parent is anxious, insecure, fearful of impending disaster, and feels inadequate to cope with the ordinary adjustive problems of life. By projecting the object of threat onto the child, he is able to mitigate his own anxiety in two ways: (1) some of the perceived threat to himself is deflected, thereby making the environment look less foreboding; and (2) he is better able to cope with the threats confronting the child than those besetting himself. He can isolate the child from painful experiences by using himself as a shield, since the frustrations facing a child are relatively concrete and avoidable; whereas he cannot insulate himself from the world and still maintain his own intense strivings. But the success he enjoys in protecting his child from danger and frustration is transferable to his own situation. Since the anxiety-ridden personality is also predisposed toward rejecting and overvaluing attitudes, overprotection may be regarded as an alternative to the latter orientations. Sometimes it occurs as a reaction-formation for covert rejecting tendencies or as a form of expiation for overt rejecting behavior. In some instances the predisposing anxiety is reinforced by such contributory factors as marital unhappiness, a long history of sterility or miscarriages, severe illness or injury in the child, and death of a previous child or close relative (Clausen, 1966; Levy, 1943; Staver, 1953).

Under and Overdomination

The simplest explanation of the origin of under and overdominating attitudes is that they reflect a temperamental disparity in self-assertiveness between parent and child. A combination of mild, self-effacing parent and aggressive, ascendent child (or vice versa) is not a statistical rarity. Frequently, however, the explanation is not as simple. A truly ascendent and self-reliant parent may have little need to assert himself with his children, whereas (as some evidence suggests) the submissive, ineffective parent who lacks self-assurance may use his relationship with the child as a means of compensating for lack of status, prestige, or authority vocationally or in the eyes of his spouse (Block, 1955). The overdominating or underdominating parent may sometimes pattern his behavior after his recollections of his own parents' way of dealing with him. On the other hand, if he believes that his parents' practices were undesirable, he may make a deliberate effort to veer to the opposite extreme. In some cases underdomination is a manifestation of passive rejection; the parent is only too happy to leave the child to his own devices as long as he himself is not bothered. Actively rejected children, however, are usually overdominated. In overvaluing parents underdomination is generally a projection of exaggerated ego aspirations. Since the parent hopes for vicarious ego enhancement through the accomplishments of a volitionally omnipotent child, he can hardly afford to frustrate the latter's will. Either orientation (but especially underdomination) may also represent adherence to a current philosophy of child rearing.

In terms of both source and expression, parental overdomination is largely the antithesis of underdomination. But although the general consequences of both attitudes are quite similar in their impact on ego maturation, much greater possibility for heterogeneity in the child's response exists in the case of the former. This heterogeneity results from variations (1) in the brusqueness or kindliness with which the overdomination is administered, and (2) in the self-assertiveness of the child. The first variable governs the acceptability of the overdomination to the child. The second variable determines the type of resistance that will be offered if overdomination is unacceptable, that is, active (rebellion) or passive (sabotage).

EARLY SOCIAL DEVELOPMENT IN THE FAMILY

Parents as Cultural Representatives

Especially during the early years, the child is not exposed directly to a representative sample of the culture at large but to a restricted, family-biased version of it. The parent is under obligation both to interpret the culture to the child and to serve as its official representative in dealing with him. The parent is under pressure to produce and deliver an individual who is a reasonable facsimile of the prevailing cultural pattern. If he himself—within acceptable limits of deviancy—has assimilated the values and expectations of his culture with respect to the goals of child rearing, relatively little difficulty ensues in playing the role of cultural representative. If, however, his personal values and attitudes are at variance with cultural norms he is often resentful and ambivalent about this role, sometimes showing open defiance but more often conforming verbally while following covertly his own inclinations.

In what ways does the child's indirect exposure to the culture through his parents differ from the more direct kind of exposure that he later receives at the hands of other socializing agents? First, the family presents a highly idiosyncratic picture of the culture to the child. Parents are always selective in the cultural alternatives they choose to transmit and in their perceptions of cultural norms.

Furthermore, they not only deviate deliberately in varying degrees from cultural prescriptions but also improvise their own prescriptions in the more unstandardized aspects of parent-child relationships. In any event, salient features of their own idiosyncratic personality traits are always expressed in their dealings with the child. Second, the *specific* models of behavior presented by the parents differ qualitatively from *other* specific models the child perceives in the wider community. The idiosyncratic features of the latter tend to lose their individual identity in the composite role protraits that eventually emerge; but because of their *primacy,* the models provided by mother and father retain their idiosyncratic properties. Their particular specificity constitutes in itself and becomes equivalent to other general categories or abstractions in which only commonalities are retained while non-distinguishing specificities are discarded. Finally, the home environment is not only a social one but is also intensely personal and intimate. Rewards and punishments come with simple directness from persons, never from abstract symbols (Cameron, 1947). Home, therefore, can never be more than a rough preview of what the child can anticipate from the wider culture. He can only predict that it (the culture) will treat him more objectively, casually, and impersonally; he can expect no special privileges, no special concern with his welfare, and no favored treatment. But apart from these negative forecasts, he is much more at a loss regarding the kinds of behavior he may anticipate from others, since he is confronted on the outside by a much larger array of persons about whose attitudes he knows substantially less.

Initial Social Behavior in the Home

The child's first social behavior occurs within the family circle in relation to adults rather than to other children. Considering his immaturity in other spheres—perceptual, cognitive, language, and motor—it is unusually well developed. This precocity reflects the operation of potent, genically determined capacities for social responsiveness, including specific predispositions for such stereotyped expressive characteristics as smiling, cooing, and gurgling in response to the human voice and face. Sensitization to the social environment is shown by earlier recognition and differentiation of and emotional responsiveness to persons than to inanimate objects (Tagiuri, 1969).

The child's social responsiveness is also facilitated by his dependency, which requires that his needs be satisfied from the very beginning in an interpersonal context. He becomes accustomed and responsive to the behavior and communicative acts of others in the course of having his needs satisfied by them. Initially, however, until the child becomes *psychologically* dependent, the objective dependency situation primarily influences the *parents'* social behavior. It is conceivable, nevertheless, that even before he appreciates the mother's causal relation to the satisfaction of his needs, her status as substitutive reward and signal of imminent gratification facilitates his social responsiveness to and recognition of her. Once he perceives his helplessness and dependence on her availability for his continued physical survival his very sense of security acquires social reference. He now initiates social interaction with adults, responds affectively to their presence and absence, discriminates between friendly and angry expressions, and shows fear when a stranger approaches. During this time he also acquires needs for the affection and stimulation that parents provide; and during the satellizing period, he becomes dependent on their acceptance and approval for security and adequacy feelings. It is little wonder then that social relationships with persons—through which all other needs are satisfied —should become important needs in their own right.

Impact of Intrafamilial Experience on Later Social Development

One of the most important consequences of early parent-child relationships is the pronounced tendency for the child's later interpersonal relations with peers and other adults to reflect the influence of social attitudes, expectancies, and adjustive techniques experienced in dealings with his first socializers, his parents. To the child the world of interpersonal relations is completely unstructured at first; and for the first few years of life most of the differentiation of this unstructured field occurs in the home. Hence, in the absence of any other frame of reference for basing his expectations of what people in the outside world are like and for reacting to them, it is most natural for him to use the model provided by his parents and to employ adaptive techniques previously utilized in the home situation. Moreover, habituation to *particular* satisfying features of the parent-child relationship creates needs for them in the child, needs which can only be satisfied by conditions analogous to those that produced them in the first place.

The child's capacity for forming wholesome interpersonal relationships outside the home, therefore, is influenced by the following aspects of the intrafamilial situations: (1) a base of friendly relations with parents which lead him in advance to expect the best from people unless given cause to feel otherwise; (2) the extent to which his parents either do not create unique, unrealistic needs and expectations in him that only they are willing and able to satisfy, or encourage the development of special adjustive techniques to the exclusion of the more usual and adaptive abilities necessary for most social situations; (3) the availability (neither insufficient nor excessive) of family support, assurance, and guidance should he encounter difficulties with others; (4) the absence of home attachments that are so strong as to be preemptive; (5) the lack of personality traits or adjustive habits from the parent-child relationship that other children find offensive; and (6) the avoidance of predispositions (instilled by home training) to withdraw from extrafamilial social experience to the point where the learning of realistic social roles becomes impossible.

The child's social behavior is also profoundly affected by whether or not he has undergone satellization, which in turn is an outcome of the parent-child relationship. To the satellizing child, group membership provides derived status and constitutes an intrinsic ego support. He experiences a certain spontaneous joy and enthusiasm in group activity, which follows from the "we-feeling" associated with group relatedness. To the non-satellizer, on the other hand, the field of interpersonal relations is just another arena in which he contends for extrinsic status and ego aggrandizement. There is no identification with or self-subordination to group interests, and no possibility of deriving spontaneous satisfaction out of gregarious activity. A similar type of dichotomy prevails in the relationships satellizers and non-satellizers respectively establish with teachers and other adults.

The rejected individual has strong needs for volitional autonomy but finds it difficult to assert himself effectively in interpersonal relationships. Not only has he failed to master customary roles and techniques necessary for adult self-assertion but he also *feels* incapable of playing these roles convincingly. This is partly a result of the low degree of empathy that rejecting parents manifest in relation to their children (Guerney, Stover & De Meritt, 1968) and a direct carry-over of the child's feeling of helplessness in coping with the ruthless domination of parents. But in part it also reflects feelings of unworthiness attributable to his parents' negative valuation of him, lack of intrinsic self-esteem, and chronic anxiety. Rejection and derogation by parents adversely affects cognitive and linguistic abilities in rejected children (Brodie & Winterbottom, 1967; Hurley, 1965; Kinstler, 1961). Because he does not appear adequate to protect his own interests and avoid being taken advantage of, he invites aggression from others; but in view of his genuine needs for volitional independence, he resents any subservience to which he is subjected and may eventually react explosively. More typically he withdraws from conflictful social situations and intellectualizes his aggression; and if he can overcome his haunting fear of further rejection, he may even try to establish satellizing-like relationships with non-threatening persons.

During childhood, rejected individuals are alternatively described as shy and submissive on the one hand, and as aggressive, quarrelsome, non-compliant, and resistive to adult guidance on the other hand (Baldwin et al., 1945; Baumrind, 1966; Becker, 1964; Hatfield, Ferguson & Alpert, 1967). Without a secure home base to which they can return, they tend to adjust less successfully than accepted children to novel and stressful social situations (Becker, 1964; Heathers, 1954; Shirley, 1942). Juvenile delinquency is significantly more frequent in homes characterized by lack of parent warmth and rejection (Becker, 1964; Medinnus, 1965). Children's control over aggression and their reactions to their own transgressions are all characterized by a low degree of internalization when they have been exposed to extreme parental rejection or punitiveness (Bandura & Walters, 1963a; Sears et al., 1957). Where rejection is prolonged but passive (e.g., as in foundling homes), children tend to establish emotionally shallow interpersonal relationships and to display social immaturity.

The underdominated child is encouraged to assert himself, but at the same time no demands are made on him to develop the mature personality traits necessary for realistic implementation of volitional independence. Because he has little direct experience with the restrictive features of reality and is not required to learn the limits of acceptable conduct, he cannot easily choose realistic roles and goals. As a result of being conditioned to a relationship in which all of the yielding is done by the other party, he comes to think of himself as a unique person to whom others just naturally defer. In his relations with other children and adults, he tends to be domineering, aggressive, disobedient, petulant, and capricious (Becker, 1964; Levy, 1943). He is unwilling to defer to the judgment and interests of others, always demanding his own way upon threat of unleashing unrestrained fits of temper (Levy, 1943). But despite his conspicuous lack of social success outside the home, he still tends to persist in this type of domineering behavior, partly because he is so thoroughly overtrained in it and partly because of the imperious need to dominate, which he has acquired from the parent-child relationship (Cameron, 1947; Levy, 1943). The overvalued child for very similar reasons develops the same type of social behavior but has stronger needs for volitional independence and ego aggrandizement. Hence, although he never basically abandons his grandiose aspirations and desire for deference, he is more highly motivated to modify the strategy of his interpersonal behavior in order to establish the overtly satisfactory social relationships he recognizes as important in the quest for status and power. The extrinsically valuing parent who overvalues his or her child's achievements is frequently characterized as critical or hostile, often to the point of rejecting the child or pushing the child beyond intrinsic ability levels (Crandall, 1967). Part of parents' overvalued striving for their children appears to be related to lack of self-acceptance in themselves (Medinnus & Curtis, 1963).

Because of constrictive and dominative home environments respectively, both overprotected and overdominated children fail to learn the social skills necessary for adequate self-assertion and self-defense. Unable to defend their rights successfully, they are continually fearful of being duped and exploited by others. Since the peer group is unwilling to satisfy their special needs for protection and direction, they tend to withdraw from peer relationships and to seek the company of parents and adults who can play the roles their needs demand. Overprotected children are generally submissive, dependent, compliant, shy, anxious (Becker, 1964; Levy, 1943; Radke, 1946), and inadequate in meeting stressful situations (Shirley, 1942). They are extremely dependent on their mothers and experience great difficulty in making friends (Levy, 1943). Overdominated children exhibit the same traits and in addition tend to be well-controlled, dependable, polite, self-conscious and introverted (Baldwin, 1948; Becker, 1964; Radke, 1946; Siegelman, 1966; Walsh, 1968). Autocratic, harsh, and capricious overdomination, however, may not be accepted by the child, and hence may lead to active rebellion in ascendent, extraverted children and to passive sabotage in docile, introverted children. These latter two groups probably account for the reported frequency of quarrelsome, uncooperative, uninhibited, and inconsiderate behavior in children from autocratic homes (Becker, 1964; Symonds, 1949). Children from "democratic homes" tend to be active, competitive, and socially outgoing, both in friendly and in aggressive and domineering ways, and to enjoy high acceptance from their age-mates. In contrast to overdominated children, they show originality, intellectual curiosity, and constructiveness in school activities (Baldwin, 1948; Becker, 1964).

DISCIPLINE*

The Need for Discipline

Although much cultural diversity prevails in the severity and techniques of discipline, the phenomenon itself is encountered in all cultural settings. In the child's development, there are several authority holders who make differential demands on his behavior (Dubin & Dubin, 1963) but the earliest authority agents in our culture are clearly parents. The need for discipline occurs in those situations where the child is concerned with routines of daily living, in establishing sibling and adult relationships, and in displaying behavior that adults deem appropriate (Clifford, 1959). We have already elaborated on the reasons for believing that every noteworthy advance in personality maturation is accompanied by some change in the expectations of significant persons in the child's environment, which change is enforced in part by some coercive form of pressure. On both counts parents occupy a strategic position. Not only do parents change their own expectations as a result of altered needs and new perceptions of the child's behavioral capacity, but they also channel through these changing cultural expectations new standards for appropriately mature behavior at different age levels. In either case, the parent is one of the most appropriate agents for applying whatever coercive measures are necessary for effecting conformity of the child's behavior to changed patterns of expectations. Direct experience with limiting and restrictive factors in the environment is necessary for learning to conform to a reasonable degree with social norms of acceptable behavior, for learning to set realistic roles and goals, for learning to make reasonable demands on others, and for acquiring responsibility, self-control, and the capacity for deferring need satisfaction. Since these aspects of socialization are not written into the genes, they are not acquired spontaneously. To be sure, the removal of all pressures for conformity can undoubtedly eliminate most interpersonal conflict and negativism, but it still must be demonstrated that normal personality maturation will then also occur under such ruleless conditions.

---

*As used in this section, discipline refers to the imposition of standards and controls by others on the child's behavior. The relative absence of discipline is equivalent to maximal permissiveness (underdomination) in the handling of children.

It is also profitable to distinguish between the effects on the child of restrictive, subjective authority and of an authority that is warm and issue-oriented (Baumrind, 1966). The former is more likely to be associated in the child with negative affect, disaffiliativeness, and rebelliousness (Baumrind, 1966).

Discipline is also necessary from the standpoint of the child's emotional security. Without unambiguous standards of social reality in relation to which he can orient his behavior and control his impulses, he feels confused and insecure. The absence of external standards places too great a burden on his limited degree of self-control and attitudinal sophistication. In a completely permissive environment, he is afraid of the consequences of his own uninhibited behavior—of both the retribution and the guilt; and in the absence of punishment there is also very little opportunity for reducing guilt feelings.

Ambiguous control also cannot be avoided unless discipline consists of punishment as well as reward. It is unrealistic to expect that in the early and middle years of childhood approval for acceptable behavior automatically endows its logical opposite with negative valence. The child does not make inferences so easily and does not typically operate at the level of logical consistency that this approach assumes. Especially during the early years the positive valence of an attractive but forbidden activity is not effectively reduced until such time as explicit evidences of reproof are administered. Reproof can have a variety of consequences depending on the way it is administered (Aronfreed, 1968b; Baumrind, 1966; Hoffman, 1963). The use of disciplinary techniques that attempt to change the child's behavior by appealing to his need for affection and self-esteem appear to foster a more internalized moral orientation, whereas physical coercion and shame lead to externally controlled and authority-regulated conduct in children (Aronfreed, 1968a; Bronfenbrenner, 1961; Hoffman, 1963). More important than love withdrawal is the use of induction techniques where parents focus on the consequences of the child's actions for others (Aronfreed, 1968b; Hoffman & Saltzstein, 1967).

Democratic Discipline

Proponents of extreme permissiveness frequently equate their philosophy with democratic discipline and assert that other forms of discipline are synonymous with authoritarianism. The arguments and evidence used in this latter connection only discredit autocratic types of control (overdomination)—*not* all types of non-permissive discipline. This evidence merely supports the need for democratic methods of control rather than for maximally permissive (laissez-faire) methods (underdomination), the effects of which are no more desirable than those of overdomination. There is also no rational basis for believing that the parents' authority role is necessarily incompatible with a relaxed and cordial parent-child relationship. Most children recognize their parents' right to impose controls and do not question the legitimacy of disciplinary measures. A democratic approach to discipline does not require the parent to renounce his prerogative of making final decisions or to refrain from imposing "external" standards and restraints on the child:

> Authoritarian control and permissive non-control may both shield the child from the opportunity to engage in vigorous interaction with people. Demands which cannot be met or no demands, suppression of conflict or sidestepping of conflict, refusal of help or too much help, unrealistically high or low standards all may curb or understimulate the child so that he fails to achieve the knowledge and experience which could realistically reduce his dependence upon the outside world. The authoritarian and permissive parent may both create, in different ways, a climate in which the child is not desensitized to the anxiety associated with nonconformity. Both models minimize dissent, the former by suppression and the latter by diversion or indulgence. To learn how to dissent, the child may need a strongly held position from which to diverge and then be allowed under some circumstances to pay the price for nonconformity by being punished. Spirited give and take within the home, if accompanied by respect and warmth, may teach the child how to express aggression in self-serving and prosocial causes and to accept the partially unpleasant consequences of such actions. (Baumrind, 1966, p. 904).

Characteristics

In contrast to authoritarian discipline, which is harsh, tyrannical, vengeful, and power-oriented in terms of control measures (Becker, 1964; Brody, 1965; Hart, 1957; Hoffman, 1960), democratic discipline avoids any attempt to intimidate the child and repudiates the use of punishment as an outlet for parental aggression. It does not propose to eradicate the distinction between parental and filial roles. The parent is recognized as the more mature and dominant party in the relationship; his judgments are given more weight and his demands more authority. Nevertheless, no exaggerated emphasis is placed on status differences, and all artificial barriers preventing free communication are removed. Respect is always a two-way proposition: the child's rights and opinions—and especially his dignity as a human being—are never disregarded. The child is encouraged to participate in the determination of goals and standards whenever he is qualified to do so, and maximal reliance is placed on inner controls. Verbal exhortations are reinforced by personal example.

Democratic discipline is also as rational and as unarbitrary as possible. The parent provides explanations for decisions and permits the child to present his point of view; and even when the latter is too young to understand reasons, the parent tries to use a reasonable tone of voice. For many reasons, however, a wholly rational approach is unfeasible since (1) cognitive limitations make it impossible to render many explanations intelligible to the child; (2) many parental requests cannot be justified on the basis of reason but must nevertheless be heeded on the grounds of either necessary conformity to cultural tradition or of superior experience and judgment; and (3) many emergency situations in childhood require complete, immediate, and unquestioning obedience.

Other Aspects of Parental Discipline

Methods of parental control must obviously be adapted to meet changing conditions of personality organization and maturity. In the presatellizing period parents are largely dependent on physical restraint, reward, and punishment. During the satellizing stage, they can rely more upon approval and disapproval, prestige suggestion, personal loyalty, and moral restraints of conscience and guilt feelings. Later, in the desatellizing period, the child is less disposed to conform on the basis of personal allegiance and desire for approval; considerations of expediency and ego enhancement become more salient at this time. With increasing age, therefore, effective discipline becomes more rational and less authoritarian. It is more acceptable to the older child if the parent acts as an impersonal agent of the culture in interpreting and enforcing social norms than if he continues to serve as a personal source of authority and to demand obedience as an axiomatic right. Parents also instigate less resistance if, wherever possible, they bring children into line by letting age-mates apply "lateral sanctions" than by applying hierarchial sanctions themselves.

Although the effects of inconsistent discipline are difficult to assess because "inconsistency" refers to a multitude of different combinations and orderings of parental responses to children's behavior (Becker, 1964; Walters & Parke, 1966), it is nevertheless safe to suggest that effective discipline is unambiguous, consistent, and relevant to the misbehavior to which it is applied. Arbitrary and inconsistent rules can exist within and between parents (Becker, 1964) and tend to be cognitively unclear (Baldwin, 1955); hence they are learned with great difficulty. Rules are also inevitably ambiguous if the parent fails to define the limits of acceptable behavior, neglects to differentiate clearly between filial and parental prerogatives, and handles every situation as a special case according to the demands of expediency. The ambiguity surrounding the limits of unacceptable behavior is further enhanced by an habitual tendency to avoid issues by distracting the child. Two other favorite techniques of the ineffectual parent are self-insulation (pretending unawareness) and empty verbalism when an occasion for discipline arises. Half-hearted verbal reproof that is not accompanied by effective disciplinary action actually reinforces misbehavior by guaranteeing to the child that he can expect no *real* interference from his parents. The behavioral outcome of inconsistent discipline is the high frequency of antisocial behavior, conflict, and aggression in the child (Becker, 1964; Walters & Parke, 1966). By contrast, consistent paternal discipline is associated with independence and assertiveness in boys and with affiliativeness in girls (Baumrind & Black, 1967).

DEPRIVATION OF AFFECTION

The literature on the development of affection in children is eclipsed by the vast number of studies reporting the adverse effects of emotionally-depriving parents on the development of their children. Many of these studies were summarized by Bowlby (1952) and, although they were lacking in sophisticated design and extremely impressionistic and subjective in nature, they nevertheless ingeniously took advantage of uncontrived deprivation occurring in foundling homes or resulting from wartime dislocation.

Maternal Deprivation

The early studies on maternal deprivation indicate that after six to nine months of age prolonged or severe deprivation of maternal care, or abrupt separation from the accustomed mother figure during the first three years of life, often (but not necessarily) leads to extremely serious developmental consequences. In the preschool period the immediate effects may be described as follows: (1) retardation in motor, language, and intellectual development (Freud & Burlingham, 1944; Haggerty, 1959; Provence & Lipton, 1962; Spitz, 1945, 1949, 1951a, 1951b); (2) malnutrition and an unusually high infant mortality rate despite excellent medical care (Spitz, 1945, 1951b); and (3) a behavioral syndrome of agitation and weepiness followed by apathy, passivity, disinterest in the environment, stereotyped rocking movements, hostility, and increased susceptibility to infection (Fischer, 1952; Roudinesco, 1952). The latter syndrome, designated as "anaclitic depression" (Spitz & Wolf, 1946) appears typically after abrupt separation from the mother and generally disappears shortly after her return (Fischer, 1952, Spitz & Wolf, 1946).

Before considering the long-term effects of deprivation or separation, several comments should be made concerning the conceptualization of the effects of deprivation. First of all, the earlier studies, because of their design problems, can be considered as only suggestive in nature (Yarrow, 1964b). Second, the research literature has treated maternal deprivation and maternal separation as synonymous topics with the result that the effects attributed to maternal separation are often due to other deviating conditions of maternal care (Yarrow, 1961). Finally, the meaning of the deprivation or separation experience—and subsequent experiences after separation—will vary with individuals and with experiential factors (Yarrow, 1964b) such as the developmental stage of the child at the time of separation (Casler, 1961; Prugh & Harlow, 1966; Yarrow, 1964b), the character of the relationship with the mother prior to separation (Yarrow, 1964b), the nature of the institution and the possibilities for adequate caretaking (Ainsworth, 1966; Casler, 1961; Yarrow, 1964b), the reason for the separation (Ainsworth, 1966; Casler, 1961), and the set of individual differences vulnerable to the experience of separation (Yarrow, 1964b).

The early research literature on "maternal deprivation" has been applied to a variety of different conditions, which, singly or in combination, produce the general consequences already reported. At least three major conditions of deprivation have already been explored but, in many instances, not distinguished from one another. First of all, deprivation can occur when an infant or young child lives in an institution where he receives no maternal care, and consequently has insufficient opportunity for interaction with a mother-figure (Ainsworth, 1966). Second, deprivation can also occur when an infant or a young child lives with a mother or caretaker, but does not have sufficient interaction with her (Ainsworth, 1966). This type of deprivation, where mother or caretaker is present but not interacting, has been labelled "masked deprivation" (Prugh & Harlow, 1966). Lastly, deprivation may occur because of the child's inability to interact with a mother-figure—presumably the result of repeated breaches of ties with mother figures or previous deprivation experiences (Ainsworth, 1966).

The concept of "maternal deprivation" can now be distinguished from "maternal separation" if we consider the latter as covering those situations where there are discontinuities in a relationship already formed (Ainsworth, 1966). The distress due to discontinuities in attachments may, in many instances, be different from the effects of deprivation, unless the separation leads to a deprivation experience (Ainsworth, 1966).

LONG-TERM EFFECTS OF SEPARATION AND INSTITUTIONALIZATION

When relationships are found between early separation experiences and later personality characteristics, a cautious attitude concerning statements about causality is required (Yarrow, 1964). Most of the evidence on the long-term effects of deprivation is derived from studies that are retrospective in nature (Ainsworth, 1966). The retrospective study identifies a cluster of symptoms or personality characteristics and explores the history of the individual(s) displaying this syndrome to discover the likely antecedents or conditions that possibly led to these symptoms or personality characteristics (Ainsworth, 1966; Yarrow, 1964). Bowlby (1944), with a sample of 44 juvenile thieves, did the classic study relating delinquency to early deprivation experiences. Fourteen of these 44 youths were characterized as "affectionless characters" and a retrospective historical analysis revealed that 12 of these 14 children were separated from their mothers during infancy or early childhood. Several other studies have supported this finding, revealing a higher incidence of maternal deprivation in children characterized as psychopathic or sociopathic personalities (Bender, 1947; Earle & Earle, 1961). Summaries of the research literature that uses the retrospective design reveal a significantly higher incidence of separation in the diagnostic categories of schizophrenia, neurosis, depression, and psychoneurotic and psychosomatic disturbances (Ainsworth, 1966; Yarrow, 1964). At the same time, discrepant evidence mitigates against any general conclusion concerning deprivation and separation; several studies report no significant differences in the incidence of early separation experiences between disturbed patients and normal controls (Howells & Layng, 1955; Schofield & Ballan, 1959). The time of the separation may be an important consideration since the loss of the mother is only a factor in psychotic disturbances if it occurs before 10 years (Gregory, 1958); and severely disturbed children usually have entered the institution before the end of the first year whereas more stable institutional children had the separation occurring after two years of age (Pringle & Bosio, 1958; Pringle & Bosio, 1960).

The follow-up study provides firmer evidence than the retrospective study because the separation experience can be carefully documented and a follow-up history charted (Yarrow, 1964). However, follow-up studies reveal similar results and discrepancies as do the retrospective studies. Children hospitalized in foundling homes from the earliest months to three years of age and then placed with foster parents were followed through adolescence and compared with matched controls who had not been subjected to the institutional experience (Goldfarb, 1945b). The former had several distinctive characteristics: they tended to have a persistently depressed IQ (median 75); they exhibited special retardation in language skills and conceptualization; they were severely distractable, unable to concentrate, hyperactive, and uncontrollable; they showed little ability to anticipate the consequences of their behavior or to acquire normal inhibitory control; and they displayed temper tantrums and aggressive, impulsive, antisocial behavior without appropriate anxiety. Their emotionality and interpersonal relationships were shallow, they demanded attention and affection indiscriminately, they adjusted poorly with their peers, and they showed conspicuous lack of executive and volitional independence (Goldfarb, 1945b). Similarly, Provence and Lipton (1962) reported that children from adopted homes had difficulty in forming close affectional relationships and had problems with impulse control and conceptual thinking. However, as with the retrospective studies, the follow-up studies do not always reveal such severe outcomes. Several studies indicate that severe personality disturbance is not an inevitable outcome of maternal deprivation and is highly dependent on other factors in combination with the separation event (Beres & Obers, 1950; Bowlby, Ainsworth, Boston & Rosenblith, 1956; Freud & Burlingham, 1944; Hellman, 1962; Maas, 1963).

The present findings permit no general conclusions concerning the long-term effects of maternal separation on later personality characteristics. The varied and discrepant results that are obtained may be due to the fact that such studies involve many variables beside the simple event of maternal separation. The earlier conclusion that the young infant is sensitive to the most subtle nuances of parental attitudes, that permanent psychological damage results unless extremely high levels of mothering are maintained, must certainly be qualified in light of the ongoing research. The separation experience cannot be considered the sole etiological factor (Yarrow, 1964b) and several qualifications should be kept in mind. First, the effects of separation have not been established prior to six months of age, and most observers agree that the period from nine months to three years is the most crucial in this regard (Bender, 1950; Bowlby, 1946; Bowlby, 1952; Schaeffer & Emerson, 1964; Spitz, 1945, Spitz; 1949; Spitz, 1951b; Yarrow, 1964b). Prior to this time insufficient perceptual and conceptual maturity exists for the infant to center significant interpersonal relationships or to appreciate the meaning and consequences of loss of attachment (Schaeffer & Emerson, 1964).

Second, the degree of trauma concurrent with separation appears as an important factor in the ultimate outcome (Yarrow, 1964). The subsequent experiences may be crucial because separation can have mild consequences if the child is provided with a mother-figure rather than the insufficient interaction experiences characterized by institutional care (Trassler, 1960).

Finally, aside from the fact that the effects of deprivation and separation can be reversed, it is important to distinguish between rejection and outright neglect. The former attitude does not necessarily imply lack of personal attention or inadequate stimulation; and it can only be perceived by older, more perceptually mature infants.

Other Aspects

MULTIPLE MOTHERING

The fact that separation from parents frequently leads to a new type of environment (i.e., institutional) in which there are several caretakers taking on the mother's role has led to a considerable amount of speculation concerning the diffusion of the mother's role (Yarrow, 1964b). The often deleterious effects of the institutional environment has fostered interest in the study of cultures where multiple-mothering is the rule rather than the exception, and in caretaking arrangements that exist outside institutional settings.

The Israeli kibbutzim offer a culturally acceptable way of raising children that involves a type of multiple-mothering arrangement. The kibbutz practice frequently involves the separation of the mother from child in early infancy where a substitute-mother (metapelet) takes over many of the mother's child-rearing duties. In contrast to the institutional living previously discussed, the mother maintains contact with her child (often breast-feeding him for several months) and the parents visit the infants regularly (Yarrow, 1964b). Kibbutz children do show early developmental retardation; but this may be the result of less stimulation in this setting as compared with the home (Rabin, 1958). However, from the late preschool years onward, such children manifest no intellectual retardation and no apparent personality problems. Rabin (1958) also reports one study in which the children were considered more mature in their emotional control and had greater overall ego strength. It is likely that kibbutz children have as much contact and interaction with their parents after infancy as do children living at home (Spiro, 1955). It may be that this early communal living with sufficient parental interaction provides an adequate means of both satellization on parents and resatellization on peers at much earlier ages than normally thought possible.

Another type of non-institutional setting where multiple-mothering is employed is the home management training house for students of home economics. Children are frequently taken out of institutions and put in these houses where they are cared for by several young women in training (Gardner, Hawkes, & Burchinal, 1961). The house mother (for the trainees) provides a sense of continuity as she shares some of the infant care responsibilities. The children are the objects of considerable attention by the trainees and eventually move to foster or adoptive homes. Follow-up study of these children during the preschool years reveals no evidence of intellectual retardation or gross personality disorder (Gardner et al., 1961). These apparently successful multiple-mothering arrangements have led some to question the view that single mother-child institutions are the only way to counteract or relieve deprivation and separation effects (Mead, 1962; 1966). Mead (1962) even suggests that multiple-mothering, when it is adequate, may help the child trust more people and therefore engender toleration for separation experiences. Ainsworth (1966) counterargues that even where multiple-mothering exists as a successful societal institution, it is likely that the infant himself is monatrophic (i.e., he tends to attach himself primarily to one specific figure even though he extends his attachments to other supplementary figures). More careful observational studies of specific family and multiple-mothering structures may help in resolving some of the present theoretical controversy (e.g., Gewirtz & Gewirtz, 1968).

Paternal Deprivation and Separation

The vast majority of the research studies dealing with separation and deprivation have dealt primarily with the mother. Interest in the father's role in the socialization process has originated in the theoretical writing stressing sex-role identification in preschoolers and in the middle years of childhood (Yarrow, 1964). The influence of psychoanalytic theory on parental separation problems was first advanced when it was noticed that there was a strong attachment to father fantasy figures among preschoolers who had had meager contact with their fathers (Freud & Burlingham, 1944). Subsequent cross-cultural studies indicate that the boys raised in societies where the father is absent during infancy have sex-role identity conflicts and display strong overcompensatory masculine behaviors to threatened feminization (Burton & Whiting, 1961). Father absence appears to affect the sexes differentially (Lynn & Sawrey, 1959). In studying the eight and nine-year old children of families of Norwegian sailors and in comparing them to intact families, it was found that the boys from the father-absent group showed immature and insecure satellization with the father and poor peer adjustment and that the girls from these families were highly dependent (Lynn & Sawrey, 1959). Father absence probably induces certain types of maternal behaviors since the mothers in the sailor families were more overprotective and authoritarian (Tiller, 1957).

Father absence has also been studied in situations where the father has been called for military duty. Stolz et al., (1954) studied families where the father was absent for the Second World War and found that boys in such families displayed more feminine fantasy and overt feminine behavior and poorer relations with their peers than boys in intact families. The return of the father also caused friction, for the male child now had to compete for maternal affection and the father was frequently upset by the boy's feminine mannerisms. Aggressive fantasy in doll play has also been reported for boys in the father-absent families of the Second World War (Bach, 1946; Sears, Pintler & Sears, 1946). Carlsmith (1964) found more feminine intellectual patterns (i.e., more stress on verbal, as opposed to mathematical items) for males coming from father-absent families, and the earlier the separation of father and son, the more feminine the patterns that were displayed.

An interesting problem is posed by the observation that there is a high incidence of delinquent behavior in children from father-absent homes (McCord, McCord & Thurber, 1962). Children in lower-class families where the father is absent by virtue of death, desertion, divorce, or imprisonment show a much higher incidence of adult criminality (McCord et al., 1962) than do children from intact families. Even medical students report a much more antisocial history when the father has been absent during early childhood (Siegman, 1966). It is clear that other factors operate, along with father absence per se, to produce antisocial behaviors, and that the presence of the father must be related to certain types of parent-child interaction for favorable outcomes (Andry, 1960). Andry (1960, 1966), in fact, indicates that delinquents tend to stay away from both parents and do not seek their advice when in trouble. A type of "masked paternal deprivation" may occur in father-present delinquent families since children in such families often prefer to deal with their mothers when they encounter trouble (Andry, 1966). Again, deprivation and separation appear to be necessary research distinctions.

The recent investigations into the families of lower-class blacks reveals a family structure, essentially matriarchical in nature, where the father is absent or demoralized through habitual unemployment (Bronfenbrenner, 1967; Moynihan, 1965; White House Commission on Civil Disorders, 1968). Black families are much more unstable than comparable white families (Hunt, 1966), and the child is frequently denied the benefits of biparental affection and upbringing; he is often raised by his grandmother or older sister while his mother works to support the family deserted by the father (Deutsch et al., 1956). One consequence of this matriarchical family climate is an open preference for girls. Boys frequently attempt to adjust to this situation by adopting feminine traits and mannerisms (Dai, 1949). Even when the father is present in the black family, sexual identification may be difficult for the boy faced with a strong feminine figure while also confronted, for satellization, with a male who is economically inadequate (Gordon & Shea, 1967).

These studies point to the fact that the father should not be ignored in the discussion of deprivation and separation effects. The treatment of specific effects in a univariate manner (i.e., just paternal deprivation or maternal deprivation), however, leads to superficial relationships that appear and disappear from one study to another. As with maternal deprivation and separation, the effects of paternal deprivation and separation exist within a complex social matrix that can also change maternal behaviors toward the child. Future studies in this area increasingly will have to treat family interaction, or lack of it, as a multivariate process instead of treating mother and father as separate and independent variables. Moreover, sibling composition of the family also interacts in different ways with father absence (Sutton-Smith, Rosenberg, and Landy, 1968).

SHORT-TERM HOSPITALIZATION

The experience of hospitalization may represent a type of separation phenomenon but the effects of separation may be compounded by many other concomitant factors. Frequently accompanying short-term separation from parents due to hospitalization is the threat of surgery, acute illness, and other fear-provoking phenomena (Yarrow, 1964b). Children under seven months of age are apparently less traumatized by hospitalization, and more responsive to strange adults, than are infants over seven months of age (Schaeffer & Callender, 1959). Also, infants over seven months show desperate clinging to their mother and considerable departure crying (Schaeffer & Callender, 1959). Early childhood is marked by developmental changes in hospital reactions; these are probably due to three-year-old children showing the most severe reaction to hospitalization, and with this reaction decreasing with age as desatellization and resatellization take place (Prugh, Staub et al., 1953). School-age children (6 to 10 years) showed less anxiety about separation and their fears were focused on painful or potentially painful hospital experiences (Prugh, Staub et al., 1953).

Return from hospital was accompanied by age differential reactions; the children under seven months stared with blank expressions and scanned the surroundings without interpersonal interests, and the older infants, who were more satellized, showed excessive anxiety about anticipated mother separation and a marked fear of strangers (Schaeffer & Callender, 1959). The traumatic experiences of hospitalization can be alleviated if the hospital designs procedures to minimize separation anxiety and fear of bodily injury (Faust, Jackson et al., 1952). Robertson (1958) has suggested that the mother be given permission to "room-in" at the hospital before and following surgery. Obviously, the short-term effects of deprivation due to hospitalization are rarely similar to the effects of extended institutionalization.

In summary, at least three major conditions of deprivation have already been explored but, in many instances, not distinguished from one another. First of all, deprivation can occur when an infant or young child lives in an institution, where he receives no maternal care, and consequently has insufficient opportunity for interaction with a mother-figure (Ainsworth, 1966). Second, deprivation can also occur when an infant or a young child lives with a mother or caretaker but does not have sufficient interaction (Ainsworth, 1966; Prugh & Harlow, 1966). Finally, deprivation may occur because of the child's inability to interact with a mother-figure; this is presumably the result of repeated breaches of ties with mother figures or previous deprivation.

INFANT TRAINING AND ADULT PERSONALITY

Empirical evidence, in general, has not supported the widely held belief that *specific infant-care practices in and of themselves* contribute significantly to enduring psychosocial and idiosyncratic differences in personality development. Our purpose in the present section is to propose possible reasons for this absence of relationship and to suggest how and under what conditions infant and early childhood experience might conceivably influence the development of intracultural (idiosyncratic) differences in personality structure as well as the distinctive (psychosocial) patterning of personality traits in different cultures.

Psychosocial Traits

Since cultures obviously tend to perpetuate themselves, that is, to produce adult individuals who develop ways of behavior consonant with prevailing norms, it is self-evident that cultural values must somehow be woven into the developing fabric of personality structure. In the course of growing up, for example, certain influences must be brought to bear on the Hopi child that reliably produce a Hopi adult who more nearly approximates the Hopi ideal of adult personality than the American or Japanese. The issue under discussion here is whether the psychosocial aspects of personality are primarily transmitted (1) via specific infant-care practices as such or as representative of broader cultural values, or (2) via more direct and recurrent exposure to implicit and explicit expressions of pervasive cultural norms during the *entire* period of development prior to adult life but subsequent to infancy.

Assuming for the moment that particular infant-care practices do not exert any specific invariant influence on personality development simply because they impinge on given erogenous zones, is it possible nevertheless that such practices consistently reflect basic cultural values and hence give rise to predictable personality outcomes on this basis? On a priori grounds alone this does not appear very likely. Since the realization of the same cultural goals and the expression of the same cultural attitudes can be achieved through different and even antithetical methods, the presence or absence of a particular practice cannot possibly have uniform attitudinal significance from one culture to another. In addition, child-rearing practices are influenced by such non-attitudinal and non-value factors as customs of marriage and family organization, economic conditions, and historical accident. Thus, in their cross-cultural survey of child training practices, Whiting and Child (1953) found that

> the practices of a society for one system of behavior are almost entirely independent of its practices with respect to another. This . . . suggests that aspects of child training . . . do not grow out of cultural attitudes toward children such as might produce general laxness or general strictness, but rather out of antecedents specific to each system of behavior.

This leaves us with the remaining possibility that cultural attitudes toward children, as well as other pervasive values, might be reflected in the *manner of administering* different practices if not in the mere fact of their presence or absence. Although careful observation would probably confirm this hypothesis, at least in part, it is still unlikely that cultural attitudes expressed in this way play an important role in structuring personality. First, during infancy the individual's contact with the culture is largely indirect and buffered by his family group. In a general way, of course, the family serves as the representative of the culture in dealing with the child. But parents differ considerably in how they interpret cultural norms relative to child rearing and in their need for conforming to such norms; and in any event, they are probably less disposed to follow the cultural prescription slavishly when the child is young and his lapses are excusable than when he is older. In addition, the actual flavor of the cultural attitude that is conveyed to the infant is undoubtedly influenced by affective and temperamental dimensions of the parent-child relationship that are intercultural in distribution (e.g., acceptance-rejection, under or overdomination).

Second, even if the cultural attitudes reflected in the manner of administering infant-care practices were expressed more proximately and less variably, they could still not be perceived and understood very effectively by the perceptually and cognitively immature infant. Hence, if this mechanism of transmission does function at all, it probably first becomes a significant factor in the postinfantile period. Environmental stimulation is not irrelevant during the first year of life but only plays a supportive role; within a wide range of cultural diversity in child-rearing attitudes, developmental outcomes remain essentially constant.

In seeking to identify the mechanisms whereby cultures transmit the psychosocial attributes of personality, it seems more fruitful, therefore, to look beyond the limited field of infant-care practices. In doing so, we expect the transmission of values, goals, interpersonal roles, and ways of perceiving and thinking to take place directly, as appropriate occasions for indoctrination arise, rather than obli-

quely and symbolically in the way parents administer the routines of child care.*
We also expect the culture not to limit its major indoctrinating efforts to cognitively immature infants but to exert socializing pressures continuously, recurrently, and in mutually reinforcing situations. Lastly, we expect psychosocial
traits to reflect certain *institutionalized* aspects of handling and timing shifts in
children's biosocial status (i.e., the amount and explicitness of recognition accorded different stages of development), the choice of socializing methods and
agents; the degree of role and status discontinuity existing between children and
adults; the extent to which new demands and expectations are geared to maturational readiness and to individual differences; and the abruptness, duration, and
anxiety level associated with transitional stages of development.

Idiosyncratic Traits

Questions similar to those we asked in considering the impact of infantile
experience on psychosocial traits may be raised about the impact of infantile
experience on the development of idiosyncratic traits. Do idiosyncratic traits
develop (1) as consequences of *specific* infant-care practices per se, (2) as consequences of *general parental attitudes* expressed in the presence or absence of
practices or in the manner in which they are administered, or (3) as consequences
of recurrent interpersonal experiences in later childhood and adolescence?

PRACTICES VERSUS ATTITUDINAL SUBSTRATE

Two basic assumptions underlie the psychoanalytic doctrine that particular
infant-care practices in and of themselves exert specific, invariant, point-to-point
effects on adult personality structure. First, it is assumed that the excess,
sufficiency, or deficiency of "erotic" satisfaction experienced when a given
practice impinges on a particular stage of psychosexual development (and its
associated libidinal drive and erogenous zone) plays a crucial organizing and
directional role in subsequent personality development. Second, it is assumed that
the type of neuromuscular activity associated with erogenous experience (contrac-
tion or relaxation, sucking or biting) influences in a predetermined way the kind of
personality trait that emerges.

It is not at all clear, however, why the satisfactions and frustrations resulting
from such experience should have more than *immediate* effects on behavior. No

*This does not mean that all indoctrination is accomplished by means of explicit training
procedures. As a matter of fact, the influence of culture is so pervasive that perhaps most indoctrination
occurs incidentally and on an implicit basis Nevertheless, incidental learning occurs most effectively in
children when it is *not* indirect (i.e., inferential from or tangential to immediate experience). As Ralph
Piddington observes in his *Introduction to social anthropology,* vol. 2, 1957, much indoctrination
occurs on an impersonal level and its effects depend as much on its content as on the way in which it is
carried out.

self-evident reasons are apparent why these effects should be lasting, generalized, or involve core aspects of personality. It is true, of course, that since much parent-child interaction occurs in relation to erogenous zones and to the satisfactions, demands, and expectations connected therewith, this experience acquires thereby wider significance for the child's biosocial status, his sense of security, and his feelings of volitional and executive dependence and independence. But if this is the case, the impact of infant-care practices on personality development must be attributed to the child's reactions to the variable attitudinal, role, and status implications of these practices and not to the experience of particular erogenous satisfactions and gratifications per se or to any inherent relationships between sucking and passivity, biting and hostility, or anal retention and stinginess.

If we accept the orthodox psychoanalytic thesis, we must then arbitrarily exclude many important sources of variability associated with the meaning of a particular child-rearing practice. We would have to assume that the feeling tones and attitudes connected with the administration of a practice and the general psychological context of role and status relationships in which it occurs make no difference—that is, that the child's past experience and present expectations and the attitudinal tenor of other parent practices are irrelevant. Hence, the more credible hypothesis at this point seems to be that the attitudinal substrate' of a practice, and its implications for biosocial status, influence later personality development rather than any immediate hedonistic consequences of that practice.

Underlying parental attitudes, however, cannot be inferred directly from the presence or absence of a practice. In the first place, the choice of a particular practice in preference to another may conceivably have no attitudinal significance whatsoever. At any rate, it rarely has any *exclusive* attitudinal significance that is patently self-evident; rather it varies in meaning from one parent to another in accordance with individual differences in personality and experience. Second, it also depends upon many factors completely unrelated to parents' attitudes or personality trends, such as social-class membership, family tradition, and child-rearing ideology. In a given parent the choice of a particular practice may thus not have much attitudinal significance or be reflective of characteristic and pervasive general attitudes. And, except in extremely homogenous populations, it is unlikely that its attitudinal significance will be similar for different individuals. It is hardly surprising, therefore, that children's personality traits in general are not significantly related to the presence or absence of particular infant-care practices in their early upbringing. Nor is it surprising that "favorable" techniques in different areas of child rearing are not highly associated with each other. Sewell, Mussen and Harris (1955) found low and generally non-significant intercorrelations among child-rearing practices, even in a quite homogeneous population, and concluded therefrom that parents "may follow what appears to be permissive treatment with respect to one practice or during one period of the child's development but employ restrictive techniques in other aspects of training."

Evidence such as this, however, does not prove that parents do not manifest characteristic, generalized, and pervasive attitudes in their child-rearing practices. It merely indicates, for the reasons pointed out above, that lack of generality and individual self-consistency is found with respect to such formal aspects of these practices as presence or absence, duration, and age of initiation and termination. If we were to observe carefully the manner in which different practices were administered, it is much more likely, as some preliminary studies suggest, that persistent and pervasive attitudinal constellations characteristic of individual parents' approaches to child rearing could be identified. Such generalized *individual* attitudes reflected in child-rearing practices are probably more effective in influencing the development of idiosyncratic traits than *cultural* attitudes are in influencing the development of psychosocial traits. A single parent can be more consistent and less variable in expressing his own personality trends than many different parents can be in interpreting and expressing cultural values. Also, unstandardized temperamental and attitudinal aspects of parent personality are communicable to children more readily and directly, less inferentially, and at an earlier age in the daily routines of child care than the stylized aspects of cultural values that ordinarily require more appropriately structured occasions for effective indoctrination.

Regardless of whether child-rearing practices per se or the parent attitudes they reflect are considered as significant in influencing subsequent personality development, it is important to avoid the frequently committed error of confusing antecedence with causality. This is the error of assuming that a particular practice (or the attitudes underlying it) *causes* a later personality trait simply because it precedes the latter chronologically. In the first place, it stands to reason that any generalized parental attitude will be expressed in *many* rather than in only one child-rearing practice. Hence, no single practice can ever be crucially determinative by itself. If consistent with a general attitudinal trend, it merely constitutes one of many supportive practices serving the same end; if inconsistent, its influence is nullified by the cumulative weight of other practices. Second, at the same time that the child is exposed to reflections of parent attitudes and values in child-rearing practices, he or she is also exposed to these same attitudes and values in other contexts both inside and outside the family circle.

The manner of administering child-rearing practices thus represents only one facet through which parental attitudes may be expressed. These same attitudes impinge on the child's personality development through other channels (e.g., formal and informal instruction, interpersonal climate within family, observation of parents interacting with other persons) not only simultaneously but also continuously and recurrently throughout the entire period of childhood. Many anthropological generalizations regarding alleged causal relationships between specific infant-care practices and various features of adult personality are thus suspect for these reasons. They are also suspect because either (1) they are frequently derived from a sample of only one culture—and hence it is not even possible to ascertain whether the observed concomitance between infant training and adult personality is statistically significant on a cross-cultural basis—or (2) they are based on cross-cultural comparisons in which the cultures are not sufficiently well matched on all other variables (apart from the specific practices under investigation) to warrant the drawing of definitive causal inferences.

LIMITING FACTORS

To whatever extent a child's personality development is influenced by broad, pervasive parental attitudes reflected in infant-care practices, three ineluctable and limiting conditions remain operative: parental attitudes cannot be communicated until an infant is sufficiently mature to perceive and react to them; the reactions that an infant exhibits are in part a function of constitutional factors; and the effects of early infantile experience on personality may be modified (reinforced, altered, reversed) by subsequent experience in later childhood, adolescence, and adult life.

We have good reason to believe that the young infant's perceptual and cognitive immaturity tends to insulate him from the influence of parental attitudes. His relatively slow rate of perceptual-social development, in comparison with that of the young of infrahuman mammals, limits his ability to perceive attitudinal cues and to comprehend their significance, to make subtle discriminations among feeling tones, and to generalize and conceptualize his interpersonal experience—or even to remember it for any length of time. It is thus difficult to accept the currently fashionable view that infants are aware of the subtlest shadings of parental attitudes by virtue of some special empathic sensitivity to covert cues communicated through bodily tensions and expressive movements. Both the logic and the evidence with respect to perceptual development indicate that children first become aware of gross and overt elements in the cognitive field and only later, as differentiation occurs, do they respond to partial, subtle, and covert cues. It is true that infants tend to be quiescent when handled by calm, relaxed, and confident mothers and to cry and fuss when handled by tense and flustered mothers who have ambivalent feelings about motherhood. But it is much more parsimonious to suppose that maternal attitudes affect the smoothness and pleasantness of handling procedures—and that the infant reacts to the immediate hedonistic and frustrating properties of the handling practices as such—than to suppose that he perceives and responds to the attitudes underlying them. Hence we conclude that until he actually *perceives* the parental attitudes that are reflected in the daily routines of child care, these attitudes can shape only his immediate behavior, not influence his personality development.

It would be a serious mistake, however, to assume that even *perceived* parental attitudes in late infancy and early childhood exert an irreversible effect on adult personality or that early favorable or unfavorable experience predetermines the outcome of later crucial stages of personality development. Although favorable infantile and early childhood experiences undoubtedly do much to insure the development of a well-adjusted adult personality, the damaging impact of serious trauma in late childhood, adolescence, and adult life cannot be discounted. Later rejection by parents, exposure to overprotective and under or overdominating attitudes, crippling disease, extreme somatic deviations in adolescence, problems of acculturation and culture conflict, severe economic hardships, etc., all leave their mark in undoing part of the desirable foundation established in childhood. Thus, despite affectionate care and early indulgence in an infant-centered home, adult Hopi life is characterized by marked discord, anxiety, suspicion, distrust, and fear of death. Eggan (1945) attributes this to abrupt restriction of aggression and to the inculcation of supernatural fears in middle childhood, to culture conflict and ambivalence about white rule, and to the rigors of exacting a livelihood from a dry rocky terrain. The same situation applies more or less in the case of the Navaho, and for very much the same reasons.

An additional source of trauma affecting later personality development lies in the tremendous contrast that prevails in certain cultures between the permissiveness of early upbringing and the severity of the demands and expectations imposed upon the adult. This consideration is vital in evaluating the suggestion advanced by Moloney and others that we import into our own culture some of the maximally permissive practices employed by some primitive peoples. Thus, prolonged and extreme mothering might be quite appropriate in Okinawa where the culture as a whole is relatively simply organized, undemanding, and noncompetitive—an ambiance that might indeed constitute *one* of the reasons for the relatively low incidence of psychosis among the Okinawans. But when the same practices are employed by immigrant Okinawan parents in the highly stratified and competitive Hawaiian culture, the incidence of psychosis is significantly greater than that among other ethnic immigrant groups of comparable socioeconomic status (Wedge, 1952).

Evidence regarding the apparently irreversible effects of certain infantile experiences on the later behavior of infrahuman mammals cannot be applied indiscriminately to human infants. In the first place, young infrahuman infants are relatively more mature, perceptually and socially, and can thus be influenced more crucially by early infantile experience. Second, personality development is more complex in human beings: a larger number of component developmental processes is involved; and as the critical phases of the different processes succeed each other, the relative importance of different interpersonal variables keep shifting. Finally, the possibilities for reversing the direction of personality development are much enhanced in human beings because of their greater ability to verbalize and generalize their experience, and because of the more important role of the environment in patterning major aspects of their development.

A final consideration affecting the impact of infantile experience is the matter of constutional differences. The active, self-assertive child, for example, neither perceives nor reacts in the same way to parental rejection or overdomination as does the phlegmatic, submissive child. And this reactive difference in turn differentially affects the perpetuation or modification of the parental attitude in question. Constitutional factors thus not only provide for interindividual variability in response to similar infantile experience but also account for much intraindividual continuity in personality structure. If a given personality trait remains stable over the years, its persistence need not necessarily be attributed to the indelible influence of infantile experience. It may be explained both by the stability of certain temperamental predispositions and by the recurrence of the same environmental factors.

A widely prevalent assumption is that *all* symptoms of behavior disorder (as well as misbehavior) are attributable to errors in child rearing (i.e., are compensatory reactions to frustration, rejection, etc.). It is necessary for parents to realize that child-rearing behaviors are not the only relevant variables involved in the production of behavior disorders. Genic and constitutional factors and transitional tensions are often potent enough to result in behavioral disturbances, even in an optimal home environment. Misbehavior also is often an experiment on the child's part to test the limits of parental tolerance or endurance. Unfortunately, many psychotherapists are guilty of unwarrantedly alienating children from parents by ascribing all psychopathology to the latter's influence.

4

The Natural History of Ego Development: Ego Omnipotence and Devaluation During Childhood

The investigation of the self-concept in early infancy is obviously fraught with serious scientific hazards. In the absence of verbal reports from the child regarding his perception of self and universe, we must have recourse to speculation and inference from the way he is treated, from the demands made upon him, from his reactive capacities, and from a subjective estimate of the degree of cognitive sophistication that determines his perception of these things. In making such inferences, the greatest single source of error is an "adultomorphic" approach, which can never be avoided completely. But despite this limitation and the probable impossibility of ever obtaining objectively verifiable data, speculation is still necessary and desirable in order to avoid important gaps in our theory of personality development. Later stages of ego development are naturally dependent in part upon beginning phases in the evolution of a notion of self—even if the infant cannot tell us what they are. Speculative formulations are as allowable here as in other theoretical areas, provided they possess some plausibility, obey the law of parsimony, are logically reconcilable with related empirical data at a later stage of development, and are uttered with the humility and tentativeness befitting their status as hypotheses rather than as definitively established facts. And in this particular instance there is the additional requirement that they be consistent with the presumed cognitive maturity of infants.

DEFINITION OF CONCEPTS

To avoid confusion later, it is necessary to distinguish at the outset between the terms *self, self-concept, ego,* and *personality,** which constitute, in the order

*The distinction between personality and ego is made in Chapter 2 (p. 19).

given, an ascending hierarchy of complexity and inclusiveness. The *self* is a constellation of individual perceptions and memories which consists of the visual image of the appearance of one's body, the auditory image of the sound of one's name, images of kinaesthetic sensations and visceral tension, memories of personal events, etc. The *self-concept,* on the other hand, is an abstraction of the essential and distinguishing characteristics of the self that differentiate an individual's "selfhood" from the environment and from other selves. In the course of development, various evaluative attitudes, values, aspirations, motives, and obligations become associated with the self-concept. The organized system of interrelated self-attitudes, self-motives and self-values that results may be called the *ego.* This constellation of ego referents in turn undergoes conceptualization: a least common denominator is abstracted that constitutes at any given stage of development the conceptual essence of the person's notion of himself as a functioning individual who is endowed with certain attributes related to role and status.

PREDETERMINISTIC APPROACHES TO EGO DEVELOPMENT

According to psychoanalytic doctrine, the ego is formed as a characterological precipitate of the id as it comes into contact with reality. (S. Freud, 1935; Hartmann, 1952, 1958). It supposedly serves both as a subjugator of socially unacceptable id impulses and as an ally of the id in satisfying its libidinal and aggressive drives through acceptable means (S. Freud, 1952, Loeveninger, 1966). Thus psychoanalytic theory does not regard the ego as completely preformed but as an experiential derivative of innate drives. It is clear that this theory follows, nevertheless, basically predeterministic lines: variability in ego development can only occur within the framework of an innately patterned sequence of prestructured libidinal drives. Ego drives do not arise autonomously in the course of changing interpersonal experience but can only be derived (sublimated) from the original source of libidinal energy. Since individual and cultural variability in the unfolding of psychosexual drives is made coextensive with ego development, the *only* kind of experience that is considered relevant to this development is that which involves frustration and gratification of erogenous drives.*

The psychoanalytic view of ego development also contains elements of preformationism as well as predeterminism. All properties of the ego are not

---

*Gesell's approach (1933, 1954) to ego development, as already pointed out, is also predeterministic. It presumes that (just as in the case of early motor development) "the basic order and the general modality if not the specific outline of differentiations are determined by intrinsic factors ('ancestral genes')". Environmental factors allegedly account for only minor variations in ego development, whereas all basic uniformities are attributed to internal "morphogenic" factors.

considered to evolve from experiential modification of the id; the existence of a rudimentary ego and of some specific ego attributes is assumed at birth before there is any opportunity for interpersonal experience (S. Freud, 1952, Hartman, 1958). Thus the neonate is said to react with anxiety to the "trauma" of placental separation from the mother (S. Freud, 1936), to be capable of volition, and to experience feelings of omnipotence (Ferenczi, 1916); and the male child is presumed to have innate attitudes of both hatred toward and identification with his father. In addition, even though psychoanalysis attributes the genesis of patterned psychosexual drives exclusively to a phylogenetic id, too many core aspects of personality related to the self-concept are implicated in the origins of sexual behavior to exclude it arbitrarily from ego structure. Hence, psychoanalytic concepts of psychosexual drives actually constitute a preformationist approach to an integral component of ego development.*

AN INTERACTIONAL APPROACH TO EGO DEVELOPMENT

Ego development may be viewed as the resultant of a process of continuous interaction between current social experience and existing personality structure that is mediated by perceptual responses. According to this interactional view, neither the direction nor the patterning of ego development are predetermined by endogenous genic factors or by the sequential unfolding of psychosexual drives. Instead, a wide range of interpersonal experience (both current and internalized within personality) constitutes the major determinant of inter and intracultural uniformities in ego development.** Such experience is prerequisite to the genesis of the ego and of ego attributes, including psychosexual drives. Its salient components are not infant-care practices that impinge on erogenous zones but rather changes in cultural demands and expectations. From exposure to influences such as these, ego drives are generated autonomously rather than being sublimated from prestructured libidinal drives.

---

*Unlike orthodox psychoanalysis, contemporary psychoanalytic ego psychology emphasizes "autonomous ego functions" (Erikson, 1950; Hartmann, 1958) and individuation from an undifferentiated ego matrix (Hartmann, 1958; Mahler, 1958, 1968). However, it is still primarily based on Freud's doctrines of aggressive and libidinal drives in the unconscious, predetermined stages of psychosexual development, infantile sexuality, the unconscious source of libidinal (id) drives, and aggressive impulses as the source of all other drives.

**Various patterning predispositions and potentialities of *genic* origin also give rise to intercultural uniformities in ego development. These genic factors, however, influence primarily those general features of human behavior that set limits to variability in ego development rather than determine the direction of such development in their own right.

MAJOR VARIABLES AFFECTING EGO DEVELOPMENT

The more important variables that participate in ego development may be classified as social (external), endogenous (internal), and perceptual (mediating). *Social* variables include all aspects of institutional, intergroup, intragroup, and interpersonal relationships and organization that affect the course of ego development. They not only comprise the current stimulating conditions that help determine the direction of behavior and development at any particular moment, but also, through a process of internalization, contribute significantly to the growing structure of personality. *Endogenous* (or internal) variables constitute the growth matrix of ego development. They are a product of all previous relevant interactions between heredity and environment, and selectively predispose or limit the direction of change in response to current experience. Internal variables include personality and temperamental traits, level of motor and cognitive capacity, physiological factors, and, most important, the prevailing state of ego organization itself. Thus, it is clear that most significant personality development is not a simple and immediate function of social experience. Always interposed between the two are both perceptual factors and the ego structure that the individual brings into the social situation.

Perceptual variables play a mediating role in the interactional process underlying ego development. Before social experience (e.g., parental attitudes, cultural norms), various competencies related to self, and different ego needs, motives, and attributes can be brought together in the same interactional field, they must first be related to perceptually (i.e., give rise to a clear content of awareness). The stimulus world, therefore, whether of internal or external origin, is not the proximate antecedent of behavior or development; the perceptual world is.* Thus, although a child's role and status in the home and his parents' behavior toward him are objective social events in the real world, they affect his ego development only to the extent and in the form in which they are perceived. This does not imply that the perceived world *is* the real world but that perceptual reality is both psychological reality and the actual (mediating) variable that influences behavior and development.

Insofar as perception itself undergoes systematic developmental changes during the life cycle, level of perceptual maturity must be considered a determining as well as a mediating variable in ego development. We have already seen the extent to which perceptual immaturity insulates the young infant from awareness of environmental threat and from the attitudinal effects of parental practices. This same perceptual immaturity, for example, does not enable the child to appreciate fully either his executive dependence and incompetence or the meaning of parental

---

*Perceptual reality considered as a dependent variable is itself an interactional product of stimulus content, cognitive maturity, and ego structure.

deference to his needs during infancy. This immaturity also obscures awareness of subtle interpersonal attitudes and of the functional and reciprocal nature of social rules and obligations within the childhood peer group. On the other hand, increasing perceptual maturity makes it possible for the self-concept and the ego to become abstract conceptual entities. Further, many of the more complex constituents of the ego, such as self-esteem, self-critical ability, and the ability to set consistent levels of aspiration exist only in very rudimentary fashion in the absence of verbal symbols.

How can we explain these evidences of growth in perceptual maturity? One obvious possibility is that perceptual maturity is a function of cognitive capacity and sophistication that tend to increase with age and experience. Here we must consider the impact on perception of increased ability to verbalize, to manipulate symbols and abstractions, and to form categorical judgments; to make more subtle differentiations within the stimulus field, to avoid animistic thinking, and to disregard irrelevant instances of concomitance in reaching judgments of causality. Some aspects of perceptual maturation, however, are probably attributable to normative modifications of ego structure itself (e.g., changed perceptions of parents and peers following upon ego devaluation).

THE NATURE AND ACQUISITION OF BIOSOCIAL STATUS

The term "biosocial status" is a convenient abstraction that makes it possible to refer to the generalized aspects of both role and status pertaining to an individual of given sex and functional age level in a relatively homogeneous cultural setting. Its *culturally standardized* attributes are anchored in the organizational procedures, requirements, values, and traditions of social groupings and institutions. Thus infants, as a group in American middle-class culture, have a stereotyped biosocial status recognizably distinct from that of male and female children, adolescents, and adults. The role aspects of biosocial status consist of significant interpersonal behavior functionally differentiated in part by adjustment to the demands and expectations of others; the status aspects delineate hierarchical position vis-à-vis others as defined by relative dominance, control, prerogatives, independence, prestige, etc. However, the actual biosocial status that any *individual* enjoys is a *particular* interactional product that is a variant of the cultural stereotype. The latter serves as an external determinant entering into the formation of personal biosocial status by generating (through appropriate representatives) specific demands and expectations to which the individual carriers of the culture react (as they do to any social stimulus) in terms of existing ego structure, idiosyncratic personality traits, and perceptual maturity.

But it is not enough to say that individuals in accordance with idiosyncratic personality dispositions and social situations enact and enjoy variants of a perceived cultural stereotype of biosocial status. Because of an all-too-easy tendency to conceive of age-level roles in a reified sense—as an ordered sequence of socially stylized masks and robes racked up in a cultural prop room all ready to don as the player moves across the stage of life—it is necessary to insist explicitly on the fact that biosocial status is for the most part an *individual achievement* in an interpersonal setting. Except for hereditary princes, few persons inherit a ready-made status; and except in the relatively rare instances of highly structured social situations, roles require considerable improvisation. Each of us must achieve our own biosocial status within the framework of the culturally standardized stereotype (Blumer, 1953).

This becomes more clear when one inquires how roles are learned. The formal concept of role implies that an individual acquires a role by learning from a model the actions, words, grimaces, and gestures appropriate for him in a given situation. But when one actually looks for this model in childhood it turns out to be little more than a reified abstraction. Does a child learn the child's role by attending the children's theatre, by reading books about children, or even by observing friends and siblings? No. In early childhood the cultural model gets into the act as a psychological reality mainly through the influence it exerts on the *parents'* child-rearing practices. In much the same manner as the young of other mammalian species, the human infant, after highly variable initial contacts with parents, siblings and others, enters into increasingly more standardized and stable relationships with them. The upshot of these repeated interactions are roles that he himself and his opposite numbers have *created*. Only as the child grows older and is exposed more directly to the symbolic values of the culture do preconceived notions and models become important in the initial structuring of interpersonal "transactions" between human beings.

Earned and Derived Status

Whenever social life is characterized by differences in roles and status and by dependence of one person on another or on the group as a whole, one of the more basic kinds of human interaction that arises under such conditions is the reciprocal relationship of identification-acceptance. This type of relationship includes in varying proportions the elements of "dominance-subordination," "leadership-followership," and "care-dependency" described by Scott for different infrahuman mammals (Scott, 1953). Much confusion results, however, from the failure to distinguish between two essentially different kinds of identification-acceptance, each of which involves a reciprocal relationship between a relatively independent and dominant individual (or group) and a relatively dependent and subordinate individual.*

One type of identification** that is very common in the canine and simian worlds and very uncommon in the feline world may be called satellization (Ausubel, 1952). In a satellizing relationship the subordinate party acknowledges and accepts a subservient and deferential role, and the superordinate party in turn accepts him as an *intrinsically* valuable entity in his personal orbit. The satellizer thereby acquires a vicarious or *derived* biosocial status (1) that is wholly a function of the dependent relationship and independent of his own competence or performance ability, and (2) that is bestowed upon him by the fiat of simple intrinsic valuation by a superordinate individual or group whose authority and power to do so are regarded as unchallengeable.

On the other hand, the two parties to the same "transaction" may relate to each other in quite a different way. The subordinate party can acknowledge his dependency as a temporary, regrettable, and much-to-be remedied fact of life requiring, as a matter of expediency, various acts of conformity and deference; but at the same time he does not have to accept a dependent and subservient status as a *person*. In turn, he can either be rejected outright or accorded qualified acceptance, that is, not for intrinsic reasons (as a person for his own sake), but for his current or potential competence or his usefulness to the superordinate party. The act of identification, if it occurs at all, consists solely in using the latter (superordinate) individual as an emulatory model so that he can learn his skills and methods of operation and thus eventually succeed to his enviable status. And accordingly, the only type of biosocial status that can be engendered in this situation is the earned

---

*Psychoanalytic ego and family therapists (e.g., Erikson, 1950; Mahler, 1958) speak of "psychological individuation" (establishment of a separate ego identity from the mother or from the undifferentiated family ego mass). However, this is only one dimension of ego development, dealing primarily with the acquisition of individuality or volitional independence, and is hardly coextensive with ego development as described in this chapter, although these authors tend to regard it as the sole significant dimension. In the first place, it does not increase linearly with age, but increases from birth to age two, then decreases until preadolescence (with transitory fluctuations at ages two and one-half, four, and six, increases abruptly at adolescence with exaggerated demands for independence, increases less agitatedly during adult life until middle age, and then begins to decline in senescence.

**Identification* is used in a global, undifferentiated sense by psychoanalytic writers (e.g., Alexander & Ross, 1958; A. Freud, 1966; Freud, 1925, 1935; Holt, 1971), by psychoanalytic ego psychologists (e.g., Adler, 1917; Erikson, 1950; Hartmann, 1950, 1958; Horney, 1937, 1939; Kernberg, 1972; Kohut, 1971; Kris, 1951; Mahler, 1951, 1958; Shafer, 1968; Sullivan, 1953), and by non-psychoanalytic psychologists (e.g., Allport, 1943; Kagan, 1958; Lewin, 1946; Maslow, 1941; McClelland et al 1953; Murphy, 1947; Murray, 1938; Sanford, et al., 1953; Sears, 1951). This distinction between these two conceptually very different kinds of identification was first made by the senior author in 1950. Identification differs from *imitation* (Bandura, 1962) and behavioral "contagion" (Redl, 1949) in involving emotional relatedness to others, not merely affect-free imitation of their behavior.

status that reflects his actual functional competence, power, or control. This non-satellizing type of identification occurs for one of two reasons: either the superordinate party will not extend unqualified intrinsic acceptance (e.g., as in the case of the rejecting parent or the parent who values his child for ulterior self-enhancing purposes), or the subordinate party is unwilling to or incapable of satellizing.

The wider significance of earned and derived status for personality structure, as we shall hypothesize in detail later, is that each is associated with distinctive patterns of security (freedom from anticipated threat to physical integrity), adequacy (feelings of self-esteem, worth, importance), and other ego attributes (level of ego aspirations, dependence and independence, etc.) Corresponding to derived status in ego structure are (1) feelings of *intrinsic* security that inhere in the affectional aspects of a satellizing relationship and (2) feelings of *intrinsic* adequacy that are relatively immune to the vicissitudes of achievement and position. Corresponding in turn to earned status are (1) feelings of *extrinsic* security that depend upon biological competence or the possession of a competent executive arm in the person of an available superordinate figure and (2) feelings of *extrinsic* adequacy that fluctuate with both absolute level of ego aspirations and the discrepancy between the latter and perceived accomplishment or hierarchical position.

EXPERIENCED VERSUS "OBJECTIVE" DEPENDENCY

It is important to realize that feelings of dependence and independence in ego structure do not correspond in point-to-point fashion to the theoretically expected "realities" of the environmental dependency situation. This is so because more proximate than these latter "realities" in determining dependency feelings are actual attitudes and behaviors of parents, plus the child's perceptions of these attitudes and behaviors. During early infancy, for example, when the child is most helpless and dependent "in fact," he is treated with most deference by his parents. Thus, despite his actual helplessness to gratify his needs or compel conformity to his wishes, considerable environmental support is given to his perception of self as volitionally independent. Perceptual immaturity adds further to the discrepancy between the child's actual biosocial incompetence and the minimal feelings of dependency he probably does experience (Ausubel, 1952).

EXECUTIVE AND VOLITIONAL DEPENDENCE

At this point it might be helpful to make more explicit the distinction between executive and volitional dependence. Both consist of affectively colored self-perceptions of limited self-sufficiency and freedom of action, but *executive* "refers to the manipulative activity involved in completing a need-satisfaction sequence, whereas *volitional* refers solely to the act of willing the satisfaction of a given need apart from any consideration as to how this is to be consummated." As perceptions also they correspond only *more or less* to their relevant stimulus content. And although these two ego attributes tend to be positively related to each other, marked discrepancies may exist between them at any point in the life cycle, especially during infancy when it is reasonable to suppose that the child conceives of himself as both volitionally independent and executively dependent.*

In addition to constituting perceived ego attributes, volitional and executive dependence—or independence—also constitute *ego needs*. Their strength varies in relation to other ego attributes (such as notions of omnipotence), to needs for earned and derived status, and to parental and cultural demands, reinforcements, and punishments. The need for executive dependence is compatible with and reinforced by the exalted (regal) self-concept of infants and with the benevolent, undemanding environment in which they live. The young child is coerced by environmental pressures and by the need for derived status to both surrender much volitional independence and to acquire more executive independence. During adolescence the attainment of executive independence is essential for achieving the volitional independence and earned status necessary for adult personality maturation.

SOURCES OF PSYCHOSOCIAL AND IDIOSYNCRATIC DIFFERENCES

Psychosocial differences in ego development reflect differences in the ways that various cultures institutionalize interpersonal relationships on the basis of age, sex, and kinship—and in the ways that they elaborate basic values and ideals of personality structure. These factors in turn influence such crucial aspects of ego development as the handling and timing of shifts in biosocial status (e.g., explicitness, abruptness, choice of socializing agents), the amounts and kinds of status that individuals are expected to seek, and the degree of personality maturity considered appropriate for different age levels. In our culture, for example, girls are expected to satellize more than boys, and women are expected to obtain a larger proportion of their current biosocial status than are men from derived rather than from earned sources. Thus, girls more than boys tend to perceive themselves as accepted and intrinsically valued by parents (Ausubel, et al, 1954), and "are more apt to be relatively docile, to conform . . . to adult expectations, [and] to be 'good' " (Parsons, 1942).** In the areas of self-aggrandizement, personal achievement, and possessions, wishes and emotional responsiveness on the part of boys exceed those of girls; in the direction of social and family relationships, physical appearance, and personal characteristics girls surpass boys (Cobb, 1954; Crandall, 1967, Havighurst, et al., 1954; Zeligs, 1942).

*This is somewhat less true today because of the influence of the women's liberation movement.

**Failure to make this distinction between volitional and executive dependence is responsible for the unexplained contradictory allegations in psychoanalytic literature that the infant both regards himself as omnipotent and feels overwhelmed by his dependence on parents.

Within the normative schema of ego development to be presented below, numerous opportunities also exist for the elaboration of idiosyncratic differences. First, one expects that children who are *temperamentally* more assertive, "thick-skinned," self-sufficient, energetic, or resistive to stress, will be less dependent on others' approval, more capable of maintaining self-esteem in the face of less earned or derived status, and in general less disposed to satellize than children with the opposite set of temperamental traits. One also expects that individuals who are genically predisposed to develop strong hedonistic needs will tend to be more resistive to pressures directed toward attentuation of these needs during the course of ego maturation, and that children who are accelerated in motor or cognitive development will be subjected to greater parental demands for mature behavior. Second, as will be seen shortly, differences in such basic dimensions of parent attitudes as acceptance-rejection, intrinsic-extrinsic valuation, and over or under-domination, hold important implications for variability in satellization, desatelliza-tion, needs for achievement, and mode of assimilating values. A third source of idiosyncratic differences in development lies in variability of perceptual sensitiv-ity. It seems reasonable to suppose, for example, that the perceptually more sensitive child is more vulnerable to the detrimental effects of unfavorable parental attitudes and is more apt to be aware of his own limitations and the realities of the dependency situation. Finally, once differences in such ego attributes as relative propensity to satellize are established, they themselves serve as important sources of variability in ego development. Thus we might predict that, everything else being equal, the more intrinsic self-esteem a child enjoys, the less need he has to strive for ego aggrandizement and the more realistically he is able to adjust his current aspirational level to prior experience of failure (Ausubel, et al, 1954).

NORMATIVE SEQUENCES IN EGO DEVELOPMENT*

In this section we propose to outline normative uniformities in the sequential course of ego development during childhood. Most of the evidence for this analysis comes from materials drawn from our own culture. Nevertheless, it is believed that sufficient intercultural commonality prevails in genic patterning predispositions, behavioral potentialities, and in intrafamilial and social needs, problems, and conditions of adaptation to make many of the hypothesized general features of ego development applicable to all cultural environments despite culturally-induced differences in details. This assumption, however, can only be verified by extensive cross-cultural investigation.

Differentiation of the Self-Concept

PREVERBAL STAGE

As a unified abstraction of its essential properties, the self-concept is a

---

*We wish to emphasize again that the theoretical propositions contained herein are frankly speculative and are offered as *hypotheses* only.

complex ideational entity that is slow in developing and usually requires the facilitating influence of language. All the same, the child possesses a functional *perception of self* (i.e., of the distinction between that which is within and that which is beyond the borders of his own body) long before he acquires any language. As in the evolution of any new percept, the basic problem is that of defining boundaries between figure and ground. In the case of the self-percept, the boundaries of the self must be delimited from the wider environment of objects and persons with which it is initially fused (Gesell & Ilg, 1943; Harvey, et al., 1961; Murphy, 1947; Sherif, 1965; Spitz & Wolf, 1946).

This latter process occurs along multisensory lines as the infant comes into contact with his physical environment. The sense of touch acquaints him with the presence of objects outside himself; kinaesthetic sensations make him aware of his own movements in space; and the sense of pain vividly informs him that transgressions of the self-not-self boundary are unpleasant. The visual *body image* as manifested by self-recognition of a portrait or mirror reflection (Garai, 1966) and by correct identification of own age, size, sex, and skin color in a series of pictures (Clark & Clark, 1947; Horowitz, 1943) first becomes a stable self-percept during the preschool period. Apparently, therefore, in the early years of childhood it serves more as an abstract symbol of self-identity than as a concrete functional datum helping the child to differentiate between himself and the environment.

Self-perception is facilitated further by the infant's reaction to the mother as a person. As early as six weeks he smiles differentially to the sound of the human voice (Bühler, 1933) even though it is not associated habitually with care and attention (Dennis, 1941); and in the third month of life he smiles and vocalizes spontaneously in response to the human face (Dennis, 1941; Spitz, 1949, 1962). Thus "mother's outline serves as an anchorage point for the slowly accumulating self-pattern" (Murphy, 1947). It provides a scaffolding for the elaboration of his own self-portrait as a person,* and as we shall see shortly, makes possible a perception of mother as a manipulator of his reality and as a causal agent in the satisfaction of his needs.

Perhaps the most poignant experience leading to the consciousness of self develops as an outgrowth of inevitable delays in the gratification of the infant's organic needs. Here the contrast between inner experience and the outside world is highlighted by the juxtaposition of awareness (1) of painful discomfort and pleasant satisfaction referable to the *body* and (2) of objects and persons in the *environment* that lead to dramatic change in the affective quality of consciousness. Later, when a sense of volition develops, the act of willing (as a directed expression of the self as an entity) and the assistance it invokes from other persons sharpens even more the distinction between self and environment. Further accen-

---

*Perception of other persons also precedes self-perception in the recognition of body image (as in mirror reflections and photographs) and in the development of language concepts dealing with persons. Perceptual discrimination between self and others is acquired more slowly when others are similar to self, as in pairs of twins.

tuation of the self-environment dichotomy accompanies the appreciation of cause-effect sequences and emerging perceptions of own helplessness, executive dependence, and volitional omnipotence to be described below.

VERBAL STAGE

The abstraction of a unified concept of self from its component percepts (cutaneous, visceral, visual, volitional, etc.) requires the intervention of language. Two preliminary steps precede the final emergence of the self-concept in its most highly developed verbal expression as the first-person singular: (1) the concept of possession, and (2) third-person reference to self. By the eighth month, "possessive emotions toward toys are manifested . . . Between the tenth and twelfth months . . . a positive sense of property becomes observable." By 21 months* this is conceptualized as "mine," a generalized term that not only includes *all personal* possessions but also excludes the possessions of others (Gesell & Ilg, 1943). This concept of possession presupposes a sharpening of the distinction between self and others to the point where objects come to "belong" to the person habitually using them.

A slightly more advanced stage in the acquisition of a verbal concept of self is completed at 24 months. At this time, the child becomes aware of entities. Before he referred to another child as "baby"; now he uses this same term or his own given name in making third person reference to himself, his possessions, and his activities. The highest degree of nominalistic abstraction in relation to the self appears at 27 months when the child uses the personal pronoun "I" (Gesell & Ilg, 1943). This "I" constitutes an abstraction of all the separate perceptions of self. It implies a genuine conceptual self-consciousness. In contrast to third-person usage, which merely indicates cognizance of himself as a *person like other persons,* the use of the first-person singular means that he designates himself as a special and unique kind of personal entity, *distinct from all other persons.* After this point is reached, a new abstract level of self-reactions becomes possible: identification with persons, goals, and values; incorporation of standards; competitive behavior; and finally, self-judgments, guilt feelings, and conscience (Ames, 1952; Gesell & Ilg, 1943; Rosenzweig, 1933; Spitz, 1949).

The Omnipotent Phase

The stage of ego development that follows the emergence of a functional self-concept may be designated as the omnipotent phase (roughly, the period from six months to two and one-half years). It seems paradoxical and contradictory that

*The Yale norms reported here were obtained from a very specialized and unrepresentative group of children. As used in this chapter they are only intended to convey a rough notion of *mean* age and sequential order of development in an unrepresentative but relatively homogenous sample of children in our culture. It is not implied that the same designated mean ages or sequences necessarily apply to all children everywhere.

feelings of omnipotence should coexist with the period of the child's greatest helplessness and dependence on adults. Yet, as we shall see shortly, the paradox is easily resolved if the non-unitary concept of dependence is first broken down into its easily discriminable executive and volitional components. When this is done, self-perceptions of volitional independence and executive dependence are seen as quite compatible with each other under the biosocial conditions of infancy. Unlike the psychoanalytic doctrine of infantile omnipotence (Ferenczi, 1916), which assumes the existence of both a preformed ego and of volition at and even prior to birth, the present theory conceives of omnipotent feelings in infants as a naturalistic product of actual interpersonal experience (parental deference) and cognitive immaturity. It is self-evident that the child's perception of his relative omnipotence cannot be demonstrated empirically prior to the advent of language. And even then, it can only be inferred from rampant expressions of imperiousness and possessiveness that are so prevalent during the latter portion of this age interval (Ames, 1952; Gesell & Ilg, 1943).

DEVELOPMENT OF EXECUTIVE DEPENDENCE*

Although completely helpless and dependent *in fact,* it is highly improbable that the newborn infant appreciates his helplessness and executive dependence. Before he can conceive of his helplessness, he has first to be capable of deliberately willing the satisfaction of his needs and perceiving in a causal sense his own inability to do so. Similarly, to appreciate that he is dependent on *another* for the execution of his wishes requires that he perceive the latter as a person and the succorant acts of this person as causally related to his need-satisfaction sequences. In the first few months of life, however, crying is not volitional, mother is not perceived as a person, and the child probably has no conception of causality (Piaget, 1952, 1954). It is true, of course, that the mother is always present before and during the act of need reduction, and that after the first month of life merely holding the infant without offering him nourishment is sufficient to still his hunger cry. But at this early stage of development, it is more credible—for the reasons given above—to suppose that the mother, by virtue of habitual association with need reduction, serves as a signal of imminent need satisfaction and perhaps as a substitutive satisfying object in her own right, than that the infant perceives his helplessness and the *causal* connection between mother's presence and the reduction of his hunger.

From the foregoing analysis, it appears that the development of a sense of volition is a prerequisite first step before a feeling of executive dependence can arise. How this development is brought about, however, must remain forever in the realm of speculation. The most plausible hypothesis we are able to suggest is that volition is a learned outgrowth of the innately determined pattern of general

*Psychoanalytic theorists and developmental psychologists and psychiatrists (e.g., Bühler, 1968, Bowlby, 1960; Erikson, 1959; Escalona, 1963; Glover, 1956; Klein, 1932; Kris, 1951; Mahler, 1968). fail to distinguish between executive and volitional dependence.

excitement in response to any intense internal or external stimulus (e.g., hunger). This reactive pattern, particularly crying, has adaptive value in that it frequently evokes maternal succorant activity that reduces the need responsible for the excitement. Eventually, after repeated experiences of the efficacy of crying in relieving the tensions of need, a causal connection may be perceived between antecedent and consequent. At this point, crying becomes a conscious, deliberately employed (volitional) device rather than an almost reflex response for relieving unpleasant sensations referable to self.

Once volition is acquired, it reciprocally facilitates the perception of causality, since the act of willing constitutes a vivid antecedent in many causal sequences. The child is now in a position to perceive that his expression of will does not lead to need satisfaction through his own manipulative activity (i.e., a perceiving of his own helplessness) but only through the intervention of an external agency (i.e., a perceiving of his executive dependence). In this instance, ability to perceive the mother as a person facilitates the perception of causality inasmuch as it is undoubtedly less difficult to conceive of a person than of an object as a causal agent and manipulator of reality.

ENVIRONMENTAL AND PERCEPTUAL SUPPORTS OF
OMNIPOTENCE

But all the while that a conception of executive independence is being developed, a notion of volitional independence and omnipotence is concomitantly engendered. Precisely when the child is most helpless, he is accorded, almost invariably in all cultures, more indulgence and deference by parents than at any other period of childhood (Whiting & Child, 1953). Parents tend to be most solicitous and eager at this time to gratify his expressed needs. In general, they make few demands upon him and usually accede to his legitimate requests. If training is instituted, it tends to be delayed, gradual, and gentle (Leighton & Kluckhohn, 1947; Whiting & Child, 1953). In this benevolent environment, therefore, much support is provided in external stimulus conditions for a perception of parental subservience to his will. Also, at this age he is not sufficiently mature, cognitively speaking, to appreciate the relatively subtle motivations (i.e., love, duty, altruism) that underlie parental deference (Ausubel, 1952). Although the child is mature enough to perceive the overt attitudes and behaviors of individuals in his interpersonal world, he does not seem to expect to receive the same degree of deference from older siblings as from his parents. His perceptual immaturity is manifested rather at the level of perceiving the more subtle, covert, or motivational aspects of attitudes. Thus, because of his personal volitional power, the child has the quite understandable autistic misperception that the parent is *obliged* to serve him, not that the parent does so altruistically out of deference to his extreme helplessness.

The infant's appreciation of his *executive* dependence does not detract essentially from his self-concept of relative *volitional* ominpotence and independence. He perceives his helplessness and dependence on others, yet when he wills the satisfaction of his needs, they seem to be satisfied. Hence his perception of dependency is limited to the executive sphere. A volitionally powerful individual has no need for executive competence so long as other competent persons are at his beck and call. In fact, it may even enhance the child's notion of his own power that success in need gratification takes place *despite* the manifest handicap of executive incompetence. He might, therefore, legitimately think, "My will must be powerful indeed if a tiny, helpless creature like myself can compel omniscient adults to gratify my desires." At the very most, perceived executive dependence qualifies the regal scope of his will by making it subject to the availability of a compliant executive arm. Feelings of executive dependence thus become satisfactorily integrated as a subsidiary aspect of the more inclusive self-image of volitional omnipotence. And despite objective biosocial incompetency, the infant's sense of adequacy (self-esteem) at this point—his feeling of personal worth, importance, and ability to control and manipulate the environment to his own ends—is predominantly of the earned type. That is, it depends upon a misinterpretation of early parental subservience to his needs and desires as a result of which he vastly exaggerates his volitional power and independence.

The self-perception of helplessness, however, constitutes a potential threat to the infant's physical safety and integrity. Hence it gives rise to an undercurrent of insecurity that can only be allayed by the continued availability of the executive arm upon which he is dependent (mother). At this stage of development his sense of security—his level of confidence regarding the future benevolence of his interpersonal environment in providing for his basic needs—is thus closely allied with feelings of executive dependence; and inasmuch as a need for security exists, it generates a parallel need for perpetuating executively dependent relationships. These dependency needs are reinforced (1) by the perceived efficacy of such relationships in providing security and in relieving hunger, discomfort, and insecurity (reward), and (2) by the perceived consequences associated with the unavailability of mother, that is, insecurity, hunger, discomfort (frustration), the alleviation of which can only be accomplished through the highly canalized device of the dependency situation. Thus when the dependency needs of infancy are not satisfied because of abrupt separation from the mother, when conditions of succorance become ambiguous or change suddenly, or when demands for executive independence are granted prematurely, there is some evidence that young children later show either residual overdependence (Hartup, 1963; Sears et al., 1953; Stendler, 1954) or overanxiety about dependence on adults (Whiting & Child, 1953).

The Ego-Devaluation Crisis

As long as the infant is helpless in fact, parents are content to be indulgent and deferential in treating him, expecting only that he grow and realize the phylogenetic promise of infancy. In part this attitude is indicative of solicitousness and altruism; but it is also the only realistic expectation they can have in the light of his actual incapacity for responding to their direction. They are naturally desirous of being liberated from this subservience as soon as possible and of assuming the volitionally ascendent role that is warranted in the relationship. In addition they begin to feel the social pressure and the responsibility of training the child in the ways of his culture. But typically in all cultures, they wait until he attains sufficient motor, cognitive, and social maturity to enable him to conform to their wishes.

The age deemed appropriate for ending the stage of volitional independence and executive dependence varies between two and four in different cultures. In our own middle-class society it is closer to two than four (Whiting & Child, 1953). At this time parents become less deferential and attentive. They comfort the child less and demand more conformity to their own desires and to cultural norms. During this period, the child is frequently weaned, is expected to acquire sphincter control, approved habits of eating and cleanliness, and to do more things for himself. Parents are less disposed to gratify his demands for immediate gratification, expect more frustration tolerance and responsible behavior, and may even require performance of some household chores. They also become less tolerant toward displays of childish aggression. In short, all of these radical changes in parental behavior tend to undermine environmental supports for infantile self-perceptions of volitional independence and omnipotence.

Increased cognitive sophistication also contributes to ego devaluation by enabling the child to perceive more accurately his relative insignificance and impotence in the household power structure. He begins to appreciate that his parents are free agents who are not obliged to defer to him and who satisfy his needs only out of altruism and good will. He begins to see himself as dependent upon them both volitionally and executively. Now volitional independence is no longer perceived as compatible with executive dependence. As a consequence of ego devaluation, the situation is precisely reversed: increased *executive* independence is required along with greater *volitional* dependence. From this point on, perceived lack of executive independence is no longer regarded as a regal badge of omnipotence but as a condition necessitating dependence on the will of others.

The Satellizing Solution to Ego Devaluation

The devaluing pressures described above precipitate a crisis in ego development that is conducive to rapid discontinuous change. They tend to render the infantile ego structure no longer tenable and to favor reorganization on a satellizing basis, since in no culture can the child compete with adults on better than marginal terms. The only stable, non-marginal status to which he can aspire and still retain a reasonably high level of self-esteem requires the adoption of a volitionally dependent and subordinate role in relation to his parents. Since he cannot be omnipotent himself, the next best is to be a satellite of persons who *are*.

By so doing he not only acquires a derived status that he enjoys by the fiat of being accepted and valued as important for himself (i.e., irrespective of his competence and performance ability), but also, by perceiving himself as allied with them, he shares vicariously in their omnipotence. His sense of security now becomes less a function of having competent persons available to satisfy his physical needs than of maintaining an emotionally and volitionally dependent relationship with stronger, protective, and altruistic persons, which implies among other things the provision of whatever succorance is necessary. He is also relieved of the burden of justifying his adequacy on the basis of hierarchical position or actual performance ability, which at the very best is marginal and, in any event, is subject to unpredictable fluctuations.

The satellizing solution to the ego-devaluation crisis is more stable and realistic, and less traumatic, than any alternative solution open to the child at this time. Since feelings of adequacy (self-esteem) are largely a function of achieving status commensurate with level of ego aspiration, the retention of grandiose aspirations of volitional independence and omnipotence in the face of a reality that constantly belies these pretensions will obviously make him chronically vulnerable to serious deflation of self-esteem. On the other hand, there are limits to the degree of ego devaluation that is consonant with the maintenance of feelings of adequacy. If the child's ego aspirations are lowered to the point necessary to bring them into line with his *actual* ability to manipulate the environment, the resulting abrupt and precipitous trauma to self-esteem will probably be even greater than if the untenable pretensions to omnipotence are retained. By satellizing he thus, avoids both unfavorable alternatives and maintains the maximal degree of self-esteem realistically compatible with the cultural status of children.

PREREQUISITES FOR SATELLIZATION

From the foregoing it is apparent that satellization cannot occur in just *any* kind of home environment. Before the child can accept volitional dependency and seek a derived status, he must first perceive himself as genuinely accepted and valued for himself; for in the absence of these two parental attitudes, the potential advantages of satellization (i.e., the acquisition of a guaranteed and stable derived status and the assurance of intrinsic security and adequacy) are vitiated, and the child has little incentive for relinquishing the aspirations of volitional independence and becoming subservient to the will of another. Acceptance of volitional dependence on powerful figures is a hazardous venture indeed unless one feels assured in advance of their benevolent intentions. The rejected child also cannot acquire any derived status when his parents, instead of extending emotional support and protection, regard him as an unwanted burden. Rejection is the most extreme method of indicating to the child that the omnipotent and omniscient parents consider him unworthy.

Similarly, the advantages of a derived status cannot accrue if the parent only values the child in terms of his potential eminence.* Sooner or later the child realizes that he is not valued for himself but in terms of his potential capacity for gratifying frustrated parental ambitions. In this case, however, the infantile ego structure is more tenable and less subject to the usual pressures forcing devaluation. The overvaluing parent has no interest in deflating infantile notions of omnipotence and grandiosity. He interprets these characteristics as portentous of future greatness, and continues through indulgence and adulation to provide an environment that helps to maintain for some time the fiction of infantile omnipotence.

Several other variables related to the personality characteristics of parent and child tend to make the process of satellization more or less difficult or prolonged but do not affect ultimate outcomes crucially. An unduly submissive or permissive parent who fails to impress the child with the distinction between their respective roles and prerogatives tends to prolong the phase of omnipotence. The child is spared the pressure of parental demands for conformity to their will and standards, and hence exhibits less need for ego devaluation. But if he is truly accepted and valued for his own sake he will eventually perceive his actual biosocial status and choose satellization as the most feasible solution to the problem of maintaining childhood self-esteem in an adult dominated society. Reference has already been made to the effect of temperamental variables in the child on tendencies to satellize.

CONSEQUENCES OF SATELLIZATION

Satellization has profound consequences for all aspects of ego structure and for the future course of personality development. Part of the satellizing shift in source of biosocial status involves abandonment of notions of volitional omnipotence and independence and of the centrality of self in the household social economy. But to compensate for this the child acquires a guaranteed source of derived status from which he obtains intrinsic feelings of security and adequacy. Thus children who perceive themselves as more intrinsically valued tend to undergo more ego devaluation: they conceive of their capacities in less omnipotent terms and are less tenacious about maintaining unrealistically high levels of aspiration in a laboratory task after cumulative experience of failure (Ausubel, et al, 1954). School children ranked high on acceptance tend to be characterized by

*Evidence from the study of children's perceptions of parental attitudes (Ausubel, et al., 1954) indicates that it is possible for extrinsically valuing parents to be perceived as accepting (although for ulterior motives). The same evidence, however, supports the logical supposition that the rejecting parent cannot possibly extend intrinsic valuation to his child. In general, acceptance and intrinsic valuation are highly correlated. And since extrinsically valued children are almost invariably overvalued, the latter term alone will be used henceforth in referring to children who are overvalued for ulterior purposes. It is not rare, however, for accepted, intrinsically valued children to be overvalued (Ausubel, 1952; Ausubel, et al., 1954).

"willing obedience" and relative lack of self-sufficiency and ego defensiveness (Sanford, 1943).

Another product of satellization that is related to but distinguishable from its devaluing features (i.e., changes in status, aspiration level, volitional independence) has to do with the *object* or *content* of the child's conformity to parental volitional direction. It encompasses the training goals underlying the new parental demands and expectations to which the child is conforming. These goals may be designated as *ego maturity* goals since—irrespective of later changes in source of status, independence, and volitional control—they remain as constant objectives of personality maturation throughout the desatellizing and adult as well as the satellizing period of ego development. Although there is much intercultural variability in the ideals of personality maturity, the needs of individual and cultural survival require that infantile hedonism, executive dependency, and moral irresponsibility be attenuated in all cultures. With respect to all of these components, the infant is characteristically at one pole and the mature adult at the other. Thus, although there are characteristic fluctuations in ego-status goals throughout the life cycle, there is a continuous increase in ego-maturity aspects of personality from the satellizing stage until senesence when some decline may set in.

Hence, as children increase in age beyond the period of infancy, they are expected to grow in ability to develop non-hedonistic motivations, to plan in terms of larger and more distant goals, and to forego immediate satisfaction in order to gratify more important, long-term aspirations. Second, they are expected to develop more executive independence. Growth in motor capacity for self-help is not always matched by equal *willingness* to carry out the often tedious and time-consuming manipulations necessary in gratifying needs. Parents, however, are unwilling to serve indefinitely as the executive arm of their offspring's will, and demand that children acquire a certain measure of self-sufficiency in the ordinary routines of living. In contrast to younger children, for example, older children are less apt to request a helping hand in walking a plank blindfolded (Heathers, 1953). Lastly, it is expected that children will internalize parental standards, accept the moral obligation to abide by them, and regard themselves as accountable to parents for lapses therefrom.

During the satellizing period the child is motivated to undergo change in these areas of personality development in order to obtain and retain parental approval, since only in this way can he feel sure that the derived status he enjoys will continue. His sense of security and adequacy become increasingly dependent upon conformity to parental expectations of more mature behavior. Highly accepted children are judged as willing to exert much "conscientious effort" to hold the approval of "admired authorities" (Sanford, 1943); and children who perceive themselves as intrinsically valued at home are rated by teachers as more executively independent and more able to postpone the need for immediate hedonistic gratification (Ausubel, et al, 1954). It has also been shown that task-oriented children, who presumably satellize more and have less need for ego aggrandizement, exhibit more emotional control and make fewer demands on adults (Gruber, 1954).

Finally, satellization has important implications for the mechanisms by which norms and values are assimilated from elders and from membership and reference groups. The essential motivation directing the satellizer's organization of his value system is the need to retain the acceptance and approval of the persons or groups that provide his derived status. Hence he develops a generalized set to perceive the world in the light of the values and expectations he attributes to the latter individuals. Children who perceive themselves as most intrinsically valued by parents are least apt to make value judgments deviating from perceived parent opinions (Ausubel, et al., 1954). Later, this orientation is reinforced by the desire to avoid the guilt feelings that are associated with repudiation of parental values. Value assimilation is thus an unconditional act of personal loyalty in which both considerations of expediency and the objective content of what is internalized are largely irrelevant, that is, from a motivational standpoint. The satellizing child identifies uncritically with the moral values and membership groups of his parents, even when these are only meaningless symbols. Thus, irrespective of his actual experience with black children, the white child of five and six tends to assume his parents' attitudes, favorable or unfavorable, toward blacks (Horowitz, 1936; Radke-Yarrow, et al., 1952).

NEGATIVISTIC REACTIONS TO DEVALUATION

Ego devaluation is not usually brought about smoothly and painlessly. Typically, although not invariably, the child first resists the threatened loss of his infantile ego status by more vigorous and aggressive assertion of its grandiose-imperious features before acknowledging that the advantages of a derived status offer him a more tenable biosocial position (Ausubel, 1950; Gesell & Ilg, 1943; Reynolds, 1928). This leads to resistive or negativistic behavior that tends to reach a peak between two and three years of age (Gesell & Ilg, 1943; Reynolds, 1928). The sources of resistance to ego devaluation are many: the inertia of existing personality organization; the insecurity and loss of immediate status involved in any rapid transition; the loss of advantages associated with present status and the disadvantages perceived in the new status; aggression and counteraggression.

The two- or three-year old has been accustomed for some time to living with the prerogatives and immunities of his omnipotent ego structure. Hence, he is understandably reluctant to part with an orientation that placed him at the center of his universe and to accept instead the role of dependent satellite. To retain parental approval he must inhibit hedonistic impulses, surrender volitional independence, and conform to parental standards; and until the prospects for satellization are entirely certain he must contend with the marginality and anxiety of transitional status. Rage, however, is a more conspicuous component of the child's response to ego devaluation than anxiety, providing the latter takes place in a generally benevolent and accepting atmosphere. Such an atmosphere mitigates anxiety by providing a pervasive sense of security and opportunity to satellize. Finally, negativism during this period constitutes a form of counteraggression against the often aggressive and interfering behaviors that parents use in pressing their training demands. Thus it tends to be less intense when either parent or child happens to be temperamentally unassertive or submissive.

Issues regarding self-help are frequent excitants of negativism. The child vigorously resists attempts to abolish the executive dependence and "baby ways" that are part of his omnipotent self-concept. On the other hand, denying him the opportunity for self-help is also a common precipitant of resistiveness. We may hypothesize here, however, that the child's ire is aroused not so much because desire for executive independence per se is frustrated but because of interference with his notion of volitional independence, that is, with his perceived prerogative to do a particular task by himself *if he* so chooses (Ausubel, 1950). The birth of a sibling is often such a traumatic event because the dethroning and transfer of indulgent attention to a new child comes at a time when the ego is already bearing the brunt of a violent devaluing process. Thus sibling rivalry tends to be less severe if the younger child is born either before or after (i.e., less than 18 or more than 42 months) the crucial stage of devaluation in the older sibling (Sewall, 1930). Girls apparently manifest less negativism at this age than do boys (Goodenough, 1931) for two reasons. First, because they perceive themselves to be more accepted and intrinsically valued by parents and to have a more available like-sexed person with whom to identify, they can acquire more derived status. Second, they are able to obtain more subsidiary earned status than boys can by participating in female household tasks (Parsons, 1942).

In any particular instance of this kind of negativism specific normative, temperamental, or situational factors are undoubtedly important. Because of volitional immaturity, compliance may be difficult without prior or simultaneous execution of the opposite alternative of refusal. Genuine misunderstanding of requests, disinterest in particular tasks, or requiring the child to exercise control and discrimination beyond his developmental capacity also instigate negativistic behavior (Harvey, et al., 1961). At any rate, children's negativism seems more blatant than adults' since they lack the latter's language repertoire of polite evasions and circumlocutions when aroused (Reynolds, 1928).

The Non-Satellizing Solution to Ego Devluation

The satellizing solution, for the reasons given above, is hypothesized as the most acceptable and satisfactory, and hence as the most frequently chosen way in which children resolve the crisis of ego devaluation. It presupposes that they can acquire a derived status through the medium of a dependent parent-child relationship. In all cultures, however, a variable number of parents are psychologically incapable of or unwilling to extend acceptance and intrinsic valuation of their offspring. Thus, deprived of the self-esteem provided by the fiat of unconditional parental acceptance, such children must continue to seek earned status and feelings of adequacy on the basis of their *own* power to influence and control their environment. There is this important difference however: whereas formerly a grandiose earned status could easily be assumed on the basis of a misinterpretation of parental subservience to their desires, increased cognitive maturity no longer makes this possible. Although the environment may continue to provide some support for the notions of volitional independence and omnipotence, these notions must now be related increasingly to *actual* performance ability (executive competence) and hierarchical position.

If satellization is impossible, two alternatives still remain for resolving the crisis of ego devaluation: ego aspirations can either be maintained at the omnipotent level or else be reduced drastically in order to correspond to actual biosocial competence unenhanced by the derived status afforded through parental acceptance and prestige. In the first instance, no devaluation of ego aspirations takes place; in the second, devaluation is complete. Although the latter alternative (complete devaluation) is conceivable under certain circumstances, it is not very probable. First, it involves an overly drastic, abrupt, and traumatic depreciation of self-esteem. To aim high is in itself an enhancement of self-esteem, whereas immediate capitulation to the most unpalatable ego status available implies defeat and degradation. Second, various factors in the parent-child relationship operate against complete devaluation. An individual who fancies himself omnipotent does not react passively but with counteraggression, bitterness, and vengeful fantasies to the hostility, aggression, and humiliating depreciation of his self-esteem implied in rejection by parents. By setting his sights on power and prestige, he hopes someday to obtain revenge and negate parental judgments regarding his worthlessness. In the case of the extrinsically valued (overvalued) child, complete devaluation is also an unlikely outcome. The parent who intends to aggrandize his own ego through the child's future eminence does all in his power to perpetuate the fiction of the latter's infantile omnipotence by maintaining a worshipful and deferential attitude. Thus, only where rejection takes the more passive form of prolonged emotional neglect and deprivation (as in foundling homes) is the child apt to undergo complete devaluation instead of attempting the preservation of omnipotent aspirations. If the neglect is thoroughgoing enough, no real need for devaluation exists since omnipotent fancies do not develop in the first place; and in the absence of overt parental aggression, the maintenance of grandiose aspirations as a mechanism of counteraggression and revenge is unnecessary.

CONSEQUENCES OF FAILURE IN EGO DEVALUATION

The child who fails to satellize generally fails also to undergo ego devaluation. The infantile personality structure that is not presented with the prerequisite conditions for reorganization tends to persist despite various shifts in biosocial status. Unable to achieve feelings of security and adequacy on a derived basis, he continues to seek their extrinsic counterparts. Feelings of adequacy continue to reflect earned status, whereas feelings of security remain a function of the parents' availability in providing for his basic needs until he possesses sufficient power, position, and prestige to feel unthreatened in facing the future.

Under these conditions the child is not obliged to relinquish aspirations for volitional independence, renunciation of which is implicit in the self-subordination of anyone who satellizes (i.e., who derives his status by the mere fact of dependent relationship to or acceptance by another). It is true that increased capacity to perceive the social environment more realistically compels him to revise somewhat both these aspirations and his self-estimate in a downward direction. But even though a discrepancy between aspirational level and current status is inevitable for some time, his high ego aspirations still tend to persist. In the absence of satellization, which guarantees a derived intrinsic status, the acquisition of extrinsic (earned) status becomes a more compelling necessity. Hence, because of this compensatory need for high earned status, exaggeratedly high levels of ego aspiration remain tenaciously resistant to lowering despite their relative untenability in the present. The child hopes to close the gap in the future; and even in the meantime the maintenance of a high aspirational level in and of itself elevates self-esteem. Lending some empirical support to these speculations are the findings (1) that children who perceive themselves as extrinsically valued by parents tend to have more omnipotent conceptions of their capacities and to maintain a tenaciously high level of aspiration on a stylus maze task despite persistent failure (Ausubel, et al., 1954), and (2) that low acceptance by parents tends to be associated with high scores on self-sufficiency and ego defensiveness and low scores on "willing obedience" in school children and with high need for achievement in college students (McClelland, et al., 1953; Sanford, 1943; Schaeffer & Bayley, 1963).

Although both rejected and overvalued children can enjoy no derived status, and although they fail to undergo substantial devaluation in terms of aspirations for volitional independence and omnipotence, rejected and overvalued children show important differences between them during their childhood years. In an austere and hostile home environment the rejected child cannot possibly acquire any earned status or entertain any immediate aspirations for it. Hence, not only does he not enjoy any current self-esteem but he must also project all his aspirations for power and prestige either outside the home (e.g., school, peer group) or into the more distant future. The need for survival also compels a humiliating outward acceptance of an authority and control he resents. In such generally insecure surroundings, the catastrophic impairment of self-esteem to which he is subjected (because of his worthlessness in parents' eyes) tends to make him overreact with fear to any new adjustive situation posing a threat to his sense of adequacy.* Nevertheless, hypertrophied ego aspirations are carefully nurtured within and

---

*The anxiety is chronic in rejected non-satellizers, with acute exacerbations, when they are confronted with novel or threatening new adjustive situations.

there is no inner yielding of independence and no true subordination of self to others. Throughout his life he continues to search for an intrinsically accepting parent surrogate (teacher, relative, spouse, friend, mentor, boss) who will enable him to achieve some degree of derived status or intrinsic self-esteem and thus enable him to relax in part from his relentless drive for achievement-oriented success. Fear of further rejection tends to make him, nevertheless, overcautious in approaching parent surrogates. Further, unable to cope with parental anger and punitiveness, and afraid to retaliate in kind, he fails to learn adequately how to express anger when necessary, or how to assert himself or defend himself from the attacks of peers or other adults. He may thus let himself be used as a "doormat" for years and then suddenly explode intemperately, thereby jeopardizing his vocational or marital security.

The environment of the overvalued child, on the other hand, provides abundant satisfaction of both current needs for earned status and immediate aspirations for volitional independence and omnipotence. The child is installed in the home as an absolute monarch and is surrounded by adulation and obeisance. Hence he suffers no impairment of current self-esteem and has no current cause for neurotic anxiety. These eventualities first threaten when the protection offered by his unreal home environment is removed and his hypertrophied ego aspirations are confronted by peers and adults unbiased in his favor. Because of his obnoxious, egocentric, and overbearing personality, he tends to be rejected by peers——expecting the same deference he receives from parents. Only later, when he recognizes the need for more adequate peer relationships for furthering his exaggerated ego aspirations, does he become less personally obnoxious.

Satellizers and non-satellizers also differ markedly with respect to motivation for achieving ego maturity goals (i.e., executive independence, attenuation of hedonistic needs, development of moral responsibility). In contrast to the satellizing child who merely assimilates these goals and standards of parental training through a process of value assimilation, the non-satellizer is primarily motivated in his orientation to values by considerations of expediency and attainment of earned status. He responds to the prestige suggestion of authority figures not because he feels any need to agree unconditionally with them but because he acknowledges their suitability as emulatory models and stepping stones to power and prestige. Children who perceive themselves as extrinsically valued tend to disagree more with perceived parental opinions (Ausubel, et al., 1954), and children who fail to identify emotionally with their parents only assimilate the latter's values superficially (Finney, 1961; Zucker, 1943).

The non-satellizer, therefore, does not accept the unconditional obligation to abide by all internalized values but tends to be selective in this regard. The basis of this selectivity is the expediential criterion of potential usefulness for ego enhancement.* Thus, the curbing of hedonistic impulses and the acquisition of

---

*As will be pointed out later, this factor makes for instability in ego-maturation attributes. Once the non-satellizer abandons his quest for earned status (e.g., reactive depression, reactive schizophrenia), he regresses to childhood levels of ego maturity.

executive independence are regarded as essential for ego enhancement and, therefore, become invested with moral obligation. Hence, with respect to these attributes of ego maturity, rejected school children tend to be rated just as favorably as their accepted contemporaries (Ausubel, et al., 1954); whereas, in the light of these same criteria, extrinsically valued children, who are under little external pressure from parents to conform to standards of mature behavior, are temporarily retarded (Ausubel, et al., 1954), probably at least until their status depends more on persons outside the home. On the other hand, values such as truthfulness and honesty do not always serve and sometimes oppose the interests of self-aggrandizement. In such instances, as suggested by the higher incidence of delinquency in children who are made to feel rejected, unloved, and unwanted, the sense of obligation may selectively fail to operate unless buttressed by either strong convictions of equity or by coercive external sanctions.

The Satellizing Stage

After the negativistic reaction to ego devaluation subsides, the child who finds it possible to satellize is less self-assertive and more anxious to please and conform. He is more responsive to direction and can be bargained with or put off until "later" (Gesell & Ilg, 1943). He perceives his own power and position to be much depreciated, and he feels quite dependent upon parental approval. In their eyes he is a "good boy," that is, relatively docile, obedient, and manageable. But progress toward satellization does not proceed in a straight line. Changing capacities engender new self-perceptions with resulting fluctuations in disposition to remain content with a satellizing status.

EARLY FLUCTUATIONS

The four-year-old is more conscious of his own power and capacity. Marked strides have taken place in intellectual, motor, and social growth, and he is much less dependent on his parents. He learns new ways of manipulating persons and social situations and establishes a modicum of independent status for himself outside the home in the world of his peers. With increased self-consciousness of capacity comes a resurgence of infantile ego characteristics; and possessing still but a rudimentary self-critical faculty, he tends to exaggerate his newly acquired abilities. This tendency toward self-overestimation is facilitated by the child's intoxication with initial successes, his exposure to competitive cultural pressures, and his history of grandiose thinking only recently left behind. Apparently there are times when he even believes he is capable enough to regain volitional independence and to cast aside satellization in favor of seeking an extrinsic status on the basis of his own competence. Deference to parental authority can become burdensome, especially when it is so obvious to him that he "knows better." Parents are also always interfering with his desires for immediate pleasure.

At the age of four the child thus becomes expansive, boisterous, obstreperous; he is less anxious to please, obey, and conform (Gesell & Ilg, 1943). His behavior shows resistiveness to direction and is typically "out-of-bounds." He is "bigger" than everyone and can do everything (Gesell & Ilg, 1943). Now for the first time he becomes intensely competitive in his play and desires to excel others (Ames, 1952; Gesell & Ilg, 1943; Greenberg, 1932; Leuba, 1933; McKee & Leader, 1955). Everything that he has or can do is compared with the possessions and abilities of others, and the decision regarding relative superiority is invariably made in his favor. He is acutely resentful of the privileges accorded older siblings. His concern with power and prestige is also manifested by his preoccupation with possessions, by interference with and teasing of other children and household pets, and by snatching of toys (Murphy, 1947). With the growth of language his resistance assumes more verbal, subtle, and symbolic forms. Threats, boasts, contentiousness, deceit, and delaying and stalling tactics replace temper tantrums and open aggression.

It is important to distinguish between the negativism current at four from the variety prevailing at two and one-half. The goals of the latter are to perpetuate a highly autistic brand of omnipotence that reflects a very immature grasp of the social reality in which the child lives. The basis of parental subservience is completely misinterpreted and no incompatibility is perceived between executive dependence and volitional omnipotence. At four, however, omnipotent pretensions are given a more legitimate and realistic basis. Executive competence is accepted as prerequisite for volitional independence, but because of an inadequate self-critical faculty, a very minimal degree of executive ability is inflated to the point of omniscience. Resistance is provoked when the exuberantly self-confident child tries to capture volitional control from the parent but meets with rebuff. At this age also self-assertion is no longer an end in itself; stimulated by competitive pressures, the child seeks to demonstate his own superiority and to reveal the weaknesses of others. But despite his bold front, the expression of negativism begins to acquire moral implications that were previously absent. This is revealed by a growing tendency to disclaim responsibility for resistive behavior; to ascribe it to accidental causes, to coercive agents operating on him, or to other persons; and to rationalize it as desirable or as a form of self-defense.

At other times, however, the four-year-old becomes painfully aware that he is only a child. When his bluff is called, his inescapably dependent biosocial position brings him back to reality with a thud. He is thus torn between two opposing forces—a longing for volitional independence based on an exaggerated self-estimate of his executive competence, and a frightened desire to return to the protection of his dependent status as he stretches his wings too far and falls. This conflict is generally resolved in favor of the need to retain parental approval and derived status (i.e., in the case of emotionally accepted, intrinsically valued children). The eventual triumph of satellization is not only aided by the development of a more realistic self-critical faculty but is almost an inevitable product of the child's dependent biosocial status in all cultures. The acceptance of parental control is also facilitated by the growing prestige authority of the parent in the child's unstructured attitudinal field, by the operation of guilt feelings in the child, by the latter's rationalization of compulsory parental demands as elective desires of his own, and by the liberal application of rewards, threats, and punishment.

LATER ASPECTS

Five, like three, is also a relatively quiet, well-conforming age that succeeds a period of negativism. As the child's self-critical faculty improves, his self-exuberance diminishes with a resulting loss of confidence in the enthusiasm for his own powers (Gesell & Ilg, 1946). He is more dependent on adult emotional support, tends to be sympathetic, affectionate and helpful, and is likely to invite supervision. The parents are idealized and appear more omnipotent than ever. The extent to which the child accepts parental value judgments is indicated by his almost tearful sensitivity to approval. A minor threat or mild show of disapproval is remarkably successful in effecting compliance. But until identification with the parent reaches a maximum at about the age of eight (Gesell & Ilg, 1946; Havighurst, et al., 1946), one more major fluctuation in level of satellization still has to occur. It is precipitated by changes in biosocial status occasioned by the child's entrance into school.

The six-year-old tends to be aggressive, expansive, boastful, and resistive to direction (Gesell & Ilg, 1946). His negativism follows the same pattern met with at age four; there is much of the same cockiness and blustering self-assurance based on an exaggerated notion of a recent gain in competence. But this time there is more real cause for crowing and ego inflation. For the first time he is conceded an official status in the culture that is independent of the home. For several hours every day he now enjoys—at least in part—an extrinsic status that reflects his relative competence in mastering the curriculum. In addition, the authority of his parents is undermined by the termination of their reign as sole dispensers of truth and moral values. At the same time, school exerts a sobering influence on the child since it also makes greater demands for mature behavior. Hence there is an improvement in such attributes of ego maturity as independence and reliability (Stendler & Young, 1950).

School does not have the same impact on all children. The satellizer tends to react to the teacher as a parent substitute, but the approval he receives from her is less unconditional and more related to performance ability than that which he receives from parents. In the total economy of his personality, also, the earned status he achieves at school still plays a relatively peripheral role in comparison to the derived status provided by his home. The rejected child finds in school his first major opportunity to obtain any status whatsoever, whereas the overvalued child almost inevitably suffers a loss in appreciation at the hands of his classmates.

Satellizing and non-satellizing tendencies are not mutually exclusive or all-or-none characteristics. Superimposed on the satellizing child's quest for intrinsic status is a greater or lesser striving for a subsidiary extrinsic status. Similarly, rejected non-satellizers are more or less able to form satellizing-like attachments to non-parent individuals who qualify better for this relationship. In addition to these individual differences, typical normative changes also take place in the balnace between satellizing and non-satellizing tendencies. Despite periodic fluctuations, the general trend between three and eight years of age is toward greater satellization. Thereafter, rapid strides in social maturity, the new source of status available in the peer group, resentment over exclusion from the adult world, the impetus of sexual maturation, and changing expectations from adults—all play a role in undermining the satellizing attitude. But even in adult life, as already pointed out, satellizing attitudes continue both to provide a subsidiary source of current status and to influence in substrate fashion level of ego aspirations, susceptibility to neurotic anxiety, and mode of assimilating new values.

SOME ASPECTS OF EGO FUNCTIONING

Ego involvement is not synonymous with ego enhancement. It merely refers to the degree of self-implication in a given task or performance (i.e., whether or not the outcome is a matter of concern or importance to the individual) and does not make explicit the motives for his concern. Thus, non-ego-involved areas in the environment are relatively peripheral and undifferentiated; failure in such areas is easily sloughed off, and success does not inspire elation. As already pointed out, since the magnitude and tenacity of aspirations vary with the degree of ego involvement in a task, the generality of aspirational (as well as of other) "trait" behavior depends upon holding ego involvement constant. Even more than success or failure in performance, the degree of ego-involvement also determines the extent to which children find tasks attractive (Nunally et al., 1965; Schpoont, 1955). Failure lowers the attractiveness of a task much less when children perceive themselves as "trying hard" to do well than when they are indifferent about performance (Schpoont, 1955).

The *motivation* underlying ego-involvement, however, is quite another matter. In many ego-involved tasks the chief object of the activity is ego enhancement, in which case we speak of *ego orientation*. Here the task is pursued as a source of either derived or earned status. On the other hand, the motivation for some ego-involved activities may be entirely unrelated to ego enhancement, being energized solely by a need to acquire mastery or to discover a valid solution to a problem. Thus human beings may become intensely ego-involved in tasks in which the outcome *per se* rather than its relation to self-enhancement is the major focus of concern (White, 1963). In such instances the person is *task-oriented*. He experiences feelings of success and failure, but not loss or gain in ego status or self-esteem.

It follows that before ego involvement can arise developmentally, the child must first possess a functional concept of self in relation to which various objects and activities in his environment are ordered in a hierarchical arrangement. When this occurs, he is able to experience success and failure whenever ego-involved goals are either gratified or frustrated. The capacity for ego-enhancing motivation, on the other hand, requires in addition that the child be able to set ego aspirations and respond with fluctuations in self-esteem to success and failure affecting these aspirations. In our culture, this is illustrated by the competitive behavior that first appears in three-year-old children and becomes increasingly prominent therafter (Ames, 1952; Gesell, 1954; Gesell & Ilg, 1943; Greenberg, 1932; Leuba, 1933); such behavior presupposes comparison of one's own and others' performance, appreciation of the concept of surpassing others, and desire to excel. It is also illustrated in the practical setting of aspirational levels for self-help in informal situations; in two to three-year-olds these aspirations adhere quite closely to level of ability (Anderson, 1940). Consistent levels of aspiration in more formal laboratory situations are not apparent, however, until about the age of five (Gesell & Ilg, 1943). For this kind of behavior, the child requires a clear notion of the immediate future, some self-critical ability (Crandall, 1967; Greenberg, 1932), and acceptance of the cultural value of aspiring to goals that are either less accessible (Wright, 1937) or are somewhat beyond his or her prior level of performance (Crandall, 1967; Rosenzweig, 1933).

Ego-oriented motivation in our culture tends to have a competitive and self-aggrandizing flavor based upon the proposition that "no one can enhance . . . himself without encroaching upon the self-enhancemnt . . . of others" (Murphy, 1947). Children typically work harder in response to prestige incentives than under anonymous conditions (Ausubel, 1951), and in response to competitive personal rewards rather than in group contests (Maller, 1929). But although all ego-oriented motivation is directed toward self-enhancement, this does not necessarily imply a desire for ego aggrandizement. Even in our own culture, many children will exert themselves tremendously under conditions that at most allow for private satisfaction with achievement (Ausubel, 1951). The Navaho child strives little for individual achievement and seeks to avoid "being singled out . . . for superior performance" (Leighton & Kluckhohn, 1947). The essential feature of earned status is that it is gained through an individual's own efforts (rather than vicariously by virtue of a dependent relationship to others) and depends upon the quality of his performance. It does not necessarily mean individual success, prestige, power, or competitive advantage. It may just as well be based upon personal satisfaction, for competence, modest security, and approval for group mindedness. In non-competitive cultures self-enhancing status may be best acquired by renouncing individual ambitions and doing a good job of self-effacing, self-denying cooperative activity directed toward the welfare of others.

Ego-enhancement motivation in our culture is clearly identified in the achievement motive (McClelland et al., 1953). The *achievement motive* in children is characterized by their perception of performance in terms of standards of excellence (McClelland et al., 1953). Furthermore, the perception of standards of excellence is accompanied by the experience of pleasant or unpleasant feelings about meeting or failing to meet these standards (Crandall, 1967).

Achievement motivation is by no means the reflection of a unitary or homogeneous drive. It has at least three components. One of these is a cognitive drive, that is, the need for acquiring knowledge and solving problems as ends in themselves. This drive certainly underlies the need for academic achievement to the extent that such achievement represents to the learner the attainment of the knowledge he seeks to acquire. It is completely *task-oriented* in the sense that the motive for becoming involved in the task in question (acquiring a particular segment of knowledge) is *intrinsic* to the task itself, that is, is simply the need to know; and hence the reward (the actual attainment of this knowledge) also inheres completely in the task itself since it is capable of wholly satisfying the underlying motive.

A second component of achievement motivation, on the other hand, is not task-oriented at all. It may be termed *ego enhancing* because it is concerned with achievement as a source of earned status, namely, the kind of status that an individual receives in proportion to this achievement or competence level. It is ego enhancing inasmuch as the degree of achievement determines how much earned status he enjoys, and, simultaneously, how *adequate* he feels (his level of self-esteem); feelings of adequacy in this case are always a direct reflection of relative earned status. The ego-enhancement component of achievement motivation is therefore directed both toward the attainment of current achievement, or prestige, and toward future goals (later sources of earned status) that depend on the latter.

The final or affiliative component of achievement motivation is neither task-oriented nor primarily ego enhancing. It is not oriented toward academic achievement as a source of earned status, but rather toward such achievement insofar as it assures to the individual the approval of a superordinate person or group with whom he identifies in a dependent sense, and from whose acceptance he acquires vicarious or *derived* status. The latter kind of status is not determined by the individual's own achievement level, but by the continuing intrinsic acceptance of him by the person(s) with whom he identifies. And the individual who enjoys derived status is motivated to obtain and retain the approval of the superordinate person—by meeting the latter's standards and expectations.

Some aspects of each of the cognitive, ego-enhancement, and affiliative components are normally represented in all achievement motivation; however, their proportions vary, depending on such factors as age, sex, culture, social-class membership, ethnic origin, and personality structure. Affiliative drive is most prominent during early childhood when children largely seek and enjoy a derived status based on dependent identification with, and intrinsic acceptance by, their parents. During this period, their striving for achievement is one way of meeting their parents' expectations and, hence, of retaining the approval they desire. Actual or threatened withdrawal of approval for poor performance, motivates them, therefore, to work harder to retain or regain this approval. Since teachers are largely regarded as parent surrogates, they are related to in similar fashion.

Affiliative drive is thus an important source of motivation for achievement during childhood. However, children who are not accepted and intrinsically valued by their parents, and who therefore cannot enjoy any derived status, are compensatorily motivated to seek an inordinate amount of earned status through high achievement. Thus high levels of achievement motivation typically represent low affiliative drive that is more than compensated for by high ego-enhancement drive.

During late childhood and adolescence, affiliative drive both diminishes in intensity and is redirected from parents toward age-mates. Desire for peer approval, however, may also depress academic achievement when such achievement is negatively valued by the peer group. This is a more common occurrence among lower-class and certain culturally deprived minority groups (Ausubel, 1965). Middle-class peer groups, as is pointed out later, place a high value on academic achievement and expect it from their members.

The significance of satellization vs. non-satellization in early personality development is associated with a distinctive pattern of achievement motivation. Generally speaking, the non-satellizer exhibits a much higher level of achievement motivation in which the ego-enhancement component is predominant, whereas the satellizer exhibits both a lower level of achievement motivation and one in which the affiliative component tends to predominate prior to adolescence.

The satellizer identifies with his parents in a dependent sense and is accepted by them for himself. He enjoys, by virtue of this acceptance, both an assured derived status and the accompanying feelings of intrinsic adequacy or self-esteem that are relatively immune to the vicissitudes of achievement and competitive position. He has thus relatively little need to seek the kind of status that will generate feelings of extrinsic adequacy commensurate with his degree of achievement. He does not, in other words, view achievement as the basis of his status or as the measure of his worth as a person; it is merely a means of meeting the expectations of his parents and of retaining thereby the approval that confirms for him his good standing in their eyes.

The non-satellizer, on the other hand, is either accepted on an extrinsic basis or rejected by his parents. Enjoying no derived status or intrinsic self-esteem, he has no choice but to aspire to a status that he earns through his own accomplishments. Since his feelings of adequacy are almost entirely a reflection of the degree of achievement he can attain, he necessarily exhibits a high level of aspiration for achievement and prestige—a level that is much higher, and more stable in the face of failure experience, than that of satellizers. This is obviously a compensatory reaction that reflects his lack of derived status and intrinsic self-esteem. Consistent with his higher aspirations for achievement, he manifests more volitional and executive independence than the satellizer, and is better able to defer the immediate gratification of hedonistic needs in order to strive for more long-term goals (Mischel, 1961). Similar personality differences between individuals manifesting ego-enhancement and affiliative drive orientations to learning, respectively, were reported by Atkinson and Litwin (1960) and by McClelland et al. (1953).

Consistent with the sex differences previously mentioned concerning satellization and intrinsic evluation, female achievement performance is motivated more by affiliative needs, whereas male achievement motivation is primarily ego enhancing (Crandall et al., 1964; Sears, 1962; Tyler, Rafferty and Tyler, 1962).

Other aspects of the parent-child relationship are also implicated in the development of achievement motivation. Achievement motivation tends to be higher in those children whose parents have high intellectual achievement aspirations both for themselves (Katkovsky et al., 1964a, 1964b) and for their offspring (Rosen and D'Andrade, 1959); whose parents stress independence training and high standards of excellence (McClelland et al., 1953; Winterbottom, 1958); and whose parents, when present in problem-solving situations with their offspring, exhibit greater participation, instigation, encouragement, and disapproval (Katkovsky et al., 1964b; Rosen and D'Andrade, 1959). Achievement motivation is also apparently stronger in instances where an achievement-oriented mother is dominant in the home: a dominant, demanding, and successful father, on the other hand, is perceived by his sons as providing a competitive standard that is too overwhelmingly superlative to be challenged successfully (Strodtbeck, 1958). In summary, review of the literature on achievement motivation and parental determinants bears out the prediction that non-satellizing (i.e., extrinsically valued) children seek earned status through ego-enhancing motivation. The studies suggest

> that high levels of active parental involvement, particularly along cross-sex, parent-child lines provide the basis for achievement motivation performance on intelligence tests, and intellectual achievement behaviors in free play . . . . In each case, part of that involvement was reflected in negatively-valued parental behaviors or attitudes such as rejection, criticality, hostility, or "pushing" the child beyond his ability, and this was particularly true of mothers of achieving children of either sex. (Crandall, 1967, pp. 179-180)

Significant normative fluctuations (as well as individual differences) in the balance between earned and derived status occur throughout the course of ego development. But, as already indicated, initial ways of relating to others tend to persist, especially if they occur at critical periods of socialization. Thus, although it is true that as the satellizing child grows older he increasingly strives for earned status, he will, even as an adult, continue to enjoy the residual sense of intrinsic worth that his parents earlier conferred on him, and will continue to satellize in some aspects of his current interpersonal relationships.

Level of Aspiration

Much insight into ego organization and functioning can be gained by observing the extent to which individuals take past performance into account in setting their level of aspiration for future performance. Children with adequate amounts of self-esteem (well-adjusted, academically successful children) respond to cultural pressure for achievement by aspiring to levels somewhat above the level of prior performance (Crandall, 1967; Ringness, 1961; Sears, 1940). However, since they do not have compensatorily high ego aspirations, they neither respond beyond the range of present capacity, nor cling rigidly to high aspirations after failure experience. In this way, they minimize feelings of failure associated with a marked discrepancy between aspiration and performance levels.

Individuals with relatively little self-esteem (e.g., especially unsuccessful non-satellizers), on the other hand, are coerced by their high ego aspirations into maintaining tenaciously high levels of aspiration despite realistic considerations to the contrary. They find surrender of their high aspirations more traumatic than the immediate feelings of failure accompanying performance that is below aspirational level; also, merely in the maintenance of their high levels of aspirations, they find a source of ego enhancement. If they can manage to disinvolve their egos from the task, however, they tend to aspire to unrealistically low performance levels that they can always surpass, and thus at least spare themselves immediate failure experience (Sears, 1940). In the long run, however, they fail to achieve either any social recognition or any genuine feelings of self-esteem and succumb eventually either to chronic or acute neurotic anxiety.

In support of the above interpretation of level of aspiration behavior are the following findings: (1) boys, since they possess less derived status than girls, generally tend to set higher levels of aspiration and are more willing to take risks (Crandall and Rabson, 1960; Slovic, 1966; Walter and Marzolf, 1951); (2) handicapped or socially stigmatized children who presumably have a compensatory need for high extrinsic status—for example mentally retarded, physically handicapped, and asthmatic children (Little and Cohen, 1951; Ringness, 1961; Wenar, 1953), black children (Boyd, 1952), individuals of low social and economic status (Gould, 1941), and children who fail chronically in school (Sears, 1940)—tend more than control groups to aspire unrealistically beyond present level of performance; (3) children or adolescents who perceive themselves as extrinsically valued (Ausubel, et al., 1954), who have high prestige needs (Ausubel, Schiff and Goldman, 1953; Ausubel, Schiff and Zeleny, 1953), and who have unrealistic ambitions (Hausmann, 1933; Sears, 1941) all tend to adhere to high levels of aspiration in the face of persistent failure experience.

Egocentricity, Egoism, and Subjectivity

By egocentricity is meant the extent to which the individual's self (in contradistinction to *other* persons, things, and events) is central as an object of attention in his psychological field. At the superficial level of saliency of awareness it merely connotes preoccupation with self and relative indifference to external events.* At a deeper level of value, concern, and importance, i.e., as a high degree of ego involvement in self and of relative inability to relate emotionally to others, it is more appropriate to speak of egoism or narcissism. Narcissism, along with relative disinvolvement from external concerns, poor object relations, and introversion, are the dominant preschizophrenic or schizoid personality traits** that precede withdrawal from adult reality and mature ego-status and ego-maturity goals during schizophrenic episodes.

Although egocentricity and egoism are probably related positively to each other, they are determined by different kinds of factors. Egocentricity-sociocentricity depends upon social maturity, social poise and skill, gregariousness, introversion-extraversion, loquacity, etc.; egoism is more a function of magnitude of ego aspirations. Thus it is conceivable that an outgoing, sociable person may be sociocentric but egoistic (superficially interested in others and their affairs, yet not *really* concerned with their welfare), and that a shy, introverted person may be egocentric but capable of genuine concern for and warm attachments to others once he knows them well enough to drop his shyness.

In the course of intellectual, social, and personality maturation, both egocentrism and egoism tend to diminish with increasing age. In communicating with others, children gradually increase in ability to perceive, pay sustained attention to, take into account the feelings and viewpoints of others, and to interchange ideas as well as talk to each other (Ames, 1952; Gesell & Ilg, 1946; Piaget, 1932). As they grow older in their play they tend to become more aware of the presence and needs of others, more cooperative, considerate, and altruistic.

Closely related to but distinguishable from egocentricity is the young child's overly *subjective* approach to the interpretation of his experience, his perceptual autism, and his lack of reality testing (Piaget, 1929, 1932; Sullivan & Hunt, 1967). As he advances in age, he becomes increasingly able to approach questions of equity from a less personal and more detached point of view, to argue from the standpoint of a hypothetical experience (Gesell & Ilg, 1946; Inhelder & Piaget, 1958; Piaget, 1929). His pictorial representations of reality come to resemble more and more the model rather than the artist (Belves, 1950).

---

*When the self, its attributes, and its experiential contents are the focus of psychological self-analysis, the term *introspection* is applicable. It is a prime characteristic of introverts.

**Actually shyness and asociality, which are typically considered the pathognomonic preschizophrenic traits in children in the United States, are rarely associated with adult schizophrenia (Morris, Soroker, & Buruss, 1954; Robins, 1966)

5

Ego Development in Adolescence and Adult Life

THE EGO-MATURATION CRISIS: DESATELLIZATION

Before ego development can be complete, one more important maturational step is necessary: emancipation from the home and preparation to assume the role of a volitionally independent adult in society. But before adult personality status can be attained, ego maturation must achieve a new balance between the dichotomous needs for independence and dependence—a balance that is closer to the volitional independence and self-assertiveness of infancy than to the docility and submissiveness of childhood. This involves largely a process of desatelliza- tion: the path away from volitional independence trod during early childhood must be largely retraced. Although the consummatory aspects of desatellization must be postponed until late adolescence, important preparatory aspects are accomplished during middle and late childhood.

In terms of the needs arising out of the child's dependent biosocial status, satellization is the most felicitous of all possible solutions to the crisis of ego devaluation. However, beginning in late childhood and extending throughout adolescence, a second major shift in biosocial status precipitates a new crisis in ego development—the maturation crisis—which demands a reorganization of com= parable scope and significance. Confronted by changing biosocial conditions and under pressure to become more volitionally independent and acquire more earned status, the satellizing organization of personality becomes just as untenable and unadaptive as the omnipotent organization was at an earlier date. But since the home and parents still continue to function as the major status-giving influences in the child's life until adolescence, the actual crisis phase (transitional disequilib- rium, disorientation, marginality, and anxiety) is postponed until that time.

Despite much intercultural diversity in the specific content and method of ego maturation, the *general* goals of personality maturation tend to be similar in most cultures. Ego maturation encompasses two essentially different kinds of personality changes—changes in (1) ego-maturity goals and in (2) ego-status goals. *Ego-maturity* goals include the attenuation of hedonistic motivation; the acquisition of increased executive independence and frustration tolerance; the development of greater moral responsibility, more realistic levels of aspiration, and more self-critical ability; and the abandonment of special claims on others' indulgence. Beyond infancy there is continuity of cultural expectation regarding these goals for individuals of all ages, the only differences being in the purposes they serve and in the *degree* of development expected. Thus, progress toward ego-maturity goals is made during the satellizing as well as the desatellizing period. During the latter period, the motivation underlying the attainment of these goals tends to shift from the retention of derived status and parental approval to perception of such attainment as prerequisite to the achievement of higher standards of volitional independence and earned status. In deciding whether to assimilate new values, the desatellizing child is more prone than the satellizing child to use such criteria as expediency and capacity for enhancing ego aspirations instead of the criterion of blind personal allegiance (satellizing orientation). This new approach to value assimilation (which also characterizes the non-satellizer at *all* ages) will henceforth be referred to as the *incorporative* orientation.

The *status goals* of ego maturation, on the other hand, are discontinuous from early childhood to late childhood, adolescence, and adult life. They include the acquisition of greater volitional independence and earned status; heightened levels of ego aspirations; the placement of moral responsibility on a social basis; and the assimilation of new values on the basis of their perceived intrinsic validity or their relation to the major goals of the individual. With respect to these goals, the child is not expected to be a miniature adult. Volitional independence, for example, achieves a high point during infancy, drops to a lower point during middle childhood, and starts rising again during late childhood. The child obtains the major portion of his status from derived sources and the adult his from earned sources; and although this reversal is not completed until adolescence, the balance begins to shift during middle and late childhood. Hence, insofar as the realization of ego-status goals is concerned, the stage of satellization represents a period of retrogression rather than of progress. But even though desatellization restores many of the ego-inflationary features of the infantile period, this doesn't mean that the adolescent is back in the same place he left at the close of infancy; for supporting this gain in ego enhancement is considerable growth in cognitive sophistication and executive competence, much real accomplishment in the goals of ego maturity, and fundamental changes in social pressures and expectations. The concept of maturation can be defined only in terms of a pancultural norm indicating the direction in which certain aspects of personality structure must change if the desired goal of an acceptable adult member of society is to be realized. This cultural ideal of personality maturity influences in turn prevailing expectations relative to changes in goal structure during adolescence, the latter being inevitably fashioned in terms of enhancing the former (Ausubel, 1952).

The essence of this concept of maturation, that is, acquiring the motivation to achieve greater volitional independence and a more earned source of ego status, is obviously incompatible with a relationship of satellization. The satellizing orientation must be weakened before the individual will strive to seek status on the basis of his proficiency in the virtues and competencies valued in his particular culture.

Once these basic maturational goals are internalized, they can be implemented only if a number of other personality attributes are simultaneously modified in the appropriate direction.

For example, the enhancement of earned status requires that an individual pay less attention to the immediate gratification of hedonistic needs and concern himself more with planning for long-range prestige goals; that he acquire greater competence in implementing decisions by himself; and that he at least give the appearance of conforming to the moral standards of his social group.

The adolescent is required to give greater self-reference to considerations involving his own competence and his status in the group. Accordingly, he finds it necessary to adopt much more of the incorporative orientation in the learning of more mature goals and values—because only within the framework of this learning orientation can he efficiently enhance the objective of extrinsic status. When related to this goal, the criteria of blind loyalty, personal allegiance, and craving for personal approval cannot be very reliable motivations for the acceptance of new values. More efficacious and realistic in this situation are such criteria as expediency and perceived superiority in expediting the gratification of particular status needs. The overt satellizing orientation is also frowned upon socially because it conflicts with the maturational ideal of greater volitional independence which is so crucial for the success of the new approach to status problems.

The following is a summary of the characteristic features of adolescent ego maturation that appear in related contexts in preceding or succeeding sections of this volume:

EGO MATURATION TASKS DURING ADOLESCENCE

A. The Acquisition of Greater Volitional Independence.
   1. Independent planning of goals and reaching of decisions.
   2. Assimilation of new values on the basis of their intrinsic validity or their relation to major goals of the individual, rather than on the basis of loyalty to parents or parent surrogates.
   3. Greater reliance on non-parental (that is, societal) sources of ego support.
   4. Aspiring to more realistic goals and roles—adopting a level of ego aspiration that is more consonant with ability and environmental possibilities.
   5. Increased frustration tolerance, the ability to withstand more intense and

prolonged experience with frustration without marked loss of self-esteem, collapse of aspirational level, or deterioration of performance.

6. Emergence of an adequate self-critical faculty—the ability to evaluate own performance critically, to perceive deficiencies and inadequacies in this performance, to become cognizant of discrepancies between an objective standard and own efforts to attain it.

7. Abandonment of special claims on others' indulgence.

B. Reorganization of Goal Structure on a Less Devalued Basis.

1. Greater need for obtaining earned (as opposed to derived) status.
2. Heightened level of ego aspiration.
3. Increased self-valuation.

C. Replacement of Hedonistic Motivation by Long-Range Status Goals.

D. Acquisition of Increased Executive Independence.

E. Acquisition of Moral Responsibility on a Societal Basis.

Pressures toward Desatellization

No sooner is the dependency of satellization achieved than new conditions are created that undermine it and alter the shifting balance of dependence-independence. First among the factors impelling change toward personality maturation is the cumulative impact of progress in cognitive and social capacities, which in turn induces modification of parental and societal expectations. During the period of middle childhood, there is an unspectacular but steady gain in the child's ability to comprehend abstract relationships, to reason, and to generalize. His level of sophistication in perceiving the attitudes, needs, and feelings of others; the relative status positions of various persons (including himself) in the group; and the distinguishing criteria of social class status are all gradually pushed forward. By understanding more thoroughly the nature of the environment in which he lives, he thus feels less awed by its complexity and more confident to navigate alone and unguided. He feels that he now possesses a sufficient fund of social and intellectual competence to qualify for a more mature and responsible role in the affairs of his culture, to engage in the status-giving activities that he formerly regarded as the exclusive prerogative of adults. Hence he tends to wish more than younger children for such status-conferring attributes as good looks, stature, mental ability, and popularity (Cobb, 1954); to prefer difficult tasks that he cannot complete to easier ones that he can (Rosenzweig, 1933); and to be less hedonistic and authority-conscious in his emotional responsiveness to different situations. But this time, unlike the situation at four, he really possesses sufficient executive competence to warrant a serious and legitimate quest for more earned status and greater volitional independence.

Ego maturation in response to parental expectations of more mature behavior may ordinarily be expected to lag initially because of the phenomenon of perceptual constancy in the child. The prepotency of habitual expectations may temporarily force *altered* parent behavior into *familiar* perceptual molds despite manifest changes in stimulus content. The rate of ego maturation is also held back by ambivalent feelings in the child, who is naturally reluctant to part with the protection and security of dependency. This ambivalence is probably greater in children with strong needs for hedonistic gratification (who find long-range striving difficult) and in sedentary, shy, "thinskinned," and introverted children to whom self-assertion comes painfully.

Lastly, ego maturation is a function of cultural expectations and of the availability of mature role-playing experience. These latter factors reciprocally influence each other as well as generate pressure and opportunity for personality reorganization on a more mature basis. Largely for these reasons, when ego maturation in our culture is appraised in a cross-cultural context the acquisition of ego *status* goals (e.g., volitional independence, greater earned status) is seen to lag markedly behind the acquisition of ego-*maturity* goals (e.g., greater frustration tolerance, sense of responsibility, and long-term goals; more executive independence, more deferral of immediate hedonistic gratification) (Winterbottom, 1953).

THE CENTRALITY OF SELF DURING ADOLESCENCE

There are a number of reasons for believing that the concept of self occupies a more prominent place in the individual's psychological field during adolescence, and that considerable upward revision of self-estimate and a heightened level of ego aspiration take place. In contrast to the carefree and extraverted self of later childhood, the adolescent self becomes a more crucial and clearly delineated object of awareness. The adolescent appears concerned with more precise verbalization of his feelings about himself. For all practical purposes, diaries are almost an exclusive adolescent (and feminine) phenomenon (Kuhlen, 1952). Daydreaming is more common in postpubescent than in prepubescent girls of comparable age (Stone & Barker, 1939). Developmental studies of personality structure using the Rorschach Test agree that adolescents are more introspective and given to fantasy, and more introverted and concerned with exploring subjective experience than indivduals of younger or older age groups (Hertz & Baker, 1943; Hertzman & Margolies, 1943; Thetford et al., 1951). Increased awareness of and interest in other traditional symbols of selfhood such as the body (Jersild, 1952; Stolz & Stolz, 1944), grooming (Silverman, 1945), and one's name (Eagleson, 1946) are also characteristic of adolescence. Concern with intellectual status and social relations have considerable self-reference and are important sources of self-esteem in the adolescent (Jersild, 1952). Awareness of one's own sociometric status is enhanced during adolescence (Ausubel et al., 1952). Finally, adolescent preoccupation with sexual matters can be partly explained by the usefulness of the opposite sex as a contrast medium for self-expression and sharper definition of individuality.

Adolescence is a period of inflation of ego aspirations and self-estimate. In contrast to the early crisis of devaluation, it may be regarded as a time of ego revaluation. All of the maturational tasks of adolescence—the acquisition of volitional independence and earned status, emancipation from parents, achievement of economic independence, release from dependence on parents in assimilating values, learning a biological sex role, emphasis upon executive independence and long-range status goals, the acquisition of adult body form—have ego inflationary implications. This supposition is confirmed by analysis of the content of adolescent fantasy, which casts the ego in heroic and amorous roles (Forman, 1935; Hollingworth, 1928) with emphasis upon vocational success and material gain (Shaffer, 1936; Washburne, 1932). Analysis of the inferred goals of high school students (Brown & Martin, 1941), and the fact that the vocational goals of adolescents tend to be at a higher level than are justified by a realistic consideration of aptitude and job opportunities lead to the same conclusion.

ADOLESCENT PERSONALITY COMPARED WITH THOSE OF INFANCY AND CHILDHOOD

The tasks of adolescent personality development overlap sufficiently with those of infancy and childhood to make a more detailed comparison profitable.

To begin with, the crisis of maturation just like the crisis of devaluation precipitates an extended period of developmental disequilibrium. All of the difficulties attending a transitional stage of ego development must be endured again. A secure and established biosocial status is exchanged for a new status that is unsettled, marginal, conflictful, and uncertain of attainment. A highly differentiated and familiar psychological field must be abandoned for one that is uncharted, ambiguous, undifferentiated, and fraught with unknown implications. The quest for orientation must be begun anew. It is no wonder then that resistance to change will come from within as well as from without.

Second, adolescence resembles infancy more than childhood in that a new biological drive (sex) must undergo initial socialization. This emergent phenomenon presents a problem that has not arisen since early infancy, and the control of this new source of hedonistic motivation is comparable in many ways to the early regulation of hunger, thirst, and bladder and bowel evacuation.

Third, there is a reactivation of the issues of dependence vs. independence, of self-assertion vs. subservience, which have lain relatively dormant since the crisis of devaluation.

Again violent fluctuations in these dichotomous needs are the order of the day until a new equilibrium is found. But the general trend of change is in the opposite direction. The pendulum swings closer to the infantile goals of volitional independence and mastery of the environment than to the subservient attitude of childhood. This does not mean that the young adult is back in the same place that he left at the close of infancy; for behind this shift in ego development is considerable growth in perceptual ability and executive capacity as well as fundamental changes in social pressures and expectations. Thus, the position that was abandoned as untenable after fierce resistance from three to five is now given a new basis in reality. Henceforth the tide of battle turns after the turbulent struggles of adolescence and enables the young adult to hold permanently to volitional and executive independence (Ausubel, 1952).

Rank and his followers emphasize the shift in the independence-dependence balance during adolescence. This shift, however, is, in and of itself not coextensive with the process of adolescent personality maturation; it is only one component aspect of the more general constellation of changes catalogued in this section, and cannot be appreciated properly apart from them. For example, the need for greater volitional independence is accentuated by higher ego aspirations, greater self-valuation, and increased demands for earned status. The adolescent individual who (1) has more modest ego demands, (2) values himself more modestly, and (3) is more content with vicarious status can also tolerate considerably lower levels of volitional independence with much greater equanimity than his more ambitious contemporary with a more grandiose self-concept.

As in the crisis of devaluation, negativism is a prominent aggressive response of the individual to the insecurities and anxieties of the rapid transition in biosocial status. In devaluation, however, the general direction of change is toward a decrease in status, whereas in the new situation the reverse holds true.* More important is the difference in the cause of the disproportion between status and capacity that gives rise to much of the conflict-provoking negativistic behavior. In the earlier period, the two and three-year-old demands volitional freedom far out of proportion to his executive capacity. The adolescent on the other hand, receives too little volitional independence in relation to his ability. Status deprivation exists in both instances; in the first case this is attributable to the unrealistic aspirations of the child, but in the second to the inability or unwillingness of parents or social order to provide status commensurate with capacity.

The same difference underlies a general similarity between infancy and adolescence in still two other areas. The adolescent like the presatellizing child is more concerned with earned (in contrast to derived) status, but has a more realistic claim in actual executive competence. Similarly, the adolescent's higher self-valuation is more realistically grounded in environmental supports.

Finally, in comparison with the satellizing child, the adolescent resembles the presatellizing child in owing to personal loyalty relatively little of his feelings of accountability to parental moral standards. But, unlike the situation in infancy, these feelings are based on more abstract propositions, are directed by societal sanctions and guilt feelings, and do not owe their force to more tangible applications of reward and punishment.

*However, the status of the infant is heading toward greater stability and security in childhood, whereas the transition from childhood to adolescence involves a comparable loss in these areas.

On the other hand, adolescence is in several respects more nearly continuous with the direction of personality development during satellization. During adolescence, childhood trends toward greater executive independence, toward increased reliance on long-range goals, toward greater overall moral responsibility (despite the shift in the basis for these), and toward greater conformity to societal demands (Thetford, et al., 1951) are extended. Hedonistic motivation is further attenuated.

But this time the motivation is different. It reflects a need for attaining recently internalized and more mature goals that would be frustrated by preoccupation with pleasure-seeking activities, rather than a need for gaining parental approval (Ausubel, 1952). And although the adolescent shift toward earned status is more reminiscent of infancy, there is continuation of the childhood trend to seek such status on the basis of actual executive competence.

PREPARATORY ASPECTS OF PERSONALITY MATURATION IN ADOLESCENCE

From the standpoint of *ultimate* criteria of maturity, the satellizing era of middle and late childhood is a period of mixed progress. The attenuation of hedonistic motivation, the gain in executive independence, and the enhancement of feelings of moral responsibility are all steps toward adult maturation. But in relation to other, more crucial characteristics of mature personality structure, such as volitional independence and reliance on earned status, satellization constitutes at least a temporary setback. It is true that realistic progress toward these goals also occurs; but as already pointed out, whatever earned status is achieved occupies only a subsidiary position in the total *Gestalt* of biosocial dependency.

Childhood may be regarded as a period of apprenticeship in acquiring the *qualitative* aspects of personality maturity that are necessary for individual and cultural survival. Adolescence, on the other hand, is more a period of apprenticeship in attaining the prerogatives and behavioral capacities associated with volitional independence and earned status. Thus, much of the personality development necessary for maturity is achieved before adolescence or exists at a near-threshold level, and is, therefore, a function of the quality of training for maturation provided during this period.

Factors Bringing About Preparatory Maturation

First among the factors impelling change toward personality maturation is the cumulative impact of progress in perceptual and executive capacities, which in turn induces modification of parental and societal expectations. During the period of middle childhood, there is an unspectacular but steady gain in the child's ability to comprehend abstract relationships, to reason, and to generalize. His level of sophistication in perceiving the attitudes, needs, and feelings of others, the relative status positions of various persons (including his own) in the group (Ausubel et al., 1952; Parten, 1933), and the distinguishing criteria of social class status (Stendler, 1949), is gradually pushed forward. Hence, the first precondition for acquiring more mature behavior patterns—readiness for learning—is satisfied.

But as a result of widespread acceptance of the doctrines of Gesell and the advocates of ultrapermissive education, it is commonly believed that maturation is solely a spontaneous process, generated from within when the child is ready to move on. The application of external pressures is held to be unnecessary and unwise, and productive of resistiveness. But, although the removal of external coercion will eliminate negativism, it will *also* obviate the possibility of maturation.

Gains in maturity do not arise spontaneously and automatically out of the needs of the child. They are more than a reflection of increased readiness to undergo training as a result of increased capacity proceeding from growth, although this factor must also not be ignored. In every noteworthy maturational advance relative to ego structure there is some change in the expectations of significant persons in the child's environment, a change that is also enforced by some coercive form of pressure (Ausubel, 1952).

Just as important for maturation as appropriate revisions in expectations is sufficient opportunity for learning mature and responsible behavior. Without the requisite experience and practice, maturation can evolve no more readily through response to altered external expectations alone, than through spontaneous generation from changed conditions of internal readiness.

By inducing personality maturation in the child, parents play a strategic role in the changing environmental expectations. The new demands they set reflect their own needs and desires as well as their changed perceptions of the child's growing capacities for responsible behavior. Also channeled through them are changing cultural expectations of appropriately mature behavior at various stages of development. And in either case, it is they who apply whatever coercive measures are required to effect the necessary degree of conformity. The parent is unwilling to serve indefinitely as the executive arm of his offspring's will. At the termination of infancy, he welcomes the increased self-sufficiency of the child since it frees him for other tasks, and approves of the shift in ascendence-submission, which gives him greater control and direction of the latter's activities.

To enforce conformity to his new expectations the parent can rely upon reward and punishment, approval and disapproval, prestige authority, and the moral restraints imposed by the child's guilt when he strays from the path of internalized duty. Also at the parent's disposal is the power to extend or withhold the appreciation that chiefly motivates the child's early bids for extrinsic status. Although it is true that external controls and extrinsic considerations (reward and punishment) generally tend to be replaced by some form of self-discipline, the process of internalization is a very gradual one and, by definition, presupposes the original existence of external controls, since obviously nothing can be internalized that does not first possess an external form. And even after internalization is fairly well established, the presence of external controls in the background serves a salutory effect.

In the new face he presents to his child, the parent is for the most part playing the role of cultural representative. "Reality training is important . . . among all people who survive" (Leighton & Kluckhohn, 1947). Under an economy of scarcity, everyone must develop certain minimal skills and a willingness to work. When life is more abundant, the child's actual economic contributions to family survival may be deferred until early adulthood, but in any case he is no longer permitted the self-indulgence and irresponsibility of earlier years. At the very least, a large share of self-help is demanded.

> As in the post-weaning period the (Navaho) child learns that he cannot indefinitely continue to have his way, so between five and eight, he has to acquire a sense of responsibility. Every society has to teach its members that they can not always indulge themselves and that they have duties toward others. The difference lies in when, and how, and by whom the child is disciplined. White society's training in some types of self-restraint . . . comes early. The Navaho child is "beaten down" later after he is sure of the fundamental affection of his relatives.
>
> The sanctions for appropriate behavior are eventually referred to some social norm. Parents in our culture appeal to children not to shame *them* by their misbehavior in the eyes of the neighborhood, but the Navaho parent says, "If you behave like that people will make fun of you."*

In contrast to the extreme indulgence with which they are treated in infancy and early childhood, Navaho children are severely rebuked and even whipped if they take shelter during a storm while out herding and lose track of the sheep. Neglect or abuse of livestock is the least forgivable of childhood misdemeanors. When children first begin to help with the herding at six or seven, they tend to ride and chase the sheep and goats and otherwise disturb and distract them from feeding. Harsh scoldings break them of these habits quite quickly . . . The culprit is dressed down properly, and an effort is made to shame him into more responsible conduct. . . .

The growth of a sense of responsibility is facilitated by the custom of setting aside each year a sheep or two which, with their increase, belong to the child himself. The young herder feels, then, that he isn't just doing a job for his father and mother—he is also looking after his own property. His own interests become involved in his learning to care properly for the flocks . . .

The period from six through the early teens is a time for learning skills as well as for developing responsible behavior. Besides the chores of chopping and bringing in firewood, emptying ashes, hauling water, husking corn, etc., instruction in more specialized tasks begins. From about the age of eight on, children of the two sexes tend to be separated a good deal of the time. Each is trained in certain skills by their elders of the same sex.

*This, and the following quotation, reprinted by permission of the publishers from Dorothea Cross Leighton and Clyde Kay Maben Kluckhohn, *Children of the people: The Navaho individual and his development*. Cambridge, Mass.: Harvard University Press, Copyright, 1947, by the President and Fellows of Harvard College.

The culture not only regulates (1) the general direction of preparatory maturation, which is typical of most human societies, and (2) the more specific aspects that are idiosyncratic to its particular values and traditions, but also places "limits upon the personal punishments and even the scoldings which may be imposed on children" (Leighton & Kluckhohn, 1947). Within this general pattern, however, there is considerable room for individual family differences, both in the emphasis placed upon different goals of maturation and in the type, severity, and feeling tones behind the controls used to effect their realization.

ESTRANGEMENT OF PARENT AND CHILD IN URBAN CULTURES

In rural and primitive cultures, the home serves as both the source of subsidiary extrinsic status and the training institution for developing more mature and responsible behavior.

In modern urban cultures, however, children have little opportunity for exercising independence, responsibility, and identification with the world of adult concerns, necessitating a complete separation of the activity and interest systems of child and adult. Because such children are given no responsibilities in the workaday world of adult concerns, they evolve a complete set of prestige-giving values of their own.

In almost all spheres of life, our culture goes to great extremes in emphasizing contrasts between the child and the adult . . . The child must be protected from the ugly facts of life, the adult must meet them without psychic catastrophe; the child must obey, the adult must command this obedience. These are all dogmas of our culture, dogmas which, in spite of the facts of nature other cultures commonly do not share.

We think of the child as wanting to play and the adult as having to work. . . . But in many societies . . . when the child can run about it accompanies its parents . . . doing tasks which are essential and yet suited to its powers; and its dichotomy between work and play* is not different from that

*The distinction between work and play is also less marked in primitive cultures. Curle (1949) suggests that the segmentation of life in modern civilization as a result of rapid social change, the greater availability of leisure time, and the greater freedom of individual choice in heterogeneous societies has brought this about.

its parents recognize, namely the distinction between the busy day and the free evening. The tasks it is asked to perform are graded to its powers, and its elders wait quietly by, not offering to do the task in the child's place. (Benedict, 1938)

This absence of absolute dichotomy between child and adult prevails among the Navaho.

Children and adults do not belong to two separate worlds. The same set of standards prevails in most things for all ages, from the child (as soon as he can talk) to the very old people . . . . [At the same time] Navaho practice is to expect only so much from children at each age level. The white tendency is to project adult standards down into all except the earliest childhood.*

Ruth Benedict reports essentially the same situation for the Cheyenne Indians.

The essential point of such child training is that the child is from infancy continuously conditioned to responsible social participation, while at the same time the tasks that are expected of it are adapted to its capacity. The contrast with our society is very great. A child does not make any labor contribution to our industrial society except as it competes with an adult; its work is not measured against its own strength and skill but against high-geared industrial requirements. Even if we praise a child's achievement in the home we are outraged if such praise is interpreted as being of the same order of praise of adults . . .

In urban societies, on the other hand, the culture is not organized to provide children with many important opportunities for extrinsic status. Mature roles must be learned by a course other than gradual participation in family or communal responsibilities. "Denied a place in adult reality they [children] must find other outlets for the independence and mature interests which personality growth has stimulated (Benedict, 1938)." They are obliged to find sources of earned status in peripheral activities (school, peer group athletics) far removed from the main current of status in the adult world. They supplement this with the vicarious status that can be obtained through identification with the glamorous exploits of prominent figures in public life, and with whatever satisfaction can be gained by carrying on covert guerrilla warfare with adults and adult standards.

Thus, the child's interests and concern become "oriented more toward his contemporaries than toward his parents." In his peer group he is given a chance to obtain the mature role-playing experience from which adult society excludes him and which his parents are unable to furnish. Identification with this group also

*Reprinted by permission of the publishers from Dorothea Cross Leighton and Clyde Kay Maben Kluckhohn, *Children of the people: The Navaho individual and his development.* Cambridge, Mass.: Harvard University Press, Copyright 1947, by the President and Fellows of Harvard College.

provides a substitute source of derived status; from it he receives ego supports that reduce his dependence upon parental approval. And "by attributing the prerogatives of judgment, decision, choice and initiative to a group fashioned in his own image, he . . . effectively demolishes his exclusive association of these powers with parental figures and thus paves the way for eventually assuming them himself".

School serves a very similar function. It provides both a new subsidiary source of primary status based upon academic ability, and a fresh source of derived status that challenges the parent's monopoly of this commodity and of omniscience as well.

All of these factors—availability of other sources of derived status, reduction of absolute dependency on parents for ego support, need for going beyond the home for extrinsic status, the child's own greater competence, and the emergence of a new authority to challenge his parent's omniscience—tend to break down "the deified picture" he nurtures of his parents. And as the parent's omnipotence declines, his power to confer by fiat an absolute intrinsic value on the child begins to ebb. This stimulates an intensified quest to satisfy status needs beyond the home.

The net effect of this urban displacement of the home as a training institution for personality maturation is threefold. (1) Desatellization from parents is undoubtedly accelerated by their devaluation, although not until adolescence is over is the child "sufficiently free of the attitude of subservience to evaluate them with critical detachment" (Ausubel, 1952). (2) The lack of actual role-playing experience in the adult world cannot be completely compensated for by the various substitutes available in school, peer group, and hero-worship activities. Lacking the stimulation of genuine social expectations of mature behavior in the adult sense, and sufficient opportunity for suitable practice, the individual must inevitably lag in ego maturation (Ausubel, 1950). (3) Finally, this situation cuts the child off affectively from the adult world for as long as he is a child.

Thus, a long process of estrangement between children and adults begins that persists until the former attain adulthood themselves. Insurmountable barriers to commonality of feeling, to mutual understanding, and to ease of communication are often built up. This alienation is not unaccompanied by resentment and bitterness. Although outright resistance to adult authority is usually withheld until adolescence, there is reason to believe that the preadolescent's apparent conformity is only a veneer that hides the smoldering rebellion from view. This is suggested by the often contemptuous and sneering remarks he makes about adults in his own company; and perhaps were it not for compensatory outlets in movies, comics, and opportunities for fighting with peers and bullying younger children, it would come more into the open (Murphy, 1947). Because girls are able and expected to satellize more and longer than boys and can also achieve more earned status at home and in school, they tend to be more conforming to and less at war with adult standards and values.

PUBESCENCE: CONSUMMATORY FACTOR IN
PERSONALITY MATURATION

The preparatory changes in personality maturation catalogued above, as well as the factors bringing them about, are not to be minimized in evaluating the total maturational change from the close of infancy to the beginning of adult life. Yet the transition can not be consummated merely by the cumulative impact of these same factors, namely, parental and cultural needs for personality maturation; increased executive competence of the child; new sources of derived status and ego support; the weakening of dependency ties on parents; the deflation of parents and the continued progress toward desatellization; and the achievement of an independent, subsidiary source of earned status. This is true even where children are not relegated to a separate and discontinuous world of status opportunity, but contribute to the economic sustenance of the family. The conclusion is inescapable that whatever independence and earned status children can earn before pubescenece can occupy only a subsidiary role in the larger *Gestalt* of biosocial dependency. The gains in these areas are primarily a by-product of the training in responsibility and the attenuation of hedonistic impulses that constitute the main maturational business of childhood.

The personality maturity of adolescence and adulthood are *qualitatively* different from the maturity of childhood. In our own culture, this qualitative difference is explicitly recognized in the dichotomy characterizing the types of status activities and opportunities for independence available to children and adults respectively. In cultures that do not erect such dichotomies, this qualitative difference prevails nevertheless as a result of a transcendental leap that becomes effective at a crucial transitional point on a continuous quantitative scale. This point is reached when, in the total economy of ego organization, earned and derived sources of status exchange positions as subsidiary and dominant (or peripheral and central) figures in the *Gestalt*.

Pubescence plays the role of crucial catalytic agent in shifting the direction of the source of status, and hence in inaugurating the consummatory aspects of personality maturation. It is the cue for reversing social expectations about the major type of status that the child may appropriately seek. Hence in relation to the pubescent individual,

the social value of derived status depreciates while the corresponding value of extrinsic status increases. The adolescent, thus, not only finds that he is increasingly expected to establish his status through his own efforts, but also that the latter criterion tends to displace the childhood criterion (i.e., of derived status) as the chief measure by which his social milieu tends to evaluate him. Simultaneously, social pressure is put on the parents to withdraw a large portion of the emotional support which they had hitherto been extending to him by way of conferring intrinsic status. (Ausubel, 1952)

In addition to the fact that by his own volition and under cultural pressure the parent acts to provide less derived status, his power to do so is also impaired. Continued widening of the child's social horizon tends to effect an increasing devaluation of the parent's stature. This process is accelerated by (1) the now more glaring inability of the parents (in comparison with other cultural agencies) to furnish an extrinsic source of status, and (2) the more critical and objective appraisal the child can make of his parent when he is freed of the bias and "halo effect" implicit in an attitude of subservience.

Pubescence also exerts a catalytic effect on the child's strivings for personality maturation. In the face of the altered cultural expectations that puberty induces, he feels that his aspirations for greater status and independence are more legitimate. But even apart from these social sanctions and pressures, his reactions to his newly attained adult physical form, reproductive power, and biological sex drive cannot do otherwise than generate aspirations for the status with which these attributes are patently associated.

MECHANISMS OF DESATELLIZATION

This discussion obviously relates to children with a history of satellization during the childhood era. The mechanisms whereby non-satellizing individuals undergo personality maturation will be given separate treatment.

DESATELLIZATION THROUGH RESATELLIZATION

Within the satellizing orientation itself, we have delineated two different patterns of maturation. The more familiar type is characteristic of modern urban civilization. It involves a gradual replacement of parents by age-mates as the essential socializing agents. The age-mates not only supply the child's needs for extrinsic status and the opportunity for mature role-playing experience but also displace the parents as the persons in relation to whom any residual remnants of the satellizing orientation are maintained (resatellization). This pattern, as already pointed out, involves considerable devaluation of and desatellization and alienation from parents, yet also carries with it relatively slow and inefficient maturation during preadolescence and the middle years of childhood. But

> although this substitution of age-group standards for home standards is often regarded as a phenomenon rooted so deeply in the psychology of maturation as to be inevitable, cross-cultural investigations show this is not so. In Samoa the young boys and girls are given increasing status in the community as they reach and pass adolescence, but there is no period when they rebel against the authority of the head of household and substitute instead a set of counter and antagonistic standards. (Mead, 1940)

Frank (1944) makes the same observation: "In a static, tradition-bound society, the process of emancipation does not necessarily imply a supplantation of the family as the principal medium through which the culture operates." "Here the family could still serve as the primary source of goals and standards while the adolescent's position in relation [to parents] merely shifts from a dependent to an independent role. That is, the adolescent could still learn most of what he needs to know as an adult from his parents, but would assimilate this knowledge for use in the role of an independent person in his own right" (Ausubel, 1952)

In addition to the factors already mentioned as contributing to devaluation of parents and renunciation of their standards is the fact that the

> role we give to parents that they must pose as better and more complete representatives of their culture than they really are also exposes growing children to almost inevitable disillusions. Furthermore the notion that children are different in kind from adults fosters attitudes in children's and adolescents' groups which are qualitatively different from the attitudes of the adults. (Mead, 1940)

The gap thus created between children and parents under these circumstances is further widened by the rapid rate of social change. Adding to the psychological and social distance already present are the very different worlds in which the two generations grow up, producing an actual discrepancy in the content of the values each accepts. Hence, "the children who continue to adhere to the standards set up by their parents carry the stigma of being 'old-fashioned,' 'out of date,' 'prigs,' 'prudes,' or lacking in social consciousness" (Mead, 1940).

What are some of the outstanding consequences of this substitution of age-mate for parental socialization? Besides inducing more complete devaluation, it also accelerates desatellization. The mere fact that individuals of their own generation assume the function of setting standards, a power that had always been regarded as the prerogative of omniscient elders, serves to devalue parents as suitable foci for satellization, and to sanction the legitimacy of their own assumption of this power. But this very same factor leads also to another quite different result:

> There is a difference in the positive self-valuation of the individual who is attempting to meet standards represented by remote and highly respected persons . . . and the individual who is striving hard to meet the standards of persons who inspire no great respect . . . The rejection of parental standards in favor of the late-recognized and antagonistic age-grade standards results, therefore, in an attenuation of self-respect and a weakening of the internalized standards of behavior upon which the operation of our culture is still postulated. (Mead, 1940)

According to Margaret Mead, age-mate socialization has important reciprocal repercussions on social change. An entire revolution of standards becomes possible merely by appealing to the readiness of youth to reject parental ways in favor of a new set of mores. Such change, however, which is founded on no other basis than the need to conform to group norms, does not necessarily bring progress.

The quantity of the surrogates replaces their quality, for a single individual or pair of individuals, who are highly respected as different in kind and better than the child, is substituted the *number* of age mates who approve and follow a certain course of behavior. (Mead, 1940)

Thus is lost an important potentiality for social progress inherent in the older system of socialization by parents, namely, the "striving to avoid the self-reproach of failing to realize an unobtainable ideal, the picture of the parent . . . conceived in childhood" (Mead, 1940).

The repudiation of parental standards in favor of less idealistic age-grade norms also makes youth reared on an earlier diet of satellization more susceptible to demagogic influence. As Mead points out, this readiness to accept alien doctrines is not unaccompanied by feelings of *guilt* in rejecting prior loyalties (Mead, 1940).

And it is this element in their character structure which leaves room for the leader; a parent surrogate who will lift their conformity to the mob on a higher level again and make them feel less guilty of apostasy toward their own infantile acceptance of their parents' dictated systems of morality. (Mead, 1940)

As we shall see later, however, the greater readiness of the adolescent to accept age-grade in preference to parental norms does not necessarily make for a complete overthrow of the standards previously accepted; for the new norms presented by the peer group tend to hew more closely to the values of the social class in which the adolescent claims membership than to the alien values of a different social class. The same values that the child rejects because they are proposed by the parent are eagerly accepted when advocated by the peer group in slightly different form but with essentially the same content.

DESATELLIZATION THROUGH THE ACHIEVEMENT
OF EARNED STATUS

More important for the outcome of desatellization than the issues of who is the basic socializing agent and who—parents or peer group—becomes the focus of residual satellizing trends is the mode of acquiring status. The satellizing orientation is abrogated primarily by the displacement of derived by earned status as the chief source of self-esteem in the adolescent individual. However, the major socializing agent must inevitably constitute the source of the extrinsic status in question. Hence we find the same split between rural and primitive cultures on the one hand, and urban cultures on the other, in the manner in which extrinsic status is obtained.

Generally speaking, adolescence is less prolonged in cultures in which adolescents gain extrinsic status by participating in the same types of economic activities as their parents. But in cultures characterized by age-mate socialization, parental sources of status are not available to adolescents, adolescence is extremely prolonged, and earned status is achieved in peripheral functions far removed from the main economic currents of the social order. We have already referred to the latter situation as interim status. Although from a long-range standpoint the goals of this type of status have only temporary "stop-gap" significance, they do constitute distinctive objects of striving in their own right during the adolescent period.

Here, arises another source of discontinuity between children and adults. Three discrete value and status systems must be learned before adult life is reached. And during adolescence the individual is obliged simultaneously to satisfy the need for immediate age-mate status while keeping an eye toward the more long-range goals of adult status.

In either setting it is important to realize that earned status does not necessarily mean individual success, prestige, power, or preeminence. It may just as well be competence that is not compared with another's, modest security, safety, approval for group-mindedness, maintenance of "face." Thus, among the Navaho,

> the youngster is not urged to strive for individual achievement. There is no promise of personal success for the able and hard-working or the good and righteous. On the other hand, a sense of worthlessness is never drummed into a child so that his whole subsequent life is a struggle to justify himself . . . To accept authority over his fellows or to take initiative in any obvious fashion has for the Navaho the psychological meaning of separating him from the social group to which he looks for both support and regulation . . . But a sense of responsibility is none the less real for being divided and shared, for being—to the white person—vague and unfixed . . . . The majority seem to be only interested in safety . . . . They themselves will sometimes say, "All we want is enough to eat for ourselves and our families." . . . The predominant drive is for moderate material well-being.*

From this we may conclude (1) that the magnitude of residual intrinsic adequacy feelings available to adolescents and adults is partly a function of a societal norm, the mean value of which varies from culture to culture, with considerable room for individual family differences; (2) that the drive for extrinsic status is inversely related to the magnitude of these residual feelings of adequacy; and (3) that the particular orientation of the goals toward which earned status is

---

*Reprinted by permission of the publishers from Dorothea Cross Leighton and Clyde Kay Maben Kluckhohn, *Children of the people: The Navaho individual and his development*. Cambridge, Mass.: Harvard University Press, Copyright, 1947, by the President and Fellows of Harvard College.

directed—whether competitive and individualistic or cooperative and group-related—is conditioned by the prevailing value system of a culture or subculture.

In both types of socialization patterns (age-grade and parental) a transitional variety of earned status is evident. That is, the child's initial quests for extrinsic status are largely bids for parental approbation and as such must be considered modified manifestations of satellization. If they elicit appropriate signs of appreciation from parents, their continuation as ends in themselves is encouraged.

DESATELLIZATION THROUGH THE EXPLORATORY ORIENTATION

Two modes of assimilating values have already been discussed, the satellizing orientation and the incorporative orientation, as characteristic of childhood and adulthood respectively. The incorporative is naturally an accompaniment of the quest for greater extrinsic status since it utilizes a criterion of ego enhancement as the preparatory set in reacting to new value experience. The satellizing orientation, on the other hand, is predicated upon personal loyalty and the need to retain parental approval or at least to avoid the guilt engendered by repudiation of parental standards. Common to both orientations, however, to a greater or lesser degree, is a subjective bias favoring the generation and perpetuation of a given type of status (earned or derived), and a relative indifference to objective considerations impinging on the empirical or logical validity of the value in question.

A third type of learning orientation (exploratory) is not status-oriented in either sense, but is directed toward objective problem-solving regardless of the status implications involved.

> In every person's psychological world there is a . . . sphere of value-laden, ego-involved learning experience in which the task itself and not its relation to ego status is the primary focus of concern. Where task-oriented goals or values are concerned, levels of aspiration operate, success or failure is experienced, but self-esteem is not necessarily affected since ego status is not at stake. The basis of the exploratory [orientation] lies in the active curiosity which is manifested by human beings from the earliest days of infancy. (Ausubel, 1952)

The utilization of the exploratory orientation is obviously limited during childhood, for as soon as the implications of independent objective investigation are pursued to their logical conclusion, the danger always exists that they will conflict with values tied to primary allegiances, and hence precipitate an avalanche of guilt feelings (Ausubel, 1952).

But as subservience to parental values wanes, the exploratory orientation can be used more freely, and continued use promotes desatellization by de-emphasizing considerations of personal loyalty in value assimilation.

Unfortunately, however, the development of the exploratory orientation is severely curtailed in the course of age-mate socialization. The adolescent's marginal status and his dependence on the peer group for status permits very little deviation from group values, and hence little opportunity for independent exploration. The adolescent who ventures beyond certain severely circumscribed limits is quickly ostracized from the peer society. On the other hand, when the adolescent owes his opportunities for earned status to his elders, there are similar pressures to make him conform to traditional values. In both instances the exploratory orientation tends to be sacrificed because of the adolescent's need to conform to the standards of the agents who control the sources of his status. The very operation of this factor, in other words, is merely another manifestation of the incorporative orientation.

EGO-MATURING INFLUENCES

DESATELLIZING FACTORS IN THE HOME

The central developmental task of desatellization is the regaining of the volitional independence surrendered in the course of satellization. Hence desatellization, can best be implemented by (1) encouraging the exploratory orientation and by discouraging the satellizing orientation in the assimilation of values; (2) developing multiple sources of intrinsic security and adequacy through satellization with persons and groups outside the home; and (3) developing skills in independent planning and goal-setting by providing opportunities for practice, and appropriate conditions for learning realistic roles and goals, adequate frustration tolerance, and realistic self-criticism.

Children can only feel free to pursue the exploratory orientation in the learning of values if they are absolutely sure that they are *unconditionally* accepted by their parents. This requires that they be allowed to accept the values of our culture rather than having them crammed down their throats with withdrawal of parental emotional support as the ever-threatening penalty for disagreement. But even if unconditional acceptance is assured, disapproval must be used reservedly since it inevitably leads to guilt feelings in the child. Hence parental disapproval should not be administered automatically whenever the child's attitudes deviate from the parents'—as if disagreement *per se* were evil. It should be reserved for instances of serious deviancy which would lead, if left uncountered, to personality distortion or maladjustment. Disapproval and guilt feelings, as already indicated, can be used to discourage blind and uncritical reflection of parental viewpoints; and the praise that is usually reserved for this situation can be dispensed when evidence of independent and critical thinking is presented.

The dependent aspects of satellization can also be minimized if the child can find derived status in multiple sources rather than in his parents alone. Under such circumstances the one source is no longer so precious. He need not tread so warily to avoid arousing disapproval. Fortified by the ego support he receives from friends, grandparents, older siblings, teachers, group leaders, etc., he can afford more often to assert his independence and risk arousing parental ire. Even if these additional sources of intrinsic status play only a subsidiary role in relation to parents, they may often spell the difference between complete subservience and occasional defiance.

This condition for the development of mature behavior has been grossly violated by the present-day fetish of permissiveness* in child rearing. The tremendous vogue enjoyed by this doctrine can in part be explained as a reaction to the rigid and authoritarian parental practices that were fashionable in the preceding two decades. In part, it is a by-product of the recent overemphasis placed upon frustration as an etiological factor in the behavior disorders and an invariable and unqualified evil. More specifically it has been rationalized on the basis of evidence that has applicability to young infants only, and by reference to the analogy of the more permissive and democratic approach to the learning of values advocated above and practiced in the more progressive schools.

However, it is one thing to advocate self-demand feeding schedules because of the low frustration tolerance of infants, and their recognized exemption from stringent social demand, and quite another matter to suggest the indefinite prolongation of this policy into the early and later years of childhood. Similarly, there is no incompatibility between granting children greater freedom in accepting values on the one hand, while insisting on the other that their behavior be confined within certain broad limits imposed by the social expectations and prohibitions relative to their age group.

It seems unreasonable to expect that a child can ever orient his goal structure realistically in relation to obstacles and barriers without some direct experience with frustration. In order that he acquire sufficient frustration tolerance to persist (despite inevitable setbacks in the pursuit of long-range goals) in maintaining his essential independence and in avoiding an excessively lax and uncritical appraisal of his accomplishments, he must learn the meaning of failure and the means of grappling with it. Exposing the child to unnecessary or pointless frustration or to frustration beyond his developmental capacity for coping with same will no doubt only impede the growth of this tolerance. But the extreme permissive viewpoint embodied in the underdominating parent—who conceives of her ''parental role as intended to insure the fact that her child suffers not the slightest'' impediment in implementing his desires lest he become ''emotionally insecure''—leads to the very same result.

Purposeful and persistent avoidance of frustration creates for the child a

*For purposes of highlighting the chief issues involved, this critique of permissiveness is based upon the most extreme presentation of this philosophy of child rearing (e.g., Gesell & Ilg, 1943; Spock, etc.) that can be found in books of child care and school discipline. The reader should bear in mind, however, that all shades and degrees of permissiveness short of authoritarianism exist. In fact, the authors would regard their own position as a limited endorsement of permissiveness if judged against the impersonal overstrict and rigid Watsonian criteria of child rearing popular in the interval between World Wars I & II.

conception of reality which is so distorted that he becomes exclusively
conditioned to living in a hedonistic environment. Under these conditions,
maturation, which involves adjustment to a reality fashioned in good part
from the fabric of frustration, becomes an utter impossibility. (Ausubel,
1952)

The development of frustration tolerance, therefore, requires that a child be
encouraged to solve his own problems and learn through his mistakes, that his
course through life not be continually smoothed by systematic elimination of the
problems that confront him. He must learn to take responsibility for the consequences of his behavior when mistakes are made and failure ensues. Parental
"whitewashing" does not develop frustration tolerance but reinforces the immature tendency to cope with failure and misbehavior by rationalizing, disclaiming
responsibility, and abandoning even minimal standards of self-criticism.

Another undesirable outcome of indiscriminate permissiveness is that a child
finds it difficult to perceive self and self-role realistically, to deal adequately with
the child-adult relationship, and to evolve goals that are realistically related to
probability of success and amount of motivation at his disposal. The conditions
under which self-role can be realistically learned require a clear appreciation of
what can be included legitimately within the appropriate age-sex-subculture role
and what must perforce be excluded from it. The attitude of unvarying permissiveness fulfils neither condition. By advocating unrestricted freedom for the child in
setting his goals, by refusing to impose limitations on behavior that is socially
unacceptable, and by denying the legitimacy of status differences between children and adults, the overly permissive parent or teacher makes it impossible for the
child to perceive the boundaries of his role.

In some extreme cases, exposure to this variety of childrearing leads to
complete unrealism regarding the demands that an individual can legitimately
make on others and their moral obligation to help him (the "Prince" or "Prin-
cess" complex). The child perceives his biosocial incompetence, and satellizes in
the sense that he accepts a derived status and a dependent position in relation to his
parents. But the latter cater excessively to his dependency needs, indulge his desire
for executive dependence, fail to impose or enforce any demands or restrictions,
and scrupulously avoid making any distinction between child and parental roles.
As a result of this extreme underdomination, he develops the notion that he is a
very precious and privileged person. His parents *have* to do things for him and
have to help him—not because his will is omnipotent or irresistible, but because he
has a special claim on their indulgence. Eventually this orientation is extended to
the world at large: "The world owes me everything I need. People are obliged to
help me; it is my natural due. After all, they can not let *me* fend for myself or suffer
pain and deprivation. In the case of other people, yes, but not *me*. In *my* case it is
different. It would be too cruel, too unfair." Such individuals approach even
complete strangers with the unabashed plea, "I'm in a terrible fix, you've simply
got to help me, or I won't be responsible any longer for what I do."

In no culture can the distinction between parental and filial role be eradicated. The parent is required to be more dominant and ascendent in the relationship than the child. His judgments must be given more weight and his demands more authority. The welfare and safety of the child require that he sometimes defer completely and comply immediately with parental requests. The parent has a right to expect unconditional obedience in times of danger without offering explanations for his demands. Where differences are irreconcilable, and issues of parental responsibility or social principle are involved, the parent's view should prevail. But the adherents of unqualified permissiveness refuse to face these issues squarely because to do so would mean repudiating the theoretical basis of their child-rearing doctrines. On the other hand, they cannot ignore these considerations completely—because the practical pressures of meeting everyday situations and occasional crises, and of minimally satisfying cultural demands require the adoption of more directive and authoritarian attitudes than are consistent with their underlying philosophy. What results, therefore, is an unsatisfactory compromise that only adds to the ambiguity of the learning situation.

This compromise approach is reflected in many different attitudes of the overly permissive parent. He persistently refuses to define or clarify the acceptable limits of child behavior and handles each situation as it arises according to the demands of expediency. In this way he feels that he remains true to his doctrines while still in a position to cope with special situations. But the child exposed to this treatment cannot generalize in any consistent fashion about the limits of behavioral acceptability. The parent, for example, fails to make clear that his demands upon the child have a different status than the child's demands upon him, but on occasion acts as if this were the case by using force or threats. The child who has been-indoctrinated with the principle of equality of status is thereby justified in concluding that either the general principle still holds but was unfairly violated by the parent, or that he, too, can exercise the same prerogatives as the parent with respect to the employment of force and threats. The same parent may permit his child to participate in activities far beyond his developmental capacities, but will cut them short on some pretext, if embarrassing or unfortunate consequences ensue, rather than let him learn the fitting generalization that he is not yet equipped to handle certain situations.

The ambiguity surrounding the limits of unacceptable behavior is further enhanced by the parental tendency to avoid issues, which might arise from opposing the child's desires, by resorting to distraction. While this technique is occasionally defensible—when the child is ill, unduly fatigued, hungry, or excessively irritable—it effectually prevents him from learning what constitutes out-of-bounds behavior if used habitually as the path of least resistance. Much less objectionable is the widely accepted practice of saying, "You can't do this, but you may do this." This tactic avoids the error of ambiguity and is a feasible method of handling many difficult situations. But if used compulsively (as implied by the popular permissive dictum, "Say 'no' to a child as infrequently as possible, but if you must, always offer him a positive alternative"), it conditions him to an environment which is highly unrealistic in terms of the social prohibitions that will inevitably limit his behavioral freedom. The restrictions imposed in most real-life situations have only a negative aspect. This does not mean that positive alternatives cannot be found or that the child should not be encouraged to search for same; but if they are available or can be applied, it should be made clear that in most cases they originate as a product of the frustrated individual's resourcefulness and are not inevitably given in the prohibition itself.

Two other favorite techniques of the overly permissive parent are self-insulation and empty verbalism when an occasion for discipline or restraint arises. Obviously, if a parent cannot see or hear anything objectionable he cannot be expected to interfere. If, on the other hand, the behavior is so flagrant that self-insulation is impossible, half-hearted verbal disapproval can be given. The parent then feels that by voicing his objections he has discharged his parental duty even if the child continues this behavior during and after the time that the reproof is being administered. Actually,however, unless he takes active measures to halt or punish the objectionable activity and to prevent its occurrence in the future, he is really condoning it. The child perceives that the disapproval is only verbal since the parent does not feel strongly enough about the matter to enforce his demands, an option that is obviously within his power were he disposed to use it. Hence, all the while that the latter stands disclaiming against the unacceptable behavior and doing nothing about it, reinforcement is continually provided by the assurance that the misbehavior is condoned and that the rewards motivating it will not be taken away. Unenforced verbal commands become in effect stated guarantees of immunity from interference and punitive action. The upshot of this situation is that the child becomes positively conditioned to verbal disapproval, and not only ignores its purported intent but also feels encouraged by it.

The conclusion is thus inescapable that the important goal of consistency in discipline cannot be achieved unless the child understands unambiguously what his environment demands and expects of him. This absence of ambiguity can be realized only if reinforcement is provided at both ends of the range of behavioral acceptability. It may be true that reward and approval are more efficacious in motivating the learning of acceptable behavior than are punishment, restraint, and disapproval in discouraging undesirable behavioral patterns. Nevertheless, neither is sufficient by itself. From a developmental standpoint, it is naive and unrealistic to assume that in the early and middle years of childhood the learning of desirable rewarded behavior automatically endows the logical opposite with a negative valence. Each valence must be separately established in order to encourage activity at one pole and discourage activity at the opposite pole; for until such time as the negative valence is established by active measures of reproof, the unacceptable behavior has a natural positive valence in the eyes of the child and competes in attractiveness with the benefits adhering to approved behavior. He will, therefore, be constantly tempted to sample the advantages of the former; and if not discouraged by disapproval, can legitimately interpret tolerance as license to continue.

In due time, of course, interaction, synthesis, and mutual reinforcement ensue when only one of the reciprocal pairs described above is either rewarded or punished as the case may be. In the case of older children and adults, endorsement of the "good" alternative carries with it an implied condemnation of the "bad." But this implication is never as thoroughgoing as the advocates of the self-consistency theory of personality would have us believe. Tennyson's dictum that a man must hate evil before he can love the good is true in the sense of absolute logic, but implies a level of logical consistency that is rare in the typical person's organization of values and attitudes. The temptation to test the limits of tolerance for unacceptable behavior, to see how much one can "get away with" before incurring retribution, to take advantage of laxness, certainly declines with maturity, but nevertheless is present in all of us irrespective of whether a generally wholesome conscience is operating. Hence, consistent and unambiguous discipline requires explicit definition of the limits of unacceptable behavior, reinforced by tangible evidences of disapproval, especially in the early years of life when ability to generalize values is limited.

The same need for explicit restraints holds true for similar reasons when we consider the growth of internalization of social prohibitions in relation to the problem of consistent discipline. It is true that the only effective and durable type of discipline we can hope to establish is a self-discipline based upon internalization of external restraints. The control that relies primarily upon constant supervision, force, fear, or threat is certainly consistent enough in its implications but contributes little to ego maturity. This does not mean, however, that in order to promote self-discipline external prohibitions must be completely removed. The process of internalization occurs only gradually and is never complete. Other controls, therefore, must be visible enough in the beginning, can be relaxed somewhat as maturity increases, but must always be held in readiness in the background to reorient goals when the child strays from the path of reality. In this sense controls serve not as the chief supports of realistically oriented and socially acceptable behavior but as limiting factors that restrain impulsive flights toward caprice and fancy. Like policemen on the corner, they are hardly responsible for the usual decorum of the law-abiding citizen but are convenient reminders that ill-considered mischief and out-of-bounds behavior will not be passively tolerated but may, on the contrary, lead to painful consequences.

Apart from the deleterious effects on maturation that will be described more fully in later sections, there is little reason to believe (contrary to the views expressed by indulgent parents) that excessive permissiveness makes for a happy childhood and adolescence. Quite the contrary, it leads to the insecurity that follows from adhering to any unrealistic, ambiguous, or inconsistent frame of reference. Unrealistic goals usually prove to be unsuccessful. Undue demands on persons other than parents ordinarily meet with a cool reception. Expectations of receiving special consideration outside the family circle are seldom realized. Ordinary frustrations cannot be borne with equanimity but lead to precipitate abandonment of goals, petulance, and temper tantrums; and at this point another source of insecurity arises from the child's dependence upon his own inadequate control of aggressive impulses. In the absence of suitable external restraints, he has good reason to fear the consequences that his uninhibited rage may bring upon him. He might even blame his parents: "It's your fault for making me so mad"; or, "Why didn't you stop me from doing that?" But he may also blame himself for these excesses of aggression and suffer more than his share of guilt feelings.

> Since punishment is not forthcoming from parents . . . there is not infrequently the necessity for self-punishment. Much of the wild, reckless, and unconventional behavior of the overindulged child may be attributed to his demands for punishment, and his behavior becomes so extreme only because his overindulgent parents are slow in taking him to task . . . For this reason the overindulged child may frequently be so extremely rebellious and aggressive that his behavior necessitates punishment by a somewhat hesitant parent. (Symonds, 1949)

The entire complex of absent self-control, selfish unreasonableness, importunate demands for immediate gratification, unrestrained aggressiveness, rebellious self-assertion, refractoriness to routine, irresponsibility, and lack of consideration for the needs of others forms such an unattractive, unloveable portrait that social acceptance by teachers, neighbors and age-mates is difficult indeed. Thus, even this last desperate defense upon which the advocates of extreme permissiveness are thrown back—that the child is happier in such a setting—is open to serious question.

Perhaps now after three decades of overenthusiastic and uncritical endorsement of permissiveness as a panacea—as a virtue *per se,* as the epitome of the "psychological" approach to interpersonal relations—parents, teachers, and clinical workers will be able to appraise its values and consequences more objectively. This will take a certain amount of courage since the prevailing climate of informed professional opinion regards opposition to "all-out" permissiveness as unprogressive, reactionary, and tantamount to psychological treason. But in the long run, it will be rewarded by the emergence of a more rational and consistent theory of discipline than that which presently enjoys vogue as the current fad and fashion in child rearing.

For children to develop the skill and confidence necessary for competent exercise of volitional independence, they require opportunity for practicing self-direction, making plans and decisions, actually participating in mature role-playing experience, and learning from their own mistakes. Overdominated children, although mature in such respects as "conscientious efforts" (Sanford, 1953) and "orderly production" (Sanford, 1943), tend to be shy, submissive, lacking in self-confidence, and deficient in the volitional aspects of independence (Levy, 1943; Stendler, 1954; Symonds, 1949). The latter outcome also holds true for overprotected children whose parents withhold the opportunity for independent decision-making lest it lead to injury or frustration (Levy, 1943; Stendler, 1954; Symonds, 1949).

Similarly, the more impersonal the basis on which obedience and conformity are required, the less likely is the desire for independence to be inhibited by feelings of personal loyalty and guilt. Navaho parents do not demand obedience as a personal right or regard disobedience as "bad," but point out "the advantages of obedience [and] the value of taking advice and instruction from more experienced persons" (Leighton & Kluckhohn, 1947). Threats are not warnings of personal reprisal for insubordination but objective predictions of disaster for children who fail to heed prudent admonition. The authority for discipline is impersonalized and referred either to supernatural forces or to agencies "outside of the immediate family circle." If a plea for good conduct is made by appealing to shame-avoidance, it is from the child rather than from the parent that the plea for deflection of shame is made. In all of these ways, the overly dependent and personal aspects of satellization are minimized.

Even when parents are not overprotective or overdominating, inherent factors in the parent-child relationship make them ambivalent toward the child's emancipation. They tend to fear the loss of love that removal of his dependency creates (Meyers, 1946).

They have a vested interest to protect—the satisfactions, the ego supports, the feelings of power and importance that go with having another individual dependent upon them for guidance and direction. "Emancipation requires much sacrifice by parents. They must relinquish authority" and "learn the patience and restraint required to develop the capacity for self-direction in the child." This is naturally a much more difficult task for parents who are exploiting the dependent aspects of the child's attachment for them as a substitute source of status and affection in instances of vocational or marital maladjustment (Ausubel, 1952). Such feelings of ambivalence naturally give rise to parental inconsistencies in behavior and expectations which confuse the child and compound the retarding influence the ambivalence exerts on maturation.

Feelings of rivalry, often only dimly perceived, also complicate the parents' attitudes towards the child's maturation. They cannot help comparing their waning powers and motivations with the child's growing competencies and naively sanguine aspirations. If these are a source of pride, they also represent a threat which, with each passing day, brings the shadow of eventual displacement closer. "Unconsciously," therefore, they may be motivated to slow the progress of maturation. The resentment that these attitudes provoke in the child, however, may bring about the opposite effect (desatellization) by deepening the estrangement that already so frequently exists.

Not to be ignored in this picture is the possibility of serious lag between alteration of attitudes and appropriate modification of related behavior. It is a commonplace observation that underlying attitudes may remain unaltered despite formal changes in outward behavior. Less frequently recognized is the equally important tendency for old behavior patterns to persist out of sheer inertia despite modification of the attitudinal substrate. It takes time to learn the appropriate gestures, mannerisms, and inflections of a new role even if one has mastered the required shift in feeling tones. And even then the phenomenon of perceptual constancy in the child may force altered parental behavior into the same perceptual molds because of the prepotency of habitual expectations.

Hence, the child frequently fails to respond appropriately to changes in parental expectations of greater maturity, despite manifest changes in stimulus content, because he cannot reorganize into a new *Gestalt* what to him can only have a fixed and constant perceptual meaning. He thus withdraws from parents "for no other reason than the fact that they always are the ones to whom he has always *been* a helpless child" (Zachry, 1944).

Personality maturation also suffers from ambivalence of the child. He is naturally reluctant to part with the protection and security of dependency and a familiar biosocial role for the anxiety and insecurity inevitably associated with any transition in development. And, unfortunately, sufficient ambiguity prevails regarding the biosocial role considered appropriate for adolescents. Also, the period of transition is sufficiently prolonged to offer considerable support for the yearning to return to the "good old days" of childhood. This regressive alternative has a more powerful attraction both for children who have strong needs for hedonistic gratification and find long-range striving difficult and for sedentary, shy, "thin-skinned" and introverted individuals to whom self-assertion comes painfully.

Desatellization, therefore, is even under the best of circumstances, a difficult and inevitably conflictful phase of ego development. The child must contend with ambivalence, rivalry, and the inertia of habitual attitudes and behavior patterns in his parents at the same time he confronts his own ambivalence and perceptual constancy. If he becomes too independent, he provokes parental resistance and internal feelings of guilt. On the other hand, if he remains too dependent and submissive, he "loses face in his own eyes and in the eyes of his peers, feels inadequate for failure to gain extrinsic status, and develops feelings of hostility and resentment toward parents for thwarting his growth."

ADULT-YOUTH ALIENATION

The alienation of youth from the standards, status-giving activities, and training institutions of adult society, plus their compensatory immersion in a peer culture of their own making is a characteristic feature of adolescence in our culture. How is this alienation brought about and what are its effects? But first, in order to appreciate how adult-youth alienation occurs, it is necessary to understand the universal changes in personality structure that take place at adolescence. It is also necessary to appreciate why these changes do *not* typically result in such alienation in most primitive or traditional cultures but *do* result in alienation in modern Western cultures such as our own.

Everywhere, in all cultures, the metamorphosis of children into physically and sexually mature individuals and the concomitant growth of their intellectual and social capabilities generate, or set in motion, powerful pressures for certain changes to occur in their personality structure, changes that will equip them for more equal status and responsible membership in the adult community. These pressures consist of the adolescent's own recognition of the significance of his gains in physical, sexual, social, and intellectual maturity; of diminished parental and social acceptance of the appropriateness of a dependent status for more competent, adult-appearing individuals; and of the social urgency of transforming these persons into a new generation of adults capable of perpetuating the culture.

Universally, therefore, these pressures result in three major kinds of changes in the personality structure of adolescents so that they can qualify for their enhanced new role in the culture. First, they develop a need to strive more for an *earned* status based on their own efforts and competence and to strive less for an *attributed* status based on their dependent identification with and intrinsic acceptance by parents. Earned status thus becomes a more important source of their self-esteem and displaces attributed status as the principal determinant of their feelings of adequacy as persons. Second, they develop a need for volitional emancipation from their parents, that is, for exercising independence in formulating their own goals, for making their own decisions, and for managing their own affairs. Third, they are gradually expected to acquire, through appropriate training procedures, those mature personality traits and those basic skills and values that are necessary for implementing their needs for greater earned status and volitional independence. Hence, they are under greater pressure to persevere in goal-striving, despite serious setbacks, to postpone immediate hedonistic gratification in favor of achieving long-range objectives, and to display greater initiative, responsibility, executive independence, and respect for the demands of reality. Finally, they are expected to learn vocational skills, their appropriate sex roles, the basic norms and values of the culture, and the proper way of comporting themselves socially as adults.

IN PRIMITIVE CULTURES

Now in primitive and traditional cultures, these new personality needs of adolescents can be satisfied, and these new traits, norms, and skills can be acquired, *not* without some difficulty and conflict, but without serious alienation from adult society. Adolescents can acquire earned status as junior adults by participating in status-giving activities within the *mainstream* of the adult culture, and can also achieve a significant degree of volitional independence and emancipation from parents while playing more mature and responsible social, economic, and sex roles in family and community life. Thus, because they both acquire earned status and exercise volitional independence within the *adult* culture, and also simultaneously receive their training in the course of doing both these things in the same adult context, they are not alienated from adult status-giving activities, are not resentful of adult training institutions, and do not reject adult standards and authority. And since they also continue to identify emotionally with parents and

other adults, they continue to receive some measure of attributed status from such
identification and from adult acceptance of their membership in the wider culture.
This, in turn, establishes a basis for implicit loyalty to the culture and for implicit
acceptance of its values.

IN OUR CULTURE

Adolescents in our culture, naturally, have the same needs for greater earned
status and volitional independence. But the greater complexity of our technological society necessitates an extended period of education and economic dependence
on parents, prolonged vocational training, and the postponement of marriage well
beyond the age of sexual maturity. Under these circumstances, the adolescent
cannot experience any *real* volitional independence in the *adult* sense of the term,
and can obviously acquire only a token earned status outside the mainstream of the
adult culture. He not only resents his exclusion from adult spheres of independence and status-giving activities, but also tends to resent such adult-controlled
training institutions as the home, the school, and various youth organizations
because they conduct their training functions entirely apart from any opportunity
for him to exercise volitional independence, or to acquire earned status within the
context of the adult culture. Hence, he is alienated from adult status-giving
activities and from adult training institutions, and, accordingly, from adult standards as well.

TWO CONSEQUENCES OF ALIENATION

This alienation from adult society, coupled with the accompanying resentment and prolonged frustration of his needs for adult volitional independence and
adult earned status, have two serious consequences, namely, the generation of
aggressive anti-adult attitudes and the compensatory formation of distinctive peer
groups with distinctive standards, status-giving activities, and training functions
of their own. Let us consider each of these consequences in turn. The aggressive
anti-adult orientation not only promotes further retaliatory rejection of adult
standards, but also makes it more difficult for adolescents to identify with adults,
to obtain any attributed status from such identification, and currently to accept
adult values implicitly. The formation of peer groups, on the other hand, increases
the existing adult-youth alienation, reinforces the aggressive anti-adult orientation, and facilitates its overt, antisocial expression. Precisely how it does these
things deserves more detailed scrutiny.

ROLE OF THE PEER GROUP

Because all adolescents are in the same boat, so to speak; because they share
the same deprivation of their needs for adult status and independence, the same
alienation from adult society, the same resentments, and the same anti-adult
attitudes; because they feel they are not wanted, do not belong, and are excluded

from the larger scheme of things; they reach out toward each other for mutual support and for providing in *concert* the things that they want but cannot get *individually*.

Thus, since the modern urban community is unable to provide teenagers with the kind of earned status, volitional independence, and training in social skills that they desire, the adolescent peer group is constituted to gratify, in part, these crucial needs. It is the only cultural institution in which their position is not marginal, in which they are offered earned status, independence, and social identity among a group of equals, and in which their *own* activities and concerns reign supreme. The peer group is also the major training institution for adolescents in our society. It is in the peer group that by *doing* they learn about the social processes of our culture. They clarify their sex roles by acting and being responded to; they learn competition, cooperation, social skills, values, and purposes by sharing the common life. The peer group provides regularized media and occasions for adolescents to gratify their newly acquired desires for increased social contact with the opposite sex as well as a set of norms governing adolescent sex behavior.

By virtue of performing these essential functions, the peer group also displaces parents as the major source of attributed status during adolescence. By identifying with and acquiring acceptance in the group, by subordinating himself to group interests, and by making himself dependent on group approval, the adolescent gains a measure of intrinsic self-esteem that is independent of his achievement or relative status in the group. This "we-feeling" furnishes security and belongingness, and is a powerful ego support and basis of loyalty to group norms.

INCREASED ALIENATION

How does all this increase adult-youth alienation? In the first place, the adolescent's very membership in a distinctive peer group, with its own status-giving activities, standards, and training functions, puts him in a *separate* subculture apart from adult society. Second, since the peer group is composed of *his* kind of people, and since he is largely dependent on it for his volitional independence, for his earned and attributed status, for his sense of belongingness, and for his opportunities to acquire social skills and practice his sex role, he accordingly tends to assimilate its standards. As he becomes progressively more responsive to its approval and disapproval, he becomes increasingly more indifferent to adult norms and values, to adult suggestion, and to adult approval and disapproval. Lastly, the peer group's exaggerated needs for rigid conformity to its norms—as well as its power to exact conformity from its members in return for its unique ability to satisfy their needs—further accentuate the adolescent's alienation from adult society.

DEMAND FOR CONFORMITY

Why must the peer group demand so much conformity from its members? First, no institution, especially if it has status-giving functions, can exist for any length of time without due regard by its members for uniform, regular, and predictable adherence to a set of avowed values and traditions. Hence, in its efforts to establish a new and distinctive subculture, and to evolve a unique set of criteria for the determination of status and prestige, the peer group must do everything in its power to set itself off as recognizably distinct and separate from the adult society that refuses it membership. If this distinctiveness is to be actually attained, widespread non-conformity obviously cannot be tolerated. Second, conformity is also essential to maintain the group solidarity that is necessary to offer effective and organized resistance to the encroachments of adult authority. If an appeal to precedent, or to a *prevailing* standard of adolescent behavior, is to be the basis for exacting privileges and concessions from adults, a solid and united front with a minimum of deviancy must be presented to the adult world.

Furthermore, not only does the peer group increase the adolescent's alienation from the adult culture, but it also intensifies his aggressive anti-adult sentiments resulting from this alienation and from the prolonged deprivation of his needs for adult status and independence. Simply by being a member of a larger group of individuals who share the same anti-adult attitudes, these attitudes become reinforced through such mechanisms as the mutual sharing of confidences, felt wrongs, and grievances, and the mutual support and justification that group members give each other for their feelings of animosity toward the common adult foe.

Cultural Factors Affecting Adolescent Maturation

Neither the parent nor the culture are unaware of the growth in cognitive and social competence that takes place during the preadolescent years, In accordance with practical economic needs and the overall cultural training program, therefore, the child is expected to acquire a source of extrinsic status to supplement his role as dependent satellite in the family configuration.* Depending on the degree of cultural discontinuity prevailing between children's and adult's roles, he either acquires a subadult, fringe status in adult society or earned status in peripheral activities (e.g., school, peer group) far removed from the mainstream of status-giving operations in the adult world. In most primitive cultures the home serves as both the source of subsidiary extrinsic status and the training institution for developing more mature and responsible behavior. The child is assigned responsible tasks of considerable social and economic importance in agriculture, handicrafts, and household arts as well as duties for looking after younger siblings. And "the tasks that are expected of it are adapted to its capacity" (Benedict, 1938).

However, no sooner is the dependency of satellization achieved than new

---

*Achievement motivation tends to be relatively high in children whose mothers make early demands for and reward independent accomplishment highly (Child, 1954). There are also marked intercultural and social class differences in achievemnt motivation.

conditions are created that undermine it and alter the shifting balance of dependence-independence. At the same time that he enjoys the derived status of dependent child in the home, he begins to acquire an earned performance-based status in the peer group and in school. Here he is valued not for himself but primarily for what he can do and how well he can perform in comparison with his fellows. As he makes vast strides in executive competence through expansion of motor, intellectual, and social capacities he begins to perceive himself in a less dependent light. His parents loom less omnipotent and less omniscient in relation to his own abilities. He fancies himself entitled by virtue of his new capacities to greater volitional independence, to greater extrinsic status, to a more responsible role in the social order.

But the extrinsic status of childhood—even if achieved in economically significant activities, as in primitive cultures and rural environments—can constitute only a subsidiary source of status.

The sexually immature individual can nowhere acquire adult personality status no matter how vital his contribution to the economic life of the home or community. The earned status he enjoys must inevitably play a subordinate role in the larger *Gestalt* of volitional dependency and derived status, which characterize the biosocial position of children the world over.

In complex modern cultures, children have little opportunity for exercising independence, responsibility, and identification with the world of adult concerns, necessitating a complete separation of the activity and interest systems of child and adult. Such children are given no responsibilities in the workaday world of adult concerns, and evolve a complete set of prestige-giving values of their own.

One undesirable consequence of excluding children from *genuine* responsibility in the adult world is that deprived of this necessary role-playing experience, related aspects of ego maturation tend to lag behind. Study of children in grades four through twelve "reveals little evidence [of] . . . marked developmental progress in the child's amount of responsibility (Harris, et al., 1954a) or any relationship between his sense of responsibility and the number of home duties he assumes (Harris et al., 1954b). The fact that these relationships hold true for rural as well as urban children suggests that the child in our culture has no *real* opportunity for socially responsible participation. The routine assignments he carries out are so subordinate and expendable that they have little bearing on his earned status or volitional independence.

A second consequence of the displacement of the home as a training center for ego maturation is that the child becomes increasingly dependent on non-parental sources of earned and derived status. In his peer group, he is given a chance to obtain the mature role-playing experience from which society excludes him and which his parents are unable to furnish. Identification with this group also provides a substitute source of derived status providing him with ego supports that reduce his dependence upon parental approval. School serves a very similar function. It provides both a new subsidiary source of earned status based upon academic ability and a fresh source of derived status that challenges the parent's monopoly of this commodity and of omniscience as well.

All of these factors—the availability of other sources of derived status, the possession of subsidiary earned status, the need for going beyond the home for sources of extrinsic status, the child's own greater competence, exposure to a diversity of family and social climates with resulting awareness of alternative standards and ways of doing things, and the emergence of new authorities to challenge his parents' omniscience—tend to break down the child's deified picture of his parents. Thus, beginning with late childhood, glamorous figures such as movie stars and sports heroes, attractive visible adults, and composite portraits of admired adults start to displace parents as emulatory models (Havighurst et al., 1946). As the ties of dependency weaken and the perceived omnipotence of the parent diminishes, the latter's power to confer by fiat an absolute intrinsic value on the child begins to ebb; and as the parents' glory fades, less vicarious status can be reflected to the satellite.

Systematic observation of the eight-year-old indicates that he is already more outgoing and in greater contact with his environment. "He resents being treated as a child and . . . can't wait to grow up" (Gesell & Ilg, 1946). The nine-year-old is more independent, responsible, cooperative and dependable. After making a futile attempt to draw the adult into his world, he seems to accept the fact that fusion is impossible. "He becomes very busy with his own concerns and doesn't have time for routines or parents' demands." There is "much planning in great and practical detail" (Gesell & Ilg, 1946). He "may prefer work to play" (Gesell & Ilg, 1946). But these concerns are "now oriented more toward his contemporaries than his parents . . . and he verbally expresses indifference to adult commands or adult standards" (Gesell & Ilg, 1946).

There is no doubt that the cultural availability of extrinsic status is the crucial variable affecting the rate, the duration, and the difficulty of adolescent maturation. Almost all of the distinctive characteristics of adolescent development in Western civilization are derivatives of the fact that pubescent children's greater executive competence can receive no social recognition in terms of adult status-giving activity. On the other hand, in primitive rural cultures such as the Navaho, "there is no period of several years when the individual is neither a child nor an adult as the adolescent in White American society today. The Navaho's physical maturity and social maturity are more nearly coincidental" (Leighton & Kluckhohn, 1947). Our adolescents must customarily look forward to an eight-year period of subadulthood that provides a marginal, interim status in peripheral activities, and a good deal of uncertainty regarding the eventual attainment of adult status.

Such a situation is more or less inevitable in any complex culture requiring extended education and apprenticeship. The peer group is obliged, then to provide compensatory sources of status and to assume responsibility as the major training institution of adolescence. But this dichotomy need not be as absolute as it is at present. With some intelligent social engineering, adolescents even as apprentices can be provided with a good deal of status-giving experience and responsibility in projects involving the community as a whole.

The reasons for the prolonged adolescence in our culture and its grosser behavioral consequences were discussed at length. Here we shall be concerned only with what at first glance seems to be a purely self-evident phenomenon, namely,

> the precise nature of the mechanisms whereby socio-economic conditions necessitating a prolongation of the transitional period of sub-adulthood becomes translated into an actual process of retardation in the sphere of psychological development. The relationship between social status on the one hand and ego valuation on the other is a fundamental problem of ego psychology. (Ausubel, 1950)

The most important intervening variables in this process of transmutation—"the level of social expectations regarding rate of maturation and the availability of mature role-playing experience"—are intimately related. The former, in fact, is almost completely a function of the latter, which depends upon socio-economic factors influencing the need for adolescent manpower. In accordance with fluctuations in this need, society keeps shifting its view of the urgency with which adolescent maturation should take place.

> This relationship is never a one-to-one affair since a certain minimal level of status change is anticipated on the basis of pubescence alone, and a certain amount of time lag is inevitable between the onset of changed economic conditions and the evolution of new social attitudes. Nevertheless the correspondence is quite close; and in the more usual type of economic situation in our culture, conditions are such that little sense of urgency is felt regarding the rapidity of maturation. Thus, although the adolescent may desire to gain status more rapidly than he is allowed to, he feels no pressure to do so—at least from the adult segment of society. (Ausubel, 1952)

Having no other frame of reference as a guide than prevailing social expectations,

> his level of aspiration with respect to the proper rate of maturation generally corresponds to the relative urgency with which society regards the problem. Most adolescents would believe any other course to be virtually impossible, since like children, they tend to believe that prevailing social arrangements are absolutely given and hence immutable. (Ausubel, 1950)

Why do adolescents base their levels of aspiration regarding maturational progress on cultural expectations? First, as in any unstructured field, these expectations undoubtedly exert considerable influence in the form of prestige suggestion. Second, they have motivational properties emanating from their capacity to generate *transitional anxiety*. The mere existence of these expectations constitutes a threat. Adolescents are expected to mature at a certain rate or else face the possible loss of "status advantages otherwise accruing from successful maturation." The feelings of anxiety and insecurity instigated by this threat can only be reduced by suitable evidences of maturation, thereby giving rise to appropriately pitched motivations (levels of aspiration) (Davis, 1944).

When culturally induced, low levels of aspiration to maturational progress actually result in developmental retardation by "making the adolescent disinclined to seek out . . . role-playing experiences propitious for personality development." And the most proximate variable involved in this chain of events, the one directly responsible for the lagging rate of maturation, is deprivation of the necessary experience required for personality growth.

When the cultural unavailability of adult status becomes very extreme, it retards personality maturation even more directly. By ruling out access to needed experience to individuals who would otherwise obtain it by high endogenous motivation (despite social discouragement), it exerts a levelling influence negating motivational variability of other origin.

In addition to status deprivation, other social factors largely idiosyncratic to our culture, such as various types of cultural discontinuities and discrepancies in attaining adult status, also tend to retard adolescent personality maturation.

Later Impact of Non-Satellization on Maturation

As already indicated, the non-satellizer never really surrenders his aspirations for volitional independence and exalted earned status during childhood. Hence in a sense the ego-status goals of maturation are already accomplished in advance, and since the main function of most ego-maturity goals is the enhancement of self-esteem through earned status, these tend to be acquired with little difficulty. The chief exception here relates to the development of realistic goals, which is largely precluded by the non-satellizer's insistent need to maintain high ego aspirations irrespective of the situation or his level of ability. It would also seem reasonable to question under certain conditions the stability of values that were never implicitly internalized on the basis of personal loyalty but solely for purposes of relevance for ego enhancement and achievement. The obligation to abide by all internalized moral values, for example, is threatened by the fact that many such values are often in conflict with the ends of ego enhancement. As will be pointed out in Chapter 9, these children are particularly vulnerable to neurotic anxiety by virtue of their lacking an inner core of intrinsic self-esteem to protect their egos from the vicissitudes of life and because of their tendency to compensate for this lack of intrinsic self-esteem by internalizing only high levels of aspiration.

As represented by the tasks of acquiring greater volitional independence, of striving primarily for extrinsic status, of raising the level of ego aspiration, and of adopting the incorporative and exploratory learning orientations, desatellization is ordinarily the main business of adolescent maturation. Since in non-satellizers these tasks are accomplished in advance, it follows that maturation involves a less comprehensive change and is more likely to be successful. The non-satellizer with his high ego aspirations and his exaggerated needs for earned status has always regarded dependence disdainfully, as symbolic of defeat in his quest for these goals. Volitional independence had never been really surrendered, and hence does not have to be regained.

Other aspects of maturation take place for the express purpose of implementing the acquisition of earned status—provided there are "no overwhelming contraindications emanating from the non-satellizing situation itself." For example, goal frustration tolerance, self-critical ability, executive independence, and long-range goals are acquired easily enough.

> But the imperious need for superior accomplishment and pre-eminent extrinsic status effectively prevents the setting of realistic goals in many cases. Although level of ego aspiration is uniformly high in non-satellizers and is extremely resistant to lowering in the face of frustration, there is no reason for believing that the distribution of ability in this group is [uniformly high] . . . Aspirational level will, therefore, be persistently and unrealistically high except in the small minority of individuals whose abilities are commensurate with their ambitions. (Ausubel, 1952)

It would be reasonable to expect that the attenuation of immature personality traits on the basis of expediency (ego enhancement) is a much less stable arrangement than attenuation on the basis of satellization. In satellization there is implicit and unquestioning acceptance of the desirability for change. In the former instance, on the other hand, "where changes are made with specific ends in view," (1) abandonment of ends leads to reversal of change, and (2) incompatibility of the change with underlying ends often leads to sabotage of change. Thus, should either the goals of ego enhancement be abandoned (as in periods of severe personality disorganization), or should any of the goals of ego maturation be perceived as in conflict with the ends of ego enhancement, maturational regression can easily take place. The most vulnerable aspect of this type of maturation lies in the durability of feelings of moral accountability under conditions that are prejudicial to personal gain and advantage. Lacking the satellizer's implicit acceptance of the duty to abide by all internalized moral values, the non-satellizer is sorely tempted to let these values "go by the board" if the stakes are sufficiently high and the chances of apprehension and retribution sufficiently low.

If maturation is more successful in non-satellizers, it is also more stressful. The satellizer's extrinsic self-esteem is damaged by status deprivation during adolescence, but this injury tends to be peripheral because of a residual core of intrinsic self-acceptance. The non-satellizer's self-esteem, on the other hand, is wholly a creature of the environmental vicissitudes that deny or gratify the exalted ego aspirations on which he has "staked his value as a human being." Hence, the absence of intrinsic feelings of adequacy makes the damage wrought to the only type of self-esteem he knows (extrinsic) central rather than peripheral. And in addition it is only when intrinsic self-esteem is lacking do threats to extrinsic self-esteem have the power to induce neurotic anxiety.

The destructive impact of status deprivation on self-esteem and potential for anxiety response is greater in non-satellizers for still another reason besides lack of intrinsic adequacy. Because of their exaggerated needs for ego enhancement (which are highly resistant to discouragement), they find the same degree of status deprivation much more deflating to self-esteem. They are denied also the current source of derived status that adolescent ex-satellizers enjoy by maintaining in part a satellizing orientation* toward peer group, teachers, and employers. They are unable to experience the ego support and "we feeling" that is derived from the act of dependent identification with and self-subordination to group interests.

MATURATION OF REJECTED CHILDREN

Although rejected children find adolescent status deprivation more stressful than do satellizers, adolescence often presents quite a few more opportunities for status than childhood. The decreased importance of the rejecting home in comparison with the importance of school and peer group is in itself an ego inflating factor. The fact of rejection becomes less catastrophic as the importance of the rejecting figures in the psychological world diminishes. Also, in comparison with childhood, many new opportunities of achieving extrinsic status present themselves.

Rejected children do have a latent capacity for forming satellizing-like relationships to non-threatening individuals. Their original failure to satellize was due to the absence of suitable parental figures in the home rather than to disinclination. When removed from the home, the possibility of satellization is increased, although fear of repetition of rejection makes them move cautiously.

Neurotic anxiety is almost invariably present in rejected children from the beginning. Self-esteem is sufficiently impaired, both by (1) the absence of intrinsic feelings of adequacy and by (2) the catastrophic injury to extrinsic adequacy feelings implicit in the rejecting situation, to constitute the major source of threat in any adjustive situation.

The socialization of the rejected child is made difficult by his inability to assert himself adequately and to protect himself from the aggression of others. This is a consequence of a learning deficit acquired in the course of having to submit so long and helplessly to parental aggression that he cannot master the roles necessary for adult self-assertion. Aggression by others evokes an habitual response of helpless submissiveness.

*It might be noted here that non-satellizers also use the incorporative and exploratory orientations exclusively in value assimilation.

What other persons usually fail to recognize, however, is that this aggression and domination are only outwardly accepted; that quite unlike the overdominated satellizer who genuinely accepts the subservience to which he is subjected, the overdominated non-satellizer gradually accumulates a reservoir of resentment and hostility which eventually overflows with such violence as to rupture existing relationships beyond repair. (Ausubel, 1952)

Typically, the rejected child tends to be taken advantage of, appears to accept the situation meekly, and then to the amazement of others erupts violently and impulsively. To avoid this sequence of events, he prefers to withdraw from conflictful situations and to intellectualize his aggression. Either course of action, however, does little to promote effective interpersonal relationships.

MATURATION OF OVERVALUED CHILDREN

In contrast to its effect on the rejected child, adolescence usually brings a marked *loss* in extrinsic status and self-estimate to the overvalued child. He can hardly expect the same flattery and adulation in school and peer group that he was accustomed to receive at home. In fact, adolescence frequently marks the onset of neurotic anxiety; for only now is the impairment to his extrinsic self-esteem sufficiently catastrophic to predispose him to this personality disorder. But unlike that of the rejected child, the anxiety is not offset by the possibility of obtaining some derived status (and, therefore, some intrinsic self-esteem) through the belated establishment of satellizing-like relationships.* His failure to undergo devaluation and satellization was less a compensatory reaction of self-defence, than an outcome of the parent's active fostering of the infantile-ego organization. Thus, he tends to find satellization too degrading, and is usually too obnoxiously selfish, self-centered, and narcissistic either to inspire genuine love in others or to be capable of relating himself emotionally to them (Ausubel, 1952).

The overvalued child differs from the rejected child also by manifesting no incapacity for self-assertion and aggression. In fact his socialization is hindered by an excess rather than by a deficiency of these qualities. He tends to alienate associates initially by his overbearing, domineering, and importunate behavior.

But in his case the motivation is available to modify the strategy of his inter-personal relationships and to learn more acceptable social behavior, since he recognizes the importance of good social relations in the struggle for power. Through assiduous study and intelligent application of self-control he is able to acquire an agreeable set of formal manners and a superficial veneer of good fellowship to mask his formerly offensive aggression and self-seeking . . . Hence . . . he is able to learn a highly effective form of self-assertion in inter-personal relationships. (Ausubel, 1952)

*Neurotic anxiety may be allayed in the rejected child by his achievement of intrinsic status per se, and by the reduction of frustration that this permits through a lowering of level of ego aspiration.

Because of his excessively permissive upbringing, the overvalued child thus experiences more initial difficulty than the rejected child in acquiring goal-frustration tolerance, long-range goals, self-critical ability, and executive independence, and in relinquishing hedonistic motivations. But unlike the underdominated satellizer, his lack of intrinsic self-esteem, his exaggerated needs for ego enhancement, and his genuine volitional independence motivate him more strongly eventually to acquire these attributes of maturity.

Under certain unusual circumstances ego-maturity goals may be rejected by non-satellizers despite the importance of these goals for ego aggrandizement. For example, overvalued preadolescents or adolescents (especially girls) may reject the goals of adult personality maturation in retaliation for the later paradoxical increase in parental domination, restrictiveness, and control that is often related to parental fears about their daughters' precocious involvements in heterosexual experience. Such adolescents (particularly girls) frequently drop out of school, marry unsuitable mates, become hippies, or use drugs just to revenge themselves on parents—even though it frustrates their hypertrophied ego demands. In later adult life, however, they may either belatedly mature or experience reactive depression or schizophrenia because of their underlying low self-esteem and predisposition to neurotic anxiety.

THE EGO IN ADULT LIFE

As adult life approaches, exaggerated demands for volitional independence from parents give way to more temperate needs for autonomy. The adolescent's independence is now an established fact; he has no more need to be strident about it. He satellizes less in relation to the peer group, re-establishes his own individuality, is less dependent on it for his status (earned or derived), and begins to acquire more earned status in the mainstream of the adult culture. Rapprochement with parents typically occurs.

Satellizers continue to acquire derived status in relation to their bosses, spouses, and glamorous public figures; and rejected non-satellizers continue to search for "safe" persons (i.e., persons who will not reject them) with whom to establish a satellizing relationship so as to derive some supplementary derived status and thus have an intrinsic source of self-esteem independent of their compensatorily high and typically unrealistic needs for achievement. Their success in this endeavor depends on how successful a marriage they can make and on whether they can find a mentor who takes a *personal* as well as a professional interest in their careers. Overvalued non-satellizers rarely satellize in adulthood and typically seek in their children the vicarious ego-aggrandizement that they are seldom able to achieve themselves unless they are unusually able individuals. Thus the vicious cycle is perpetuated from one generation to the next.

The drive for earned status and recognition tends to peak in the middle forties for most persons (Botwinick, 1959; Bühler, 1935, 1951; Kuhlen, 1959; Low-enthal & Boler, 1967; Neugarten, 1963). Motivation, adaptiveness, venture-someness, flexibility, creativity, self-discipline, hard work and self-denial, physical stamina and intellectual acuteness, and problem-solving ability—all required for successful achievement—start to decline (Cantril, 1946; Jones, 1959; Kuhlen, 1959; Lorge, 1956; Schaie, 1955). Many non-satellizers begin to see the handwriting on the wall and their self-confidence and self-esteem begin to wane (Kuhlen, 1959; Lehner & Gunderson, 1953; Mason, 1954). With time running out, and death approaching, they begin to realize that they will never gain the success and recognition they crave in terms of their needs for self-esteem. This often precipitates the crisis of middle age, exacerbates the level of chronic anxiety, and may even precipitate panic states or a reactive schizophrenia or depression.

In some cases there is preoccupation with death. More typically, however, this inevitable end to their strivings is relegated to a "back burner", and the individual seldom comes to terms, psychologically or philosophically, with the problem of his own demise. Thus most people in Western culture die by default, so to speak, without ever evolving a deliberately formulated set of attitudes about dying.

As senescence sets in with physical frailty, ill health, slow or more precipitate deterioration of intellectual faculties and of physical stamina, a reverse process of satellization often takes place. Old people renounce their own strivings and tend to live in the reflected glory of their children's accomplishments. (Lowenthal, Riley & Foner, 1968). Ego-status goals decline inasmuch as opportunities for earned status diminish (Riley & Foner, 1968) and older persons in our culture are more the object of derision than of veneration. Self-esteem thus gradually begins to ebb until all volitional independence is surrendered; and the senior citizen often returns to the emotionally dependent status of childhood. At best he is typically accepted on sufferance in Western culture and has little to look forward to except death. His interest in life and events begins to flag (Kuhlen, 1959), and this in turn accelerates his physical and intellectual deterioration.

6
Ego Development in Segregated Black Children*[1]

Ego development refers to the orderly series of changes in an individual's self-concept, self-attitudes, motives, aspirations, sources of self-esteem, and key personality traits affecting the realization of his aspirations as he advances in age in a particular cultural setting. It obviously varies from one individual to another within a particular culture or subculture in accordance with significant temperamental traits and idiosyncratic experience. Nevertheless, it manifests a certain amount of intracultural homogeneity or intercultural difference because of culturally institutionalized differences in interpersonal relations; in opportunities for and methods of acquiring status; in prescribed age, sex, class, and occupational roles; in approved kinds of personality traits; and in the amount and types of achievement motivation that are socially sanctioned for individuals of a given age, sex, class, and occupation.

For all of these reasons the ego development of segregated black children and youth in America manifests certain distinctive properties. Black children live in a predominantly lower-class subculture that is further characterized by a unique type of family structure, by specially circumscribed opportunities for acquiring status, by varying degrees of segregation from the dominant white majority, and, above all, by a fixed and apparently immutable denigration of their social value, standing, and dignity as human beings because of their skin color. Hence, it would be remarkable indeed if these factors did not result in significant developmental differences in self-esteem, in aspirations for achievement, in personality adjustment, and in character structure. In fact, the United States Supreme Court decision of 1954 outlawing school segregation was based primarily on considerations of ego development. It recognized that school and other public facilities cannot be "separate and equal" because enforced and involuntary separateness that is

*Reference notes for this chapter are on page 337.

158

predicated on purely arbitrary criteria necessarily implies an inferior caste status, and thereby results in psychological degradation and injury to self-esteem.

In this chapter we propose to do two things. First we would like to consider the personality development of the segregated black child and youth as a special variant of the more typical course of ego development in our culture. Here the approach is normative, from the standpoint of a personality theorist interested in subcultural differences. In what ways does the ego development of segregated black children and youth differ from that of the textbook child growing up in the shadow of our dominant middle-class value system? Second, we would like to consider some kinds of, and reasons for, individual differences within this under-privileged group. Do all black children in the Harlem ghetto of New York City, for example, respond in the same way to the impact of their segregated lower-class environment? If not, why not? Are there social class, sex, and individual differences among black children? Questions of this type would be asked by a personality theorist concerned with idiosyncratic and group variability within a subcultural setting, or by a psychiatrist treating the behavior disorders of such children in a Harlem community clinic.

EGO DEVELOPMENT IN YOUNG BLACK CHILDREN

Social-class Factors

Many of the ecological features of the segregated black subculture that impinge on personality development in early childhood are not specific to blacks as such, but are characteristic of most lower-class populations. This fact is not widely appreciated by white Americans and hence contributes to much anti-black sentiment: many characteristic facets of the black's value system and behavior pattern are falsely attributed to his racial membership, whereas they really reflect his predominant membership in the lower social class. Nevertheless, these characteristics are commonly offered as proof of the alleged moral and intellectual inferiority that is supposedly inherent in persons of black ancestry, and are used to justify existing discriminatory practices.

Lower-class parents, for example, are generally more casual, inconsistent, and authoritarian than middle-class parents in controlling their children, and resort more to harsh, corporal forms of punishment (Maccoby, Gibbs, et al, 1954; Markley, 1958). Unlike middle-class fathers, whose wives expect them to be as supportive as themselves in relation to children, the lower-class father's chief role in child rearing is to impose constraints and administer punishment (Markley, 1958). Even more important, lower-class parents extend less succorant care and relax closely monitored supervision much earlier than their middle-class counter-parts (De Vos & Miner, 1958; Havighurst & Taba, 1949); Lower-class children are thus free to roam the neighborhood and join unsupervised play groups at an age while suburban children are still confined to nursery school or to their own backyards. Hence, during the preschool and early elementary-school years, the lower-class family yields to the peer group much of its role as a socializing agent and source of values and derived status. During this early period, lower-class children undergo much of the desatellization from parents that ordinarily occurs during middle childhood and preadolescence in most middle-class families. They acquire earlier volitional and executive independence outside the home and in many cases assume adult responsibilities such as earning money and caring for younger siblings. Abbreviated parental succorance, which frustrates the dependency needs of middle-class children and commonly fosters overdependence (Sears et al., 1953) has a different significance for and effect on these lower-class children. Since it reflects the prevailing subcultural norm, and since the opportunity for early anchorage to a free-ranging peer group is available, it tends to encourage the development of precocious independence.

This pattern of precocious independence from the family, combined with the exaggerated socializing influence of the peer group, although characteristic of both white and black lower-class children, does not necessarily prevail among all lower-class minority groups in the United States. Both Puerto Rican (Anastasi & deJesus, 1953) and Mexican children (Maslow & Diaz-Guerrerro, 1960) enjoy a more closely knit family life marked by more intimate contact between parents and children. In Mexican families, maternal and paternal roles are also more distinctive, masculine and feminine roles are more clearly delineated in childhood, and the socializing influence of the peer group is less pronounced (Maslow & Diaz-Guerrerro, 1960).

The working-class mother's desire for unquestioned domination of her offspring, her preference for harsh, punitive, and suppressive forms of control, and her tendency to maintain considerable social and emotional distance between herself and her children are probably responsible in part for the greater prevalence of the authoritarian personality syndrome in lower-class children than in middle-class children (Dickens & Hobart, 1959; Hart, 1957; Lipset, 1959). Lower-class children tend to develop ambivalent attitudes toward authority figures and to cope with this ambivalence by making an exaggerated show of overt, implicit compliance, by maintaining formally appropriate social distance, and by interacting with these figures on the basis of formalized role attributes rather than as persons. Their underlying hostility and resentment toward this arbitrary and often unfair authority is later expressed in such displaced forms as scapegoating, prejudice, extremist political and religious behavior, ethnocentrism, and delinquency (Dickens & Hobart, 1959; Hart, 1957; Lipset, 1959).

Much of the significant relationship between social-class status and school achievement undoubtedly reflects pervasive social-class differences in cognitive orientation and functioning that are operative from early childhood (Bernstein, 1958). Middle-class children are trained to respond to the abstract, categorical, and relational properties of objects, whereas lower-class children are trained to respond more to their concrete, tangible, immediate, and particularized properties. This difference in perceptual disposition is carried over into verbal expression, memory, concept formation, learning and problem-solving. Hence since schools place great emphasis on the learning of abstract relationships and on the abstract use of language, lower-class children, on the average, experience much greater difficulty than middle-class children in mastering the curriculum.

Racial Factors

All of the foregoing properties of the lower-class environment also apply to the segregated black community. Most authorities on black family life agree that well over 50 percent of black families live at the very lowest level of the lower-class standard (Hill, 1957). In addition, however, black families are characterized by a disproportionate number of illegal and loosely connected marital unions (Hill, 1957). Illegitimacy is a very common phenomenon and is associated with relatively little social stigma in the black community (Cavan, 1959); nevertheless, illegitimate black children, especially at the older age levels, are significantly inferior to their legitimate counterparts in I.Q., school achievement, and personal adjustment (Jenkins, 1958).

Black families are much more unstable than comparable lower-class white families. Homes are more apt to be broken, fathers are more frequently absent, and a matriarchal and negative family atmosphere more commonly prevails (Conant, 1961; Dai, 1949; Deutsch, 1960; Hill, 1957). Thus the lower-class black child is frequently denied the benefits of biparental affection and upbringing; he is often raised by his grandmother or older sister while his mother works to support the family deserted by the father. One consequence of the matriarchal family climate is an open preference for girls. Boys frequently attempt to adjust to this situation by adopting feminine traits and mannerisms (Dai, 1949).[2]

Black family life is even more authoritarian in nature than is that of the lower social class generally. "Children are expected to be obedient and submissive;" (Hill, 1957), and insubordination is suppressed by harsh and often brutal physical punishment (Dai, 1949; Hill, 1957). "Southern black culture teaches obedience and respect for authority as a mainspring of survival" (Greenberg & Fane, 1959). Surveys of high-school and college students show that authoritarian attitudes are more prevalent among blacks at all grade levels (Greenberg, Chase & Cannon, 1957; Greenberg & Fane, 1959; Smith & Prothro, 1957).

Being a black also has many other implications for the ego development of young children that are not inherent in lower-class membership. The black child inherits an inferior caste status and almost inevitably acquires the negative self-esteem that is a realistic ego reflection of such status. Through personal slights, blocked opportunities, and unpleasant contacts with white persons and with institutionalized symbols of caste inferiority (i.e., segregated schools, neighborhoods, amusement areas, etc.)—and more directly through mass media and the reactions of his own family—he gradually becomes aware of the social significance of racial membership (Goff, 1949).

As a consequence of prejudice, segregation, discrimination, inferior status, and not finding himself respected as a human being with dignity and worth,

> the black child becomes confused in regard to his feelings about himself and his group. He would like to think well of himself but often tends to evaluate himself according to standards used by the other group. These mixed feelings lead to self-hatred and rejection of his group, hostility toward other groups, and a generalized pattern of personality difficulties. (Jefferson, 1957, p. 146)

Segregation

> means that the personal worth, of either a white or black person, is measured solely by his group membership regardless of individual merit. Such a measure is realistically false and of necessity distorts the developing self-image of black and white children as well as their view of each other. Under these psychological circumstances the black child, for example, is burdened with inescapable inferiority feelings, a fixed ceiling to his aspiration level which can constrict the development of his potentialities, and a sense of humiliation and resentment which can entail patterns of hatred against himself and his own group, as well as against the dominant white group. (Bernard, 1958, p. 151)

The black child perceives himself as an object of derision and disparagement (Goff, 1956), as socially rejected by the prestigeful elements of society, and as unworthy of succorance and affection (Deutsch et al., 1956); and having no compelling reasons for not accepting this officially sanctioned negative evaluation of himself, he develops a deeply ingrained negative self-image (Bernard, 1958; Wertham; 1952).

It does not take long for black children to become aware of the unfavorable implications of their racial membership. In interracial nursery schools, most children show some type of racial awareness at the age of three (Stevenson & Stevenson, 1960), and this awareness increases rapidly between the ages of three and seven (Stevenson & Stevenson, 1960). Once aware of racial differences, they soon learn that "skin color is important, that white is to be desired, dark to be regretted" (Landreth & Johnson, 1953). Very significantly, racial self-recognition develops later in black than in white children (Morland, 1958; Stevenson & Stewart, 1958); in the light of doll play evidence indicating that they resist identifying with their own stigmatized racial group (Clark & Clark, 1949), this delay in racial self-recognition can only be interpreted as reluctance in acknowledging their racial membership. As a result of the black militancy movement since 1963, however, seven and eight-year-old black children now seem to prefer black dolls (Ward & Braun, 1972).

All of the sociometric rejection and maltreatment experienced by black children in a mixed group cannot, of course, be attributed to their inferior caste status alone. Some of the victimization undoubtedly reflects the dynamics of a majority-minority group situation. Thus, when white children are in the minority, the values, judgments, and verbal expression of the black majority tend to prevail (Rosner, 1954). Under these conditions, blacks curse whites but the latter do not openly retaliate despite revealing anti-black prejudice to white investigators (Rosen, 1959).

In addition to suffering ego deflation through awareness of his inferior status in society, the black child finds it more difficult to satellize* and is denied much of the self-esteem advantages of satellization. The derived status that is the principal source of children's self-esteem in all cultures is largely discounted in his case, since he can only satellize in relation to superordinate individuals or groups who themselves possess an inferior and degraded status. Satellization under such conditions not only confers a very limited amount of derived status but also has deflationary implications for self-esteem. We can understand, therefore, why young black children in the past resisted identifying with their own racial group, why they sought to shed their identities (Deutsch, et al., 1956), why they more frequently chose white than black playmates (Stevenson & Stewart, 1958), why they preferred the skin color of the culturally dominant caste (Clark & Clark, 1947; Goodman, 1952; Landreth & Johnson, 1953), and why they tended to assign negative roles to children of their own race (Stevenson & Stewart, 1958). These tendencies persisted at least into late adolescence and early adult life, insofar as one can judge from the attitudes of black college students. These students until relatively recently tended to reject ethnocentric and anti-white ideologies and to accept authoritarian and anti-black propositions (Steckler, 1957).

The situation is now rapidly undergoing change. Ninety-six black undergraduates in one study gave blacks a significantly higher rating than white Protestants (Polite, Cockrane & Silverman, 1974). In another study black college students accepted more anti-white ideology and less anti-black ideology than a comparable group of students sampled in 1957 (Banks, 1970). Lessing and Zagorin (1972) found that students with a high black-power orientation placed a higher evaluation upon black persons and a lower evaluation upon white persons. The improvement in self-concept has been accompanied by rising material expectations and a corresponding decline in fundamentalist religious beliefs (Gift, 1970–1971).

In general, a program of black studies has not had a statistically significant effect on the self-concept (Grant, 1973; Fisher, 1972–1973). According to one study black students' self-perceptions in the future differed significantly from their self-perceptions in the past and present. (Krate, Leventhal & Silverstein, 1974). However, Hauser (1972) found that self-images of blacks were relatively un-

---

*It is not suggested, by any means, that satellization is precluded in the black child.

changed over a period of years, whereas the self-images of whites underwent significant change over the same period of time.

EGO DEVELOPMENT IN OLDER BLACK CHILDREN AND ADOLESCENTS

Social-class Factors

During middle childhood and preadolescence the ego development of the segregated black child also reflects the influence of both general social-class factors and of more specific racial factors. As already pointed out, early experience in fending for himself both in the wider culture and in the unsupervised peer group, as well as in exercising adultlike responsibilities, accomplishes precociously much of the desatellization from and devaluation of parents characterizing the ego development of middle-class children during this period.

In these developments, the school plays a much less significant role among lower-class than among middle-class children. The lower class child of school age has fewer illusions about parental omniscience for the teacher to shatter, and is coerced by the norms of his peer group against accepting her authority, seeking her approval, or entering into a satellizing relationship with her. School can also offer him very little in the way of either current or ultimate earned status. His parents and associates place no great value on education and do not generally encourage high aspirations for academic and vocational success, financial independence, or social recognition. It is hardly surprising, therefore, that lower-class children are less interested in reading than are middle-class children, have lower educational aspirations, take their school work less seriously, and are less willing to spend the years of their youth in school in order to gain higher prestige and more social rewards as adults.

Even if they equalled middle-class children in the latter respects, academic achievement would still be quite a valueless reward for a child who soon comes to realize that professional status is often beyond his grasp. Hence, anxiety regarding the attainment of internalized needs does not drive the lower-class child to excel in school. Also, because of low achievement and discriminatory treatment, he fails to obtain the current rewards of academic success available to middle-class school children. On what grounds could a child immersed in an intellectually impoverished environment be expected to actualize his genic potential for verbal and abstract thinking, when he is unmotivated by parental pressures, by ambitions for vocational success, or by the anxiety associated with realizing these ambitions?

Lower and middle-class adolescents differ markedly both in their social-value systems and in their vocational interests. Middle-class youths and their parents are more concerned with community service, self-realization, altrusitic values, and internalized standards of conduct (Kahn, 1959; Staffire, 1959), and prefer demanding, responsible, and prestigeful occupational pursuits (Pierce-Jones, 1959a; Pierce-Jones, 1959b; Sewell & Strauss, 1957). They also make higher vocational interest scores in the literary, esthetic, persuasive, scientific, and business areas than do lower-class adolescents. The latter adolescents and their parents, on the other hand, place greater stress on such values as money, security, respectability, obedience, and conformity to authority, and tend to prefer agricultural, mechanical, domestic service, and clerical pursuits.

The lower-class child's *expressed* levels of academic and vocational aspirations often appear unrealistically high (Deutsch et al., 1956), but unlike the analogous situation in middle-class children, these do not necessarily represent his *real* or functional levels of striving. They more probably reflect impairment of realistic judgment under the cumulative impact of chronic failure (Sears, 1940) and low social status (Gould, 1941), as well as a compensatory attempt to bolster self-esteem through the appearance rather than the substance of aiming high. Lacking the strong ego involvement that the middle-class child brings to schoolwork, and that preserves the attractiveness of academic tasks despite failure experience (Schpoont, 1955), he quickly loses interest in school if he is unsuccessful. Finally, since he does not perceive the eventual rewards of striving and self-denial as attainable for persons of his status, he fails to develop to the same degree as the middle-class child the supportive traits of ego maturity necessary for the achievement of academic and vocational success. These supportive traits include habits of initiative and responsibility and the "deferred gratification pattern" of hard work, renunciation of immediate pleasures, long-range planning, high frustration tolerance, impulse control, thrift, orderliness, punctuality, and willingness to undergo prolonged vocational preparation (Havighurst and Taba, 1949; Pawl, 1960; Schneider & Lysgaard, 1953).

Despite having less deep-seated anxiety with respect to internalized needs for academic achievement and vocational prestige, children of lower-class families exhibit more signs of personality maladjustment than do children of middle-class families (Hollingshead & Redlich, 1958; Sewell & Haller, 1959; Srole et al., 1962). This greater degree of maladjustment is largely a response to the greater vicissitudes and insecurities of daily living; to the greater possibility and actual occurrence of failure in an educational and vocational world dominated by middle-class standards in which they are greatly disadvantaged; to inner tensions engendered by conflict between the values of the family and those of the dominant middle-class culture; to feelings of shame about family background that are associated with impulses to reject family ties; to feelings of guilt and anxiety about these latter impulses (Sewell & Haller, 1959); and to the personal demoralization and self-derogation that accompany social disorganization and the possession of inferior social status (Ashmore, 1954; Hollingshead & Redlich, 1958; Srole et al., 1962). In most instances, of course, the symptoms of maladjustment are uncomfortable rather than disabling; but the generally higher level of anxiety, and the more frequent occurrence of motivational immaturity in lower-class children and adolescents, also increase the incidence of such serious disorders as schizophrenia and drug addiction (Ausubel, 1952a; Hollingshead & Redlich, 1958; Srole et al., 1962). Proneness to delinquency is, of course, higher among lower-class adolescents because of greater family and social disorganization; the deep-seated resentments and aggressive impulses attributable to socio-economic deprivation; the influence of organized, predatory gangs; the tacit encouragement of dishonesty by the lower-class value system; and the slum-urban teenage cult of thrills, kicks, self-indulgence, violence, and non-conformity.

Racial Factors

All of the aforementioned factors inhibiting the development of high level ego aspirations and their supportive personality traits in the lower-class are intensified in the segregated black child. His overall prospects for vertical social mobility, although more restricted, are not completely hopeless. But the stigma of his caste membership is inescapable and insurmountable. It is inherent in his skin color, permanently ingrained in his body image, and enforced by the extralegal power of a society whose moral, legal, and religious codes proclaim his equality (Wertham, 1952).

It is proper to speak of a stigma as being "enforced" when the stigma in question is culturally derived rather than inherent in the physical existence of the mark *per se* (that is, a mark of inferiority in *any* culture such as lameness or blindness). Dark skin color is a stigma in American culture only because it identifies a culturally stigmatized caste. When we speak of the stigma being "inherent in his skin color," we mean that it is a stigma which the black inherits by virtue of being born with that skin color in a culture that places a negative valuation on it. Hence the stigma "inheres" in the skin color. But this does not imply that dark skin color is inherently (i.e., apart from a particular set of cultural values) a mark of inferiority; the stigma is only inherent for the individual insofar as he acquires it by cultural definition rather than by anything he does.

Hence, since a culturally derived stigma refers to an identifying characteristic of a group that has been relegated to an inferior status position in society, the stigma can only be perpetuated as long as the culture provides some mechanism for *enforcing* the low status position of the group in question. In the absence of cultural enforcement, the stigma would vanish inasmuch as it is not inherent in the characteristic itself but is merely a symbol of membership in an inferior caste. In American society (unlike the Union of South Africa), there are no laws that explicitly create an inferior caste status for the black; even segregation statutes accorded him a separate rather than an inferior status. Hence the "mark" is enforced extralegally by preserving through social practices the social inferiority of which the mark is but a symbol.

If this situation exists despite the authority of God and the Constitution, what basis for hope does the black child have? It is not surprising, therefore, that, in comparison with lower-class white children, he aspires to jobs with more of the formal trappings than with the actual attributes of social prestige; that he feels impotent to strike back at his tormentors; that he feels more lonely and frightened when he is by himself; and that he gives more self-deprecatory reactions when figuratively looking at himself in the mirror (Deutsch, et al., 1956). He may have less anxiety about realizing high-flown ambitions than the middle-class child, but generalized feelings of inadequacy and unworthiness make him very prone to overrespond with anxiety to any threatening situation. Thus, until the last decade, in view of the general hopelessness of his position, lethargy, apathy, submission, and passive sabotage have been more typical than aggressive striving of his predominant reaction to frustration (Rosen, 1959; Siegel & Federman, 1959).

Rosen compared the educational and vocational aspirations of black boys (age 8 through 14) and their mothers to those of white, Protestant Americans, French Canadians, American Jews, Greek-Americans, and Italian-Americans. The mean vocational aspiration score of his black group was significantly lower than the mean scores of all other groups except the French Canadian. Paradoxically, however, 83 percent of the black mothers aspired to a college education for their sons. Rosen concluded that although blacks have been

> exposed to the liberal economic ethic longer than most of the other groups . . . their culture, it seems, is least likely to accent achievement values. The Negro's history as a slave and depressed farm worker, and the sharp discrepancy between his experience and the American Creed, would appear to work against the achievement values of the dominant white group. Typically, the Negro life-situation does not encourage the belief that one can manipulate his environment or the conviction that one can improve his condition very much by planning and hard work. (Rosen, 1959, p. 55).

> Negroes who might be expected to share the prevalent American emphasis upon education, face the painfully apparent fact that (apart from the token black) positions open to educated Negroes are scarce. This fact means that most Negroes, in all likelihood, do not consider high educational aspirations realistic, and the heavy drop-out in high school suggests that the curtailment of educational aspirations begins very early. (Rosen, 1959, p. 58)

Ethnicity was found to be more highly related to vocational aspirations than was social class; sizable ethnic and racial differences prevailed even when the influence of social class was controlled. These results are consistent with the finding that white students tend to prefer ''very interesting jobs'', whereas black students are more concerned with job security (Singer & Stafflre, 1956).

The relatively low vocational aspirations of black children are apparently justified by the current facts of economic life. Blacks predominate in the unskilled occupations, receive less pay than whites for equivalent work, and exceed the percentage figures for whites in degree of unemployment (Frumkin, 1958; Siegel & Federman, 1959). In skilled occupations, blacks are excluded at all educational

levels: higher educational qualifications in blacks are less frequently associated
with higher-level vocational pursuits than they are in the case of whites (Turner,
1953). Thus,

> from long experience Negroes have learned that it is best to be prepared for
> the absence, rather than the presence of opportunity—or, at most, to prepare
> and strive only for those limited opportunities which have been open in the
> past . . . Like most other people, Negroes tend to accept the views that
> prevail in the larger society about their appropriate role in that society,[and
> aspire and prepare] for only those positions where they are confident of
> acceptance. (Smuts, 1957, p.451)

Black children and lower-class white children who attend schools with a
heterogeneous social class and racial population are in a more favorable developmental situation. Under these conditions, the unfavored group is stimulated to
compete more aggressively even to the point of unrealism (Boyd, 1952; Smith,
1960), with the more privileged group in everyday contacts and in aspirational
behavior (Boyd, 1952). In their self-judgments they compare themselves with
actual models, who in fact are only slightly better off than they are, and hence do
not feel particularly inferior (Deutsch, et al, 1956). Black children in segregated
schools, on the other hand, are not only deprived of this stimulation, but in
comparing themselves to other children paradoxically feel more depressed and less
able to compete adequately, despite the fact that their actual contacts are confined
to children in the encapsulated community who share their socio-eonomic status.
Apparently then, they must used idealized mass media models as the basis for
comparison.

Black children are placed in the same ambivalent, conflictful position with
respect to the achievement values of Western civilization as are the children of
many native peoples experiencing acculturation and the sociocultural impact of
rapid industrialization. On the one hand, exposure to the new value system and its
patent and alluring advantages makes them less able to accept the traditional values
of their elders; on the other hand, both loyalty to their families and the excluding
color bar established by the dominant group make it difficult for them to assimilate
the new set of values (Ausubel, 1960; Ausubel, 1961b; De Vos & Miner, 1958;
Omari, 1960). Resentment and hostility toward the rejecting whites, as well as
disillusionment regarding white middle-class values and institutions, predispose
them arbitrarily and indiscriminately to repudiate the aspirations and personality
traits valued by the dominant culture. These negativistic tendencies are even
manifested in speech patterns; minority group children tend to reject the accepted
model of speech that is symbolic of superordinate status in a social order that
accords them only second-class membership (Anastasi & Cordova, 1953).

Further abetting these tendencies toward resistive acculturation are many
organized and institutionalized forms of nationalism and counterchauvinism.
Among the Maori, ''resistance took the form of unadaptive but adjustive mes-

sianic and magical cults, emphasis on moribund and ceremonial features of the ancient culture, and indiscriminate rejection of progressive aspects of European culture" (Ausubel, 1960, p. 221). Numerous parallels can be found among American blacks—for example, the Father Divine and black Muslim movements.

One of the most damaging effects of racial prejudice and discrimination on the victimized group is that it provides an all-embracing rationalization for personal shortcomings, lack of striving, and antisocial conduct.

> Some Negroes use the objective injustice of creating scapegoats as an opportunity to relieve or ward off feelings of personal inadequacy, self-contempt, or self-reproach by projecting all the blame onto white prejudice and discrimination. For other Negroes, however, reaction-formation becomes a main defense against the negative racial image . . . Thus they may develop extremes of moralistic, prudish, and compulsively meticulous attitudes [to disprove the stereotype].
>
> The Negro child is offered an excuse for anti-social behavior and evasion of social responsibility through feeling deprived of the social rewards for self-denial which are part of a healthy socialization process. But since these reactions are at variance with the democratic ideal of many other teachings to which children of both races are exposed at home, at church, and at school, they arouse of necessity feelings of inner conflict, confusion, anxiety, and guilt. These constitute liabilities for optimal adjustment.
>
> A continuing set of small incidents, closed doors, and blocked opportunities contribute to feelings of insecurity and mistrust and lead to the building of faith only in immediate gratifications and personal possessions. (Bernard, 1958, p. 152)

Withdrawal from Competition

An important factor helping to perpetuate the black's inferior social status and devalued ego structure is his tendency to withdraw from the competition of the wider American culture and to seek psychological shelter within the segregated walls of his own subculture. Such tendencies are particularly evident among middle-class blacks who, instead of providing the necessary leadership in preparing their people to take advantage of new vocational opportunities in the emerging desegregated culture, often seek to protect their own vested interest in segregation. Black businessmen, professionals, and teachers, for example, largely owe their clientele, jobs and incomes, to the existence of segregated institutions; furthermore, in the segregated community they do not have to meet the more stringent competitive standards prevailing in the wider culture (Frazier, 1957; Record, 1957; Turner, 1954). An additional complication is the fact that even though they "cannot escape altogether the discrimination and contempt to which blacks are generally subjected", they tend to identify with the values and ideology of the white middle-class and to dissociate themselves from other blacks. Together with pride of race and grudging affirmation of their racial identity, members of intellectual black families "are led to assert their superiority over other blacks, and look down on those who are 'no account,' shiftless, and 'mean'" (Record, 1957, p. 240).

Personality Adjustment

The destructive impact of prejudice, discrimination, segregation, and an inferior caste status on self-esteem, in addition to the usual mental hygiene consequences of lower social-class membership, result in a much higher incidence of behavior disorders in blacks than in whites. Personality disturbance is also more highly correlated with intelligence test scores in blacks than in whites (Greenberg & Fane, 1957; Srole et al., 1962; Wilson & Lantz, 1957). Quite understandably, both high anxiety level (Palermo, 1959; Roen, 1960) and suppressed feelings of aggression (Karon, 1958) are prominent symptoms of black maladjustment. Overt expression of these same aggressive impulses leads to a juvenile delinquency rate that is two to three times as high as among white teenagers (Dintz et al., 1958; Douglass, 1959). The occurrence of delinquent behavior is abetted by the high rate of unemployment (Conant, 1961) and by many characteristic features of lower-class black family life, such as illegitimate births, broken homes, desertion, neglect, employment of the mother, intrafamilial violence, harsh punishment, and tolerance for minor dishonesties (Cavan, 1959). Under these circumstances, aggressive antisocial behavior may be considered both a form of individual and social protest (Douglass, 1959), as well as an effective means of obtaining and maintaining status in the peer group of the lower-class black subculture (Clark, 1959). Drug addiction, on the other hand, represents a particularly efficient type of "dead-end" adjustment for the hedonsitic, motivationally immature adolescent who refuses to face up to the responsibilities of adult life (Ausubel, 1961a; Finestone, 1957).

Sex Differences

One of the most striking features of ego development in the segregated black community is the relatively more favored position enjoyed by girls in comparison to the middle-class model. We find girls in the *segregated* black community showing much greater relative superiority in academic, personal, and social adjustment (Deutsch, et al., 1956). They not only outperform boys academically by a greater margin, but also do so in all subjects rather than only in language skills (Deutsch, 1956). These girls have higher achievement needs (Gaier & Wambach, 1960; Grossack, 1957) and a greater span of attention; they are more popular wth classmates; they show more mature and realistic aspirations; they assume more responsible roles; and they feel less depressed in comparing themselves with other children (Anastasi & DeJesus, 1953). Substantially more black girls than black boys complete every level of education in the United States (Smuts, 1957). Adequate reasons for these differences are not difficult to find. Black children in this subculture live in a matriarchal family atmosphere where girls are openly preferred by mothers and grandmothers, and where the male sex role is generally deprecated. The father frequently deserts the family and in any case tends to be an unreliable source of economic and emotional security (Dai, 1949). Hence the mother, assisted perhaps by her mother or by an older daughter, shoulders most of the burdens and responsibilities of child rearing and is the only dependable adult with whom the child can identify. In this environment male chauvinism can obtain little foothold. The preferential treatment accorded girls is even extended to opportunities for acquiring ultimate earned status. If the family pins all of its hopes on one child and makes desperate sacrifices for that child, it will often be a daughter in preference to a son. Over and above his handicaps at home, the black boy also faces more obstacles in the wider culture in realizing his vocational ambitions, whatever they may be, than the black girl in fulfilling her adult role expectations of housewife, mother, nurse, teacher, or clerical worker (Deutsch, et al., 1956).

It seems, therefore, that black girls in racially encapsulated areas are less traumatized than boys by the impact of racial discrimination. This is precisely the opposite of what is found in studies of black children from less economically depressed and less segregated environments (Goff, 1949; Trent, 1954). The discrepancy can be attributed perhaps to two factors: the preferential treatment accorded girls in the encapsulated community is more pervasive, unqualified, and continuous; and the fact that, unlike black girls in mixed neighborhoods, these girls are less exposed to slights and humiliation from white persons. However, because of less tendency to internalize their feelings and greater openness in their social organization, black boys are able to adjust more easily than girls to the initial impact of desegregation (Campbell & Yarrow, 1958).

INDIVIDUAL DIFFERENCES IN REACTIONS TO THE SEGREGATED BLACK ENVIRONMENT

Only extreme cultural determinists would argue that all children in the encapsulated black community necessarily respond in substantially identical ways to the impact of their social environment. Although common factors in cultural conditioning obviously make for many uniformities in personality development, genically determined differences in temperamental and cognitive traits, as well as differential experience in the home and wider culture, account for much idiosyncratic variation. Would it be unreasonable, for example, to anticipate that an intellectually gifted black child in this environment might have a different fate than an intellectually dull or average youngster; that an active, assertive, outgoing, and tough-skinned child might react differently to discriminatory treatment than one who is phlegmatic, submissive, sensitive, and introverted?

Differences in early socializing experience with parents are probably even more important, especially since they tend to generalize to interpersonal behavior outside the home. At this point it is worth noting that, generally speaking, racial discrimination affects children *indirectly* through their parents before it affects them directly through their own contacts with the wider culture. This indirect influence is mediated in two ways. General parental attitudes toward the child are undoubtedly determined in part by the parent's own experience as a victim of discrimination. Some racially victimized parents, seeking retribution through their children, may fail to value them intrinsically and instead place exaggerated emphasis on ego aggrandizement. Others may be so preoccupied with their own frustrations as to reject their children. Still others may accept and intrinsically value their children, and through their own example and strength of character encourage the development of realistic aspirations and of mature, self-disciplined behavior. Parents also transmit to their children some of their own ways of responding to discrimination, such as counteraggression, passive sabotage, obsequious submission, or strident counterchauvinism. Individual differences such as these undoubtedly explain in part why some blacks move into unsegregated neighborhoods and transfer to unsegregated schools when these opportunities arise, whereas other members of the race choose to remain in the segregated environment. The decision to transfer or not to transfer to an unsegregated school, for example, was found to be unrelated to both social class status and academic ability (Crockett, 1957).

Much interindividual variability therefore prevails in the reactions of children to minority group membership. Fortunately, sufficient time is available for establishing some stable feelings of intrinsic adequacy within the home before the impact of segregation on ego development becomes catastrophically destructive. It was found, for example, that black children who are most self-accepting also tend to exhibit more positive attitudes toward other black and white children (Trent, 1954), and that black college students who identify most with their own race tend to be least prejudiced against other minority groups. Hence, while appreciating the general unfavorable effects of a segregated environment on all black children, we may conclude on the more hopeful note that the consequences of membership in a stigmatized racial group can be cushioned in part by a foundation of intrinsic self-esteem established in the home.

Counseling

Because of current grave inadequacies in the structure of the lower-class urban black family, the school must be prepared to compensate, at least in part, for the deficiencies of the home, that is, to act, so to speak, *in loco parentis*. Teachers in predominatly black schools actually perform much of this role at the present time.

It is apparent, therefore, that trained counselors must assume the role of parent substitutes during preadolescence and adolescence. They are needed to offer appropriate educational and vocational guidance, to encourage worthwhile and realistic aspirations, and to stimulate the development of mature personality traits. In view of the serious unemployment situation among black youth, they should also assist in job placement and in cushioning the transition between school and work. This will naturally require much expansion of existing guidance services in the school.

Research has shown that black children's distrust of white counselors and authority figures in general have made it

difficult for a white counselor to create an atmosphere wherein a Negro could gain insight . . . .

The fundamental principle of counseling—to view the social or personal field as the client does—is difficult to attain in such a situation. The white person can only imagine, but never know, how a Negro thinks and feels, or how he views a social or personal situation. The cultural lenses which are formulated from unique milieux are not as freely transferable as it is assumed, or as we are led to believe. (Phillips, 1957, p. 188)

7

Conscience and Guilt

Values refer to ways of striving, believing, and doing whenever purpose and direction are involved or choice and judgment are exercised. Values are implied in the relative importance that an individual attaches to different objectives and activities; expresses in his moral, social, and religious beliefs; and shows in his aesthetic preferences. They underlie sanctioned ways of behaving and interacting with people in a given culture and the kinds of personality traits that are idealized. Values therefore are important factors in determining goals and goal-seeking behavior, standards of conduct, and feelings of obligation to conform to such standards and to inhibit behavior at variance with them. They help to order the world of the child differentially in terms of degree of ego involvement (i.e., to determine his interests), orient him to his cultural milieu, influence the content of his perceptions, and sensitize him selectively to perceive certain classes of objects and relationships.

THE TRANSMISSION OF VALUES

Three component problems are involved in the intracultural transmission of values. First, we must consider the external patterning factors to which the child is exposed and which influence him selectively to interiorize certain values in preference to others. Second, we must identify the mechanisms through which the external standards are interiorized. Third, we must reckon with the sanctions (both internal and external) that maintain values in relatively stable form once they are internalized.

External Patterning Factors

The young child's world of value judgments is largely unstructured for lack of relevant experiential frames of reference and, hence, is very susceptible to the influence of prestige suggestion from significant figures in his environment. First through his parents and later through other socializing agents, he is exposed to both explicit and implicit indoctrination. The latter occurs insidiously through recurrent and unobtrusive exposure to the underlying value assumptions of family and culture. Thus, young children tend to identify with the value symbols of their parents' membership and reference groups long before they are sufficiently mature to comprehend the meaning of these symbols. Preschool and early school-age children, for example, assimilate the racial and religious prejudices of their parents quite independently of any actual contact with the groups concerned, and they identify with parental religious and political attitudes without any rational understanding of the issues involved (Hirschberg & Gilliland, 1942; Proshansky, 1966).

Several studies have provided experimental evidence of children's susceptibility to prestige suggestion. Direct person-to-person influence in the form of modeling has been shown to modify children's moral judgments (Bandura & McDonald, 1963) and self-imposed delay of gratification (Bandura & Mischel, 1965). Prestige suggestion is more effective (1) in contexts where the authority's opinion is rationalized rather than arbitrary; and (2) in ambiguous judgmental situations where the child has little past experience, an indefinite and unformed evaluative frame of reference, and no incontrovertible sensory evidence before him (Ausubel et al., 1956). Children naturally vary greatly in their susceptibility to prestige suggestion, but the question of whether suggestibility can be considered a general personality trait is still unsettled. Evidence from studies with adults indicated that degree of susceptibility is inversely related to self-sufficiency, self-assertiveness, and relative indifference to others' approval. In accordance with a social sex role, which includes being more docile, conforming, and submissive to adult authority, girls tend to be more responsive than boys to prestige suggestion (Ausubel et al., 1956; Duncker, 1938; Messerschmidt, 1933; Patel & Gordon, 1960).

Mechanism of Interiorization

We may distinguish, on the basis of the degree of motivation involved, between two essentially different ways of interiorizing the values of other persons or of groups. As an individual simply habituates to a given set of norms, values underlying these norms may acquire an aura of axiomatic rightness and may be accepted as self-evidently valid. Here no particular needs of the individual are satisfied. A simple mechanical type of imitation belongs in the same category; the expressed values of one person serve as a stimulus instigating acceptance of comparable values by another. This process is facilitated in group situations and is very similar to behavioral "contagion". However, whenever such imitation involves a more active *need* to be like other persons or to conform to their expectations (apart from fear of punishment), it is more proper to speak of motivated interiorization or identification. Identification, therefore, is a motivated form of imitation in which both the *interpersonal relationship* (direct or fantasied) between imitator and imitatee and the imitated act itself are highly significant for the learning that ensues.

Although identification implies an underlying motive in one person's acceptance of another's values, the term itself without further qualification does not specify the type of motivation that is operative. In order to designate more precisely the individual's motivational orientation to value assimilation, the terms *satellizing* and *incorporative* (non-satellizing) will be used. In each case the child responds to prestige suggestion but does so for different reasons. The non-satellizer (in contrast to the satellizer) does not accept prestige authority blindly and uncritically from a person or group out of personal loyalty or desire for derived status, but because the authority of the suggester is respected as relevantly influencing the outcome of his quest for earned status. The purpose of his hero worship is not to be a loyal and devoted camp follower but to emulate and displace the hero, and to use him as a guide and stepping-stone to ego enhancement. Conformity to group norms in his case is more a matter of expediency, and of obtaining the status advantages of group reference or membership than a reflection of a need for self-subservient belongingness or "we-feeling" (Ausubel, 1952; Kagan, 1958; Whiting, 1960). The *exploratory* orientation to value assimilation, on the other hand, is a more task-oriented, objective, problem-solving approach that ignores considerations of earned and derived status and places major emphasis on objective evidence, logical validity, and equity in determining the acceptability of different value positions.

External and Internal Sanctions

After the child is exposed to and assimilates values from significant persons in his environment, both external and internal sanctions operate to keep them relatively stable and to insure (in the case of moral values) that behavior is kept compatible with them. At the disposal of parents, teachers, and peer groups are such forms of control as reward and punishment, approval and disapproval, ridicule, withdrawal of love and respect, depreciation of status in the group, and ostracism. From within, a parallel set of controls is operative. The child feels apprehensive about the consequences of deviation (e.g., possible loss of present status and the threat of not attaining future status goals) from his internalized values. He learns gradually to respond with feelings of shame to the negative evaluation of himself by others, acquires a feeling of *obligation* about inhibiting behavior that is at variance with his value structure, and feels guilty when he fails to do so. The need to avoid these highly unpleasant guilt feelings and to retain feelings of belongingness in and acceptance by the group eventually becomes one of the most effective of all behavioral sanctions. In the case of satellizing children, personal loyalty is also an important factor in preventing deviancy from internalized standards.

DEVELOPMENTAL TRENDS IN VALUE ASSIMILATION

Since socialization is a gradual and cumulative process, it is hardly surprising that with increasing age children show progressively closer approximation to adult moral, social (Cruse, 1963; Eberhart, 1942; Lockhard, 1930; Pressey & Robinson, 1944), and aesthetic norms (Thompson, 1962), and correspondingly greater agreement among themselves (Watson, 1965). Paralleling this trend is a gradual increase in the conformity aspects of personality as measured by Rorschach responses (Thetford, Molish, & Beck, 1951). This greater conformity to adult standards naturally depends in part upon increased ability to perceive what is expected and to discriminate between finer shadings of behavioral standards. There is progressive improvement in the ability to perceive another's sociometric status (Ausubel et al., 1952; Horowitz, 1962) and to discriminate between the behaviors that teachers approve and disapprove of (Witryol, 1950) and between different degrees of seriousness of offense against property (Eberhart, 1942). Children also become progressively more aware that they are expected to conform to adult roles, and to inhibit aggressive, socially deviant behavior (Griffiths, 1952). Further consequences of the growth in cognitive capacity are the increasing tendency for values to be organized on an abstract basis, thereby permitting greater generality and consistency from situation to situation (Hartshorne & May, 1930; Hoffman, 1963; Kohlberg, 1946); and the improving ability to differentiate value judgments from factual judgments (Weir, 1960).

Although much interindividual variability prevails at any given age level, the growing importance of attaining earned status during the desatellizing period increasingly tends to favor a shift from the satellizing to the incorporative and exploratory motivational orientations in value assimilation. In interiorizing new values and goals, therefore, such considerations as ego enhancement, expediency, social recognition, and status in the group become more relevant than adult approval or personal loyalty; and satisfaction of these considerations demands much more critical examination of values prior to internalization. Accordingly, the evidence indicates that suggestibility in children decreases as a function of age (Campbell, 1964; Messerschmidt, 1933; Reymert & Kohn, 1940). The adoption of the exploratory orientation is also greatly facilitated during the desatellizing stage by the opportunity of following objective evidence and principles of equity to their logical conclusions without incurring such heavy burdens of guilt and disloyalty and without being so concerned about the possible loss of derived status.

Reflective of this shift in value assimilation is the increasing sensitivity of children to the disapproval of such authority figures outside the home as the school superintendent (Bavelas, 1942), the decreasing importance of the parents as emulatory models (Bray, 1962; Ugurel-Semin, 1952), and the increasing replacement, as models, of the parents by glamorous, historical and public figures (Havighurst et al., 1946). As shown by the steadily diminishing correlations from the age of 10 to 16 between children's reputations for various traits and the closeness of affectional ties with families (Brown et al., 1947), parents become increasingly less influential than other socializing agents in determining children's values (Campbell, 1964). Values acquire a wider social base as increased exposure to new social environments, coupled with less subservience to parental views, enables the older child to perceive the standards of his home as merely special variants of subcultural norms. Hence, with increasing age, his values tend to become more typical of the culture at large, and less typical of his own family.

With increasing age, children also tend to adopt a less subjectivistic approach to values. They consider them from a less personal and a more detached point of view, show greater ability to argue from the standpoint of a hypothetical premise, and think more in terms that transcend their own immediate experience. There is a decline in egoism and an increase in altruism (Handlon & Gross, 1959; Ugurel Semin, 1952; Wright, 1942); children become more aware of the needs, feelings, and interests of others and more able to consider a situation from another's point of view. For example, the reason offered for the unacceptability of stealing tends to shift from fear of apprehension and punishment to the perceived injury it causes others (Eberhart, 1942; Kohlberg, 1964).

MORAL DEVELOPMENT

Morals constitute that part of our cultural and personal value systems concerned with the proper ends of man's activities and strivings, with questions of good and evil, and with responsibility or accountability for behavior. Thus, the learning of moral values is only a component aspect of ego development and obeys all of the principles regulating the assimilation of any ego-related value (Kohlberg, 1964; Loevinger, 1966; Lorimer, 1968; McCullough, 1969; Wilson, Williams & Sugarman, 1967). From a developmental standpoint, we can see no theoretical advantage in divorcing moral development from ego development or in postulating the existence of a separate layer of personality such as the Freudian superego. Hence, in our analysis of the development of conscience, we shall be concerned with the same type of variables as those that determine the outcome of other aspects of ego development.

Importance for Personality Development

During the past three decades or more, psychology—the science of behavior—has attempted to evade coming to terms with ethics, the science of ends, norms, good, right, and choice. The focus of psychological concern has been on adjustment as an end in itself, the contention being that moral values are subjective and unverifiable. According to this view, moral judgments are matters of arbitrary preference and opinion beyond the pale of science; no objective psychological criterion is possible. Behavior may be appraised as constructive or antisocial, but never as good or evil. The purpose of psychology is to explain conduct, not to judge it; questions of accountability are held to be irrelevant in the light of psychological determinism, and hence the proper concern of only jurists and philosophers.

In reply to this line of argument, let us first say that to ignore ethical considerations is to overlook one of the most significant components of human conduct. Whether the psychologist chooses to recognize it or not, most purposeful behavior in human beings has a moral aspect, the psychological reality of which cannot be ignored. The goals of human development, insofar as they are determined by man and culture, are always predicated upon certain moral assumptions. Thus, the development of the individual is invariably influenced by coercive exposure to the particular set of assumptions that his culture espouses and that he himself eventually assimilates.

Second, empirically validatable ethical propositions can be discovered once we accept certain basic philosophical value judgments regarding the proper ends of development that are themselves phenomenologically unverifiable. If, for example, we grant that self-realization is the highest goal toward which man can strive, it will then be possible to establish which behavioral alternatives are most compatible with this goal and hence most ethical. But even if the primary value judgments are not empirically verifiable, they must still be predicated upon empirically determined human capacities for the kind of norms that are advocated. It is futile to speak of life goals that are motivationally unsupportable or of standards of maturity that only angels can reach. The same criterion obviously applies also to principles of accountability that must be grounded on attainable norms of moral development.

Finally, moral behavior is of interest to the child development specialist because it has a developmental history. It undergoes orderly and systematic age level changes and manifests psychobiological uniformities and psychosocial as well as idiosyncratic variability. In terms of the underlying psychological processes involved in conscience development, we deal with genically determined potentialities. However, the actual acquisition of moral behavior, the normative sequences, and variability in development are largely determined by experiential and sociocultural factors.

By means of a developmental and cross-cultural approach, it becomes possible (1) to determine the limits that define man's capacity for acquiring moral behavior and the sequential steps involved in moral growth; (2) to predict the various types of delinquent behavior that may arise as a consequence of aberrant moral development; and (3) to determine under what conditions individuals may be held morally accountable for their misdeeds.

Behavior and Ethics

Modern psychology and psychiatry have tended to drift away from concern with problems of ethics and moral values. The moralizing orientation in psychotherapy is treated with scorn in present-day textbooks of psychiatry and psychology; and if the directive and non-directive schools of thought agree on any one thing, it is that there is no room for moral judgment in the therapeutic situation. The focus is on adjustment. The therapist, we are told, cannot say that behavior is good or bad; he can only express an opinion on the quality and efficacy of an adjustive mechanism. When he can divorce himself completely from ethical judgments and can concern himself only with understanding the psychopathological origins and adjustive significance of deviant behavior, he has allegedly attained the ideal therapeutic attitude. The thesis that will be presented below—which in many ways parallels the position of Fromm (1947)—is that not only is it impossible for a psychotherapist to ignore the question of moral judgment but it is also undesirable and artificial for him to attempt to do so.

Far from being unrelated, the problems of behavior and ethics are inextricably bound together. To appraise a man's personality and ignore his moral character is equivalent in many respects to evaluating the setting of a ring while overlooking the diamond. True, the psychologist has a ready explanation for this apparent paradox. Moral values, he contends, are subjective and unverifiable. Every man to his taste and to his opinion; no objective psychological criterion is possible. We can only describe a man's personality traits with the aid of existing measuring instruments, hazard a guess as to how they developed, try to evaluate their adjustive value, and provide a plausible explanation for their antisocial components.

If you press him further by saying, "Yes, but what I really want to know is whether Mr. X is a decent and trustworthy man? Is he intellectually honest? Would he take unfair advantage of me? Is he able to control his unconscionable impulses? These factors are more important in getting along with him than knowing that he is introverted, tends to think in abstract terms, possesses an I. Q. of 120, has superior computational ability and is a compulsive father." At this point, the psychologist usually becomes defensive, and insists that moral judgments are not only beyond the pale of science, but can also impair irreparably his objective findings. "If you are interested in those subjective aspects of personality," he concludes, "why don't you ask his former employer. He can tell you. He's not a scientist."

The same psychological abhorrence of ethical judgment can be seen in our modern orientation toward antisocial conduct, crime, and delinquency. Criminality is regarded as either a psychological or a social disease. There are no delinquent individuals, only delinquent parents or delinquent social systems. When one really understands why a criminal behaves as he does, the psychological evaluation is complete. Whether he is good or bad or whether he is morally accountable are arbitrary value judgments, matters of social policy or legal philosophy that do not concern the psychologist. To the latter, the delinquent is a product of his heredity and environment, an individual who had no other choice but to act as he did; and in the light of this psychological determinism moral responsibility and retribution are necessarily irrelevant, inconsistent, and illogical. Behavior can be appraised as unfortunate or antisocial but never as evil. So long as it can be explained in psychological terms, it cannot be perceived as evil, since such an evaluation implies a value judgment that lies beyond the scope of behavioral assessment.

In the history of psychology, as Fromm (1947) points out, this moral relativism is a comparatively recent development. Aristotle, Spinoza, and Dewey, for example, all held that ethics can only be based on a science of behavior, and that "objectively valid value propositions can be arrived at by human reason."

Two problems are paramount in all ethical systems: (1) What shall man live for? Toward what goals shall he strive? What is involved in true self-realization? What is mature behavior? (2) Is man morally accountable for his behavior? Under what circumstances can he be exempted from moral accountability? Can antisocial behavior be reduced to psychological terms alone? If so, does psychological understanding obviate the necessity for moral judgment? In both instances, no valid or realistic ethical principles can be predicated apart from what is known about the behavioral capacities of human beings. It is futile to speak about life goals that are motivationally insupportable. The meaning of self-realization can be understood only in terms of purposeful strivings that can be related to the biosocial matrix from which human behavior emerges. The degree of maturity that man may conceivably attain cannot possibly exceed the maximum level that is defined by optimal interaction of the relevant variables involved in his personality development. The question of moral accountability can only be answered in relation to the problem of moral development or conscience formation, which in turn is an important facet of ego development.

These two core problems of ethics, therefore, are not beyond the domain of psychological investigation. As a matter of fact, they can and will be solved only as quickly as the science of human behavior itself advances. And if we admit the possibility of discovering objectively valid and verifiable principles of behavior, we must likewise be committed to the proposition that value judgments "built upon the science of man" have an equal claim to objective validity.

Importance for Socializing Process

Moral obligation is one of the most important psychological mechanisms through which an individual becomes socialized in the ways of his culture. It is also an important instrument for cultural survival since it constitutes a most efficient watchdog within each individual serving to keep his behavior compatible with his own moral values and the values of the society in which he lives. Without the aid it renders, child rearing would be a difficult matter indeed. If children felt no sense of accountability to curb their hedonistic and irresponsible impulses, to conform to accepted social norms, or to acquire self-control, the socializing process would be slow, arduous, and incomplete. The methods of sheer physical force, threat of pain, deprivation and punishment, and withholding of love and approval—all used in combination with constant surveillance—would be the only available means for exacting conformity to cultural standards of acceptable behavior. And since the interests of personal expediency are not always in agreement with prescribed ethical norms, since the maintenance of perpetual vigilance is impractical, and since fear alone is never an effective deterrent against antisocial behavior, a social order that is unbuttressed by a sense of moral obligation in its members can enjoy precious little stability.

The need to conform to established cultural norms, however, is only one component of the more general problem of moral obligation. As it stands, this type of obligation refers only to those contemporaneous aspects of moral behavior that are subject to change as society itself changes. The process of simple cultural transmission of values is complicated today by the comparatively frequent influx of new values that challenge moral preconceptions (Hemming, 1957).

In more mature forms of morality, then, obligation stems more from a reasoned judgment based on some personal principles than from simple conformity to prevailing cultural norms. The cultural basis of conscience development in the individual may be found in the potent need of both parents and society to inculcate a sense of responsibility in the child. Not only the physical survival of its members but also the perpetuation of its selective way of life is contingent upon the culture's degree of success in this undertaking. Thus, the attenuation of infantile irresponsibility might be considered part of the necessary process of ego devaluation and maturation that presumably characterizes personality development in all cultures. Socialization demands the learning of self-control and self-discipline, the subordination of personal desires to the needs and wishes of others, the acquisition of skills and self-sufficiency, the curbing of hedonistic and aggressive impulses, and the assimilation of culturally sanctioned patterns of behavior. Moreover, in its most mature aspects, socialization demands that the individual govern his behavior by *rules* that he arrives at rationally before conforming to them. It seems highly unlikely that any of these propensities could become thoroughly stable before conscience is firmly established. Indeed, the very notion of *character* formation assumes adherence to the directive role of conscience in moral behavior.

PSYCHOLOGICAL COMPONENTS OF CONSCIENCE

The term *conscience* is an abstraction referring to the cognitive-emotional organization of an individual's moral values and to other psychological processes involved in keeping conduct compatible with internalized moral standards.

It presupposes, first, that he is able to assimilate certain standards of right and wrong or good and evil and accept them as his *own*. The assimilation of moral values does not necessarily mean that these values will influence conduct in any stable and systematic fashion until a sense of *obligation* evolves to conform to them in his own *personal* behavior and to feel *accountable* for lapses therefrom. The sense of obligation is itself a moral value and must undergo internalization; developmentally, however, this step occurs *after* the interiorization of other ethical values. That is, the child believes that certain actions are good or bad and applies these designations to *other* persons' conduct before he feels that he ought or ought not to do them himself. But unlike other values, moral obligation has the regulatory function of compelling adherence to internalized norms of behavior. Hence this core value of his moral system not only makes possible the implementation of other values but also welds them together into an organized system. It gives generality and genotypic consistency to moral conduct by entering into every moral decision he makes. For example, the disposition to refrain from committing an act of dishonesty depends on more than the strength of honesty impulses in a given context. The *total* inhibitory control that can be exercised in this situation is rather the strength of the particular moral value (honesty) weighted by a general factor that is the strength of the moral obligation to abide by *all* internalized values.

The operation of conscience also presupposes the capacity to *anticipate* the consequences of actions in advance of their execution and to exercise volitional and inhibitory control in order to bring these anticipated consequences into line with perceived obligation. The acquisition of such inhibitory control is naturally a very gradual process that parallels the growth of the self-critical faculty and of the ability to endure postponement of immediate hedonistic satisfaction.

The final psychological process involved in the operation of conscience is the self-critical faculty. Without this capacity for realistically appraising one's own intentions and behavior in the light of internalized moral principles, it is neither possible to inhibit immoral actions nor to experience guilt after they are executed. The importance of the self-critical faculty in the development of conscience can be seen in the fact that the latter remains in a rudimentary state until the former is reasonably well advanced (age five to eight). When self-criticism can be employed, guilt feelings become possible, since these are a reaction to the perception of a discrepancy between one's own behavior and the moral standards in relation to which a sense of obligation exists.

Guilt is thus less of a psychological process underlying or necessary for the operation of conscience than it is a cognitive-emotional reaction of the individual to the actual functioning of conscience in a situation where perceived disparity exists between behavior and obligation. The core ingredient of guilt is the feeling of shame, which Gardner Murphy (1947) describes as a "collapse in the usual mechanism of adequate self-portraiture and an immobilization in helplessness with or without an appeal for renewal of status." In addition to shame, guilt includes the feelings of self-reproach, self-disgust, self-contempt, remorse, and various characteristic visceral and vasomotor responses. Phylogenetically, shame is not a distinctively human response since it undoubtedly occurs in animals such as dogs who are able to enter into satellizing-like relationships with human beings.

On an emotional plane at least, it is thus possible to think of conscience in animals, provided the animal's capacity for abstraction is kept sufficiently low.

Through the processes of retrospective association and anticipation guilt tends to be incorporated into the behavioral system of conscience and to furnish it with some of its most distinctive identifying features and substantive qualities. Behavior leading to guilt evokes the anticipation that retribution will be inevitable either through the suffering inherent in guilt feelings, the seeking out of social punishment as means of guilt-reduction, or the functioning of a supernatural agency. The inevitability of punishment, therefore, is one of the characteristic properties of conscience reactions.

Guilt Reduction as Motivation

Guilt feelings will be discussed later as a cause of symptomatic anxiety. In the everyday behavior of human beings, self-justification constitutes an impelling and ubiquitous motivation. The picture of self as shameful and contemptuous is highly threatening to self-esteem and is productive of considerable anxiety. Hence we can expect that guilt-reduction mechanisms will for the most part parallel those we will later catalogue for anxiety reduction.

The most commonly used mechanism of guilt reduction is repression. Contrary to Mowrer's (1950) assumption, however, repression of guilt is not the primary cause of even symptomatic anxiety, but is mainly a consequence of it. Conscious guilt is repressed because it is anxiety-producing. This repression in turn intensifies the anxiety not because of some mysterious reason associated with "the return of the repressed," as Mowrer claims, but because repression obviates the possibility of punishment, confession, expiation and other guilt-reducing mechanisms. It is true that repression can never be complete, as demonstrated, for example, by the appearance of repressed guilt feelings in dreams. This incompleteness of repression, however, does not provide a convincing explanation for the conversion of guilt into anxiety since we know: (1) that conscious guilt can be productive of anxiety; and (2) that repression interferes with the evolution of guilt reduction mechanisms.

Projection of guilt is a more effective means of guilt reduction, since in this fashion accountability is not merely repressed but is actually disowned by perceiving the blame elsewhere. This, of course, involves distortion of evidence similar to what happens in rationalization. Through depersonalization, amnesic states, and states of multiple personality it is possible to divorce segments of behavior from the sense of personal identity and thereby to disown all connection with the associated guilt. Obsessions displace concern away from the genuine source of guilt feelings and monopolize the field of consciousness with relatively innocuous material, whereas compulsions may often symbolize a form of expiation. In another type of displacement noted by Fromm (1947), "a person may feel consciously guilty for not pleasing authorities, while 'unconsciously' he feels guilty for not living up to his own expectation of himself.''

More direct forms of guilt reduction include punishment, confession, and expiation, all of which are extensively employed by various religions. Social punishment, namely, that form of punishment imposed from without or made known to others, can confer almost complete absolution. Confession involves the preliminary phase of punishment: self-culpability is exposed to others so that their condemnation can be secured in place of self-condemnation that has less guilt-reducing properties. A variant of this mechanism is found in the self-accusatory, auditory hallucination. It is more guilt-reducing for a latent homosexual to hear external voices accusing him of being a "loathesome fairy" than to accuse himself of the same tendency. A patient of the senior author ceased hearing such voices after gaining insight into this mechanism, but soon began to hear motors humming. When in turn this symbolic substitution was understood, the motors vanished only to be replaced by overt symptoms of anxiety. Expiation is a form of punishment emphasizing restitution or exaggeration of the particular moral trait or virtue in relation to which a sense of guilt is experienced. A typical example of the latter variety is the adjustive mechanism known as reaction formation, for example, the mother who feels excessively guilty for rejecting tendencies may become inflexibly oversolicitous toward her child.

Various formal and culturally stereotyped varieties of guilt reduction are also available, such as verbal magic, pseudoremorse, and hypocritical religious observance. Thus, many persons tend to believe that if they make a formal, verbalistic show of remorse, confession, and self-castigation, their guilt is absolved. The insincerity of this maneuver is revealed by the fact that their remarks are offered as a preface to the actual execution of the behavior that is verbally condemned.

The more morally bankrupt certain people become—the more incapable of experiencing genuine feelings of guilt—the more they seek out the formal moral respectability that comes with ritualistic religious observances. They wish to continue their immoral practices and still enjoy a reputation for righteousness. Sometimes, of course, they must suffer continuous chastisement by hearing their hypocrisy berated by the clergy. But even this does not phase them. Furthest from their thoughts is a desire for genuine reform, and at the same time they are too shameless to be offended by moral reproach. What happens, therefore, is a sentimental orgy in which tears of pseudoremorse and self-pity are shed as their calumny is exposed; and once having shed these tears they are convinced that they are morally acquitted and entitled to pursue the same unprincipled path.

It is not necessary to believe, however, that all guilt feelings are intolerable and must somehow be repressed, disowned, rationalized, confessed, expiated for, etc. In the same sense that there is tolerance for conscious anxiety, there is tolerance for conscious guilt, the degree of tolerance, of course, being subject to wide individual differences. Man's portrait of himself need not be free of all moral blemishes. Hence, a good deal of ordinary guilt can be acknowledged on a conscious level and taken in stride without any efforts made toward guilt reduction. There is reason to believe that the intrinsically secure person who is moderately self-sufficient possesses more guilt tolerance than either the insecure or the overly dependent individual.

In our culture we tend to underestimate man's capacity for moral depravity.* We tend to assume that people could not conceivably be guilty of certain immoral intentions and practices because if they were, "How could they possibly live with themselves?" And if we do admit such a possibility, we reveal the impact of psychoanalytic doctrine and moral relativism on our thinking by blaming "unconscious motives" and by absolving the individual from moral accountability on the grounds that he is the innocent product (victim) of his heredity and environment. "How could he have possibly acted in any other way?"

Several alternative explanations, however, should be considered. First, most people can tolerate more conscious guilt than we are willing to concede; we have exaggerated man's need for perceiving himself as completely untainted in a moral sense. Second, many times when we think that a person should be experiencing guilt feelings he really is not for one or both of two good reasons: (1) no real internalization of moral obligation has taken place; or (2) self-criticism is inhibited to the point where no discrepancy can be perceived between behavior and obligation, regardless of how flagrant the disparity may appear to others. It is necessary to differentiate this latter situation from instances in which (3) guilt is actually experienced but wrongdoing is still denied because of pride, inability to admit being in the wrong, and outright intellectual dishonesty; and (4) guilt occurs but is rationalized away without conscious awareness of distortion or misrepresentation of facts.

The mental hygiene value of keeping guilt on a conscious level parallels the advantages of dealing with anxiety on the same basis: The possibilities of evolving constructive solutions are greatly enhanced. In the case of the former, this means learning to bear and live with one's quota of guilt while taking such realistic preventative and restitutive measures as are indicated. Where legitimate compromises with moral principles are clearly necessary, the reasons for them should be unambiguously perceived and acknowledged as such rather than rationalized on a more acceptable basis. In this way it is possible to retain one's moral code intact under the most trying of circumstances. Unless the reasons for unavoidable moral expediency are kept clearly in mind, habituation to and corruption by convenient deviations from responsibility tend to occur; and what may start out as a reluctant maneuver under duress ends up by becoming an individual's characteristic mode of ethical behavior.

---

*The reason for this cultural reluctance to perceive unethical tendencies in others is partly a historical reaction to the witch-hunting proclivities of previous generations, and partly an institutionalized defense against insecurity, that is, there is less reason to be fearful if people are perceived as more benevolent than they really are.

Children generally in contradistinction to adults are not capable of making this type of adjustment. Being unable to appreciate or evaluate the issues involved in making inescapable moral compromises, they are more likely to actually assimilate rather than simulate acceptance of the inferior ethical alternative represented by the compromise. We witnessed just such a situation in Germany during the Second World War. Many adults were able to survive the Hitlerian years morally unscathed, whereas the children who grew up at the time remained completely indoctrinated.

In our present moral climate where expediency enjoys such vogue, the practitioners thereof try to rationalize its use by exaggerating the cultural necessity for conformity, upholding deference to authority, and advocating unprincipled opportunism if one is to "get ahead." Granted the moral neutrality of these injunctions, how *far* "ahead" does one wish to get in "hunting with the hounds"? How *far* is one willing to curry favor with those who push others around? At any rate, there is more tolerance in our culture for independence and non-conformity than persons who act upon such injunctions are willing to concede, and even some chance of winning admiration in the process.

When this is pointed out, the last defense that will usually be offered is insecurity. Although this may be ostensibly true, it is not the sole reason. Unprincipled ambition is the main motivation, as proved by the fact that the attainment of security usually does not put an end to but rather intensifies moral expediency.

Conscience and Superego

It is customary for many psychiatrists and clinical psychologists—even those who are not psychoanalytically oriented—to use the Freudian term "superego" as if it were synonymous with conscience. This practice is not only exceedingly imprecise but is also highly misleading, since superego does not refer to the developmental conscience described above as a part of the ego, but rather to a separate, reified layer of personality derived from a specific, inevitable, and universal event in psychosexual development.

Throughout our discussion of conscience development we have stressed Sherif and Cantril's proposition that

> There is for the individual no psychological difference either in the genesis of or the function of "moral" codes (which psychoanalysts separate out as the "superego") and other norms of behavior the individual learns. The emerging developing ego is in large part composed of all these interiorized social values. (1947)

The values subsumed under conscience are merely internalized in an ethical context and are more closely related to such factors as self-criticism, obligation, self-control and guilt feelings.

The rationale for the superego as something special and apart from the rest of the ego is poorly conceptualized in psychoanalytic literature. It is not clear whether the ego or the superego has the function of testing reality and of clearing the way for the expression of id impulses. The distinctions between ego, superego and ego ideal are also obscure and are defined differently by various analysts. Confusion exists as to whether the superego is a product resulting "from the repression of the Oedipus complex [or] is itself the mechanism which effected the repression."

The superego according to Freud (1935) arises in relation to the child's task of repressing Oedipal wishes, namely, sexual desires for the parent of the opposite sex and hostility toward the rival parent of the same sex. In order to effect this repression, the child identifies with the moral standards of the father, a task made easier by the fact that this event "takes place in the prehistory of every person" (1935). The final outcome of this repression and of the incorporation of the father's moral tabus against sexual expression leads to the formation of the superego, which in effect becomes the "heir to the Oedipus complex" (1935).

Evidence for the existence of an Oedipus complex is entirely impressionistic and is based upon retrospective clinical material. No unequivocal empirical findings are available to indicate that hostility toward parents of the opposite sex is derived from sexual rivalry; in fact, studies of preference for parents in young children invariably show that the mother is preferred by both boys and girls (Simpson, 1935). The alleged universality of the Oedipal complex has been undermined by Malinowski's findings (1927), which suggest that hostility between father and son is not present in a culture where the maternal uncle happens to be the authority figure. The phylogenicity of such complex and specific urges and identifications is also highly untenable on theoretical grounds.

The concept of superego, lastly, ignores all of the developmental evidence available on the growth of conscience—from complete infantile amorality to a sense of moral responsibility based first on fear of punishment, later on uncritical satellization, and finally on rational notions of moral reciprocity and functionalism. It is a static concept that makes no allowances for shifts in the nature of a conscience as its

original frames derived from the parents sooner or later prove themselves inadequate for any satisfactory adjustment to the group situation. These frames are, then, at least in part, discarded in favor of new standards imposed on the individual by his relationship to others in the group . . . Moral codes can and do arise spontaneously in children's social groups . . . . These results of Piaget together with the data from cultural anthropology which show the extreme variation of the Oedipus complex even within a single culture indicate that the psychoanalytic concept of the universal development of a 'superego' in human beings has no basis in fact as a special part of the ego with a special function (Sherif & Cantril, 1946).

Normative Changes in Conscience Development

Although none of the conditions necessary for the emergence of conscience can ever be satisfied at birth, all human beings are potentially capable of acquiring conscience behavior under minimally favorable circumstances. Culture may make a difference in the form that this behavior takes and in the specific kinds of stimuli that instigate it. But the capacity itself is so basically human and so fundamental to the sanctions by which social norms are maintained and transmitted to the young in *any* culture that differences among individuals within a culture would probably be as great as or greater than differences among cultures. Thus, despite the probable existence of many important, culturally conditioned differences in children's acquisition of guilt behavior, there are presumptive grounds for believing that considerable communality prevails in the general patterning of sequential development. Such communality would be a product of various uniformities regarding (1) basic conditions of the parent-child relationship, (2) minimal cultural needs for socialization of the child, and (3) certain growth trends in cognitive and personality growth from one culture to the next (Ausubel, 1955).

Normative shifts in conscience development reflect both gains in cognitive maturity and age-level changes in personality organization. Significant personality factors include alterations in dependency relationships, ego-status needs, and mode of assimilating values. Significant cognitive factors include increased capacity for perceiving social expectations and the attributes of social roles, and increased ability to discriminate, generalize, formulate abstractions, and take multiple perspectives. Growth in self-critical ability and in capacity for a less egocentric and more objective approach to values involves both cognitive and personality variables. Interaction between these two sorts of variables is responsible for most developmental changes in the basis of moral obligation and in notions of moral law, justice, and culpability; because of the many psychological components of conscience, however, it is entirely conceivable that some aspects of moral development are influenced more by one type of factor than by another. MacRae (1954), for example, found that children's disapproval of moral transgressions was positively related to measures of parental authority, whereas conceptions of equity and culpability were not. In general, cognitive capacities seem more important as prerequisites for reaching certain normative levels of moral functioning than as determinants of interindividual differences.

COGNITIVE CHANGES

The importance of cognitive factors in conscience development is seen in the capacity for making *moral judgments*. Consideration of the moral judgments (i.e., knowledge of the difference between right and wrong) of children stresses the fact that we are dealing with a conscious cognitive or intellectual process quite different from the Freudian unconscious superego (Wilson et al., 1967).

After conscience is stabilized by the development of an adequate self-critical faculty, total character (e.g., helpfulness, truthfulness) scores do not improve consistently; in fact, during this age period of 10 to 13, older children are significantly more deceitful than younger children (Hartshorne & May, 1930). Improvement is shown only in those aspects of conduct that depend on knowledge of societal moral standards and in motivational traits that are necessary for the acquisition of greater earned status (Hartshorne & May, 1930); Terman, 1925). This situation probably reflects in part the characteristic moral confusion and expediency of our culture. Children gradually learn that the triumph of honesty is not inevitable. Thus it does not follow that good deeds necessarily result from good words. To complete the picture of conscience development, therefore, we must view the impact of cognitive factors within the general framework of the child's socio-affectional relations.

True, relatively few adolescents and adults, as both Havighurst and Taba (1949) and Kohlberg (1958, 1963) have shown, acquire moral beliefs and reach moral judgments either by formulating a generalized and self-consistent code of conduct or by invoking logically universalizable and consistent ethical principles. This largely reflects the prevailing climate of moral expediency in the wider culture, the ubiquitous tendency in the adult world to solve moral conflicts by appealing to platitudinous slogans and dogmatic doctrine, and "the fact that the teaching of what is right and wrong is done with reference to isolated, concrete acts of behavior; relatively little effort is made to help them develop a coherent moral philosophy" (Havighurst & Taba, 1949). However, we can hardly conclude that, because most North American teenagers and adults, unlike European intellectuals, do not have an explicitly formulated moral *Weltanschauung,* their moral values operate on an unconscious and purely affective level. In the light of the previously cited developmental data, it seems more plausible to suppose that a subverbal set of rational principles is operative on an implicit basis. But even when an individual *can* identify the rational principles underlying his moral decisions, the influence of Freudian tradition on psychological thought is so strong that they are usually discounted. The argument here is that the simultaneous identification of motivation for a given theoretical position, belief, or course of action ipso facto either invalidates its logical basis or rationale or renders it irrelevant.

RELATED CHANGES IN EGO DEVELOPMENT

Our discussion of ego development in a moral context rests on the assumption that moral development is a subset of general ego development which can be conceptualized independently (Loevinger, 1966). The essential similarities between moral and ego-development theorists are seen in the three-stage developmental process that all embrace (Kohlberg, 1969). This three-level process in moral and ego development implies: (1) a first level at which rules and the expectations of others are external to the self; (2) a second level at which the self is identified with or equated with the rules, stereotypes, and expectations of others, especially authorities; and (3) a third level at which the self is differentiated from conventional rules (Kohlberg, 1969). In our ego development framework, level one is the presatellizng ego, level two involves early and late ego satellization, and level three is the desatellizing stage. The reason for discussing ego development here is that the *cognitive-judgmental* component of conscience development is incomplete without considering the *executive aspects* that are closely related to ego development considerations. The following discussion will therefore consider "conscience" development under our *general ego development* theory as advanced in Chapters 4 and 5.

In the *presatellizing stage,* conscience for the most part involves little more than the development of inhibitory control on the basis of learning to anticipate and avoid punishment. Previous experience with a given type of unacceptable behavior leads the child to expect pain, deprivation, isolation, or disapproval if such behavior is repeated, and leads to feelings of insecurity in contemplating it. Inhibition of such behavior, therefore, is rewarding since it reduces insecurity. During this stage, children obey prohibitory commands but do not consistently honor unenforced positive requests. Such conduct is devoid of any moral implications since it only indicates submission to authority rather than genuine acceptance of it. Cognitively, the presatellizing period roughly corresponds to Piaget's egocentric stage and Kohlberg's premoral level. Thus consciousness of rules in terms of obligation has yet to be developed, and the primary motivating force is fear of punishment. Contrary to Piaget's interpretation, our own position agrees with Kohlberg's (1964) view that it is fear of punishment rather than respect for the rules of adults which is the primary motivating force at this stage. The premoral level of "punishment and obedience orientation" and early precursors of "naive instrumental hedonism," lead to a somewhat autistic definition of values in terms of private needs (Kohlberg, 1969).

During the *early satellizing stage,* the child acknowledges her or his dependence upon parents for volitional direction and decides to accept a satellizing role in relation to them, thereby acquiring gradually a need to assimilate their values. Acceptance of parental standards of rightness and wrongness depends upon this satellizing relationship to parents (Lerner, 1937; Piaget, 1932), and is facilitated by prestige suggestion and by the parent's altruistic role. But acceptance of these values does not obligate the child—in the absence of a still undeveloped sense of moral responsibility—to regulate her or his own behavior accordingly (Ausubel, 1955). Hitting, for example, is perceived as "bad" when *other* persons do it but not when gratification of the child's *own* aggressive impulses are involved (Fite, 1940).

Behavior can first be regarded as manifesting moral properties when a sense of obligation is acquired. The need to retain derived status makes the child acquiesce to the proposition that disobedience is wrong, disloyal, and hurtful to his or her parents. At this point, guilt reactions become possible, and the child becomes motivated to conform to parental standards in order to avoid the negative self-evaluation, anxiety, and remorse associated with guilt. This development takes place in children who are accepted and intrinsically valued. Parents of delinquents are typically less accepting, affectionate, and solicitous than parents of nondelinquents (Kohlberg, 1964). Moral identification is facilitated in a democratic home atmosphere by firm, consistent, and love-oriented discipline (Hoffman, 1963). In general, strength of guilt feelings in adults tends to be correlated with love-oriented techniques of punishment (Hoffman, 1963; Kohlberg, 1964).

Early satellization corresponds to the latter phases of Piagetian "egocentrism" or to the beginning of the autonomous stage. Correspondingly, the "naive hedonistic orientation" (Kohlberg, 1969) involves sufficient reciprocity in interpersonal relations to foster the early development of guilt reactions. With this development there is a greater, but by no means overwhelming, probability that there will be greater consistency between moral judgments (i.e., legislation) and moral action (i.e., execution). Thus the development of feelings of moral obligation is a gradual process. It is not only hampered by negativistic trends, but also by the slow growth of self-critical abilities and of the ability to generalize principles of right and wrong beyond specific situations. It does not arise spontaneously but, rather under the pressure of the parents' new authority role and training demands. Furthermore, it is reinforced by the parents' physical presence and prestige suggestion, by the continued application of external sanctions (reward and punishment as well as threat and ridicule), by the withdrawal of love and approval, and by the child's continued dependence on a parent for physical survival. The early stages of satellizing conscience represent a compromise between aggressive negativism and an unstable sense of moral responsibility. The preschool child strenuously attempts to rationalize his misdeeds by attributing them to accident, forgetting, real or imaginary playmates, sensory deficiency, involuntary movements, and misunderstanding.

The *late satellizing stage* is marked by the completion of the internalization and assimilation of parental values. Stabilization of the sense of moral obligation occurs primarily as a result of gains in self-critical ability. Once the child is able to appraise self and situation realistically enough to accept the dependent biosocial status that is inevitably hers or his in any culture, the child can finally acknowledge parental authority as unquestionably and unconditionally valid. Improved self-critical ability also enables the child to perceive his or her own wrongdoing in the absence of external coercive agents. Hereafter the child appears concerned with the spirit as well as the letter of moral duty, and threats of reprisal for punishment are less frequently uttered (Piaget, 1932). Now attuned to conventional moral roles and to the anticipation of praise or blame related to these roles, the child begins to operate as a controlling force on conduct. At first this role-taking ability is mainly based on natural and familial types of affection and sympathy, but then, it yields to a wider social radius where *justice* is based on regard for the rights and expectations of both rule-enforcers and rule-obeyers (Kohlberg, 1963a). Regard for rules is based on some form of organized social order (Kohlberg, 1968).

In addition to social inexperience, both a satellizing orientation to value assimilation and a cognitive inability to appreciate the functional basis of moral principles keep the child's conscience during the middle years somewhat absolutistic and heavily dependent on the conventional wisdom of older family members and authorities in the community (Kohlberg, 1964).

The *desatellizing stage* is marked by significant changes focused on the basis of moral obligation and conceptions of moral law. During this phase, feelings of moral accountability are placed on a societal basis instead of remaining a function of parent-child relationship and are referred to more abstract principles of justice and responsibility based on relationships outside the immediate family. The beginning of the desatellizing period remains conventional and "authority maintaining" in focus, but the notion of unilateral obligation and respect for adults (Piaget, 1932) gives way to reciprocal obligations that are stressed in conventional societal institutions (Kohlberg, 1964). Changes in the heterogeneity and differentiation of peer group organization and its status functions make possible a reformulation of the concept of moral law on a more reciprocal, functional, and exploratory basis.

The above changes are instigated by modification in the parent-child relationship, shifts in the child's needs for a more earned source of status, alteration in his group experience, and maturation of his perceptual and cognitive capacities. As he begins to lose his volitional dependence upon parents and to become more concerned with acquiring earned status, his satellizing orientation to value assimilation becomes increasingly less serviceable for the satisfaction of his ego needs. Since the inherent sacredness of moral standards also depends in part upon a perception of parents as infallible and omniscient beings, it begins to break down as he enters the school and community and discovers that there are other authorities, various moral alternatives, and different versions of the truth. The more he comes into contact with the variable moral beliefs of the culture at large, the more his parents' early monopoly on moral authority is challenged, and the less axiomatic their values become.

The changing nature and organization of peer group experience also promotes developmental changes in moral behavior. A primary function of the early peer group is to provide a supplementary source of derived status; and the child accepts its authority on the same unilateral and absolutistic basis as he or she does that of the parents. Prior to the age of eight, the child also operates in small, isolated, and informally organized groups in which roles are poorly differentiated and a lack of functional division of labor exists. Later, groups become larger, less isolated, and more stable. Children experience membership in several different groups exhibiting a variety of rules, practices, and values, and begin to improvise their own rules to meet new situations. As individual roles are differentiated, the need for cooperation and mutual obligations increases. The older a child becomes, the more his or her peer group becomes a source of earned status; at the same time, the parents become less and less a source of moral authority.

However, it is mostly in heterogeneous *urban* cultures that values (during preadolescence and especially adolescence) tend to acquire a wider social base and peers tend to replace parents as interpreters and enforcers of the moral code. But neither phenomenon is indispensable for the maturational changes in moral organization that occur at this time. Repudiation of parental authority and of filial ties is *not* necessary for the acquisition of mature conceptions of moral responsibility and culpability based on intention, interpersonal needs, and reciprocal obligations. All that is required from a personality standpoint is a change in status and dependency needs and sufficient social experience to appreciate the functional basis of existing authority relationships. The later phase of desatellization, therefore, differs from its predecessor only in intensity and completeness of desatellization. The transition into adolescent society makes it possible for the child to incorporate and explore more fully the gamut of moral values leading to greater tolerance and flexibility (McCullough, 1969). In some cases, the ego has achieved sufficient maturity to allow the self to become differentiated from conventional rules (Kohlberg, 1968). This increasing differentiation is marked by moral obligations and principles that are based on contract and democratically accepted laws (Kohlberg, 1969). Hence this development brings with it the ability to entertain and resolve conflicting norms, where previously conflicting norms were ignored or misunderstood (Kohlberg, 1969).

Acting conjunctively with personality factors in bringing about desatellizing changes in moral values are the various aforementioned facets of cognitive maturation. Increased ability to generalize and think in more logical and abstract terms makes possible a more objective and integrated approach to moral issues (Ausubel, 1952; Kohlberg, 1969). Much normative change in moral conduct can similarly be attributed to the fact that with increasing age, ability to take multiple perspectives extensively, flexibly, and abstractly also increases (Feffer & Gourevitch, 1960; Feffer & Suchotliff, 1966; Flavell, 1967; Strauss, 1954). There is also an increasing facility in appreciating intentions over consequences in judgment (Breznitz & Kugelmass, 1967; Kohlberg, 1963). Finally, intellectual development, in conjunction with the decline in egocentricity and subjectivism, enhances self-critical ability, making possible both the perception of finer discrepancies between precept and conduct and the judgment of one's own moral behavior on the same basis as that of others (Ausubel, 1952; Kohlberg, 1969).

A common phenomenon met with in many adolescents especially of the ascetic and overintellectual type is a variety of moral perfectionism. In some cases it is indicative of the naivete, inexperience, and impulsiveness of adolescents; and of the initial reaction to the shock of disenchantment upon being initiated into the corruption existing in certain areas of public life formerly believed to be sacrosanct. In other cases, however, it has the same significance as exaggerated cynicism, namely, as a form of aggression against adult society, in which a strong motivational "set" exists to perceive all adult behavior in an unfavorable light. The cynical adolescent then proceeds to emulate and outdo the behavior he purports to perceive in adults, while the perfectionist in an orgy of self-righteousness sets himself up as a champion of truth and virtue against a hopelessly wicked world. Not infrequently, however, the same individual oscillates between the two reactions and manifests each alternately.

INDIVIDUAL DIFFERENCES IN MORAL DEVELOPMENT

In the foregoing sketch of age-level changes in moral development, we attempted to trace sequential stages that can presumably be found in all cultural settings. Still to be considered are the psychosocial aspects of moral development and personality and the cognitive factors that account for interindividual (idiosyncratic) differences within a culture.

Parental Variables and Personality Considerations

Our discussion thus far has not treated the effects of parental antecedents independently from ego-development theory. Before considering idiosyncratic personality differences, it would be desirable briefly to summarize the relationships between moral development and parental training conditions in order to clarify the subsequent discussion.

PARENTAL ANTECEDENTS

At present, summaries of studies exploring the relationship between moral development and parental antecedents allow few definitive conclusions (Aronfreed, 1968; Becker, 1964; Hoffman, 1963; Kohlberg, 1963, 1968). Tentative generalizations, recognizing exceptions, indicate that frequent expression of warmth and affection toward the child promotes identification with parental values (Hoffman, 1963; Lidson, 1966). Although threatening and punitive parents elicit identification in their children (Hoffman, 1963), it is found that this general approach to child rearing leads to external orientations in childrens' verbal expression and application of evaluative standards (Aronfreed, 1968). There is also evidence to indicate that physical punishment and direct power assertion of parents are conducive to a moral orientation based on fear of external detection and punishment (Hoffman, 1963). In contrast, an "internal orientation" toward compliance (e.g., appeals to the child's needs for affection and self-esteem) is seen in parents who have affectionate relationships with their children (Hoffman, 1963). Affectionate parental relationships, also, seem to be related to sympathetic behavior in children (Lenrow, 1965).

Although "love withdrawal" has been frequently cited as an important mechanism in the development of "internalized controls" (Hoffman, 1963), it now appears that the "induction" of certain cognitive constraints (e.g., explaining to the child the consequences of his actions before "love withdrawal") is also an important antecedent in developing internalized guilt and internalized moral judgment (Hoffman and Salzstein, 1967; Aronfreed, 1968; Kohlberg, 1968). At present, these tentative generalizations are subject to many reservations—a probable reflection of the fact that different theoretical accounts of moral development are at variance with one another. For example, social learning theory stresses the role of "imitation" in fostering mature moral judgments (Bandura and McDonald, 1963) whereas developmental theorists confine the phenomenon of "imitation" to very short-term, situational changes in moral orientation (Cowan, Langer and others, 1968; Crowley, 1968; Lorimer & Sullivan, 1968; Turiel, 1968). The tentative conclusions concerning parental warmth and acceptance, however, are not at variance with our ego development orientation. The evidence regarding the effects of warm-accepting parental attitudes is consistent with our previous interpretation of the relationship between these attitudes and the satellizing stage of conscience development. The absence of parental acceptance and its effect on moral development will now be discussed.

PERSONALITY CONSIDERATIONS

The non-satellizer obviously fails to undergo the various changes in conscience development associated with satellization, and similarly, the changes resulting from desatellization. His moral development is less discontinuous than that of the satellizer. During early and middle childhood, the non-satellizer continues to conform to parental standards for the same expediential reasons as during infancy; he fails to develop a sense of moral obligation in relation to a general attitude of subservience, loyalty, and need for approval and retention of derived status. Fear of deprivation and loss of succorance rather than guilt avoidance keep him in line and check the overt expression of his hostility. Moral obligations are assimilated on a selective basis only, that is, if they are perceived as leading to ego enhancement. In moral judgment the saliency of this ego-enhancemnt criterion is seen in the adoption of a naive-egoistic orientation (Kohlberg, 1964). The non-satellizer's conformity to moral rules, is therefore, based on the principle of expediency; those moral obligations that lead to the acquisition of earned status are selectively assimilated (McCullough, 1969). The non-satellizer's moral value system is thus functional and based on mutual obligations leading to ego enhancement (McCullough, 1969).

During late childhood, the non-satellizer becomes capable of internalizing moral values and obligations on the basis of an exploratory orientation. Unhampered by satellizing loyalties, he finds it easier to grasp functional concepts of moral law based on equity and reciprocal obligations. In this way he too acquires the prerequisites for a guilt-governed conscience. But the stability of moral obligations that circumvent a preliminary history of satellization is highly precarious because: (1) infantile irresponsibility has never been attenuated by strong, emotionally charged feelings of obligation toward significant figures in his interpersonal world, and (2) powerful needs for ego enhancement are often in conflict with the content and goals of ethical norms. Under these conditions, nevertheless, moral obligations are seldom repudiated outright since this would require direct and inexpedient conflict with cultural sanctions (Ausubel, 1952; Kohlberg, 1964). However, two less drastic alternatives are available: (1) evading indirectly the demands of conscience and the punishment of guilt when the needs of ego aggrandizement are too strong to be denied; and (2) buttressing conscience by the mechanism of reaction formation when moral obligations are too solidly entrenched to be circumvented.

Moral obligation can be evaded indirectly either (a) by selectively inhibiting the self-critical faculty so that, when expedient, even glaring discrepancies between precept and practice cannot be perceived, or (b) by claiming superior status so that one is *above* the law for *ordinary* people. Reaction formation rigidly suppresses motives that are at variance with internalized moral obligations and substitutes more acceptable motives in their place. Thus, many loopholes for surreptitious circumvention are present. Antisocial trends for example can often be expressed under the guise of lofty ideals. At the very best, the moral behavior of the non-satellizer becomes unspontaneous, stereotyped, and unduly circumscribed. Awareness of the underlying strength of unacceptable motives encourages the erection of exaggerated defenses.

The overvalued child, who has never felt much pressure to conform to parental standards, frequently regards himself as exempt from ordinary moral obligations. The rejected child, on the other hand, is not likely to claim such unique exemptions since he has been subjected to rigorous discipline. In most instances he will acquire a strong rational conscience buttressed by reaction formation that permits occasional moral lapses through impairment of the self-critical faculty. However, the concomitance of harsh rejection by parents, of a possible doubling of the Y-chromosome, and of extreme self-assertiveness in the child may result in a total repudiation of the entire fabric of parental moral values. In such a case, the resulting personality structure and correlated type of delinquency is known as aggressive, antisocial psychopathy. When rejection is expressed in parental neglect and self-love, the child displaces the hostility he feels for his parents onto others. Such behavior is reinforced by the parents' tendency to condone it as long as they themselves are not disturbed (Bandura & Walters, 1963a). On the positive side, the rejected child possesses a latent capacity for forming satellizing-like relationships that will enable him or her to experience the type of guilt feelings characteristic of satellizing children.

Among *satellizers*, aberrations in conscience development are generally less severe. The more serious problem is presented by the underdominated child who has great difficulty acquiring a sense of moral obligation. To begin with, he is not required to inhibit hedonistic motivations or to curb aggressive impulses. The limits of unacceptable behavior are poorly defined and inadequately or inconsistently enforced (Hunt & Hardt, 1965). Second, like the overvalued child, he is sometimes treated as a specially privileged person exempt from usual responsibilities toward others, and is not encouraged to develop a realistic self-critical faculty. Capricious and inconsistent parental discipline is associated with lack of self-discipline in children (Hunt & Hardt, 1965; Sanford et al., 1943) and is more characteristic of delinquents than of non-delinquents (Glueck & Glueck, 1950; Hunt & Hardt, 1965; Kohlberg, 1964). Fortunately the motivation for immoral behavior is more likely to lie in hedonistic self-indulgence than in unprincipled ego aggrandizement at the expense of others. The chief difficulty in moral development for overprotected and overdominated children, on the other hand, lies in transferring feelings of moral obligation from parents to society and in arriving at independent value judgments. Even when delinquent behavior is present, self-critical capacity and guilt are substantially correlated with more mature moral judgment levels (Kohlberg, 1968; Ruma & Mosher, 1967). This situation has less serious consequences if the parents are alive and do not subscribe to antisocial attitudes. However, if the parents are moral deviants, uncritical loyalty on the part of the child can lead to delinquent behavior; whereas the death or removal of the parents can create a vacuum in moral responsibility.

Ascendance and viscerotonia are probably important temperamental variables influencing the course of conscience development. The more self-assertive a child is the more likely he will be to resist the imposition of parental standards upon his behavior. Similarly, the greater his need for hedonistic satisfactions, the more reluctant he will be to accept the obligation of conforming to rules aimed at minimizing these satisfactions. Dishonest children tend to be impulsive, emotionally unstable, and suggestible (Hartshorne & May, 1930; Slaght, 1928). Delinquents may also be more prone, for temperamental reasons, to utilize aggression as a defense or status-gaining mechanism (Healey and Bronner, 1936). In contrast to non-delinquents, they have been described as more restless, active, impulsive, and danger-loving (Glueck & Glueck, 1950; Healey & Bronner, 1936; Hunt & Hardt, 1965; Kohlberg, 1968).

8
Moral Development and Delinquency

CULTURAL FACTORS INFLUENCING MORAL DEVELOPMENT

Cultural and social-class variables affect the development of conscience and account for intercultural differences (or intracultural uniformities) by influencing: (1) the particular moral values that are assimilated and their mode of transmission; (2) the kinds of internal and external sanctions that are imposed; and (3) the ways in which guilt feelings are instigated and expressed. The effects of cultural and social-class types of variables are exceedingly pervasive but differ in that individuals are typically influenced by the norms of other social classes but only rarely by the standards of other cultures.

We have already observed that differential cultural environment exerts a profound influence on various aspects of ego development. Hence, it would certainly be legitimate to inquire to what extent the development of conscience is

> influenced by the value systems of the social groups to which the individual belongs, or to which he relates himself positively or negatively. The values held by the family, by the dominant groups and institutions in the community, and by persons in positions of authority and high status constitute the "moral climate" in which a young person grows up. These groups and persons are in a position to punish undesirable conduct and reward desirable conduct, and their expectations have much to do with the standards of behavior developed by the individual. (Havighurst & Taba, 1949)

A general problem arises in the impact of culture on conscience development when serious descrepancies or inconsistencies prevail between the professed (official) moral ideology and the ideology that is really believed and actually practiced. This situation is illustrated in our culture by the formal endorsement of humility, kindliness, helpfulness, and fair play, and the simultaneous overvaluation of aggressiveness, prestige, and success at any price. It is symptomatic that the rate of social and economic change has far outstripped its ideological substrate and that widespread moral disintegration and confusion have ensued. In the struggle for material success, concern for moral values and traditional moral restraints are being swept aside. The form rather than the content and intention of behavior is becoming the chief criterion of moral judgment in our society. What it means for a child to grow up in such a moral climate is something that still requires considerable investigation. We can only predict on logical and historical grounds that it will encourage expediential lack of principle and cynical acceptance of moral depravity. We can expect children to grow up hypocritical, deceitful, unconcerned with human values and the welfare of others, indifferent to injustice, and sold on the principle of getting the most out of people and valuing them solely on the basis of their market price.

At the very best this situation leads to ethical confusion and inconsistency and to a potentially heavy burden of guilt. However, because of the prestige suggestion inherent in the operation of social norms, and because of extremely high tolerance for moral ambiguity, inconsistent values may be assimilated in such a way that their incompatibility is never perceived. It is presumed by the perceiver that inconsistency in cultural values is inconceivable; hence, an advance "set" exists to perceive such values as consistent.

Cross-Cultural Differences

The findings of cross-cultural research in moral development are fraught with many of the methodological and conceptual difficulties characteristic of this type of research. Different kinship patterns, moral beliefs, moral attitudes, etc., make it exceedingly difficult to apply a common research instrument when making cross-cultural comparisons. The few studies that have been attempted, however, give us some indication of the differential impact of different socialization practices and expectancies on moral development. Although there is some evidence that the cognitive-evaluative stages of moral orientation are universal developmental processes common to all cultures (Kohlberg, 1968,), (e.g., stage sequences appear to be the same in the cultures of Taiwan, Mexico, Turkey, and the United States), both cognitive and social factors may inhibit the achievement of the highest stages in certain cultures. However, the fact that some cultures do not reach these stages does not discredit the hypothesis of a universal developmental process.

The finding that more abstract levels of moral judgment appear earlier in some cultures than in others is indicative of the effects of their different socialization and educational practices (Aronfreed, 1968). For example, Swiss children are slower in moving from "moral realism" to "moral subjectivism" than are British children (Harrower, 1935). Similar trends are found when Swiss children are compared with American children (Boehm, 1966). American children emphasize intention over consequences earlier than do Swiss children (Boehm, 1957), and also take advice from peers in preference to parents at a significantly earlier age than do their Swiss counterparts (Boehm, 1963). On the other hand, Lebanese children demonstrate moral realism much later than do Swiss children (Najarian-Svajian, 1966). These differences appear to be a result of differential timing of desatelliza- tion within these cultures. The fact that American children accept peer advice earlier (Boehm, 1963) is indicative of the possibility that American children are encouraged to desatellize sooner than are European children. This is clearly seen when the socialization practices of Russian and American families are compared (Bronfenbrenner, 1968). Whereas American children are subjected to socializa- tion procedures that encourage independence (i.e., desatellization) from parents, Russian children show greater conformity and obedience to adults, and parents discourage independence (i.e., desatellization). At present, these findings are only grossly indicative of the effects of differential socialization on the child's moral development. Concomitantly, one can also note socialization differences in moral development within a particular culture when differences of social class are considered.

Social-Class Differences

General studies and reviews have reported positive relationships between lower social-class status in children and both more absolutistic, rigid, and au- thoritarian conceptions of moral law (Boehm, 1962, 1966; Bronfenbrenner, 1962a; Dolger & Ginandes, 1946; Durkin 1959; Harrower, 1935; Lerner, 1937b; Kohlberg, 1963, 1968; MacRae, 1954) and more primitive and retaliatory notions of discipline. Middle-class children, on the other hand, react to their own trans- gressions with more self-criticism than do their lower-class counterparts (Aron- freed, 1968). This situation is undoubtedly reflective, in part, of the authoritarian lower-class parent-child relationship and of inconsistent training in the "official" moral ideology; since the latter is accepted only half heartedly and is inconsistently enforced, it must be adhered to rigidly if it is to be maintained at all. The effects of inconsistency are less compelling in middle-class families where there appears to be greater homogeneity of values than in lower-class families (Rosen, 1964). Middle-class parents behave in ways that tend to produce an internal governor in their children and also use a verbal medium of discipline and explicit withdrawal of affection (Aronfreed, 1968). Moreover, lower-class parents exercise less im- mediate control over their children's activities, and seem to give their attention primarily to overt manifestations of transgression (Aronfreed, 1968). The more direct kind of punishment utilized in lower-class families seems to sensitize children to the external consequences of transgression (Aronfreed, 1968).

Middle-class children anticipate assuming responsibilities earlier than do lower-class children (Zurich, 1963), but this may be more reflective of social stratification than of parental upbringing. The fact is that the lower-class child does not and cannot feel as much of a sense of power in, and responsibility for, the institutions of government and economy as does the middle-class child (Kohlberg, 1968). This lack of participation generates a lesser disposition to view these institutions from a generalized, flexible, and organized perspective based on various roles as vantage points, that is, law and government are perceived quite differently by the child if he feels a sense of potential participation in the social order than if he does not (Kohlberg, 1968).

Social-class differences with respect to certain aspects of moral development appear to have been diminishing over the past 20 years (Bronfenbrenner, 1962a). In some cognitive aspects of conscience development, as a matter of fact, recently obtained differences are negligible (Boehm & Nass, 1962). This phenomenon may reflect the diminution of class differences, over this period of time, in child-rearing practices.

Within a given social-class environment, not only are there distinctive educational and vocational aspirations and accepted forms of social participation for adolescents, but also characteristic moral values relating to sex, aggression, honesty, community responsibility, thrift, loyalty, etc. (Havighurst & Taba, 1949). These value systems parallel for the most part the value systems espoused by the adult members of the subculture despite the refractoriness of adolescents to adult direction; the peer culture takes over the task of enforcing this conformity since adolescents can accept its authority without resentment.

This differentiation of moral value systems on the basis of social class does not mean that complete homogeneity prevails within a given class. Actually, considerable communication and interaction occur, with the lines of influence generally proceeding in a downward direction (except in more recent years). Where a single institution such as the high school becomes the common meeting ground of a number of subcultural groups, the moral standards of the resulting adolescent peer society reflect the morality of the middle-class that controls it. Adolescents from other social-class backgrounds must either adapt to these standards or choose to remain on the periphery of social acceptance. In the light of these considerations, therefore, the proposition that a given individual must *inevitably* assimilate the particular values of his own social class is absurd, although it is true that this phenomenon is facilitated by the presence of segregation and "disorganized areas" in large urban centers (Havighurst & Taba, 1949). Equally implausible, on the other hand, is the notion advanced in some quarters that modern forms of communication have *completely* broken down class differences in moral beliefs and behavior.

It is also necessary to distinguish between official and actual moral ideologies.

The differences in moral values among the various social classes are probably greater in practice than in words. People all up and down the social scale in Prairie City tend to agree verbally with an official moral ideology, from which their actual moral behavior departs in various ways. (Havighurst & Taba, 1949)

Shame and Guilt

Several cultural anthropologists have advanced the paradoxically ethnocentric view that guilt is not universally present or prominent as a sanction in mediating and sustaining the culture (Benedict, 1946; Leighton & Kluckhohn, 1947; Mead, 1950). They contend that in some cultures sensitivity to shame largely takes the place that remorse and self-punishment have in preventing antisocial conduct in Western civilization (Leighton & Kluckhohn, 1947). Instead of acknowledging that guilt behavior can occur whenever and wherever an individual internalizes moral obligations and can exercise sufficient self-critical ability to perceive his own wrongdoing, they lay down three indispensable criteria for the development of guilt behavior. First, the child must accept the parent as omniscient and as the source of all moral authority. Second, genuine guilt feelings can only exist when shame and other external sanctions are not operative. Third, guilt must be characterized by conviction of sin and need for atonement. Behavior that does not conform to these requirements is categorized as shame.

If we accepted the first criterion, there could be no guilt behavior in the numerous cultures in which children do not regard parents as omniscient and in which the authority for moral sanctions is derived laterally or from the group as a whole (De Vos, 1960). Actual examination of the moral behavior of children and adults in such cultures (e.g., Navaho) does not, however confirm this proposition (Ausubel, 1955; Aronfreed, 1968). The same criterion would also deny the observed occurrence of guilt (1) among adolescents and adults in our own culture who accept the peer group and society (rather than parents) as the source of moral authority and (2) among non-satellizers, who never accept the moral authority of parents but who interiorize moral obligations nevertheless on the basis of abstract principles of equity (Ausubel, 1955).

The second criterion ignores the fact (1) that guilt (a negative self-judgment for violating moral obligations) is invariably accompanied by shame (a self-deprecatory reaction to the actual or presumed judgments of others), and (2) that at all stages of development, internal sanctions are reinforced by external sanctions. Hence, although shame and guilt are distinguishable from each other, they are neither dichotomous nor mutually exclusive (Aronfreed, 1968; Ausubel, 1955)

The third criterion is peculiarly specific to certain religious doctrines and beliefs about the original nature of man that prevail in cultures adhering to the Judeo-Christian tradition, and hardly applies to peoples like the Japanese who nevertheless show striking evidences of both guilt and shame in their moral behavior (Ausubel, 1955).

Religious Differences

Because religion is inextricably bound up with other environmental factors, it is difficult to isolate its impact on the moral development of children. Church membership and religious observance are intimately related to social-class status and affect the social standing and character reputation of the child and his family (Havighurst & Taba, 1949). It is also virtually impossible to separate religious from moral values in most cultures. Even if a child receives no *formal* religious instruction, he is still influenced indirectly by religious precepts in his home training, secular schooling, peer group experience, and exposure to mass media. Partly for this reason and partly because of problems of measurement, it is extremely difficult to assess the effect of religion on childrens' moral conduct and development. If we attempt to use extent of religious instruction or observance as our measure of the independent variable in studying this relationship, this difficulty becomes immediately apparent. For some children religious observance is perfunctory, and religious doctrine is almost completely divorced from every-day life; for other children religion is an important consideration in determining moral choice and regulating interpersonal relationships. However, in American society, as compared to Turkish society, there appears to be remarkable little use of religious precepts in children's moral judgments (Kohlberg, 1967). At the same time, the development of moral reasoning appears to be much the same in many different religious communities (e.g., Protestants, Catholics, Moslems and Buddhists), (Kohlberg, 1967).

Religious orientation may affect the level of moral judgment through certain beliefs or practices. Thus, Catholic and Jewish parochial school children respond to *intentions* (i.e., to distinguish between motivation of and results of actions) earlier and to a greater degree than do public school children (Boehm, 1966). In certain judgmental situations, moreover, Jewish and Catholic children can be distinguished from one another (Boehm, 1966). For example, Catholic preschool children respond at a lower level of moral judgment in the situation where a child has hurt a peer accidentally (i.e., Jewish children are more concerned with the victim's feelings whereas Catholic children are more concerned with the guilt of the accidental offender) (Boehm, 1966). These differences probably reflect differ-ent religious emphases regarding moral responsibility, since specific attendance at Sunday school appears to have a negligible effect on the child's moral reasoning (Whiteman & Kosier, 1964).

The behavioral correlates of religious observance present an equally complex picture. Hartshorne and May's finding (1930) that the child who attends Sunday school is only very slightly more honest and helpful than children who do not attend has yet to be challenged (Kohlberg, 1964). Cross-national comparisons suggest conclusions similar to the above (Kohlberg, 1967). As Kohlberg (1967) points out:

> Theft, deceit, and juvenile delinquency are low in some atheistic societies (Soviet Russia, Israeli atheistic *kibbutzim*) as well as in some Buddist and

Christian societies, while some strongly religious nations have high rates of dishonesty (Islamic Middle Eastern nations, Italy, Mexico, etc.). Although we should not conclude from these and other findings that there is no relation between religious experience and moral character, we can conclude that religion is not a necessary or highly important condition for the development of moral judgment and conduct. (p. 181)

This conclusion should be tempered by the fact that in general, the present accumulation of evidence only tells us that religious *observance* is not highly correlated with moral conduct—not that religious belief and moral behavior are intrinsically unrelated. In fact, just the opposite is indicated by the finding that Mennonite children ascribe more religious values to life situations and more moral authority to the church than do non-Mennonite children (Kalhorn, 1944), and by the finding that Lutheran adolescents in a particularly closely-knit community have high reputations for honesty and reliability despite relatively low social status (Havighurst & Taba, 1949).

Peer Group

The child's peer group, apart from the wider adult culture, exerts a significant influence on his moral development. In some ways, it is the child's first introduction to the wider social groupings that exist outside of the family (Crane, 1958). It is to be expected that peer influences will have a differential impact within the context of different cultures. Thus in Russia the *peer group* functions as an agency of control that reinforces parental values, whereas in the United States it tends, somewhat, to undermine parental control (Bronfenbrenner, 1962b, 1968). According to Piaget's theory, the peer group provides a context in which the child can learn the rules of the game, principles of equity, and self-subordination to group goals based on mutual respect and reciprocity (Piaget, 1932, 1951). Evidence indicates that children with higher sociometric status are more autonomous in moral maturity scores (Kohlberg, 1964, 1970). The type of participation in the peer group may also be an important factor since children who are given an opportunity to be rule carriers in a game appear to have more positive attitudes toward the rules of conduct involved in the game (Borishevsky, 1965). This supports the thesis that greater social participation in and control over institutions leads to greater moral maturity (Kohlberg, 1964).

Specific types of peer participation appear to have different effects. Children who are members of character-building clubs (e.g., boy scouts) surpass non-club members in such traits as cooperativeness; however, in regard to general traits, such as honesty and judgmental maturity, which are less dependent on structured group experience, no significant difference prevails (Hartshorne & May et al., 1930; Whiteman & Kosier, 1964). This evidence supports the logical inference that the peer group does not constitute in itself an important source of moral values during childhood. Its values tend to mirror those held by significant adults (parents, teachers, clergy, etc.) in the subculture in which it is embedded. The influence of the peer group is more important in providing a *situational climate* that affects the child's inhibitory control in *particular* instances in which relevant moral obligations are not thoroughly interiorized. Social stratification within some cultures affords the peer group in childhood varying degrees of influence. Thus, moral values are more peer-oriented for kibbutz children than for parent-raised children (Kohlberg, 1964); behaviorally this appears to lead to more confession for transgressions in kibbutz children (Luria et al., 1963). In our own culture, the correlation of .23 between "best friends" on deception scores increases to .66 when they are members of the same classroom and can influence each other's behavior more directly (Hartshorne & May et al., 1930). Significant differences between different classes in the same school and between "progressive" and traditional schools also point to the influence of group morale (Ausubel, 1951; Hartstone & May et al., 1930). Lower-class children become more independent of adults and more dependent on peers at earlier ages than do middle-class children (Ausubel and Ausubel, 1962; Boehm, 1962, 1966). This situational influence may be especially important in the instigation of delinquent activity. Bolstered by group suggestion and moral sanction the individual child will sometimes participate in aggressive antisocial behavior that he would never think of doing on his own. In such participation he also responds to implied threats of ostracism and to genuine feelings of loyalty to either intimate associates or to the groups as a whole. Hence, most juvenile delinquency is usually committed by groups of children rather than by individuals (Short, 1966).

Mass Media

Despite their unofficial status in our culture, the various mass media probably exert more influence on moral development than do some of the socializing agencies that have been more traditionally charged with this responsibility. The efficacy of these media in this regard can be attributed to the fact that, in addition to presenting a more dramatic version of life to children, they are also not bound by reality restraints. Because they provide unmatched opportunities for vicarious ego enhancement and satellizing hero worship, they may influence the kinds of values that children interiorize, affect the inhibitory potential of moral obligations, and shape the development of guilt feelings.

The first type of effect is illustrated by the manipulation of children's ethical standards through the showing of selected motion pictures (Jones, 1936; Maccoby, 1964; Thurstone, 1931). For example, studies of the induction of changes in both favorable and unfavorable attitudes toward certain groups have been summarized in a recent review (Maccoby, 1964). In addition, it was found that children who spend more time with the mass media are more stereotyped in their thinking (Maccoby, 1964).

The second type of effect is illustrated by scattered findings that movies and cartoons (Bandura, Ross & Ross, 1961; Blumer & Hauser, 1934; Lovaas, 1961; Mussen & Rutherford, 1961), crime magazines (Healy & Bronner, 1936; Maccoby, 1964), and comic books (Hoult, 1949; Maccoby, 1964) may be contributory factors in causing aggression and juvenile delinquency. By suggesting that cleverly executed wrongdoing may go unpunished, stories of successful aggression may release inhibitory restraints of conscience without necessarily affecting moral values or associated guilt feelings (Brodbeck, 1955; Maccoby, 1964). Other relevant factors in the influence of mass media on delinquency are (1) identification with glamorous or prestigeful figures who portray violence and ruthlessness in a laudable light (Maccoby, 1964), and (2) the suggestive presentation of detailed information necessary for the execution of criminal acts (Maccoby, 1964). In opposition to this line of reasoning, it has been argued that mass media do not create but only release delinquent and aggressive trends and that they also provide a harmless outlet in fantasy for aggressive tendencies that might otherwise be expressed in real life (Maccoby, 1964). In most instances, futhermore, right is pictured as triumphant in the end, even though it is frequently associated with violence in the hero (Maccoby, 1964). Nevertheless, it is conceivable that, depending on the way themes of violence are handled and on the particular circumstances and individuals involved, mass media may have either an inhibitory or facilitating effect on delinquent behavior (Maccoby, 1964). The present contribution of the mass media, however, seems slanted toward the darker aspects of human nature with little exploration into its creative potentialities (Brodbeck, 1962).

OTHER ASPECTS OF MORAL DEVELOPMENT

Consistency and Generality of Moral Conduct

This controversial issue has already been considered at great length in a more general theoretical context. This specific issue related to moral development centers around the question of whether there is sufficient consistency and generality of moral conduct in a variety of behavioral situations to justify a construct of moral character. Psychological studies have in general interpreted the notion of moral character to mean the sum total of a set of virtues (Kohlberg, 1964, 1968). Character traits or virtues are those personality traits that are subject to the moral sanctions of society (Kohlberg, 1964). The early studies of character development identified such traits as honesty, service, and self-control as the prominent virtues (Hartshorne & May, 1930). The focus on "actions" over "words" (e.g., judgments) has been the general approach that psychologists have employed when assessing the presence of "moral character" (Kohlberg, 1964). Thus the measurement of the character trait of "honesty" was accomplished by cumulating occurrences of obedience to rules in situations where cheating or stealing could be accomplished without apparent detection (Hartshorne & May, 1930). The presence of the character trait *honesty* would be indicated if there was high intersituational consistency and generality across temptation situations.

The earlier findings of Hartshorne, May and others (1930), however, revealed little intersituational consistency and generality across situations for any of the character traits assessed (e.g., honesty, service, etc.). These initial findings led to the pessimistic conclusions that there are no such things as stable character traits, and that consistency of behavior from one situation to another is due to similarities in the situations and not to consistent personality traits in people (Hartshorne & May, 1930). At present, the evidence warrants the tentative conclusion that although many factors indigenous to personality organization make moral conduct unusually susceptible to the influence of situational variables, much of the apparent lack of generality is a function of such measurement difficulties as variability in ego involvement, different phenotypic expressions of the same genotypic tendency, and masking effects of normative uniformities on individual differences. In support of this view is (1) evidence showing the close relationship between measurement of ego involvement and scores on objective measures of character and personality (see Kohlberg, 1964, 1968); (2) the tendency for the generality coefficients of moral traits to be higher in older children and adolescents than in young children (Burton, 1963; Hartshorne & May, 1930; Havighurst & Taba, 1949); and (3) evidence from several studies of moral conduct in children that show greater generality of function than was reported by Hartshorne and May (Burton, 1963).

> These findings suggest a core of truth to common-sense notions of general good character, and provide some justification for adding up measures of various aspects of moral conduct into a total assessment of moral character. Common sense seems to exaggerate this consistency, however. (Kohlberg, 1964, p. 387)

The Problem of Moral Accountability*

When Oscar Wilde wrote his famous "Ballad of Reading Gaol," decrying any man's right to pass moral judgment on the actions of his fellowman, little did

*Recognition of the phenomenological reality of moral accountability and guilt does not, of course, rule out the possibility of utilizing these psychological phenomena for therapeutic or re-educative purposes. We cannot emphasize too strongly, however, that this position does not endorse but stands in opposition to the current tendency in criminological thought to dichotomize the "disease" vs. "moral accountability" approaches to the causation of delinquency and the "punitive" vs. "rehabilitative" approaches to its treatment. In other words, we would insist that moral accountability enjoys an empirically verifiable phenomenological status apart from and in addition to its potential use in the re-educative process; and that acceptance of the need for re-education in the reorientation of moral behavior does not necessarily imply that the cause of immoral conduct lies solely in faulty education and that judgment of such conduct must therefore be divorced from all considerations of moral accountability.

he realize that his position would become so widely accepted only a half century later by social scientists and philosophers concerned with human behavior. The credo of the modern social scientist is predominantly deterministic. It repudiates the notion of free will as reactionary and unscientific, and it regards the practice of passing moral judgment as abhorrent, unpsychological, and tinged with the presumption of godlike omniscience. The moral character of an individual is presumed to be shaped by forces beyond his control, and therefore, immune from any judgmental process with ethical implications. Immoral behavior is held to be no different from any other kind of undesirable behavior. It can only be understood psychologically as a type of adjustment mechanism. Caroline Zachry's appraisal (1944) of delinquency a generation ago, for example, is thoroughly representative of current non-legal professional opinion.

> To isolate certain forms of emotional disturbance and to label them with a term of opprobrium is both scientifically inaccurate and inimical to the interests of youth. It presupposes an attitude of sitting in moral judgment, of attaching blame for behavior which should be considered as a symptom of disturbance.

Our main quarrel with determinism, however, rests on a more general premise. The psychologist is not required to accept the view that the will is not an independent force but merely the executioner of the dominant motive impinging upon the behavioral field—that "free will" is an illusion that confounds awareness of the outcome of the struggle between conflicting forces with the power to determine the outcome. In our study of the development of conscience, we have traced the gradual evolution of a generalized sense of moral obligation. In association with its executive arm of inhibitory self-control, this feeling of obligation constitutes a more or less consistent system of behavior with considerable generality of function that is implicated in every moral decision. The outcome of the latter is not merely a reflection of the relative strengths of a given moral value and its opposing motive but also of the strength of the generalized sense of obligation to abide by *all* moral values and the vigor of its associated volitional counterpart.

The authors are aware of the fact that a developmental theory of conscience not only provides a basis for ethical conduct and moral accountability, but also establishes a basis in the past for immoral behavior which *was* beyond the individual's control at the time that it impinged on his ethical development. This fact is undeniable and is frequently used as an argument for determinism. In the past history of every individual can be found events to explain a particular failure to behave morally in certain situations and enable one to predict how that person will act in the future. The possibility of explaining and predicting an individual's moral lapses on the basis of his or her developmental history, however, bears no relevance to the problem of moral accountability, which requires a judgment with respect to the *present* situation. Regardless of events that once transpired beyond a person's control, if that person can now recognize a moral obligation and is physically and psychologically capable of exercising inhibitory control, he or she is accountable for any misdeed committed. If, in addition, a developmental explanation is available for such a misdeed, it provides a nice demonstration of the fact that behavior, like all events in nature, has causal antecedents (i.e., is deterministic). But what has this to do with moral accountability? Acceptance of behavioral determinism does not oblige one to repudiate the doctrine of responsibility for moral behavior.

If this hypothesis is correct, moral culpability exists whenever the possibility of exercising inhibitory control is present in an ethical problem but nevertheless fails to be exercised. If motives cannot be effectively combatted by volitional restraint because of overpowering emotion, the question of accountability obviously becomes more complicated. The defense of "uncontrollable impulse" generally means that suppression was originally possible but was surrendered to indulgence under special extenuating circumstances. In such cases, culpability is present although undoubtedly in lesser degree than in instances where more deliberate choice was possible. However, lack of awareness of the "true" motives for a misdeed is no defense so long as moral restraint can be exercised. That a murderer fails to appreciate that his hostility is a reaction against parental rejection no more absolves him of responsibility for his crime than the historical fact of parental rejection itself, although our knowledge of the latter fact makes his action more comprehensible.

It is the authors' firm contention that the vast majority of immoral and delinquent acts are committed under conditions where there is clear awareness of a moral issue and reasonable opportunity for exercising inhibitory control in conformity with the perceived direction of moral duty. For example, in instances of criminal behavior committed by a non-satellizer who consciously places himself above the law, or is intellectually dishonest in failing to perceive the incompatibility of his behavior with his professed ethical code, the decision regarding culpability should be unequivocal.

The determination of moral culpability is obviously a highly intricate process requiring considerable psychological analysis. All individuals cannot be judged by the same yardstick. For example, expediency becomes a less legitimate standard of behavior as the degree of freedom from dependency increases. Also, considerations of expediency should become less influential to an individual when interpersonal relationships are based on human values than when relationships are predicated upon a person's value as a commodity to be bought and sold in the marketplace. Thus, what ostensibly appears to be a double moral standard may, when examined genotypically, turn out to be a highly consistent ethical code of behavior.

The condemnatory aspects of moral judgment to which many social scientists object so violently are inescapable if such judgment is to have any real moral significance. And, condemnation inevitably implies punishment. It need not be assumed, however, that punishment precludes rehabilitative, preventative, or therapeutic efforts if such are indicated, or that it must necessarily be administered in a spirit of vindictiveness. As long as culpability is recognized, punishment is a necessary and relevant aspect of society's reaction to delinquency, providing it is not employed to the exclusion of such principles as restitution and re-education.

If therapy alone is instituted, culpable immoral behavior cannot then be distinguishable in any way from other behavior disorders. The notion of liability to punishment following misbehavior is more than a specific product of certain forms of cultural organization. It is an inevitable component of an individual's own concept of moral value and obligation; and it lies at the root of his or her conscience formation. As a guilt-reducing mechanism, its therapeutic value should also not be minimized.

The threat of social punishment, therefore, is an important regulatory mechanism in the development of conscience. It thus serves a self-protective function in perpetuating the moral standards of a given social order. After conscience is acquired, of course, it is no longer the main deterrent for misbehavior but does continue to restrain impulsive acts of "testing the limits." In underdominated satellizers, and non-satellizers, however, it constitutes one of the chief considerations governing the inhibition of antisocial behavior throughout the entire life span of such individuals.

With respect to society's right to condemn and punish (without being accused of taking over godlike prerogatives), we must side with the judiciary and against Oscar Wilde and the prevailing opinion of social scientists. The function of holding individuals accountable for their behavior is not only a logical extension of the belief in an objectively valid system of ethics, but is also a legitimate device that society needs to protect its members from predatory individuals. The latter justification is also applicable to the incarceration of both culpable individuals who are dangerous and incorrigible, and non-culpable persons whose freedom would constitute a menace to public safety.

However, it is just as unreasonable to hold an individual responsible for symtoms of behavior disorder as to deem him accountable for symptoms of physical illness. A person is no more culpable for inability to cope with socio-psychological stress than for inability to resist the spread of infectious organisms. In those instances where warranted guilt feelings *do* contribute to personality disorder, the patient is accountable for the misdeeds underlying his or her guilt, but is hardly responsible for the symptoms brought on by the guilt feelings, or for unlawful acts committed while ill. Acknowledgement of guilt may be therapeutically beneficial under these circumstances, but punishment for the original misconduct should obviously be deferred until after recovery.

Lastly, even if it were true that all personality disorder is a reflection of sin (Mowrer, 1960) and that people are accountable for their behavioral symptoms, it would still be unnecessary to deny that these symptoms are manifestations of disease. Illness is no less real because the victim happens to be culpable for his illness. A glutton with hypertensive heart disease undoubtedly aggravates his condition by overeating, and is culpable in part for the often fatal symptoms of his disease, but what reasonable person would claim that for this reason he is not really ill? The issue of culpability is largely irrelevant in handling the personality disorders and in any case does not detract from the reality of the illness, as Mowrer (1960) seems to imply.

It is possible in most instances (although admittedly difficult in some) to distinguish quite unambiguously between mental illness and ordinary cases of immorality. The vast majority of persons who are guilty of moral lapses knowingly violate their own ethical precepts for expediential reasons—despite being volitionally capable at the time, both of choosing the more moral alternative and of exercising the necessary inhibitory control (Ausubel, 1952, pp. 465–471). Such persons, also, usually do not exhibit any signs of psychiatric didorder. At crucial choice points in facing the problems of living, they simply choose the opportunistic instead of the moral alternative. They are not mentally ill, but they are clearly accountable for their misconduct. Hence, since personality disorder and immorality are neither coextensive nor mutually exclusive conditions, the concept of mental illness need not necessarily obscure the issue of moral accountability.

DELINQUENCY

The history of social attitudes toward delinquency, including the various competing philosophies current today, reflects the dilemma society finds itself in when it is forced to make moral judgments regarding guilt, culpability, and punishment without any adequate criteria of moral accountability. For most people, delinquency is still a matter of unethical behavior based on inherited moral weakness, an indication that the individual has voluntarily succumbed to the temptation of illegitimately benefiting himself or giving vent to aggressive impulses at the expense of his fellow citizens. However, more sophisticated points of view, namely the legal, psychological, and sociological prevail at the level of expert opinion.

The law is primarily concerned with protecting the interests and safety of individuals, groups, and society. With this end in view, the most practical assumption to make is that in the absence of evidence to the contrary, unlawful acts are willfully committed and render the offending individual liable to punishment. The strict legal test for responsibility only requires that the accused person know right from wrong and be able to appreciate the nature and quality of his act. However, in deference to the recognized contribution of emotional factors to the commission of crime by mentally disordered individuals, certfiable "insanity" itself is often accepted by the judiciary as proof of irresponsibility, and "uncontrollable impulse" as at least a mitigating factor.

Proponents of the psychological and sociological schools of thought charge that the criterion of "willful and premeditated intent" is entirely irrelevant to the question of moral accountability since it is based on the premise of "free will". Our quarrel with the legal definition of responsibility, on the other hand, rests on other grounds. First, the law is too much concerned with the material and formal rights of individuals and too little concerned with intrinsic immorality. The vast majority of acts of cruelty, injustice, and treachery are lawful and unpunishable. Second, the application of the test of willfulness and intent is not made in a context of psychological analysis of the personality structure and development of the individual. Instead, the actual motivation is frequently obscured by concentration on legalistic niceties and the legal rules of evidence; and final judgment may depend more on technical points in the statutory law and on details of precedent in common law—both of which are essentially irrelevant in most cases since they are not taken into account by the offender—than on considerations of equity and justice. Criteria such as "an uncontrollable impulse" also, are vague and often applied in a mechanical fashion without careful consideration being given to their relative weight in the causation of a particular act of delinquency.

According to the undiluted sociological point of view, delinquency is an individual behavioral manifestation of social disorganization and pathology. Individuals whose opportunities for normal personality development and constructive endeavor are frustrated by virtue of poverty, unemployment, slum conditions, etc., react with antisocial behavior. Hence, the argument runs, it is society and not the individual who really is the patient. The latter is deviant only as long as he is exposed to a diseased society. As a single factor theory of delinquency, however, this formulation breaks down in failing to explain why children from optimal social environments become wayward, and why the majority of children in a given slum area do not become adult criminals despite fairly regular participation in delinquent activities during childhood and adolescence.

The psychological as well as the psychiatric and the psychoanalytic approach is similar to the sociological in de-emphasizing the role of volitional control, but differs from the latter in locating the main etiological factor in the dynamics of early personality development rather than in social pathology. Psychoanalysts contend that criminal behavior is a symptom of mental disturbance. They view the delinquent as an individual equipped with a poorly developed ego and superego but driven by powerful instinctual forces. The psychopath, for example, is seen as fixated in the early narcissistic, sexually polymorphous stage of psychosexual development (Arahamsen, 1951). Although social conditions are recognized as contributory factors, greater stress is placed upon various aspects of the early family situation which impinge upon personality development. Non-analytic psychologists are more concerned with the influence of the parent-child relationship on the latter's socialization process rather than with its effect on sexual maturation. Both, however, would agree in the belief that delinquency is primarily a problem of disordered personality development arising from unfortunate relationships between the child and significant persons in his psychological field rather than a manifestation of disturbance in grosser patterns of social organization.

In the classification of delinquency to be offered below, two basic assumptions will be made. First, delinquency like any other behavioral outcome is a result of multiple causality. Relevant variables that must be considered in every case are heredity, personality development, other psychological factors (e.g., intelligence, suggestibility), personality disorder, transitional pressures in development, emotional instability, situational factors, family and social environment, etc. Usually, however, one of these factors is prepotent in a given case, allowing it for purposes of convenience to be placed in one of the categories of the classification. Second, while allowing that psychological and social causes of delinquency can be identified, the authors are nevertheless in agreement with the moral and legal approaches to the problem in believing that the identification of the effective cause in an individual case does not necesssarily absolve the offender from moral accountability. Objectively valid criteria of culpability are discoverable.

In modern psychological thinking about criminality, there has been too great a tendency toward divorcing all behavior of its ethical content. In other words, it seems just as one-sided to ascribe all antisocial behavior to underlying psychological disturbances as to see in it only a manifestations of basic immorality. From the standpoint of individual behavior, there is a moral aspect to most purposeful human activity, the psychological reality of which cannot be ignored. And while this aspect is so closely interwoven with the aspect of psychological disturbance that the two can hardly be separated, the relative significance of each in a given case of delinquency is usually clear enough to allow some judgment as to the individual's moral and legal accountability.

In the concluding section of this chapter, several hypotheses directed toward this goal will be offered. The third and fourth main categories of this classification are outside the scope of this volume and will not be discussed here except in passing. It is to be noted that they are considered as contributors rather than as effective causes, since it is our contention that in the absence of adequate predisposing factors in personality development, they would be insufficient of themselves to produce permanent delinquency. This interpretaion is in accord with the generally accepted fact that the type of delinquency characteristic of disorganized urban areas is a transitory phenomenon for most individuals, one that is not carried over into adult life. It points to the absence of complete homogenity in exposure to moral values within a single social class; for despite geographical segregation and continual reinforcement of lower-class value systems, the moral code of the dominant middle-class is eventually adopted by the majority of erstwhile slum dwellers.

Even in the preadolescent and adolescent period, some of the youths in these areas are more heavily influenced by middle-class values than they are by the prevailing norms in their own social-class group. While this may be a consequence of exclusion from the peer culture, it may also be a cause of such exclusion. Predatory gang behavior tends to become fixed when status deprivation is perceived by the adolescent as the outcome of social discrimination attributable to

Table 2
Classification of Delinquency

I.	Delinquency Attributable to Defects in Personality Development
	A. In Non-Satellizers ("ego hypertrophy")
	1. Aggressive, antisocial psychopath
	2. Rejected and overvalued individuals
	B. In Satellizers ("inadequate personality")
	1. Underdominated individuals
	2. Overprotected and overdominated individuals
II.	Delinquency Attributable to Transitional Pressures of Adolescence
	A. Emotional instability referable to hormonal changes, somatic deviations, status deprivation, etc.
	B. Experimentation with moral values; moral confusion, cynicism, and disenchantment
	C. Peer-group structure and anti-adult orientation
III.	Other Psychological Factors Contributing to Delinquency
	A. Personality disorder, e.g., psychosis, neurosis
	B. Intellectual deficit
	C. Hypersuggestibility
	D. Hostility and destructiveness as defense and status-getting mechanisms
	E. Expiatory need for punishment due to underlying guilt feelings
IV.	Social Factors Contributing to Delinquency
	A. Status deprivation on basis of class membership, racial or ethnic origin, and religious affiliation
	B. Predominant exposure to delinquent moral values in home, peer group, and adult culture
	C. Segregation of underprivileged youth in socially disorganized areas with opportunity for delinquent gang activities
	D. Conditions of prolonged economic exigency, e.g., poverty, unemployment

such permanent characteristics as racial origin instead of a self-limited affliction shared by all individuals in a given age group.

Sporadic delinquency is also common enough in adolescence even without the contributing influence of adverse social conditions. Prolonged status deprivation leads to an anti-adult orientation in the peer group, which sometimes explodes violently in the form of aggressive, antisocial activity. Adolescent emotional instability takes this aggressive form more readily if it is compounded by group interaction, since group resistance is much more effective than individual rebellion and provides moral sanction and anonymity to the participant. The mere pressure for conformity to group norms in adolescence is often sufficient to provoke occasional acts of delinquency in youths who otherwise have high moral standards. However, where there tends to be no large-scale segregation by social class, as in small towns and villages, organized delinquent gangs are not generally found (Havighurst & Taba, 1949).

Another factor facilitating the development of delinquent trends in adolescents is the moral confusion and ethical laxity they perceive in the culture at large. Since at this time the sense of moral obligation becomes divorced from parental loyalties, and emulatory models for a rational and reciprocal ethical code are eagerly sought on a societal basis, the moral vacuum tends, unfortunately, to be filled by the readiest and most visible set of standards available.

When rooted in aberrations of conscience that have developed from deviant parent-child relationships, deliquency has a far more serious prognosis. In preceding sections, we have considered the developmental bases for delinquent behavior in satellizers and non-satellizers respectively, and the types of delinquent mechanisms likely to occur in each personality type. However, a relatively rare type of delinquent found among non-satellizers still awaits description—the aggressive antisocial psychopath. This type of individual corresponds to the classic description of ''psychopathic personality'' who manifests from an early age cruel, impulsive, ruthless, and vindictive tendencies devoid of any remorse or guilt feelings. Such cases are characterized by an early history of parental rejection. However, the needs for counteraggression and vengeance are so great that considerations of expediency are cast aside, and complete and overt rebellion against parental standards takes place. Not only does a sense of personal moral obligation fail to develop but also any internalization of ethical values whatsoever. The same hostile, rebellious attitude is later carried over in relation to social norms, which the individual identifies with the hateful figures of his parents. Thus, there is no possibility of developing a sense of justice or obligation on rational grounds. Even the interests of self-aggrandizement are subordinated to the need for wanton destructiveness and aggressive retaliation against moral or legal authority.

Psychological Factors in Non-Pathological Adolescent Middle-Class Delinquency

Given the various personality predispositions considered above, i.e., economic and social-class pressures, the vicissitudes of life in the urban slums, and the influence of predatory groups, it is not difficult to understand lower-class delinquency. It is more difficult, however, to explain why it is currently increasing at an alarming rate in middle-class suburbs.

Our thesis, briefly, can be reduced to these five propositions: First, the most typical causal factor in middle-class juvenile deliquency in our opinion, is *not* to be found in pathological personality structure. It inheres, rather, in the fact that adolescent development in our culture is characterized by the alienation of youth from the standards, status-giving activities, and training institutions of adult society, in their resulting aggressive, anti-adult orientation, and in their compensatory immersion in a world of their peers—a world with distinctive status-giving activities, norms of conduct, and training institutions of its own. This immersion in the peer culture both intensifies the existing alienation of youth from adult society, reinforces their anti-adult orientation, and facilitates and sanctions the overt, antisocial expression of their anti-adult attitudes that we call juvenile delinquency.

Adult-Youth Alienation

Second, adult-youth alienation, like most other complex phenomena, is *not an all-or-none matter*. It exists on a continuum. For one thing, it varies greatly from one sex and subcultural group in our society to another, as well as within any given sex or subcultural group. Thus, for example, although alienation from adult society is *generally* characteristic of adolescent development in Western culture, both the *degree* of this alienation, and the *extent* to which it is expressed in delinquency, are much greater in urban slums than in middle-class neighborhoods, and are much greater among boys than among girls. This does not mean, however, that delinquency is unknown either among girls or in suburbia.

Upon inquiring why this is so, we must appreciate the role of multiple causality in adult-youth alienation. That is, many contributory and precipitating factors, both psychological and sociological, affect both the degree of adult-youth alienation in any individual or group, as well as the possibility that it will take the form of delinquency. The degree of alienation as well as the contributory and precipitating factors in this instance are particularly potent. Lower-class adolescents are understandably dubious about the possibility of ever attaining the middle-class vocational status and living standards to which they aspire, and thus they see less point in acquiring the middle-class character traits of hard work, responsibility, initiative, self-denial, long-term striving, and restraint of sexual and aggressive urges upon which the implementation of these aspirations depends. Living currently in overcrowded, poverty-stricken, and squalid surroundings, and feeling rejected by middle-class society, also accentuate their resulting feelings of alienation from and hostility toward the glittering adult world of suburbia whose material affluence they covet, but from which they feel excluded. Adolescents in urban slums also receive very little supervision from their parents, are mostly socialized by their peers, are influenced by highly organized predatory gangs, are exposed to much family and social demoralization, and express their hostile impulses habitually in direct aggressive action rather than verbally or symbolically.

Adult-youth alienation is also more pronounced among adolescents in most racial and ethnic minority groups, because here the normal degree of conflict between older and younger generations is intensified by a greater discrepancy in the respective backgrounds of parents and children. In addition, these adolescents feel alienated from and hostile toward a social order that arbitrarily seeks to deny them their rightful place in the sun because of factors entirely beyond their control, namely, the.color of their skins or their parents' place of birth.

Alienation and delinquency are more serious problems among boys than girls, because girls are traditionally more sheltered and protected in our society;

identify more strongly with parents, teachers, and other authority figures; have less insistent needs for independence, earned status, and emancipation from the home; and are more habituated from early childhood to docility, sedateness, conformity to authority, and restraint of overt physical aggression.

More idiosyncratic psychological factors that influence the rate of juvenile delinquency include temperamental and personality traits; parent-child relationships; intelligence and school achievement; and the effect of mass media. Precisely how these factors are related to delinquency will be considered later.

Identification with Adult Society

Third, adult-youth alienation is also not an all-or-none matter in quite another sense than simply in regard to variability in its degree of expression from one person or group to another. That is, operating simultaneously with the various factors causing adult-youth alienation in varying degrees, there are also two general factors within each adolescent that maintain or increase his *identification* with adult society. One of these factors stems from his ultimate aspirations for the future; the other is a legacy from his childhood. Both serve to counteract the severity of his anti-adult attitudes and their expression in juvenile delinquency.

Thus, at the same time that adolescents, particularly those from middle-class backgrounds, are alienated from adult standards and preoccupied with achieving *vicarious* forms of adult status and independence in the peer group, they are *simultaneously* engaged in and intensely concerned with educational and other pursuits that serve as stepping-stones to *genuine* adult status and independence, and to full membership in adult society. Their *ultimate* goals are *not* high status in the peer group—that is, the distinction of being the best dancer, the most prestigeful athlete, the most successful faddist, the most popular and most frequently dated girl, the most daring drag racer, the most shockingly sophisticated or anti-adult person in the crowd—but rather, well-paying professional or managerial jobs, financial security, a comfortable home in the suburbs, marriage, and a family. They also realize that attainment of these goals requires long-term striving, self-denial, postponement of immediate hedonistic gratifications, the approval of persons in authority, restraint of aggressive impulses, and avoidance of an unsavory or delinquent reputation.

Thus, it greatly overstates the case to claim that adolescents are *entirely* oblivious of adult approval, that they completely reject adult values, standards, and aspirations, and that they manifest no feelings of moral obligation to abide by earlier assimilated norms of conduct. This much is clearly evident when we pause to consider that one of the principal functions of the peer group is to transmit from one generation to the next the appropriate social-class values, standards, and aspirations that adolescents are often unwilling to accept from parents and teachers, but *are* willing to accept from their age-mates.

The significance of these two counterbalancing factors that inhibit the development and overt, aggressive expression of anti-adult attitudes must not be underestimated. In fact, until relatively recently they were quite sufficient to limit the occurrence of middle-class juvenile delinquency to the occasional black sheep or psychopathic individual. This is not to say that occasional outbreaks of mischief, vandalism, and rowdyism, and the "sowing of wild oats", were uncommon occurrences in middle-class youth of the past. Nevertheless, compared to some of the wayward activities of middle-class youngsters today, they were milder, rarer, more sporadic, and much less widespread, and serious. There is a difference between youthful prankishness and high spirits, on the one hand, and wanton, wholesale destruction of private or public property, on the other.

Let us recapitulate briefly the substance of the first three propositions. First, the principal causal factor in middle-class juvenile delinquency is the alienation of youth from adult society and their compensatory immersion in a subculture of their own peers. This factor is the chief source of the aggressive anti-adult orientation of adolescents that is expressed under certain conditions as juvenile delinquency. Second, various contributory and precipitating factors such as sex, social class, tempermental and personality traits, parent attitudes, and intelligence, account for variability both in the degree of adult-youth alienation and in the extent of its channeling into overtly aggressive and antisocial activity. Third, two important inhibitory factors—the adolescent's concern with *ultimately* attaining adult status and the residual influence of previously assimilated values and loyalties—reduce adult-youth alienation, the development of anti-adult attitudes, and the overt expression of these attitudes in delinquency. Adequate understanding of the interaction between these various factors enables us to understand why adolescent delinquency involves only a small *minority* of youth even though adult-youth alienation is a universal phenomenon in our culture; why the rate of delinquency varies so much from one sex and subcultural group to another, as well as within a given sex and subcultural group; and why, until quite recently, juvenile delinquency among middle-class youth was a relatively rare and sporadic phenomenon.

Deterioration of Standards

The fourth proposition endeavors to explain why middle-class juvenile delinquency has become such a more serious problem in recent years. Why are the two previously identified factors that inhibit the extent and overt expression of anti-adult attitudes no longer adequate to limit the occurrence of juvenile delinquency among middle-class youth to the seriously disturbed or atypically deviant misfit? The only plausible explanatory hypothesis we can advance here is that middle-class moral values in the adult society have undergone serious deterioration since the end of the Second World War. The reasons for this deterioration are numerous, complex, and obviously beyond the scope of this presentation. We will briefly discuss only two of them that are more directly related to the character development and conduct of youth, namely, the influence of modern psychology, and the effects of chronic international tension. In elaborating this fourth proposition, we will be chiefly concerned with describing the principal characteristics of the moral deterioration that has occurred, and with showing how they have increased the incidence of middle-class juvenile delinquency by undermining the influence of the two counterbalancing factors that normally keep it under control, namely, the adolescent's acute concern with the *ultimate* attainment of adult status and the residual effects of previously assimilated values and loyalties.

Fifth, and last, it is both very easy and very dangerous to view juvenile delinquency out of perspective. In the vast majority of cases, this delinquent behavior is a transitory phenomenon that does not carry over into adult life.

We shall now consider these five propositions in greater detail, confining ourselves to those aspects of the problem that are relevant to the occurrence of delinquency in middle-class adolescents—its predisposing and contributory causes, its prevention, and its prognosis—and shall also say a few words about the issue of moral accountability and punishment.

Peer-Group Influences

We come now to the final role of the peer group as a predisposing factor in juvenile delinquency. The peer group does more than merely increase the adolescent's alienation from adult society and reinforce his aggressive anti-adult attitudes. It also facilitates the overt expression of these attitudes in antisocial behavior. Without this facilitation, juvenile delinquency would rarely occur. We know this to be a fact because the vast majority of juvenile delinquent acts are not performed by *individual* adolescents but by adolescents acting in groups. In a group setting, the individual's socially objectionable conduct is sanctioned, at least in part, both by his assimilation of the group's anti-adult norms, which provide a new internal frame of reference for judging his own behavior, and by the group's approval of his behavior. Feelings of loyalty, belongingness, and gratitude also influence him to participate voluntarily in the group's activities, even if they offend his moral scruples. Furthermore, because of the marginality of his status, and his dependence on the peer group for much of the self-esteem, independence, and security he is able to achieve during these hectic years of transition, he is exaggeratedly sensitive to the threat of forfeiting these precious satisfactions as a result of incurring the group's displeasure; and if these internal pressures *still* do not suffice to keep him in line, he is frequently coerced by threat of more serious sanctions—of being shamed, ridiculed, censured, rebuffed, physically chastised, or ostracized. Finally, in any illicit group enterprise, the following inhibition-reducing psychological mechanisms are usually present: suggestion, imitation, contagiousness of behavior; the seeming obliteration of personal identity and accountability; and the reinforcing action of mutual support, encouragement, and justification. Hence, in a group situation the individual will often commit antisocial actions that he would not dare to commit alone—even if the same aggressive sentiments were present.

Reinforced Crucial Factors

We can conclude, therefore, that without the crucial factor of adult-youth alienation and aggressive anti-adult attitudes, which are both reinforced and channeled into overt, antisocial activites by adolescent peer groups, psychopathological factors would account, at most, for the sporadic waywardness of the emotionally disturbed individual. First, juvenile delinquency is practically unknown in primitive and traditional cultures where adult-youth alienation and peer-group socialization do not exist. Second, the characteristic feature of juvenile delinquency in our own culture is that it is conducted in peer groups by individuals who are essentially sociable, loyal, and altruistic, rather than antisocial or psychologically abnormal. Most seriously disturbed adolescents do not last very long as members of a *typical* peer group, delinquent or otherwise. Lastly, the characteristic juvenile delinquent in our culture does not carry over his delinquent activities into adult life. If personality or home factors were crucial or sufficient cause of the typical juvenile delinquency with which we are familiar, they would not cease to operate in most instances with the approach of adulthood and the diminution of anti-adult attitudes.

Inhibition of Juvenile Delinquency

Thus far, we have presented a rather one-sided picture—considering only the factors that increase adult-youth alienation, aggressive anti-adult attitudes, and the expression of these attitudes in juvenile delinquency. We have not reckoned in any detail, as yet, with the factors that counterbalance these developments. In the first place, almost all youth, particularly those from middle-class backgrounds, while striving for the vicarious adult status and independence that the peer group offers, are simultaneously concerned with the *ultimate* achievement of genuine adult status and independence. This also implies that they have a strong stake in acquiring the traits necessary for the attainment of these goals and in obtaining adult approval for developing the necessary traits. Thus the middle-class peer group itself, in addition to providing its own distinctive set of standards, assumes responsibility for developing in its members the appropriate adult values, motivational patterns, and character traits that adolescents will frequently *not* learn from adults, because of adult-youth alienation, but *will* learn from their age-mates. Second, the assimilation of new peer group values does not imply complete repudiation of previously assimilated adult values. These two factors, therefore, reduce adult-youth alienation and serve as powerful deterrents to the development and overt, antisocial expression of anti-adult attitudes. Until relatively recently, they were sufficient to limit the incidence of middle-class juvenile delinquency to emotionally disturbed individuals. We have previously suggested that the decline in middle-class adult morality has undermined the influence of these deterrent factors and has thus magnified the problem of middle-class juvenile delinquency enormounsly. Let us examine this relationship in somewhat greater detail.

Decline in Middle-Class Morality

.We live today in a different kind of moral climate than that in which we, our parents, and our grandparents grew up. Greater emphasis is placed on "getting ahead" by any means, fair or foul, and on the rapid acquisition of material affluence. Affability and "ability to get along with others" count for more in advancing one's career than aptitude, competence, creativity, and the willingness to work hard. The man who conforms slavishly to the opinions of his associates and superiors, who swims with the tide, and who tacitly condones wrongdoing, is valued more highly than the man who is forthright, who has the courage of his convictions, and who follows the dictates of his conscience. Expediency is the order of the day. Such virtues as individualism, moral courage, self-reliance, initiative, personal integrity and uprightness, and concern with human values are considered old-fashioned. Slackness on the job, shoddy work, overcharging, irresponsibility, and negligence find ready acceptance in many quarters.

Now what effect has this moral deterioriation had on the two aforementioned factors that have hitherto been so effective in limiting the extent of anti-adult attitudes and the incidence of juvenile delinquency in middle-class groups? First, if the adolescent perceives adults as being able to "get ahead" without fully exemplifying the traditional middle-class virtues, he is naturally led to believe (1) that he too can achieve the adult status and the independence he craves without thoroughly acquiring these same virtues himself, and (2) that adults are not *really* concerned whether or not he acquires these virtues. Thus, he is not so highly motivated either to develop such traits as self-restraint, willingness to work hard, a sense of responsibility, impulse-control, self-denial, personal integrity, and re-spect for the rights and property of others, or to seek adult approval for so doing. Further, the middle-class peer group, which has the responsibility for transmitting middle-class standards to its members, can transmit only those standards that *actually* exist. The upshot of this lamentable situation is that the adolescent's failure fully to develop these particular traits greatly increases his suceptibility to juvenile delinquency. This is so because it is precisely such traits as a sense of responsibility, impulse control, personal integrity, and respect for the rights of others, plus the desire to obtain adult approval for displaying them, that inhibits the overt, antisocial expression of anti-adult attitudes.

Second, when adolescents realize that adults do not actually live up to the standards endorsed as axiomatically right and proper since childhood, they tend to lose both their implicit belief in these standards and any feeling of obligation to abide by them. This erosion of belief and feeling reduces power to inhibit delinquent acts. When children become sufficiently mature to interpret adult behavior for what it actually is, they are impressed more by example than by precept. Lastly, the adolescent's awareness of the grievous lack of moral courage in the adult world and of the premium that adults place on conformity and expediency furnishes him with a very poor model for holding fast to his moral convictions in the face of group pressure.

Psychology and Psychoanalysis

Much of the decline in middle-class standards can be rightly placed at the door of modern psychology and psychoanalysis. Practitioners of these disciplines have commonly extolled the value of adjustment as an end in itself, irrespective of its moral implications. Frequently, they have adopted an amoral and non-judgmental approach in evaluating human behavior; have overvalued the importance of conformity and social adustment; have encouraged an attitude of hedonism, self-indulgence, and self-preoccupation in their clients; have scoffed at conscience and moral accountability as "moralistic nonsense"; and have advocated extreme permissiveness in the home and school. This too has reduced the restraining influence of responsibility, self-control, and moral accountability on the adolescent's disposition to engage in out-of-bounds and delinquent behavior, and has increased his willingness to follow the path of expedience and conform to the delinquent suggestions of his companions.

In the past twenty years, however, there has been a gratifying reversal in these latter two trends. Beginning with the Sputnik era, "the organization man" has begun to lose some ground in American vocational life. Government, education, and industry have reluctantly faced up to the fact that social charm and affability are not adequate substitutes for competence, originality, and initiative in the battle for survival with world communism. Intellectual achievement, creativity, and non-conformity are not only tolerated these days, but have even become somewhat fashionable. Some clinical psychologists and psychiatrists are also beginning to question the axiomatic infallibility of psychoanalysis; moral accountability has ceased being a dirty expression in psychological circles; and the cult of permissiveness in home and school is definitely declining.

Tensions of Modern Life

Also contributing somewhat to the postwar decline in middle-class moral standards have been the exaggerated uncertainties and tensions of modern life, the chronic state of international crisis, and the ever-present prospect of nuclear war. Many human beings, and especially emotionally unstable adolescents, react to these threats to their identity and security by perceiving life as precarious, meaningless, and absurd, by regarding long-range planning as futile, by renouncing responsibility for themselves and others, and by embracing such philosophies as existentialism, hedonism, epicureanism, and nihilism.

To sum up briefly, our thesis thus far has been this: juvenile delinquency is essentially a manifestation of the special characteristics of adolescence in modern Western culture. It is a product of the adult-youth alienation and of the anti-adult attitudes that stem from the fact that adolescents in our society are unavoidably barred for many years from achieving earned status and exercising volitional independence within the mainstream of the adult culture, and seek, therefore, compensatory satisfactions for these needs in a peer culture of their own making. Juvenile delinquency characteristically occurs among adolescents who essentially are psychologically normal; the transitory anti-adult attitudes that underlie it are *qualitatively* different from the antisocial attitudes that are more deeply rooted in defects in moral development that characterize the atypical juvenile delinquent with a serious personality disorder or the adult criminal. The very presence of the peer group facilitates the *occasional* overt, antisocial expression of these anti-adult attitudes in almost all adolescents at one time or another; but for the most part, their expression in delinquency is inhibited, especially among middle-class groups, by the adolescent's ultimate aspirations for adult status and independence and by his earlier implicit acceptance of adult standards. Because of the postwar decline in middle-class adult morality, however, these inhibitory factors have been partly undermined among middle-class youth, and, consequently, overt antisocial expression of anti-adult attitudes has become more widespread and serious. The threshold for instigating such expression, so to speak, has been generally lowered. Thus, other contributory factors need be less potent now for the typical middle-class adolescent who engages sporadically in minor delinquencies, to step up the frequency and seriousness of these acts sufficiently to get himself classified as a juvenile delinquent.

In the next section, we propose to consider some of these contributory factors that operate in middle-class surroundings and determine whether any *given* middle-class adolescent may become a juvenile delinquent. These factors include temperamental and personality traits, parent attitudes and practices, home conditions, and the mass media.

Factors in Middle-Class Juvenile Delinquency

Everything else being equal, a temperamentally independent and assertive adolescent has greater than average needs for adult status and independence, and thus tends to experience more acute frustration from the deprivation of these needs; and if he also happens to be aggressive by temperament, he is more disposed to react to such frustration with hostile and resentful attitudes toward adult authority than in some other more indirect or compensatory fashion. Aggressive anti-adult attitudes, in turn, are more likely to be expressed in overt, antisocial behavior by those adolescents who are temperamentally restless, overactive, impulsive, volatile, venturesome, danger-loving, and eager for thrills. And since juvenile delinquency typically takes place in group settings, it naturally tends to occur more frequently among strongly extroverted, group-oriented individuals, who are more likely to be involved in group activities to begin with, and among those group members who are most suggestible and responsive to group pressures.

LOW INTELLIGENCE

Low intelligence *per se* does not seem to be related to delinquent behavior but is found more frequently among juvenile delinquents for a number of indirect reasons. It increases suggestibility, the tendency to take unwise chances in the choice of delinquent activities, the probability of being apprehended by the police, and most important of all, the possibility of school failure. Scholastic retardation tends to generate particularly potent anti-adult attitudes because the frustration involved is experienced *directly* at the hands of adult society's principal training institution. But even if adults are entirely innocent of inflicting the frustration in question, it is safe to say that, because of youth's prevailing anti-adult orientation, the aggression associated with *any* serious frustration they experience, for example, that resulting from physical defect or deviation, will be directed against adult society. It has also been observed that unclear vocational goals predispose an adolescent toward juvenile delinquency, because, under these circumstances, the uncertainty characterizing the attainment of his ultimate aspirations for adult status decreases his motivation for acquiring the middle-class traits necessary for implementing these aspirations.

INADEQUATE SUPERVISION

Juvenile delinquency occurs more frequently when adolescents fail to receive adequate supervision at home, that is, when their parents are either preoccupied with their own affairs or are utterly unconcerned about the whereabouts and activities of their children, their companions, and the hours they keep. In upper middle-class suburbs, it is now becoming increasingly more fashionable for parents to compete with each other in accelerating the social sophistication of their adolescent children and to surrender to the peer group their own responsibility for supervising, guiding, and constraining teenagers' behavior. Broken homes, as is well known, are significantly related to the incidence of juvenile delinquency. This relationship not only reflects the lack of adequate parental supervision and the absence of a suitable adult model of the same sex with whom the child can identify, but is also a consequence of the atmosphere of adult tension, conflict, and bitterness to which he is exposed prior to the divorce or separation.

Prevention of Juvenile Delinquency

What can be done to prevent juvenile delinquency? In brief, first, we think we have to live with the fact that in a modern technological society the needs of youth for genuine adult status and independence must necessarily be frustrated for many years; that, as a result, a certain amount of youth-adult alienation and anti-adult sentiment is inevitable; and that peer groups with distinctive standards, status-giving activities, and training functions will inevitably arise to provide adolescents with a vicarious form of compensatory adult status and independence as well as training for adulthood in their own independently determined setting. The most we can hope to accomplish, therefore, is to reduce the existing amount of alienation and anti-adult attitudes, and to prevent their spilling over into juvenile delinquency.

Many other specific proposals can be offered to attain these goals: improvement of understanding and communication between adults and youth; opportunity for adolescents to participate in community betterment programs; reduction of the amount of failure and frustration that adolescents experience in school; participation of youth to a greater degree in family decisions and in school government; and provision for better education for marriage and parenthood.

Although we would be the last to deny the potential value of any of these proposals, we still insist that our best hope of reducing adult-youth alienation, anti-adult attitudes, and juvenile delinquency lies in utilizing the two existing counterbalancing factors that both operate within almost every adolescent and are also reinforced by his peer group, namely, (1) his previously acquired identification with adult moral standards and (2) his motivation for acquiring those adult middle-class traits that will enable him to attain the genuine adult status and independence to which he ultimately aspires. We have seen how the postwar decline in middle-class adult morality has undermined the effect of these two counterbalancing forces that previously made middle-class juvenile delinquency a relative rarity. Thus the essence of our preventive prescription, for whatever comfort it offers, is simply this: juvenile delinquency will cease being a major problem in middle-class communities when middle-class parents reaffirm identification with the traditional middle-class virtues, and set an example of moral rectitude in everyday family, social, and vocational lives that children can respect and emulate.

Prognosis of Juvenile Delinquency

To view the total problem of juvenile delinquency in perspective, three important facts must be emphasized. First, although most juveniles participate at one time or another in some form of antisocial behavior, the vast majority of them do not become *habitually* delinquent. Second, delinquent activities constitute only a tiny fraction of the total behavior of practically all adolescent peer groups. Third, and most important of all, almost 40 years of research unequivocally refutes the uninformed assertion that the juvenile delinquent of today becomes the adult criminal of tomorrow. True, most adult criminals showed signs of waywardness in their youth; but it is also true that the overwhelming majority of juvenile offenders mature into conventional law-abiding adults. With the approach of adulthood, as youth's alienation from adult society decreases, so also, in most instances, do the accompanying anti-adult attitudes and their overt expression in antisocial activities.

All of this does not mean, of course, that we should be unconcerned about juvenile delinquency or refrain from doing everything in our power to prevent it. On the other hand, it is just as indefensible to adopt unsympathetic or vindictive attitudes toward youth, to advocate an hysterical policy of harsh reprisals, or to indulge in unfounded prophecies of impending doom. For the most part, the younger generation is *not* going to the dogs—at least not any more rapidly than the rest of society.

The need for perspective is no less important in handling the individual delinquent and his perlexed and worried parents, many of whom have been unfairly scapegoated by such fashionable slogans as, ''There are no delinquent children—only delinquent parents''. True, one must do everything possible to remove or alleviate whatever contributory causes are present. But it is also necessary for parents to appreciate the nature of juvenile delinquency in the context of adolescent development in our culture, to understand the reasons for the recent increased incidence of juvenile delinquency in middle-class groups, and to realize that the condition itself is typically transitory and self-limited in duration. Thus a very wise psychiatrist once said:

> My main therapeutic approach to the parents of [delinquent]adolescents—my main treatment, advice, and prescription to them. . .is the tried-and-true phrase of the men of the ancient Church who, when beset by the unpredictable and the seemingly uncontrollable, comforted themselves and one another with the words, 'It will pass. It will pass.' (Gardner, 1949)

9
Anxiety

The problem of anxiety provides the crucial connecting link between the two aspects of the inquiry that we have pursued so far in this book—the nature of ego development on the one hand, and the relationship between aberrant ego development and personality disorder on the other hand. In anxiety states, we see at the same time both a product of disordered ego development with many characteristic signs of ego damage, and the psychopathological core of a large variety of behavior disorders that can best be understood either as complications of or as defenses against underlying anxiety.

Yet, in no other field of psychopathology is there quite so much conceptual confusion or so little consensus of opinion regarding fundamental problems. Is there any continuity from the fear states of animals to those of man? How does fear become differentiated out of the nameless emotional matrix present in infants? What relationships prevail among fear, phobia, anxiety, and insecurity? Are there different types of anxiety that may arise in the course of ego development? Can anxiety also arise in relation to situational problems unconnected with personality development or in relation to other psychopathological manifestations? In order for anxiety to develop must there first be "conflict," "repression," or "hostility"? Is there any such thing as "free-floating anxiety," or "normal" anxiety in contradistinction to "neurotic" anxiety?

In order to answer these and many other related questions, a systematic attack upon the problem of anxiety that is conceptually consistent with the theoretical framework of this book will be attempted below. Much that is arbitrary in this approach can easily be pointed out, especially in the matter of definition and classification. But in the absence of other compelling criteria, such choices must necessarily be arbitrary, and are defensible only in terms of clarity, parsimony, internal consistency, fruitfulness for research and clinical practice, and compatibility with existing empirical evidence.

DIMENSIONAL QUALITIES OF FEAR STATES

Temporal Dimensions

Fear is a differentiated emotional experience that betokens awareness of threat to some aspect of the organism's existence, integrity, safety, or well-being. Involved is not only a subjective content encompassing the source of the danger, its object, and possible consequences, but also a specific train of visceral and somatic reactions set in motion by this special cortical experience through the excitation of intermediate and lower brain centers. The experience of fear is then completed and given further identifying characteristics when sensation of these visceral and somatic reactions reaches consciousness via sympathetic afferent and proprioceptive fibers originating in the effector organs involved.

So much then for the definition of fear as a psychophysiological or generic term, as a general category of experience sharing certain conditions and properties in common, whether we speak of fear in the specific sense or in the sense of phobia, insecurity, or anxiety. It is here, however, that commonality ends and differentiation begins as we seek to identify criteria that set apart these component derivatives of generic fear.

First of all there is a temporal distinction to be made. Every person lives in the past, present, and future. That which is presently happening, or has already happened and is being re-enacted in memory, is tainted by the mark of reality. It is logically and experientially distinguishable from the hypothetical quality that characterizes anticipated experience. Hence we must differentiate between fear as a current experience (or as a current re-enactment of an old experience) and fear as an anticipated experience incidental to events contemplated in the future. Following historical usage, it will be best to refer to the former as fear in the specific sense, and to the latter as insecurity. Where self-esteem is the object of the threat that elicits a fear state (in the generic sense) we can use the term (1) anxiety-fear to cover the present and past as relived in the present and (2) anxiety to cover the future as contemplated in the present. Fear and anxiety-fear, therefore, refer to current fear states, while insecurity and anxiety refer to anticipated fear.

In the case of "anticipated fear," it is apparent that more is involved than just an emotional content. On the eve of an impending battle, a soldier may experience insecurity, that is, an actual emotional content of fear as he anticipates the events of the morrow and contemplates the possibilities of injury or death. Yet the insecurity he experiences may *not* be manifested as an emotional content evoked by a hypothetical, anticipated experience lived in advance of any actual occurrence; rather his insecurity may be an advance "set" or exaggerated tendency to react with fear when he actually confronts the dreaded class of stimuli constituting the threat. In this case, there is not fear "content" in advance of the actual event, simply a sensitization to react with fear at the appropriate moment, or a differential lowering of his fear threshold to a specific category of threatening events. Although no useful purpose is served in differentiating between *content* and *tendency* by assigning separate terms to these two varieties of fear experience with reference to future events, it is worthwhile to keep this distinction in mind for the following reason: in discussing anxiety and insecurity, emotional contents are more likely to occur when the precise nature of an anticipated threat is known, whereas their counterparts as emotional tendencies are more apt to take place when the source of the danger is more nearly vague and ambiguous.

What is Being Threatened

In the definition of generic fear, we have implied that the object against which the threat is directed must of necessity represent something that is of vital value to the organism. Fear, in other words, is no laughing matter. It is not evoked in situations of trifling import. Life, wholeness of limb, health, reputation, freedom to pursue central goals, etc., must be at stake before an individual will react with fear to a threatening situation.

Among all these values that are subject to attack, one stands out as possessing unique and central significance—self-esteem, or the individual's feeling of adequacy and competence as a person in relation to his environment. The goal of much everyday activity as well as the motivation for most adjustive mechanisms has the enhancement or defense of self-esteem as its chief object. Hence, it seems legitimate to regard threats directed against self-esteem as eliciting a special variety of fear state, which may be termed anxiety-fear when appearing as a current emotion, and anxiety when projected into the future.

The distinction being made here between fear and anxiety differs from that usually cited in the literature on anxiety. Beginning with Freud (1921), fear has been characterized as a type of emotional response to a specific identifiable source of danger, whereas anxiety has been represented as a reaction to a vague, objectless threat to a central value of personality. Fear, Goldstein (1939) holds, is differentiated out of anxiety as the individual learns to identify specific objects in his environment which formerly lead to anxiety reactions.

Our first quarrel with this traditional distinction between fear and anxiety is its inconsistency. In the same breath, it appeals to two different differentiating criteria namely, the identifiability of the threat in fear, and the central importance of the value in anxiety. The use of bidimensional criteria to distinguish between concepts is allowable only if contrasting positions with respect to *both* dimensions are simultaneously designated for each term. It only breeds logical confusion when one dimension is reserved for one member and a second dimension for the other member of the pair.

If anxiety is elicited only when core values are threatened, are we to believe that in fear only peripheral values are threatened? Would it be accurate to state, for example, that specific dangers like an uncaged lion, the muzzle of a gun in one's back, or an approaching locomotive when one is stalled on a railroad track represents threats to values of secondary importance? True, in each case cited here life itself rather than self-esteem is at stake. But who would argue that a threat to life is any less penetrating than a threat to self-esteem? It would seem more consistent to hold that values of central importance are threatened in both fear and anxiety, but that the values differ in type rather than in distance from the core of personality.

Returning to the second criterion of identifiability, we find it just as unserviceable in differentiating between fear and anxiety. Many examples of anxiety could be offered in which the victim possesses complete insight into the nature of the threat confronting his self-esteem; and not infrequently in situations involving a threat to life or health, the individual is unable to identify the source of his dread. Hence in both fear and anxiety, the source of the threat may vary considerably in identifiability; and in each case lack of identifiability adds to the severity of emotional response and to the disorganization characterizing the adjustive effort.

The classification of fear states that has emerged so far in this analysis may be depicted schematically in Table 3.

Still within the dimension of "what is being theatened," we may distinguish two other variables of some importance. Under different conditions giving rise to fear states in the same individual (or between different individuals in the same situation), considerable variability may exist with respect to the identifiability of the particular value under attack. It may not always be apparent to the individual that the object against which the threat is directed is self-esteem, life, or health as the case may be. In addition, there may be varying degrees of displacement of the value that is subject to threat. An example of this was given in the discussion of overprotecting parents, where it was suggested that such parents deflect anxiety from themselves by perceiving that their child's safety rather than their own individual self-esteem is threatened.

Source of the Threat

In addition to asking the question, "What is being threatened?", one may further delineate the characteristics of a given fear state, by posing the query, "Who or what is threatening?" A description then of the various qualities

Table 3
Classification of Fear States

Temporal Dimension	What is Threatened	
	Self-Esteem	*Other Central Values*
Present or Past	Anxiety-fear	Fear
Future (as content or tendency)	Anxiety	Insecurity

characterizing the source of the threat adds further data on the nature of the fear state being experienced. Among the chief distinctions we hope to draw from this inquiry are those between fear (or anxiety) and phobia and between normal and neurotic anxiety.

IDENTIFIABILITY

That threats differ in their identifiability has already been pointed out in connection with the problem of classification. Since variability along this dimension prevails for all components of generic fear, it cannot be judiciously employed as a differentiating criterion. An identifiable threat (e.g., a forthcoming examination) is one that is relatively specific, unitary, and clear-cut in its implications. An unidentifiable threat, (e.g., hostility to parents) on the other hand, tends to be vague, ambiguous, generalized, and fraught with multiple implications, some of which may be contradictory. It can be readily appreciated, therefore, that unidentifiable threats produce more intense fear states and give rise to defensive behavior that is less specifically adaptive. What cannot be identified cannot be avoided; nor can specific preparatory steps be taken to contend with the threat. The organism can only place itself in a state of general alertness or mobilization, and take its chances when the dreaded situation appears on the scene. Furthermore, unidentifiable threats are less subject to experimental extinction, since it is less likely that they can be linked with innocuous consequences contiguous in time.

ACCESSIBILITY

How accessible an individual's awareness is regarding the source of the threat confronting him is obviously an important dimension of his fear experience. Historically, the role assigned to repression in the production of anxiety has just about completed a full circle, beginning with Freud's earlier theory of anxiety. Freud (1921) originally held that anxiety is "general current coin for which all the affects are exchanged or can be exchanged when the corresponding ideational content is under repression." This made anxiety the common consequence of emotional (especially sexual) repression. Later, Freud (1936) modified his position considerably, demoting repression from the cause to a consequence of anxiety. In his second theory, he contended that libidinal and hostile impulses, which potentially expose the individual to danger (social reprisal), give rise to anxiety. And it is this very anxiety that serves as a cue to repress the dangerous impulses.

Horney (1937) and Sullivan (1940) accepted Freud's modified version of the role of repression in anxiety. Both regarded repression as a self-protective means of coping with anxiety by relegating the anxiety-producing factors beyond the pale of consciousness. Hence, if parental rejection, hostility toward parents, or disapproval by parents are productive of anxiety in the child, he tends to dissociate awareness of these unacknowledgeable phenomena from the main, accessible stream of consciousness. Repression under such conditions constitutes a maladaptive defense against anxiety rather than the chief mechanism responsible for its evolution. It does not enable the individual to deal constructively with threatening situations, since the implications of threats cannot be examined openly or critically. Despite the repression, anxiety continues to be generated; and since its cause cannot be coped with consciously, "unconscious" defenses (often of a psychosomatic nature) are elaborated. This fact explains the inverse relationship invariably found between the degree of conscious anxiety and the presence of psychosomatic symptoms. In addition, by tending to become an habitual defensive mechanism that is indiscriminately overgeneralized to many inapplicable situations, repression leads to a generally inhibited individual devoid of spontaneous affective impulses.

DISPLACEMENT

Another dimension related to the source of the threat and not unconnected with the problems of identifiability and accessibility is that of displacement. Does the individual experiencing fear or anxiety perceive the actual threat? Or does that individual project his perception of the offending stimulus onto an intrinsically unrelated cause? Unlike inaccessibility, however, displacement has very definite adjustive value, at least of a palliative nature if not inherently constructive in terms of eliminating the cause of anxiety. It enables him to deny the real source of the threat and to substitute in its stead something that is less formidable and more easily manageable. Consequently, the displacement is always in the direction of greater specificity, concreteness, and identifiability since these factors together make either complete avoidance or planned defense more feasible. In short, the description of displacement just given defines the term *phobia,* which is simply a form of fear or anxiety in which the source of the threat is displaced onto a more identifiable object.

"FREE-FLOATING ANXIETY"

In contrasting anxiety to fears and phobias, it is customary to refer to it as "free-floating or "objectless." The authors contend that these qualities are more apparent than real, and that the entire notion of an affect that is unrelated to a stimulating object is a psychological absurdity. A person who is afraid must be afraid of something. A person who is angry must be angry at something. A person who is in love must be in love with somebody. That loose, undifferentiated pools of unattached affect (aggression, anxiety, or libido) float around and are at liberty to attach themselves at various times to specific objects is a relic of Hippocratian psychology in which various affects were identified with finite quantities of various body fluids that could be poured as it were out of a central reservoir into specific vessels. The modern concept of emotion, on the other hand, is that of a capacity to react in a certain way in response to an adequate stimulus, a capacity that has no corporeal content apart from its phenomenological existence during such time as it is elicited by appropriate situations.

There are, however, several plausible reasons that may help account for the apparent "free-floating" quality of anxiety. As contrasted with fears, anxieties that have not undergone displacement are relatively unidentifiable and inaccessible. These two aspects are thus largely responsible for their objectless appearance. Threats that cannot be concretized or that are banished from consciousness cannot be perceived easily as the cause of a diffuse and apparently all-pervasive affect, especially when the source of the threat is internal. But because a threat cannot be identified or made accessible to consciousness is no proof that a causal relationship does not exist between it and a given affect of anxiety.

Another reason contributing to the "free-floating" appearance of anxiety is its "tendency" component, which consists of a generalized lowering of the threshold to respond with fear to all potential threats to self-esteem. In the first place, the apparent generality of this threshold-lowering creates an illusion of unselectivity and independence from causally related objects. Actually, however, the individual becomes differentially more sensitive to only a limited variety of ego-involved situations impinging upon his self-esteem. Second, since a tendency involves no actual content but only a change in readiness to respond to a particualr gradient of stimuli, it appears objectless until it is elicited by an appropriate stimulus. Nevertheless, an illusion of content is given by a subjective awareness of this increased tendency to respond with fear, which takes the form of an uncomfortable and vague tension. As a result, the individual feels as if he experienced an affective content that cannot be related to any antecedent event in his psychological world.

Objective Magnitude of the Threat

Whenever a fear response is elicited that is proportionate to the objective degree of danger inherent in the threat, we have good reason to believe that we are dealing with normal fear or anxiety. Situations productive of normal fear or anxiety are common enough in anyone's experience, since life is full of hazards and unpredictable contingencies; and to respond to such situations with fear is to behave normally enough. Fear of this kind probably serves a useful adaptive purpose since it alerts the organism to danger and mobilizes the defensive faculties. It is purely situational in nature, since it can be relieved by removal of the inciting situation. Following the initial shock of confrontation, the organism is generally able to recover, avoid panic, and set about constructively to cope with and contain the threat. However, it is conceivable that threats of catastrophic, objective magnitude to self-esteem can last for indefinite periods of time or induce overwhelming anxiety tantamount to panic, which, since it is not disproportionate to the danger involved, must still be considered as normal anxiety. The same result could also be produced by an objective incapacity of an individual that renders him relatively helpless in dealing with minor environmental hazards. This situation is illustrated (1939) by Goldstein's aphasic patients who, when presented with relatively simple sorting problems, responded with panic or rigid and compulsive, stereotyped patterns of problem-solving.

Since the distinction between normal and neurotic anxiety hinges mainly upon the disproportionateness of the response, neurotic anxiety should be suspected in all cases where the symptoms are severe enough to result in panic, paralysis, or progressive disorganization of behavior. And if further search fails to uncover an objective threat of sufficient magnitude to account for the intensity of affect displayed, clinical investigation aimed at discovering subjective sources of anxiety is certainly warranted.

SUBJECTIVE CAPACITY FOR MEETING THREAT

If we turn now to instances where this same degree of anxiety appears in the absence of what seems to be an adequate external threat, we cross the boundary into neurotic anxiety. However, by adhering to our original conception of fear states as responses made to *serious* threats to an organism's integrity or well-being, we are compelled to look for an adequate excitant that is subjective in nature. Then, if we find an individual's self-esteem is impaired to the point where he no longer has confidence in his ability to cope with problems of adjustment, the degree of anxiety manifested by that individual no longer appears disproportionate despite the relative insignificance of the environmental threat that is perceived as the precipitating cause of the affect. In contrast to normal anxiety, where the occasion (i.e., the situation that cues off the anxiety) and the cause of the affect are nearly identical, the occasion of neurotic anxiety is merely the stimulus that creates the necessity for adjustment (May, 1950). And the cause of this stimulus is simply the impaired self-esteem that makes the individual feel inadequate to cope with the adjustive problem. Hence the situation that cues off anxiety here is the individual's fear of the further ego-deflating impact of failure on an already battered self-esteem. Since the main source of the threat is internal, and in addition is frequently unidentifiable and inaccessible, it is not surprising that such anxiety may often give the impression of being "free-floating."

These feelings of inadequacy are very similar to Adler's *feelings of inferiority,* (1917) which also represent a subjective attitude of weakness or a valuation of self as inferior apart from the objective capacities under consideration. Why an individual should regard himself as more impotent and inferior than he actually is, Adler does not make too clear. Apparently, however, he originally derives these feelings from an overgeneralization that he makes as a child from his actual position of biological dependence, organic deficiency, or membership in a social or sex group enjoying a subordinate status. Overwhelmed by the implications of this inferiority stemming from an objective fact, he develops a generalized subjective attitude of inferiority regarding his adequacy overall. These feelings of inferiority according to Adler inspire compensatory efforts aimed at achieving security through prestigeful accomplishment. Then, if these compensations are not successful, secondary inferiority feelings develop.

Significantly, Adler never took the next step of identifying impaired self-esteem with anxiety states. He connected inferiority feelings with neurosis (not anxiety) only through the distorted, excessive, and contradictory compensatory efforts that these feelings tend to inspire. Adler also made the error of assuming that infants perceive their objective, executive incompetence as proof of weakness, whereas they actually perceive themselves as volitionally omnipotent. During the childhood period, he makes the further error of identifying the child's dependence on his parents as a source of inferiority feelings rather than as a source of intrinsic security and adequacy. Dependency on parents, as has already been pointed out, leads to feelings of worthlessness and degradation only in the case of non-satellizing children.

This distinction, which Rollo May (1950) lucidly makes between the occasion and the cause of anxiety, does not imply that the two phenomena are completely unrelated. May (1950) goes on to say,

> The occasions, no matter how insignificant they may seem to be objectively, always bear a subjectively logical relation to the particular inner conflict in the individual; that is to say, the occasions are significant for the anxiety of the subject because they, and not other occasions, cue off his particular neurotic conflict.

While the authors agree that the cause and the occasion of neurotic anxiety are logically related, they do not concur in the opinion that the common denominator in this case is provided by a neurotic conflict that requires a suitable occasion for provocation. Exception is taken, as we elaborate below, to the position of Horney and May, which assumes that intrapsychic conflict is an invariable prerequisite for the occurrence of anxiety. The presence of such conflict intensifies neurotic anxiety and can give rise to symptomatic anxiety, that is, to a type of subjectively derived anxiety related to personality disturbance apart from impaired self-esteem; but all that is required for neurotic anxiety itself is sufficient lowering of self-esteem to transform objectively insignificant adjustive problems into major threats.

How then do we account for the peculiar selectivity that enables minor adjustive situation x to precipitate what appears to be, on objective grounds, a disproportionate amount of anxiety, while situation y, comparable with situation x in respect to its objective threat value, fails to arouse the faintest trace of anxiety? The most obvious explanation is that each individual's self-esteem is predicated upon a different set of status and achievement factors. If a particular situation is relevant to an area that the individual predisposed to neurotic anxiety has staked out as providing the source of *his* extrinsic status, its threat value will be differentially enhanced. An anxiety-neurotic becomes so sensitive to the slightest suggestion of a particular class of stimuli that he or she overrespond with fear whenever the faintest implication of a threat is perceived from them.

It can be readily appreciated that normal and neurotic anxiety may be frequently combined in a single situation confronting a person subject to neurotic anxiety. There is no reason for believing that the latter is immune to threats that are objectively hazardous. Such threats naturally produce even greater manifestations of panic and disorganization than threats that have no objective basis. But the casual observer is led astray in this situation since there seems to be objective justification for whatever anxiety is expressed. A definite diagnosis of situational anxiety, therefore, should never be made on the basis of observations restricted to crisis situations alone. As a matter of fact, any interpretation of anxiety should be made with extreme caution. Most individuals with neurotic anxiety have learned through bitter experience that it is socially and economically disadvantageous to betray their condition to associates. Hence they develop a number of defensive devices that attempt to obviate the necessity for adjusting publicly to potential threats; and in the event that this is impossible, other techniques are mastered for concealing the panic that seizes them. Thus, many anxiety neurotics who are clever at avoiding potentially disruptive situations and at controlling the external manifestations of anxiety—and who are fortunate enough to be placed in environments propitiously structured in terms of defending them against anxiety situations—are able to escape detection indefinitely. They can even gain reputations for being singularly secure and anxiety-free individuals.

Expressive Characteristics of Fear States

The dimensions of fear states can be described not only temporally, and in terms of various attributes of the source and object of the threat, but also in terms of the expressive characteristics of the affect itself. Subjectively, fear or anxiety may be characterized by an acute awareness of danger, a diffuse feeling of panic, premonitions of disaster or impending doom, a conscious tension that is reflective of the lowered threshold of fear reactions (equivalent to Liddell's concept of vigilance in animals), and an awareness of the autonomic components of the fear response. The autonomic aspects of anxiety, that is, increased pulse rate and blood pressure, irregular respiration, thirst, blanching of the skin, increased perspiration, flatulence, aerophagia, etc., are too well-known to require extensive cataloguing. Similarly, we do not need to dwell on various motor manifestations such as tremors, tics, blocking, and hyperkinesis.

More important for our purposes is the conscious accessibility of the fear affect itself and the relationship between degree of accessibility and severity of the autonomic and motor symptoms. In clinical practice it can be readily demonstrated that a sizeable proportion of patients suffering from anxiety neurosis are not only unaware of the source and object of the anxiety-producing threat but also fail to appreciate that their somatic or psychological symptoms bear any relation to fear. That is, some persons manage to repress all or most of the subjective components of their fear reaction. Others who are less successful at doing this accomplish the same general purpose by failing to identify the subjective phenomena as indicative of fear. They complain only of vague, uncomfortable, tense, and disturbing feelings.

> "Something is the matter with me. I feel very strange, as if something terrible were going to happen, but I can't say what."
> "You mean, you are afraid of something, you are anxious or apprehensive?"
> "No, not at all. I'm not afraid of anything. I just feel strange, that's all."

It goes without saying that both types of patients—those who have no subjective symptoms of anxiety, and those who do have them but fail to recognize their relation to fear—are completely at a loss in understanding the etiology of their somatic symptoms. They are thoroughly convinced that these symtoms are simply the product of some underlying organic pathology.

The ability to admit a large amount of neurotic anxiety tò consciousness and to manage it successfully—either through intelligent resignation (learning to live with it), creating a propitious environment, or lowering ego-aspiration level constructively and increasing intrinsic self-esteem—is very important in avoiding disabling psychological or psychosomatic defenses against anxiety. It is a well-established clinical fact that the greater an individual's tolerance for conscious anxiety, the less likely he is to fall prey to compulsions, obsessions, phobias, hysteria, hypochondriasis, or psychosomatic syndromes such as neurocirculatory asthenia or peptic ulcer. All of these latter methods of anxiety-reduction are indicative of low tolerance for anxiety and of failure in controlling it through more constructive methods.

However, the relative rarity of pure cases of anxiety uncomplicated by one or more of the disabling defenses is a tribute to the inherent difficulty of controlling anxiety on a conscious level alone. To admit anxiety to oneself is a confession of weakness that persons with impaired self-esteem can make only by willingness to withstand considerable further ego trauma. To admit anxiety to others is to invite loss of respect, as well as various forms of aggression, and victimization in those aspects of interpersonal relations in which success is a reward for self-assurance, self-respect, and self-assertion. It is true that in moments of desperation the admission of anxiety can be used as a defensive measure. The individual in effect may plead, "Please help me. I am so frightened. You have nothing to fear from such a pathetically timorous creature as I."

The danger of such appeals in our competitive society, however, is too great to permit their use under ordinary circumstances. Less traumatic and less hazardous, for example, is to express anxiety psychosomatically rather than consciously. At this level also, it affords some secondary gain, that is, it offers a socially acceptable excuse for avoiding stressful experience, provides grounds for excusing failure and lack of productivity, and sometimes elicits support, solicitude, and sympathy. Another advantage is in the provision of a convenient locus for the displacement of the source of the anxiety. The individual can now admit to a conscious anxiety attributable to concern over health. The net effect of this psychosomatic expression, therefore, is anxiety-reducing, thereby lessening the need and the possibility for its conscious management; and if conscious expression of anxiety does eventuate, it can be related to the less threatening and more acceptable cause of organic disease.

The gains thus achieved in the reduction of conscious anxiety, however, are not without their price. Of all the syndromes related to anxiety, uncomplicated conscious anxiety is the most uncomfortable, but also the least dangerous and maladaptive. So long as some habitual and rigid anxiety-reducing defense is not yet firmly established, there is hope of evolving a more constructive solution. As long as he suffers consciously, one is sure that the patient is still striving for adjustment to a world of reality on an adult level, that he has neither renounced the struggle (depression) nor succumbed to immature goals in an autistic setting (schizophrenia). He has not yet paid the price of achieving security by unduly limiting the scope of his operations or by rationalizing failure on the basis of illness. And lastly he avoids the situation of a psychologically induced invalidism that can end conceivably in chronic illness or even death (e.g., peptic ulcer, chronic ulcerative colitis).

The distinctions that have been made in this section between various types of anxiety are summarized in Table 4. Each type will receive extended treatment in later sections.

RELATIONSHIP BETWEEN INTRINSIC AND EXTRINSIC SYSTEMS OF SECURITY AND ADEQUACY

When the adolescent finally begins to derive the greater portion of his or her security and feelings of adequacy from extrinsic sources, what is the fate of their intrinsic counterparts, which for so many years occupied such a central position in ego organization? Two suggestions have already been offered in answer to this question: (1) the hypothesis that satellization leaves a permanent residue in personality structure; and (2) the claim that extrinsic status is the major *current* source of adequacy feelings in adult life.

These statements imply that as a consequence of experiencing feelings of intrinsic security and adequacy over a prolonged period of time, a permanent change occurs in the way in which an individual tends to value himself and to estimate the extent of the jeopardy menacing his future safety. Hence, a certain residual or underlying *quality* of security and adequacy feelings carry over into the future despite the absence of adequate current experience that could give rise to them. (Actually, of course, the adult who satellized as a child continues to form many satellizing-like relationships as an adult; and generally speaking, he tends to be loved and accepted for himself by his family and by several associates. At the same time, these sources for feelings of security and adequacy constitute only a

Table 4
Classification of Anxiety States

I. Source of Threat is Objectively Hazardous
    A. *Normal (Situational) Anxiety:* Source of threat lies essentially in an objective hazard or in an objective incapacity of unusual magnitude. Affective reaction is proportionate to the objective threat involved.
II. Source of Threat is Mainly Subjective: An adequate objective hazard is absent, and the affective reaction is disproportionate to the precipitating objective threat:
    A. *Developmental Anxiety:* Source of threat emanates from personality defects arising in the course of ego development.
        1. *Neurotic (Ego-Hypertrophy) Anxiety:* Source of threat is related to ego hypertrophy, i.e., a history of failure in ego devaluation with residual impairment of intrinsic self-esteem, and a predisposition toward impairment of extrinsic self-esteem.
        2. *Maturational Anxiety:* Source of threat is related to residual defects in ego maturation.
    B. *Symptomatic Anxiety:* Source of threat is not primarily related to residual defects in ego development but to other psychopathological mechanisms associated with symptom formation, e.g., repression, hostility, conflict.
III. Source of Threat is Both Objective and Subjective:
    A. *Transitional Anxiety:* Anxiety arises during periods of crisis in ego development, but is self-limited in duration and in relation to extreme external and internal pressures for personality change, rather than in relation to residual defects in ego structure. The sources of threat come from new social expectations, loss of established bisocial status, lack of current status, uncertainty regarding the attainment of future status, and internalization of new developmental aspirations.

---

small fraction of the adult's *total* current experience and all of its important ego-related variables.)

It appears, then, that feelings of intrinsic security and adequacy constitute a fairly stable, ongoing cluster of attitudes related to self, which persist into adult life and interact with current variables that influence extrinsic security and adequacy as well as their correlates. The precise relationships that prevail between these two systems are undoubtedly highly complex. The authors however, are inclined to the view that in individuals endowed with such feelings of intrinsic security and adequacy, the range of fluctuation that is possible (for resultant levels of security and adequacy) in response to extrinsic factors is both narrow and peripheral. That is, the intrinsic feelings of such an adult tend to remain fairly constant regardless of the environmental vicissitudes met with in later life. Even in the face of prolonged and consistent reverses in those areas of activity reflecting adversely on extrinsic security and adequacy, he or she stands a good chance of remaining basically secure and adequate.

Applying this principle specifically, the amount of intrinsic security possessed by an individual predetermines to a large extent his capacity to benefit from extrinsic security. The intrinsically insecure person who strives desperately to make himself secure with money, power, and influence seldom impresses anyone as succeeding in this goal regardless of the enormity of his material success. The same holds true with respect to feelings of adequacy as illustrated in the following analysis of Lord Byron's triumphs by Gardner Murphy, (1947):

> But all of these left him hungry for simple acceptance, for regard for himself as a person which no one knew how to build within him. His fundamental sickness was lack of self-acceptance, self-love, status and prestige in his own eyes. Were it not for this, the admiring majority who loved his verse would have sufficed. . .The trouble was that his inner response to himself was rejection, and those who rejected him fed that scorn of self which consumed him throughout his life. There was no quest for power as such; there was a never-satisfied quest for serenity in contemplating himself.

Existing levels of intrinsic security and adequacy are also inversely related to the intensity of the individual's needs for their extrinsic counterparts. The reason for this is fairly self-evident: A person endowed with a reasonable level of self-acceptance has something upon which he can fall back in difficult times. He possesses a basic core of self-esteem that enjoys an absolute, market-free value; he is not obliged to justify his existence entirely on the basis of extrinsic criteria of competence and superiority. Were he to lose all of the emoluments of his extrinsic status he would still retain the basic framework of his self-esteem.

A good cultural illustration of this principle can be seen among the Arapesh, who because of heightened feelings of intrinsic self-esteem seem to be almost completely unmotivated by needs for power, competitive distinction, and hierarchical status (Mead, 1939). Similarly in working with gifted children in our own culture, the senior author found a wide range in the distribution of responsiveness to an incentive of personal prestige and recognition that appeared to be correlated negatively with magnitude of intrinsic self-esteem (Ausubel, 1951). On the other hand, children who seemed to enjoy greater intrinsic feelings of adequacy than their fellows were more responsive to motives such as inherent interest in the subject matter, intellectual curiosity, etc.

The fact that intrinsically secure and adequate individuals are not susceptible to catastrophic impairment of self-esteem and are not driven by ego aspirations that are unrealistically high and resistant to downward modification also makes them highly invulnerable to neurotic anxiety. In contrast to the intrinsically insecure and inadequate group, their anxiety can usually be traced to an objectively hazardous threat rather than to a subjective threat derived from a breakdown in feelings of adequacy.

Relationship Between Security and Adequacy

One of the earliest and best known efforts to bring some order out of the conceptual chaos enveloping this field was Plant's attempt to differentiate between the concepts of security and adequacy (Plant, 1937). *Security,* according to Plant, is a product of the home and consists of the feelings that a child acquires as a result of being valued for himself. *Adequacy,* on the other hand, is Plant's term for the feeling of self-regard that a child develops as a consequence of the things he can do and the reputation he acquires for doing same. A typical source of adequacy, therefore, would be the school. Plant summed up this distinction neatly by referring to security as "who-status" and to adequacy as "what-status."

Unfortunately, Plant's choice of a differential criterion for distinguishing between security and adequacy was a most unhappy one; for, it created more confusion than it actually dissipated. The main difficulty was that *both* concepts, as he defined them, refer to feelings based on a valuation of the child's worth; both, therefore, are definitions of different *types* of adequacy, corresponding almost identically to the definitions we have given above for intrinsic and extrinsic adequacy respectively. The authors contend that it is less confusing to distinguish between the two types of adequacy by merely appropriate qualifying adjectives (i.e., intrinsic and extrinsic, a distinction that would also hold true in the case of security); and to reserve the differentiation between security and adequacy for the more crucial distinction that can be made between two different categories of ego-related values, namely, the future safety of self (security) as against its relative worth and importance (adequacy).

Another difficulty inherent in Plant's position is clearly illustrated by his assertion that rural children have more security (who-status) than urban children, that the latter try to compensate for this lack of security by striving for greater adequacy (what-status). However, it would really be more accurate to state that rural children have greater opportunities to acquire extrinsic feelings of adequacy (what-status) by serving in economically useful roles and that urban children compensate for these absent opportunities by retaining as much intrinsic adequacy as long as possible.

Still another difficulty with Plant's distinction between security and adequacy is its failure to recognize the interdependence as well as the difference between the two concepts. Actually, they are not nearly so distinct as Plant would have us believe. The intrinsic forms, for example, are both products of parent attitudes reflecting unconditional acceptance and intrinsic valuation of the child. In fact, the most tenable hypothesis regarding the relationship prevailing between the two concepts is that each interacts with and influences the other and that adequacy can best be understood as the component portion of security that is concerned with the *value* of self.

This latter relationship can be more readily appreciated if we approach it from its negative aspects, that is, the relationship between inadequacy and insecurity. In our previous discussion of anxiety, we had assumed that when a threat to adequacy reaches a certain intensity, an affect of fear (anxiety) is elicited; and that frequently the source of such a threat emanates from the impairment of self-esteem itself (neurotic anxiety). We are now ready to answer explicitly the question that underlies this assumption: why does a threat to self-esteem lead to an expression of fear affect?

There are two chief reasons. First, a challenge to the individual's sense of adequacy raises the question of whether he is sufficiently competent to manipulate his environment for purposes of satisfactory adjustment and maintenance of biosocial position. If the threat then becomes increasingly more formidable, he feels incompetent to cope with adjustive problems and on the verge of being overwhelmed by environmental vicissitudes. It is at this point that he reacts with fear in contemplating the future. Anxiety, therefore, results primarily because of a threat to self-esteem that is serious enough in its implications to jeopardize his future safety. It can, therefore, be considered a subtype of the more inclusive term, *insecurity,* in which the threat, instead of being projected more directly at various aspects of the individual's safety, is deviously aimed at the same target through the more indirect route of undermining his sense of adequacy in coping with his environment.

Second, after undergoing several experiences in which self-esteem is impaired (but not necessarily in a catastrophic sense), the individual begins to realize that such states of anxiety actually interfere with problem-solving activity, and hence, potentially menace his safety. He, therefore, has still another good reason to be fearful (insecure) about threats directed against his self-esteem. On the other hand, it is evident from the foregoing that a strong sense of adequacy provides the same two reasons—only in reverse, namely, hope and confidence—for enhancing his sense of security.

Looking at the relationship between security and adequacy from the other direction, we find that enhancement of security also leads to increased feelings of adequacy. It is a well-known clinical fact that the threshold for anxiety responses can be markedly raised by placing an individual in a generally secure environment. Let us recall that one important reason for the minimal presence of transitional anxiety in the crisis of ego devaluation is the fact that the devaluing process is usually carried out with a general concern for the gratification of a child's dependency needs. Conversely, however, where the general climate of ego devaluation is characterized by parental rejection, hostility, and capriciousness in satisfying a child's needs, transitional anxiety is quite intense and becomes continuous with neurotic anxiety. Similarly in adult life, in the absence of any specific threat directed against self-esteem, a decrease in general security will result in a pronounced lowering of the threshold for anxiety reactions.

Security and Adequacy in Non-Satellizers

Because non-satellizing children are not unconditionally accepted and valued for themselves, they obviously cannot acquire any intrinsic feelings of security and adequacy. The best they can hope for is to achieve their extrinsic counterparts; and since complete ego devaluation represents too abrupt and traumatic an alternative for them to accept during the crisis of ego devaluation, this requires the acquisition of power and prestige commensurate with the exaggerated ego aspirations residual from infancy. These hypertrophic ego demands also play a current compensatory role in that they are largely powered by the absence of intrinsic adequacy; and although they do eventually predispose the individual to frustration and further loss of self-esteem, they do generate, in of themselves, feelings of extrinsic adequacy. Security also is sought in the same general manner—through extrinsic safeguards—although the rejected non-satellizer (within the limits imposed by his fear of further rejection) often tries to establish satellizing-like and other types of emotional relationships in which he can feel accepted for himself.

Earlier we suggested that in the absence of intrinsic adequacy, the attainment of extrinsic self-esteem can only be peripheral, and, hence, not very satisfying. In addition, chronic frustration, with its disrupting effect on performance efforts, is more or less inevitable, inasmuch as the ego-aspiration level tends to be tenaciously and unrealistically resistant to lowering in the face of failure because the individual is unable to become reconciled to a lower prestige status. Also, in possessing a highly developed self-critical faculty, the individual will gain little by way of ego enhancement since the technique of overvaluing the worth of his or her own performance has not been learned.

Nevertheless, the chances for accomplishment are greater than could normally be expected from the individual's level of ability because of (1) the large amount of prestige motivation generated by hypertrophic ego demands, and (2) a very high tolerance for goal frustration. This is the one bright spot in an otherwise dismal picture, since it allows for the possibility of creating environmental conditions that are relatively secure and hence propitious for the maintenance of anxiety on a tolerable level.

The absence of intrinsic security and adequacy is itself the crucial predisposing cause of neurotic anxiety; and if brought about by early parental rejection with resulting catastrophic impairment of self-esteem, the other necessary etiological factor (the precipitating cause) is concomitantly supplied. If not, either later parental rejection, or some other catastrophic blow to self-esteem will almost certainly supervene at some later date and thus make the occurrence of neurotic anxiety almost inevitable. The likelihood of this occurrence is, of course, greatly increased by the presence of exaggerated ego aspirations that set the stage for large scale deflation of self-esteem at some time or another.

A realistic therapeutic expectation in anxiety states, therefore, is to reduce anxiety to a minimum, to ward off acute attacks, and to keep the patient comfortable at as high a level of productivity as possible without developing somatic symptoms or other objectionable defenses. The restoration of security and adequacy on the same basis as can be expected in persons with a history of satellization is a forlorn hope that one should never try to realize; and if the dynamics of anxiety neurosis were fully appreciated by psychotherapists, it is something that probably never would be attempted.

NEUROTIC ANXIETY

Etiology

We have defined neurotic anxiety as a form of developmental anxiety (occurring in an individual with a history of failure in ego devaluation) in which the essential source of the threat to self-esteem arises from a catastrophically impaired sense of adequacy. It manifests itself as a tendency to overreact with fear to any stimulus that threatens to impair self-esteem further. Such stimuli generally consist of a limited group of adjustive situations having special reference to prestige areas in which there is selective ego involvement or painful memories of an especially dismal or humiliating nature.

This definition makes explicit both the predisposing and the precipitating causes of neurotic anxiety. The condition could not occur in the absence of a particular disturbance of a normal parent-child relationship, which leads in turn to a failure in ego devaluation with its consequences of non-satellization, to a failure to acquire intrinsic security and adequacy, and to a retention of hypertrophic ego aspirations. First, an individual with intrinsic security and adequacy can never suffer a sufficiently catastrophic blow to self-esteem, since such environmental debacles can result only in deflating consequences confined to the peripheral reaches of self-esteem. Second, in the case of rejected children, the catastrophic impairment of self-esteem inheres in the act of rejection itself. And third and last, if the catastrophic event must occur later, it is rendered almost inevitable by virtue of the individual's vulnerability to (1) core involvement of his self-esteem (in the absence of intrinsic adequacy) and (2) large-scale collapse of his goal structure because of the presence of grandiose ego aspirations.

Hence, the very occurrence of neurotic anxiety becomes both a prerequisite for its further existence and a discouraging prognostic indicator that the underlying pathological condition will be indefinitely perpetuated as a chronic disturbance punctuated perhaps by sporadic acute exacerbations. The authors firmly believe that the predisposing and precipitating factors mentioned above constitute the sole necessary ingredients required for initiating the mechanism of neurotic anxiety. True, the factors of repression, hostility, and conflict that figure so prominently in other theories can complicate and intensify existing neurotic anxiety. But these same factors can also occur independently in the form of symptomatic anxiety. The only other psychopathological channel that can conceivably lead to neurotic anxiety is the occurrence in mild satellizers of a particularly traumatic blow to self-esteem that has permanent implications (e.g., a disabling or disfiguring disease). But even in such cases, it is doubtful whether the anxiety is either as intense or as irreversible as in the more usual sequence of etiological events.

In the overvalued child, the same susceptibility to catastrophic impairment of self-esteem holds true, since intrinsic security and adequacy cannot be acquired so long as that child realizes that he or she is not valued as a unique individual but only as a channel for bringing greater glory to the parent. Thus, like the rejected child, the child who is prized for extrinsic reasons is driven to seek extrinsic security and adequacy through superior achievement compatible with his or her hypertrophic ego demands, a fact which sets the stage for later traumatic devaluation of self-esteem. However, although the extrinsically valued child shares all of the predisposing causes to neurotic anxiety with the rejected child, he has yet to experience the catastrophic blow to self-esteem which is the essential precipitating factor, an event that may be deferred for many years or conceivably may never take place at all.

As long as the attitude of parental overvaluation is maintained, extrinsic adequacy can be kept at a reasonably high level. There is always the danger, however, that the parent might change over to a rejecting attitude as a result of growing weary of his subservient role, or of deciding that the child either does not have sufficient ability to succeed, or is a less promising candidate than a younger sibling. If all of these hazards are successfully avoided, increasingly greater danger awaits him outside the home, as his parents become progressively less able to provide the extrinsic status he requires. Once he leaves the biased atmosphere of the home, he finds prejudice directed against him rather than in his favor because of his unpleasant self-centeredness and aggressiveness. Disastrous collapse of the grandiose goal structure usually tends to occur in the formative years when crucial decisions regarding educational and vocational ambitions have to be made, except perhaps in those rare cases where large-scale frustration can be prevented or delayed by unusual ability, wealth, or family connections.

Anxiety as Ego Damage, Defense, or Physiological Change

As a central value in personality organization, the enhancement and defense of which is one of the most powerful drives motivating human behavior, it is only to be expected that threats directed against self-esteem will provoke a wide variety of responses. These responses may be divided into three general categories: defense, escape, and ego damage. Defense efforts include reactive attempts to enhance threatened self-esteem; to make the self appear strong, competent, and masterful; to excuse, explain, and rationalize failure; etc. Escape mechanisms provide opportunities for withdrawing the self beyond the reach of possible threats. Ego damage, on the other hand, includes current and residual reactions (i.e., threats against self-esteem), all of which in and of themselves have no adjustive value but are merely reflective of the disruptive and disorganizing effects that such threats can have on personality structure.

Depending on its intensity and relation to actual impairment of self-esteem, anxiety may be considered either a defense reaction or a manifestation of ego damage. When a threat to adequacy becomes sufficiently serious to challenge the safety of an individual, it elicits the affect of insecurity. Moderate amounts of this affect in a reasonably secure and adequate person have adjustive value in that they facilitate the mobilization of the individual's adaptive efforts. However, if anxiety reaches the proportions of panic, behavior becomes hopelessly disorganized and maladaptive.

If the threat is pushed still farther, it may very well gain its goal, that is, an actual impairment of self-esteem may result. This may be the outcome of a humiliating defeat, of a loss in biosocial status, or of extreme frustration in an ego-involved area. It is clear, however, that this impairment and the accompanying anxiety can only be considered as evidence of ego damage that serves no adjustive fuction *per se,* although in creating a need for anxiety reduction, it gives rise to many defense and escape mechanisms. Again, in persons who are intrinsically secure and adequate, such damage is peripheral and transitory. But in the case of neurotic anxiety, impaired self-esteem is a permanent and relatively irreversible form of ego damage, in much the same sense as the replacement of functional cardiac muscle by fibrous tissue in coronary disease of the heart.

This residual damage is severe enough to constitute the main source of threat in neurotic anxiety, since in the absence of sufficient confidence in one's ability to cope with adjustive problems, any insignificant environmental threat to self-esteem appears extremely menacing. Returning to our analogy of the heart, we could say that in persons with normal hearts, the source of the threat of cardiac failure lies in excessive environmental demands, for example, sustained overwork, insufficent rest. Once the heart is severely damaged, however, its adaptive powers to stress are seriously impaired, and any additional burden, no matter how trivial, is dangerous. And just as the main source of the threat of heart failure in organic heart cases lies *within* the damaged heart muscle, the main source of the threat of collapsed self-esteem in anxiety neurosis lies *within* the individual's impaired self-esteem. The threat of "failure brings collapse because life has been structured in terms of self-enhancement, and because the struggle to earn a favorable view of the self has been unremitting." (Ausubel, 1952)

If ego damage does not go beyond the stage of anxiety, however, the individual may be considered fortunate indeed. In fact, the psychopathologist working in a hospital for mental diseases rarely finds any signs of pure, uncomplicated anxiety; and when he does, he regards them as excellent prognostic indicators. Anxiety is a sign that vigorous striving for adult adjustment in a reality setting is still in progress. Besides indicating that the patient is not yet utilizing some of the more objectionable defenses, it conveys the more important assurance that he has not availed himself of the relief from anxiety that can be obtained from succumbing to further ego damage. This relief is available when the individual finally decides that he needs it badly enough to relinquish the self-esteem he has been defending at such cost. It can be gained either by accepting defeat and ceasing to strive (depression), or by ceasing to strive for adult goals on a reality level (schizophrenia). Both alternatives result in extensive damage and personality disorganization.

Agitation. This is an intermediate stage between anxiety and its two psychotic complications, more usually depression. It is indicative of the fact that anxiety bordering on panic has become so severe and continuous that even the everyday routines of living can no longer be managed successfully. All of the individual's organized defenses have broken down; and disorganization is so rampant that primitive fear of death, which ordinarily can be repressed at only minimal levels of self-esteem, stalks brazenly across the stage of consciousness. When anxiety reaches this point, the pressure for yielding to one of the two psychotic solutions promising relief from this agony becomes almost unbearable.

Anxiety in Rejected and Overvalued Individuals

One of the most striking differences between rejected and overvalued children in their anxiety manifestations is the latency of the condition in the case of the latter. This is due to the postponement of the catastrophic blow to self-esteem, an event that in rejected children occurs at the close of infancy. Related to this difference is the fact that the overvalued child enjoys a superfluity of extrinsic adequacy at home, while the rejected child is enveloped in a stern, hostile environment that emphasizes persistently his worthlessness, thereby widening continually the gap between aspirations and reality. The rejected child, therefore, carries within him a greater burden of repressed hostility, bitterness, and resentment. No wonder, then, that much of his motivation has a negative quality, being inspired by considerations of revenge and an "I'll-show-them" attitude.

The blow that results in catastrophic impairment of self-esteem is also much more devastating in the case of the rejected child because it occurs at a time when ego defenses are weaker, and because the ego has not as yet had any opportunity to be fortified by experiences productive of extrinsic adequacy; nor, in view of the child's complete dependence on his parents at this stage of development, is there any possibility of obtaining other sources of extrinsic status. His self-esteem, therefore, is more completely shattered and hence less able to be benefited by gains in extrinsic adequacy. Regardless of the objective magnitude of success achieved, he can never quite take himself or his accomplishments very seriously; for indelibly engraved in the innermost reaches of his self-esteem is an unshakable conviction of being a worthless, despicable little creature whom even his own parents could not accept.

In contrast, the overvalued individual in periods of remission from acute attacks of anxiety is buoyant, exuberant, self-confident, and full of self-assurance. He does not suffer at all from inability to take himself or his success seriously. But this expansiveness, which he manifests in "good times," makes him less able to weather subsequent acute attacks of anxiety than the rejected individual, the very invariablity of whose depressed self-esteem protects him from the impact of violent and abrupt fluctuations in fortune.

In terms of the possibilities for improvement that depend on more than superficial factors in a situation, the rejected individual also shows to advantage. He still enjoys the option of establishing satellizing-like relationships with others, and is generally capable of being loved for himself. The resulting feelings of intrinsic security and adequacy that he gains from such experiences not only reduce his current load of anxiety, but also make it possible for him to lower his ego-aspiration level. The overvalued individual, on the other hand, finds satellization too degrading, and is usually too obnoxiously selfish to inspire genuine feelings of love for him in other persons.

Because of his extended training in the ways of infantile omnipotence, the overvalued child is also more reluctant to surrender the prerogative of executive dependence. However, when he realizes the expediency of acquiring executive independence, he is not hampered as is the rejected child by overt anxiety in the learning of new motor, social, and intellectual skills. Nevertheless, in periods of acute anxiety in later life, he is more apt to regress to the position of demanding assistance from others.

We have also seen that the rejected individual, trained in the habit of repressing self-assertive and aggressive feelings, develops introverted and withdrawing tendencies, tends to avoid situations involving conflict, and intellectualizes his aggression. As a result, he fails to master effective social techniques of expressing aggression, a circumstance that makes him vulnerable to exploitation by others and generates more hostility that requires repression. This seething internal reservoir of repressed hostility in turn intensifies existing anxiety. The overvalued individual, on the other hand, has had abundant experience in giving vent to hostile feelings. His problem is to learn how to make his aggressive tactics seem less offensive and ruthless than they really are.

SYMPTOMATIC ANXIETY

We have chosen to identify the term "neurotic anxiety" with the principal type of anxiety induced by a subjective threat. This is the traditional anxiety neurosis, the origin of which we have related to a primary defect in ego devaluation that predisposes an individual to catastrophic impairment of self-esteem. It is this damage to self-esteem that constitutes, in turn, the subjective threat. Apart from *situational* (normal) anxiety, however, there are still three types of anxiety induced by subjective threats that we have yet to consider. When the source of the threat is related to defects in ego maturation, it may be called *maturational* anxiety. When it is related to normal developmental pressures found in transitional (crisis) periods of ego development, it may be termed *transitional* anxiety. And finally, when it is associated neither with normal developmental pressures nor with residual developmental defects but with other psychopathological mechanisms, it may be termed *symptomatic* anxiety. This last type of anxiety may be discussed under the subheadings of repression, hostility, conflict, and guilt.

Repression*

A principal source of symptomatic "anxiety" arises when an individual discovers within himself attitudes, motivations, etc., that are personally or socially unacceptable. Anxiety originates in this case from the existence of internal impulses that, if expressed, would expose the individual to loss of self-esteem. Since in most cases, however, the individual's safety (rather than his self-esteem)

*See the section on accessibility in the earlier part of this chapter.

is involved, it is usually more accurate to refer to the resulting effect as symptomatic *insecurity*. Repression plays no part in generating this anxiety; it is employed merely as a defensive measure to protect the individual from the consequences of executing his dangerous impulses.

It is in connection with this particular function of repression that anxiety is often referred to as a "danger signal" (Masserman, 1946). It enables an individual to avoid danger situations that arise from dissident elements within himself and that are at odds with cultural standards and their internalized counterparts. So long as man remains dependent upon his culture he can neither flee nor express himself with complete disregard for social conventions. Hence, it is likely that repression will continue to play the highly important role of enabling the individual "to avoid the danger situation of which anxiety sounds the alarm" (Freud, 1936). Other defenses are both possible and undoubtedly more desirable, but none perhaps is so easily available.

Hostility

Hostile feelings offer an excellent example of internal impulses that place the individual in jeopardy by inviting social reprisal. But for other reasons as well, it is productive of symptomatic insecurity and anxiety. In all instances of dependency, a condition that prevails to a greater or lesser degree throughout the lifetime of every individual, feelings of hostility arouse the danger of alienating the person on whom the individual is dependent for his safety, support, security, livelihood, etc. (Horney, 1937). The rejected child, for example, feels tremendously hostile toward his parents, but at the same time fears his hostility because he cannot risk alienating them further on account of his dependency. The satellizing child is also made insecure by his hostile impulses since his parent's approval of him as well as his derived status is thereby endangered.

Feelings of hostility also generate insecurity (in situations where there is no dependency also) because of the expectation that it will lead to retaliation or counteraggression. This fear of retaliation (as evidenced by a sharp increase in the repression of hostility) becomes much more pronounced after the development of conscience, a fact which suggests the hypothesis that the child might feel less threatened by corporal punishment, deprivation, and loss of succorance than by the shame and discomfort associated with guilt feelings. Because of the self-reproach implied in attitudes of guilt, the pretty, unsullied picture of self results in anxiety as well as insecurity. For the same reason, the child also feels that such parental reprisals are justifiable and deserved rather than the mere reflection of superior force.

Because hostile impulses endanger the individual's safety and derived status as well as expose him to counteraggression and the trauma of guilt, the need for their repression is thus strong. Other self-protective measures, however, are also available. The provocation for hostility can be obviated if no cause for anger or affront is ever perceived. Some children, for example, are able to interpret all parental aggression as not only justifiable but also as a disguised form of benevolence. Many adults in our culture are also unable to perceive any malevolence, especially in people of superior status; and if this becomes too obvious to deny, they always have a ready excuse at hand or some basis for claiming the other's "good intentions." Another method of securing safety under such conditions, as Horney (1937) points out, is to hedge in one's hostility by various neurotic trends such as exaggerated compliancy, unobtrusiveness, or dependence. A quite different approach is to seek safety in power and independence, that is, to become so powerful and independent of others that safety is possible *despite* one's hostility.

If repression is chosen over other self-protective measures, all of the same reasons that we discussed above, which explain why repression is productive of symptomatic anxiety, also apply in this case. In addition, repression tends to become overgeneralized as a defensive device because of its easy availability, and to find application indiscriminately in all situations where hostility might arise. Hence, even in situations which require agressive behavior and in which hostility is not particularly dangerous, it is still repressed. This results in the production of the familiar overinhibited individual who represses all hostile feelings lest their expression, even on a single occasion, expose him to danger. By selectively failing to perceive actions in other persons that normally elicit a hostile response, he may even allow himself not to develop feelings of hostility. The rejected child, as indicated previously, is so overtrained in repressing hostility that he or she often fails to learn socially effective techniques of self-assertion. An unfortunate by-product of this passive, compliant attitude toward aggression by others is that it encourages the latter to continue their ruthless, exploitative actions.

Since hostile impulses are productive of guilt feelings in satellizers (and sometimes in rejected individuals), strong efforts are usually made to disown or justify them. Both aims can be simultaneously accomplished by projecting the hostility onto others. If this mechanism is successful, one either rids oneself of hostility by planting it elsewhere or justifies its presence on the grounds of self-defense. Although guilt-engendered anxiety can be obviated in this fashion, a new source of anxiety is created, however, in the form of a hostile, threatening environment.

We wish to emphasize, nonetheless, that anxiety arising from hostility is only symptomatic anxiety, which in terms of origin, intensity, expressive characteristics, and prognosis is quite distantly removed from neurotic anxiety. Hostility, to be sure, arises almost invariably in situations leading to the development or expression of neurotic anxiety. But the primary threat responsible for the neurotic anxiety is not derived from hostile impulses, but from gross impairment of the individual's self-esteem. Also, in such cases where satellizing loyalties are not implicated, hostility does not arouse guilt but fear of reprisal; hence, insecurity is a more appropriate term for the secondary affect engendered by the hostility.

If we turn now to the other side of this relationship, it becomes evident that

Horney was also correct in her proposition that anxiety causes hostility (1937). It is extremely plausible to suppose that an anxious individual will feel hostile toward persons who are in some way responsible for his anxiety; and this is confirmed by clinical observation. However, as already indicated, we cannot go so far as Horney in believing that hostility inevitably inheres in the fact of dependency (1937).

Anxiety may also lead to hostility in order to provide the anxiety neurotic with a more self-consistent orientation toward life. Hence, in order to justify his anxiety, he is motivated to perceive the world as hostile, which requires him in turn to develop feelings of hostility. This reaction may also be interpreted as a form of displacement of the source of the anxiety from a subjective to an objective focus. The latter form is obviously more acceptable and more manageable.

We must also examine the occurrence and value of aggression as a defensive technique in anxiety states. As an occasional device designed to enhance self-esteem on a relative basis by deflating the status of others, it is a very common phenomenon. As a permanent form of defense against anxiety, it is more rare because it tends to generate too much anxiety and leads to extreme social unpopularity. A more likely defense against anxiety is repression of hostility, and the assumption of a sympathetic, uncritical attitude toward others in the hope that they will reciprocate and thus create a situation propitious for anxiety reduction. Hostility is more apt to be exhibited in anxiety-ridden individuals after they become more secure in a given situation.

In any event, we can be sure that the anxiety neurotic is unable objectively to evaluate the merits or faults of individuals who either threaten or enhance his precarious security. His perception of the former is ten times as black as reality, and his perception of the latter is equally fallacious in the opposite direction. This is confirmed by empirical evidence which indicates that the better adjusted, more successful and self-accepting individual, as well as the individual who is ranked high in a given trait is more prone to estimate his own and others' abilities realistically and in accord with group ratings (Cogan, Conklin, & Hollingsworth, 1915; Jackson, 1929, Perry, 1940; Sheerer, 1949, Weingarten, 1949). Level of aspiration also tends to be more realistic after an experience of success than after an experience of failure (Lewin et al., 1944; Sears, 1940).

Conflict

Not long after Horney had declared that the danger inhering in hostile impulses and their repression constituted the source of "basic anxiety" (1937), she modified her position considerably to place greater emphasis upon conflict between "neurotic trends" as the important etiological factor (1945). Such conflict according to Horney, arises between contradictory personality trends through which the individual seeks safety. The reason for conflict is that on one hand a person may seek feelings of adequacy through self-enhancement, that is, through self-assertive, independent, aggressive, and power-seeking measures; and on the other hand, he or she may be so fearful of the consequences to self-esteem if such efforts should fail that security is sought through dependence, conformity and the hedging in of hostile impulses. These two approaches to acquiring security and adequacy are obviously mutually exclusive. A decision to "play it safe" by behaving in a compliant, passive, and dependent fashion poses a threat to a person's hope for ego enhancement through independence and aggressive action; whereas a decision in favor of the latter undermines security by threatening a trend that guards against the expression of hostile, aggressive impulses. Whichever choice one makes, therefore, leads either to feelings of insecurity or inadequacy. The same conflict is present in the choice between strivings for prestige and fears of failure; between desires to be loved and fears of rejection; between needs for the expression of hostility and independence and fears of alienating persons on whom one is dependent; between desires for material success at any cost and inhibitions stemming from moral considerations.

Besides the insecurity or inadequacy that follows from choosing an adjustive mechanism that automatically threatens an alternative device through which safety or self-enhancement is sought, conflict tends to increase helplessness by fostering confusion, indecision, stalemate, and hence failure to take any action whatsoever. Horney (1937) maintains that this dilemma is especially true since these "neurotic trends" tend to be compulsive in nature. It is quite understandable, therefore, that any factor inducing paralysis of decision or action undermines an individual's confidence in his capacity to cope with his environment, and hence is productive of anxiety.

It is important, however, to distinguish the aspect of conflict that threatens security and adequacy from the aspect that merely results in neurophysiological and psychological tension as a consequence of frustrating needs. Conflict frequently leads to frustration of needs when two needs are incompatible. if one is chosen, the other must either be denied or repressed. If a stalemate ensues, both needs are frustrated.

We can summarize this discussion by reiterating what has already been said in relation to repression and hostility as etiological factors in anxiety: Conflict is a secondary and symptomatic form of anxiety that can either occur independently, or can intensify existing neurotic anxiety. In individuals who are basically secure and adequate, conflict cannot produce more than transitory and peripheral anxiety; and in cases of anxiety neurosis, conflict would be unable to precipitate serious bouts of anxiety if the patient were not already rendered specially vulnerable by virtue of his impaired sense of adequacy. It is the latter factor, therefore, that must be accounted the major source of the threat in neurotic anxiety.

Guilt

Feelings of guilt arise when an individual perceives that his behavior is not in harmony with internalized moral values. They are especially intense and painful when the moral values concerned are the product of deep emotional loyalties typically formed in the course of a satellizing relationship. Hence, just as neurotic anxiety tends to be characteristic of intrinsically insecure and inadequate individuals, severe guilt reactions are more commonly found in persons with a history of childhood satellization. Nevertheless, guilt is found frequently enough in non-satellizers, and anxiety in satellizers. Guilt feelings are a very common cause of symptomatic anxiety in intrinsically adequate individuals.

We have already seen that one important reason why hostile impulses inspire anxiety is the fact that they also give rise to guilt feelings that are responsible in turn for the resulting anxiety. The relationship between guilt and anxiety is simply this: the condition for experiencing guilt is a perception of one's behavior that is incongruous with the pretty, idealized picture of self that we all nurture. The resulting necessity for acknowledging the culpability and debasement of self is the cause of the shame and discomfort of guilt, feelings that are feared more than physical punishment.

Guilt feelings also greatly intensify the fear of punishment or reprisal for misbehavior. If there were no guilt feelings involved, the individual would merely be apprehensive on the basis of his objective chances of being caught and punished. But if he feels guilty, he also believes that he deserves punishment and *should* be punished. The threat of punishment is thus removed from the sphere of objective probability alone, and becomes fraught with moral implications. When punishment is felt to be justified it tends to be perceived as inevitable, since the individual fears that if he is not caught he might very well give himself up in order to be at peace with himself again. It is a well known fact that guilty persons frequently seek punishment, since punishment is the one sure method of reducing guilt feelings in our society. Repression, therefore, intensifies anxiety derived from guilt feelings because it tends to diminish the inevitability of punishment.

It should also be apparent by this time that, contrary to Mowrer's theory (1950), guilt alone cannot cause neurotic anxiety. Like repression, hostility, and conflict, it only gives rise to symptomatic anxiety, which is transitory, self-limited, and peripheral in persons who are intrinsically secure and adequate. Feelings of guilt cannot destroy basic self-acceptance unless it is already undermined. And in the case of more serious guilt reactions, there is always the safeguard of confession and willingness to accept punishment as a means of guilt reduction.

MATURATIONAL ANXIETY

By maturational anxiety is meant the anxiety that is experienced by certain individuals in relation to various residual maturational defects in their personality development. Although such individuals have satellized normally and possess intrinsic feelings of security and adequacy, they have failed to undergo complete ego maturation because of exposure to unfortunate parental practices. Their anxiety, therefore, stems from difficulties associated with relinquishing derived status and striving for an extrinsic sense of adequacy; hence it is on a different plane of centrality and intensity than neurotic anxiety. Furthermore, in many cases, a poorly developed self-critical faculty forms part of the picture of faulty maturation, with the result that the individual's self-esteem is protected from deflation by an incapacity for perceiving his own incompetence.

The overprotected individual feels threatened at adolescence by the prospect of losing parental protection and the adequacy of his derived status. But even throughout childhood, his sense of security is undermined somewhat by lack of confidence in his parents' ability to protect him because of their overt fearfulness. This exaggerated apprehensiveness in viewing the environment, overtrains an individual in anticipating physical danger from the most innocuous situations. She or he tends to lack confidence in being able to handle situations adequately since parental doubts about competency are thoroughly assimilated. However, as already pointed out, a person's failure to acquire a self-critical faculty minimizes the possibility of feeling threatened by his or her own incompetence. Such a person's outlook on life is usually much more sanguine than is warranted by envisioning objective circumstances.

The underdominated individual is similarly protected by an immature self-critical faculty from experiencing threats to self-esteem that ordinarily arise from rebuffs and frustrations attending the pursuit of unrealistic goals and expectations. More serious, therefore, is the threat to such a person's security and adequacy arising from the absence of effective internal and external controls over his or her aggressive impulses.

The overdominated individual experiences a limited type of anxiety related principally to feeling incapable of volitional independence. Accepting the parents' view of his or her basic incapacity to make effective decisions, the overdominated individual suffers insecurity derived from fear of losing the volitional direction of the person on whom he or she depends. Because dominating parents are generally hypercritical of the child, he does not gain the protection of an impaired self-critical faculty. Yet, his possession of intrinsic security and adequacy, as well as the possibility of becoming volitionally dependent on others after leaving the parental home, protects him or her from severe (neurotic) anxiety.

Sometimes a satellizing child has hypercritical and perfectionistic parents who are not particularly overdominating but who erect impossibly high standards despite the fact that they accept and value him for himself. Such children, although they feel intrinsically adequate, never manage to attain unqualified feelings of extrinsic adequacy. They do not suffer from neurotic anxiety but always seem to carry with them lingering doubts as to their capacity for adequately meeting external criteria of competency. Thus, the extrinsic picture of ego adequacy that starts in early childhood from the comments of parents tends to have a pervasive influence. Since this holds true in the case of an intrinsically adequate child, how much more traumatic it must be in the case of a rejected child, whose very existence is accepted negatively by his parents!

A form of maturational anxiety is also found in individuals whose quests for extrinsic status were not sufficiently appreciated by their parents. Having failed to obtain the approbation of the most significant persons in their interpersonal environment, they are unable ever to feel completely satisfied with their achievements. Success, recognition and acclaim all tend to have a hollow ring. The same result occurs also in the case of individuals with laissez-faire parents who adopt an attitude of complete indifference toward the accomplishments of their children.

TRANSITIONAL ANXIETY

Transitional anxiety arises during periods of crisis in ego development. Its source lies in pressures that are inherent in the very nature of developmental transition. Hence it occurs universally in all individuals and at every age when rapid personality change is required. The relevant factors entering into the threat are new social expectations regarding the abandonment of an old and the gaining of a new biosocial status; needs to accomplish new developmental tasks during an intermediate period of disorientation and lack of definite status; and uncertainties whether the new status will ever be attained. In addition to these objective pressures, there is also a subjective component of the threat that is derived from internalization of the developmental tasks imposed by the culture.

Transitional anxiety, therefore, first arises during the crisis of ego devaluation. In an atmosphere of benevolent parental acceptance, it tends to be minimal, self-limited, and overshadowed by the more spectacular evidences of negativism. The threat to the child of losing his volitional omnipotence is dampened by his high level of security. Hence, with fear of loss of succorance at a minimum—and uninhibited by feelings of guilt—aggression is the most natural emotional reaction to frustration of his omnipotent pretensions.

The next important crisis inducing transitional anxiety occurs during adolescence. On the one hand, as both Rank (1936) and Fromm (1941) stress, there is fear of losing protection, dependence, and derived status, and the parallel fears of individuation, freedom, autonomy, and responsibility. On the other hand, failure to gain independence and release from his dependent security leads to feelings of inadequacy and guilt, and to social disapproval (1936). Rank also points out that the adolescent becomes so jealous of his hard-earned autonomy that he becomes reluctant to part with any of it by forming genuine love attachments requiring emotional relatedness to others (1936).

Transitional anxiety during adolescence, therefore, comes from three diverse sources. First, there are various temporal pressures inhering in the nature of adolescent transition, especially in our culture, that is, abruptness of onset, prolonged status deprivation, discrepancies in the rate of growth of various component aspects, etc. Second, there is fear of autonomy and the loss of a sheltered protected existence. Fromm (1941) points out that this anxiety can be alleviated by forming new emotional relationships with others or by escaping from the new possibilities for freedom. The former tendency, however, is combatted by the fear of surrendering newly gained autonomy. Last, and most important, is the anxiety that is derived from the myriad factors that threaten the adolescent's acquisition of adult status—the cultural conditions that prolong dependency and effectively deny him or her opportunity to play mature and responsible roles.

These unusual social conditions in our culture intensify the normal dread and uncertainty regarding the attainment of adult prerogatives which all cultures inculcate in adolescents to keep maturation moving in the appropriate direction. This is what Allison Davis means by "socially-adaptive anxiety" (1944). Implicit in this dread is both the fear of social disapproval if failure should occur and the fear of losing the advantages pertaining to the new status. True, in our complex, heterogeneous culture, all adolescents do not share the *same* transitional anxiety, but they all experience dread in relation to the hazards associated with attaining the specific goals appropriate to their social-class membership.

SITUATIONAL ANXIETY

Situational anxiety is the normal type of anxiety that arises in relation to objective threats to an individual's self-esteem. It is a self-protective reaction limited to the duration of the situation that elicits it and is proportionate to the objective magnitude of the threat involved. Three types of situational anxiety will be considered: that which (1) originates in a cultural situation; (2) follows from special individual incapacities; and (3) inheres in all constructive, problem-solving activity.

Cultural Factors

Cultural factors produce or alleviate anxiety in many different ways. First, just as a child may be intrinsically valued for himself by his parents, an adult may be more or less valued for himself by his society. The intrinsic worth of a human being can be extremely high, as in the Arapesh culture, or it can be almost nil, as in our society, where a person's value is mostly a reflection of the price he or she fetches in the marketplace (Fromm, 1947). This distinction by Fromm is an exceedingly valuable one but is in serious error by assuming that the self-esteem of all will be similarly affected by its dependence on market value. Actually, the impact of this situation on an individual's self-esteem is peripheral in the case of satellizers and central in the case of non-satellizers.

Nevertheless, if we bear the latter difference in mind, it is legitimate to say that the level of extrinsic status toward which a person feels impelled to strive is inversely related to the intrinsic cultural valuation of a person (or directly related to the emphasis placed upon his or her market value). In our society, maximum value is placed upon the goals of social prestige and hierarchical status; and it is in the struggle for these goals that an individual either attains or fails to attain extrinsic adequacy (Kardiner, 1945). The more violent the competition for these individual goals, the greater the amount of intrasocial hostility that is generated (Kardiner, 1945), the less ego support an individual can derive from group relatedness, and the greater his psychological isolation (Fromm, 1947).

Thus, although "no society has the power to give absolute security and protect the child or the adult completely against the loss of love" (Murphy, 1947), in our particular culture the vicious cycle of "competitive striving, intrasocial hostility, interpersonal isolation, anxiety, and increased competitive striving" (May, 1950) is exceptionally acute. It was this situation that Horney had in mind when referring to "basic anxiety as a reaction to living in a basically hostile and chaotic society" (1937).

Another cultural factor influencing the level of situational anxiety has to do with the *availability* of the degree of extrinsic status for which a particular culture motivates its members to strive. If, for example, as in our culture, adolescents and adults are drawn into a mad race for competitive status, and the possibility of many individuals acquiring such status is greatly limited, it stands to reason that situational anxiety will be relatively intense and widespread. This is especially true in periods of economic depression when youth spend many years of apprenticeship, education, training, and self-subordination only to find unemployment at the end of the arduous and anxiety-laden trail. But even in normal times, adolescents must tolerate prolonged status deprivation; and the bitter pill is not made any easier to swallow when it is compounded by an apparent capriciousness in the cultural distribution of rewards. The theory that success is the inevitable reward for conscientious work, self-denial, and superior ability bogs down as adolescents begin to see rewards monopolized by individuals whose sole entitlement to them springs solely from wealth, inherited position, family connections, a highly developed capacity for double-dealing and sycophancy, or portions of several or all of these factors.

In addition to the situational anxiety that can be attributed to general status deprivation, economic depression, and differences in accessibility to cultural rewards on the basis of social-class membership, special groups of adolescents and adults in our culture experience further cause for anxiety in social and economic discrimination related to their sex, race, religion, and ethnic and national origin. Furthermore, situational anxiety tends to be accentuated during periods of rapid social change, war, international tension, political upheaval, and deterioration in public and private morality. Orderly social organization ordinarily provides the individual with many safeguards and forms of security, for example, protection against violence, tyranny, and chaotic disorganization. As the social fabric deteriorates, the individual is required to erect his own defenses against the dangers that ensue.

And, as happens not infrequently, the more prolonged and intense the situational anxiety, the more engrained and operative become some subjective components. The threat to self-esteem finally leads to an impairment of the sense of adequacy, which is peripheral in the case of satellizers* and central in the case of non-satellizers. This in turn becomes a further source of threat, especially when a person attributes unwarrantedly the failure he or she experiences because of cultural factors to personal ineptitude instead. These feelings of inadequacy must be differentiated from the anxiety derived from objective organic or intellectual deficiencies that constitute a threat to self-esteem insofar as they either expose an individual to ridicule and ostracism, or predispose him to failure in various adjustive situations. We have seen, however, that adolescents who are overvalued often tend to exaggerate the importance of such defects and, as a result, they may perceive the greater part of the source of threat as subjective rather than as objective. Except in cases of permanent crippling or disfigurement, however, organic defects are seldom severe enough to produce neurotic anxiety.

"Constructive" Anxiety

Many writers (Freud; Goldstein; May; et al.) on the subject of anxiety point out that anxiety inheres inevitably in all constructive activity leading toward self-actualization. The development of any individual's capacities depends on his willingness to experience frustration; to solve new problems; to risk the possibility of failure; to face unpleasant, threatening situations; and to abandon established positions of security for exploration in uncharted fields. This means that individual as well as group progress can only take place if there is a positive disposition to accept and "move through" the burden of anxiety inherent in each new learning situation.

ANXIETY AND MOTIVATION

In our particular culture, it is quite evident that whether desirable or not, anxiety is one of the most common motivating devices employed by parents, teachers, employers, etc. It is undoubtedly true that positive motivations such as job satisfaction, joy in craftsmanship and creative effort, and desire to be socially useful are much more wholesome than anxiety reduction, but few motivations *today* are as compelling as the fear of losing one's job. The source of anxiety motivation lies not only in various natural contingencies (e.g., sickness, death, starvation) that threaten existence, but also in a series of cultural derivatives arising from fear of physical punishment, guilt, disapproval, social reprisal, ostracism, and loss of status. "Socially-adaptive" anxiety, for example, helps

---

*Although peripheral, situational anxiety in satellizers may present severe psychophysiological, motor, and subjective scars (including insomnia) requiring prolonged psychotherapy and pharmacological treatment.

provide the adolescent with motivation to attain the general developmental goals appropriate for his age group and the more specific goals appropriate for his social-class membership; it is powered by the threat of failure to acquire the status prerogatives associated with successful maturation.

However, to acknowledge the potency of anxiety motivation is not to assert that it is the only or the chief source of motivation. This would be committing the same error as Freud, who failed to see any motivation arising except in a negative fashion—as the product of sublimation or reaction formation. Motivation can be derived from many positive sources such as curiosity, interest, ability, etc. And even if the original source does happen to be related to anxiety reduction, it is possible that in the course of pursuing the activity that it inspires, other more positive motivations might develop and assume, in time, the more dominant energizing role.

It is in non-satellizers, however, that anxiety reduction really occupies the central position in the motivational picture. There is a relentless drive for extrinsic adequacy and ego enhancement to fill the void of absent intrinsic self-esteem and to allay the anxiety that arises from its impairment. The tremendous amount of motivation for prestige generated by hypertrophic and tenacious ego demands leads to greater accomplishment than can otherwise be expected either from the given level of ability or from the tendency toward disruption of performance efforts because of anxiety and overreaction to frustration. In non-satellizers, goal-frustration tolerance is extremely high, and performance as well as self-esteem frustration tolerance are relatively low; while in satellizers exactly the reverse situation prevails.

The more realistic and intelligent non-satellizer spares himself continual frustration by refusing to expend his prestige motivation indiscriminately in all directions, including those areas in which his natural endowment is poor. By selectively disinvolving his ego from prestige aspirations in such activities and channelizing his drive into areas where he is apt to face little competition (Ausubel, 1951), the realistic and intelligent non-satellizer manages to maintain extrinsic self-esteem at a higher level and anxiety at a lower level than the non-satellizer who sees a threat to himself in anyone's accomplishments and feels obliged to compete with every individual who crosses his path. Hartogs (1950) found that in simple paper and pencil tests, anxiety patients "showed an unduly high initial level of aspiration with the following goal-levels kept intentionally low." His results can easily be interpreted as evidence of the high level of ego aspiration prevailing in anxiety neurotics before they are fully aware of the nature of the task and the threat it entails, which is followed by protective ego disinvolvement once frustration is experienced.

BEHAVIORAL CORRELATES OF ANXIETY

INTELLIGENCE

Research evidence indicates almost uniformly that there is a low but significant negative correlation between anxiety and intelligence (Cowen et al.,

1965; Feldhusen, Denny & Condon, 1965; Penney, 1965; Ruebush, 1963; Sarason et al., 1964). Although stability of anxiety scores decreases as intervals between testings increase, marked changes in anxiety are inversely related to changes in I.Q. during the early elementary school years (Hill & Sarason, 1966). These findings are consistent with the inverse relationship between anxiety and novel problem-solving; they suggest that, in a threatening test situation, the negative effects of anxiety on complex learning tasks overshadow its positive motivational effects on test performance. Another plausible interpretation is that the low-I.Q. individual may feel generally anxious as a result of his inferior school achievement. A less likely interpretation is that anxiety may actually depress the development of intelligence rather than merely depressing performance on an intelligence test.

EFFECTS OF ANXIETY ON LEARNING

We have postulated that neurotic anxiety is the overreaction of an individual with impaired self-esteem to the threat anticipated in adjustive situations. The threatening implications of the latter are derived from their capacity to further impair self-esteem in the face of an inner feeling of inadequacy to cope with them. Normal anxiety, on the other hand, is the fear evoked by anticipation of objectively hazardous threats to self-esteem. Normal subjects do not display anxiety when confronted with ordinary adjustive situations because they do not lack confidence in their ultimate capacity to acquire the necessary adaptive responses.

The relationship between anxiety and learning is complicated by the fact that although high-anxiety individuals exhibit more than average *motivation* (i.e., although they tend originally to manifest an excess of ego-enhancement drive and are further driven to achieve as the only practicable means of reducing anxiety), their high level of anxiety also tends to have a disruptive effect on *novel* problem-solving (Ruebush, 1963). Thus, it has been generally found that anxiety facilitates rote and less difficult kinds of meaningful reception learning, but has an inhibitory effect on more complex types of learning tasks that are either highly unfamiliar or are more dependent on improvising skill than on persistence (Ausubel, Schiff & Goldman, 1953; Caron, 1963; Castenada et al., 1956; Lantz, 1945; McGuigan, Calvin & Richardson, 1959; Marks & Vestre, 1961; Palermo et al., 1956; Pickrel, 1958; Russel & Sarason, 1965; Sarason et al., 1960; Stevenson & Odom, 1965; Tomkins, 1943; Zander, 1944). These complex types of learning situations are obviously highly threatening to anxious individuals and tend to induce a disabling level of anxiety. It does appear, however, that anxiety may *enhance* the learning of complex tasks when they do not seriously threaten self-esteem, that is, when they are not inordinately novel or significant (Van Buskirk, 1961; Wittcock & Husek, 1962), when they produce anxiety only in a moderate degree, or when the learner possesses effective anxiety-coping mechanisms (Cox, 1968; Horowitz & Armentraut, 1965; Suinn, 1965). The learning of complex verbal materials in a typical school setting, for example, seems to be a relatively familiar and non-threatening task when compared to novel problem-solving situations. Consistent with these findings are the observations that highly anxious subjects, as compared with less anxious subjects, have poorer visual discrimination of pictures of social scenes (Knights, 1965), show less curiosity (Penney, 1965), exhibit more rigidity and earlier perceptual closure (Cohen, 1961; Smock, 1958), and evince less preference for novel toys (Mendel, 1965).

EFFECTS OF ANXIETY ON SCHOOL ACHIEVEMENT

As one may reasonably anticipate, the effect of anxiety on school achievement is comparable to its effect on learning, except that on a long-term basis its disruptive influence is much less intense. School achievement tasks, after all, tend to lose their threatening implications as students gain experience in coping with them. Nevertheless, highly anxious children are more negative in their attitudes to school-related concepts (Barnard, 1966). At the elementary-school level, anxiety generally depresses scholastic achievement (Cowen et al., 1965; Feldhusen & Klausmeier, 1962; Hill & Sarason, 1966; Lunneborg, 1964; Reese, 1961; Sarason et al., 1964). In high school, as the motivational effects of anxiety become stronger relative to its disruptive effects, the negative correlation between anxiety and academic achievement decreases, particularly in boys; it is either weaker or entirely absent when grades are used as an index of achievement (Sarason, 1961, 1963; Walter, Denzler & Sarason, 1964). In highly structured learning tasks such as programmed instruction, a positive relationship has been reported between anxiety and achievement (Kight & Sassenrath, 1966; Traweek, 1964). This finding is consistent with the fact that anxious pupils, particularly when compulsive, do much better in highly structured learning situations where novelty and the need for improvisation are minimal.

THE SELF-CRITICAL FACULTY

Another important factor that affects the individual's extrinsic sense of adequacy, the probability of frustration, and the level of anxiety manifested is the state of his or her self-critical faculty. The presence of this faculty allows an individual to evaluate, with varying degrees of severity or lenience, the acceptability of personal behavior, the degree of status acquired, and the quality of productions achieved. It reflects, in part, the influence of maturational factors and various parental attitudes and, in part, the level of his or her self-esteem and the critical standards prevailing in the environment. Although tending to remain fairly stable and consistent in line with long-range personality trends, the self-critical faculty also retains a certain adaptive flexibility. In persons who are intrinsically secure and adequate, it tends to be more lenient and to fluctuate less than among non-satellizers, in whom it is ordinarily not only more severe but also more variable.

We first meet the self-critical faculty (or the lack of it) in the pre-satellizing period when the infant is able to entertain grandiose conceptions of his volitional power, *partly* because of his very limited capacity to perceive his status realistically. Afterwards, improvement in this ability becomes one of the precipitating causes of the crisis of ego devaluation. Nevertheless, self-critical ability is still rudimentary as evidenced by the child's tendency to overvalue the extent of his executive competency in the second stage of negativism. It is only when the self-critical faculty becomes a more important determinant of daily behavior (at approximately five years of age in Gesell's population—Gesell & Ilg, 1943) that this type of negativism really begins to subside and give way to a more consolidated and homogeneous form of satellization.

During the succeeding years, the further development of the self-critical faculty becomes a progressively more crucial aspect of personality maturation. This growth is facilitated by parental practices that require the child to take responsibility for the consequences of his inappropriate behavior or inadequate performances. Undue laxity in excusing misbehavior or in evaluating inferior performance favors the emergence of an impaired self-critical faculty. The acquisition of greater volitional independence on an adult and realistic level presupposes the ability to recognize imperfections in performance; otherwise the individual feels completely satisfied with a highly inferior product, aspires to nothing better, and initiates no efforts looking toward improvement.

Because of overly uncritical parental attitudes, insufficient drive for adequate performance, and low goal-frustration tolerance, both the overprotected and the underdominated child are unable to acquire sufficient self-critical ability; and since this failure in turn has adjustive value in minimizing the possibility of frustration and protecting against the loss of self-esteem that would otherwise result in view of the individual's objective incompetence, additional motivation is provided for the arrested development of this function.

With respect to overdominated and overcriticized children, just the opposite situation prevails. Such children are required to live up to a high standard of excellence in order to meet with full parental approval. Because of their strong internalized needs to turn out high-quality performance and their reasonably high goal-frustration tolerance, they are able to learn adequate self-appraisal; in fact, in the light of these needs, the development of a superior self-critical faculty becomes a definite asset. In non-satellizers with exaggerated needs for prestige accomplishment, a severe self-critical faculty is even more expedient and imperative, but operates selectively in relation to performance; where moral behavior is involved, leniency of self-judgment is the more expedient alternative.

The non-satellizer's impaired self-esteem and lack of intrinsic self-acceptance also tend to make him adopt a harsh view toward himself. The same is true of the underappreciated child who assimilates his parent's tendency to regard his achievements with lack of enthusiasm.

We have already cited evidence to show that self-estimate tends to be disturbed in the poorly adjusted individual, and after experiences of frustration. It is also less accurate with respect to abilities that are rated low by other persons, and in areas marked by conflict or insecurity. The precise interpretation of an overly severe self-critical faculty offers many difficulties, since in various cases it can be indicative of a disturbed parent-child relationship, situational tensions, excessive ego demands, perfectionism, vanity, and impaired self-esteem.

The experience of a decade in the pharmacological, neurosurgical, and electroshock treatment of psychopathological conditions in which the self-critical faculty is exaggeratedly severe (i.e., anxiety, agitation, and depression) has provided us with considerable information about the neuroanatomical substrate of the self-critical faculty. The most drastic of these measures, prefrontal lobotomy, which almost invariably reduces anxiety, agitation and depression, after other less radical forms of intervention fail, seems to exert an almost specific inhibitory effect on the self-critical faculty by interrupting thalamo-cortical fibers that connect the orbital quadrant of the thalamus to the frontal cortex (Ausubel, 1948; Lowenbach & Suitt, 1950). Electroshock therapy that has a similar effect results in cortical damage; but the exact locus of this damage has not yet been definitely determined.

Neurophysiological evidence from animal experimentation also suggests that the pharmacological locus of the euphorogenous action of narcotic drugs is the thalamo-cortical tract. The adjustive value of narcotic drug addiction probably depends at least in part on the inhibition of the self-critical faculty, which permits the inadequate personality to retain extrinsic feelings of adequacy despite his manifest incompetency (Ausubel, 1948).

The evidence cited above shows that it is possible to change the psychological expression of the self-critical faculty by bringing physical influences to bear on its anatomical substrate. It is realized, however, that such change is normally effected on a psychological plane alone—in the course of ego defense measures or as the outcome of ego damage. Defensively, enhancement of adequacy feelings can be obtained by inhibiting the self-critical faculty as in manic states, inadequate personalities, and certain forms of moral delinquency. Exaggeration of the self-critical faculty, on the other hand, is usually a manifestation of ego damage, that is, anxiety, agitation, and depression. Under certain conditions (to be described below), however, it may serve a defensive function, for example, in compulsive perfectionism, and in the "self-frustration" mechanism.

DEPERSONALIZATION AND FEAR OF DEATH

One of the most mysterious phenomena that psychology is obliged to explain is the apparent indifference that the individual as well as his culture displays to the certainty of death. In the entire animal kingdom, man alone has a highly conceptualized sense of personal identity, man alone can contemplate the implications of death, and man alone is capable of resenting the fact that his personal identity is presumably a function of his physical integrity. Why is it that an individual in our culture, knowing or suspecting that his ego identity will vanish at death, can absorb himself so completely in the affairs of the world as if he were settling matters of ego status for all eternity? Here is a man of seventy sitting in his business office and maneuvering with intense application and consummate shrewdness to outwit a rival in a business deal that may bring him several thousand dollars profit. How can he concern himself with such trivia when tomorrow he himself, on whose behalf all this frantic competitive activity is expended, may pass into nothingness? If psychologists explain his efforts as mechanisms of ego defense and enhancement, how can they explain his indifference to this primal fact, the greatest danger of all, which not only threatens to obliterate all previous efforts but also the ego itself?

The most plausible answer to this enigma that we can offer at the present time is that normal feelings of insecurity about the prospect of death (apart from immediate tangible threats) are repressed below the threshold of awareness, providing that a certain minimal level of self-esteem is maintained. When neurotic anxiety becomes acute, fear of death tends to become a troublesome symptom. At this point, the patient is usually in a state of agitation. However, once he is resigned to failure and the defeat of his ego aspirations, and renounces all striving (depression), he even looks forward to death and becomes suicidal. Death fears, therefore, are a good prognostic sign in psychotic depressions as well as in reactive schizophrenia, where the ego, by virtue of regression to infantile concepts of self and of removal from the arena of reality, is removed beyond the reach of the threat of death.

An example of morbid concern with problems of death can be found in present-day devotees of spiritualism. This cult reflects a positive protest against and a denial of human mortality and the dependence of the ego on a neuroanatomical substrate. Beneath this attempt to remove personal identity from any relationship with biological processes lies a haunting fear of death and a severely damaged self-esteem. Religious doctrines of the hereafter, on the other hand, are reflective of extreme cultural anxiety that afterwards becomes institutionalized. Hence, normal individuals who believe in the hereafter espouse such beliefs as articles of faith in a formal sense or as matters of genuine conviction rather than as a defensive measure against overt and obsessive fears of death.

Depersonalization

Depersonalization refers to a breakdown in personal identity or awareness of self that occurs under conditions of extreme stress, and quite frequently in relation to anxiety states. However, considerable confusion has arisen about the interpretation of this phenomenon because of (1) failure to identity the quality of self-awareness preceding the onset of symptoms of depersonalization; and (2) failure to differentiate between the adjustive and ego damage aspects of depersonalization.

Goldstein (1939) contends that anxiety, as experienced by an individual in the catastrophic situation, leads to a disintegration of self-awareness and of the relationship between self and the outside world. This in turn makes him unable to evaluate his environment realistically and to identify the source of the threat.

While we tend to agree that this type of depersonalization is symptomatic of acute panic, we point out that the phenomenon occurs quite late in the course of anxiety states, either as a desperate defense measure or as an indication that considerable ego damage has already taken place. Initially at least, an accentuation of self-awareness is generally the rule in severe anxiety states. We have seen that self-preoccupation is one of the pathognomonic signs of acute anxiety and one of the main factors responsible for inducing an attitude of rejection in parents. Under such conditions, the individual *is* unable to evaluate his status objectively, but this is a consequence of impaired self-esteem, excessive self-criticism, and overreaction to environmental threats rather than a reflection of self-dissolution.

The same viewpoint that anxiety helps to consolidate the ego before it leads to ego deterioration is implicit in Sullivan's concept that in the experience of having to distinguish between those impulses that generate approval and those that are productive of disapproval (and, hence, anxiety), the self is more clearly delineated (Sullivan, 1940).

Under conditions of increasingly greater stress or more devastating anxiety, depersonalization may develop either as an adjustive device or as a sign of extreme ego damage. Personal identity becomes detached from extremely degrading experiences as a means of protecting the individual from a damaging loss of self-esteem. For example, an unwilling prostitute may try to divorce her ego from any connection with the experiences relative to prostitution (Sherif & Cantril, 1946).

Amnesic conditions, fugues, and "multiple-personality" states also illustrate the adjustive value of depersonalization. In such cases, however, the individual does more than feel that a given experience is unreal or is not happening to him. He represses or dissociates an entire body of interrelated experience from the main current of his self-awareness. Thus, he is able to eat his cake and have it too: he can express a host of unacceptable impulses and, at the same time, escape any connection of them with his sense of personal identity.

The adjustive value of this type of depersonalization becomes clear when, under the strain of even greater stress, the other variety of depersonalization appears. Here ego damage is so great that the old self is depersonalized and replaced by a new. The individual no longer regards degrading, regressive, or infantile behavior as unreal or apart from himself, but accepts it as a characteristic product of his "new self" operating in a new framework of "reality." This acceptance of the regressive self as his new personal identity, as indicative of what he really *wants* to be, is a sign of the extreme ego deterioration that takes place during the transition between the acute and chronic forms of reactive schizophrenia.

Hence, we have to distinguish between (1) depersonalization as an adjustive mechanism that consists primarily of a dissociation of personal identity from humiliating and unacceptable experiences happening to self, and (2) depersonalization as a symptom of ego damage in which marked changes in personality occur. That is, the individual becomes depersonalized in the sense of acquiring a new and different personal identity but accepts this new identity (with all of its regressive and unacceptable features) as his "real" self. The former is illustrated by the depersonalization occurring in certain cases of acute anxiety (after accentuation of self-awareness); in conditions of involuntary or ambivalent participation in degrading experiences; in amnesias, fugues, and in cases of "multiple personality." The latter type is illustrated by the depersonalization occurring in chronic cases of reactive schizophrenia when the regressive picture of self is accepted as real. "Adjustive" depersonalization, therefore, is a hopeful prognostic sign in early cases of such schizophrenia. Although there is some adjustive value (escape) in the extreme personality regression and the complete withdrawal from reality found in this entity, such a fabulous price is paid in terms of personality disorganization that it seems more appropriate to regard it as a form of ego damage complicating neurotic anxiety.

DEFENSES AGAINST ANXIETY

The basis of many defense mechanisms lies in the need for anxiety reduction. Defense efforts are elicited even before anxiety appears—when self-esteem is threatened. And when the threat becomes intense enough to evoke the affect of anxiety, the original need for defense becomes even more imperative. As a means of bringing together some of the various materials in this chapter on defenses against anxiety, a brief cataloguing of the various defenses will be attempted below. More extensive discussion will be provided in Chapter 10.

Four types of defenses will be distinguished: (1) direct forms of ego enhancement of an aggressive, compensatory, and independent character; (2) conciliatory, submissive, and dependent forms of defense; (3) various indirect and devious means of ego enhancement, which attain their goal without primary reliance on either aggressive or submissive tactics; and (4) mechanisms that provide escape from anxiety situations.

Direct means of ego enhancement include: (a) pursuing strong prestige drives for money, success, power, superior status, etc.; (b) manifesting boastful, blustering, supercilious, and belligerent attitudes, or the simulation of tremendous calm, poise, nonchalance, and indifference to social conventions; (c) attacking aggressively the opinions, behavior, or reputations of other persons in the hope of showing to advantage in relation to the deflation of their stature; (d) unleashing destructive tendencies as a means of demonstrating one's power to influence the course of events; (e) finding substitute gratification in the achievements of other individuals who are regarded as ego extensions of self, for example, the overvaluing parent.

Conciliatory forms of defense are types of behavior that reveal themselves in (a) an attitude that is sympathetic, charitable, and tolerant towards others as a means of soliciting comparable lenient treatment from them; (b) an effort to stress one's anxiety and helplessness as a bid for sympathy and immunity from aggression; (c) a repression of hostile impulses in order to insure one's safety; (d) a failure to perceive the hostility of others lest one feel obliged to retaliate and hence risk one's security; (e) a justification on hostility in others for the same reason; (f) a need to be liked by *everyone* in order to feel secure, which goes as far as entering into relationships indiscriminately with all-comers; (g) an exaggerated conformity to social demands; (h) an excessive compliancy to authority; (i) a complete surrender of individuality in group activity; (j) an abandonment of individual initiative and the prerogatives of independent action; (k) an endeavor at forming satellizing-like relationships with others; (l) a suppression of self-assertive and hostile tendencies by reaction formation.

Indirect and devious defenses against anxiety are legion in number: (a) rationalization of failure and escape from competitive striving through psychosomatic symptoms of anxiety, hypochondriasis, fatigue states, and hysterical conditions; (b) displacement of the source of the threat to a more concrete, identifiable, and manageable danger (phobia); (c) monopolization of consciousness by a displaced and innocuous source of threat (obsession); (d) displacement of the object or target of the threat to another person, (e.g., the anxious parent who overprotects his child); (e) minimization of frustration and loss of self-esteem through ego disinvolvement, depersonalization, and impairment of the self-critical faculty (e.g., mania); (f) delusional distortion of the environment (ideas of grandeur and persecution); (g) rejection of unacceptable impulses by justifying them (e.g., projection); (h) compensatory ego gratification through regression in goal maturity; (i) compensatory ego satisfaction through compulsive eating, activity, or sexuality; (j) reliance on compulsive rituals to provide security; (k) compulsive rigidity, inflexibility, and perfectionism in performing tasks in order to eliminate excessive fear of uncertainty, tentativeness, and improvisation; (l) undue advance preparation in meeting new situations; (m) reliance on familiar and stereotyped methods of problem-solving.

Escape mechanisms include: (a) avoidance of new, potential anxiety situations; (b) repression of or denial of anxiety; (c) adopting an impersonal, third-person reference to problems productive of anxiety; (d) withdrawal from social situations that generate anxiety (e.g., asceticism, intellectualization, absorption in fantasy); (e) self-insulation from emotional involvement in interpersonal relations to avoid the possibility of rejection; (f) finding a part-time escape from reality (e.g., alcoholism); (g) constriction of the field of activity to limit the magnitude of areas from which threats can arise; (h) self-frustration to avoid anxiety situations or the necessity for accepting a realistic half-loaf solution to grandiose ego aspirations.

PROGNOSIS OF ANXIETY

The development and nature of neurotic anxiety is such that predictions regarding prognosis must be made separately for young children, on the one hand, and all other age-groups on the other. Only in terms of the former is the question of reversibility (cure) relevant. The very best the latter can look forward to is palliation. With respect to the possibility of reversibility, the issue in essence is whether or not, and under what conditions, the effects of parental rejection or overvaluation can be reversed.

Since the child is almost always reluctant to accept the verdict of rejection, and is more than receptive to any change for the better in the parents' attitudes, it is the variables affecting the probability of such change that are crucial in deciding the prognosis of childhood anxiety caused by rejection. This brings us to the distinction already suggested between (1) "benign" parental rejection, which is not strongly predetermined by personality factors in the parent, and hence fluctuates greatly with situational conditions; and (2) "malignant" rejection, which exhibits greater constancy of expression because of prepotent personality predispositions. The hypothesis has already been offered that the former type of rejection is manifested most frequently by parents who were themselves rejected as children, while the latter type is manifested most commonly by parents who were themselves exposed to overvaluation.

Parents who themselves were rejected as children tend to retain a capacity for relating themselves to others (especially their own children), which can be fulfilled under favorable conditions (i.e., minimal anxiety); whereas parents who were overvalued as children tend never to acquire this capacity. The rejected parent is also influenced more by moral considerations, shows more sensitivity to public opinion, and tends to be less self-indulgent. There is thus a possibility for sufficient change to occur in the rejected parent's attitudes to enable the child to satellize, to acquire intrinsic security and adequacy, and to remain free of neurotic anxiety. All of this can happen provided that it does not come too late in the relationship between a child and a parent who endured rejection as a child. In the senior authors' experience, almost complete elimination of anxiety has been accomplished with child patients until the age of seven. In cases of malignant rejection, however, the author has never succeeded in effecting comparable results except in instances where a substitute parent (usually an interested relative) could be provided; it is futile for the therapist himself to attempt this role since he cannot provide sufficient sustained ego support to induce satellization.

The therapist's task of changing parental attitudes is lightened considerably if the parent is intelligent, has insight into the meaning of his attitudes and their effects upon the child, feels guilty about them, and is sincerely desirous of improving the parent-child relationship. Even more important, however, are those situational factors that regulate the current level of parental anxiety. A harassed, panic-stricken, self-preoccupied parent cannot benefit sufficiently from therapy to change the quality of the parent-child relationship. The relevant situational factors, in turn, are largely dependent upon other personality traits of the parent, such as ability, capacity for disguising anxiety, etc.

Parental overvaluation—including the variety practiced by parents who had been rejected themselves—is a much more difficult attitude to change. First, it has high adjustive value for the parent and tends to become a fixed, canalized defense against his anxiety. Second, overvalued children do not generally exhibit overt anxiety and are less likely to be brought to the attention of a therapist. Third, the overvalued child finds his grandiose ego aspirations quite tenable in his environment and is not disposed to satellize.

Prognosis for Palliation of Anxiety

If cure cannot be effected in early childhood, the therapist can still attempt palliation. The value of such a goal should not be deprecated since success often means the difference between psychological invalidism on the one hand, and sufficient freedom from anxiety to do creative work and experience some personal happiness on the other. The important errors to guard against are (1) unrealistic expectations of cure in adult cases of neurotic anxiety and (2) failure to take sufficient cognizance of the important role of situational factors. The first error is quite universal among psychotherapists, and the second error is committed in different ways by psychoanalytic and non-directive therapists. The former tend to ignore the current situation until insight is secured, and then attempt to have the patient apply this insight toward the solution of his everyday problems. But all along, an unfavorable environmental situation is operating to increase the anxiety and prevent the patient from acquiring and utilizing the potential benefits of insight. If at the end of a two-year period of therapy, an adult patient is still economically and volitionally dependent on his parents, has no way of earning a living, and has not even made a start in the direction of formulating his vocational goals, he is psychologically in a worse position than he was before beginning therapy.

Non-directive therapists, on the other hand, are too rigid and fanatical (in practice if not in theory) about upholding the necessity for self-direction, about avoiding transference and dependence on the therapist, and about avoiding any manipulation of the environment. While these latter goals might be desirable on a long-term basis, they cannot be striven for in the early stages of treatment when the disorganized, anxiety-ridden patient requires some active ego support and directive guidance. Furthermore, (1) the acquisition of insight is seldom possible without employing a developmental approach, and (2) the patient's avoidance of a realistic adjustment is encouraged by an attitude of complete permissiveness (e.g., the therapist expressing no judgments whatsoever, letting the client set his own limits in the relationship, etc.).

The following important good prognostic signs should be looked for by the psychotherapist: (1) a history of parental rejection rather than overvaluation; (2) the absence of psychosomatic symptoms and the presence of high tolerance for conscious anxiety; (3) the absence of fixed defensive techniques such as phobia, hysteria, compulsions, etc.; (4) the lack of excessive repressed hostility and resentment; (5) the presence of realistic ego disinvolvement without undue constriction of the individual's psychological world; (6) a degree of insight into the nature of the threat and the meaning of symptoms as well as ability to recognize the special factors that precipitate bouts of anxiety; (7) an attitude of "learning to live with" unavoidable anxiety, avoiding insoluble situations, and making advance preparations (within reason) for threatening situations that are manageable; (8) the presence of hopeful situational factors such as secure employment, opportunity for creative expression, and wholesome interpersonal relationships; and (9) the possession of other personality traits and abilities that help an individual create a secure environment for himself.

Unfavorable prognostic indicators include agitation, depersonalization, and overt fear of death. The most fateful of all unfavorable prognostic signs is evidence that the patient is ceasing to strive or is striving for regressive goals in an unrealistic setting.

10

A Developmental Approach to Psychopathology

In this chapter we shall attempt a systematic application of the dynamics of ego development to the pathogenesis of the behavior disorders. To a very large extent, this has already been accomplished in the chapters on developmental crisis and failure, anxiety, and conscience formation. What must now be done is to classify behavior disorders more formally so we can perceive more readily the relationships of the various diagnostic categories to their developmental matrices, and to each other.

The proposed system of classification is based on the dual assumption (1) that developmental factors in ego formation represent the most significant variables in the etiology of behavioral pathology and (2) that these factors account most meaningfully for the differences in onset, symptomatology, and prognosis which appear in the recognized clinical entities. These assumptions by no means rule out the importance of genic, neuroanatomical, neurophysiological, constitutional, and situational factors, or other aspects of personality development. By definition, however, classification in science aims at defining relationships between phenomena in terms of the most prepotent variable responsible for their evolution and at doing so with the least possible degree of overlap among the categories as they are established.

GENERAL PSYCHOPATHOLOGY

Without attempting to present a definitive exposition of general psychopathology, it will be helpful nevertheless to relate the developmental approach to the more general context of variables in which it is embedded.

Determinants of Behavior Disorder

If we are to abide by the general proposition that any complex behavioral outcome must be considered a resultant of various influences impinging upon an individual's psychological field, what relevant variables should be considered in assessing the possibility that he or she may or may not develop a behavior disorder or a particular type of behavior disorder? The following is a partial list of factors that should be taken into account: (1) genic predisposition as determined by single (dominant or recessive) genes or by polygenes; (2) constitutional defense factors (based on multifactorial genic patterns) that are inadequate to provide sufficient resistance to mental disease; (3) the objective magnitude of the adjustive stress or deprivation confronting the individual; (4) predispositions arising from aberrant ego development, for example, lack of ego devaluation or maturation; (5) frustration tolerance, that is, the amount of frustration an individual can withstand before succumbing either to disruption of performance ability, loss of self-esteem, or lowering of aspiration level; (6) various subjective factors that determine to what extent deprivation will either be interpreted or reacted to as frustration, that is, general level of prestige aspiration, specific ego involvement in a given activity, capacity for selective ego disinvolvement; (7) the self-critical faculty, that is, the ability or tendency to evaluate oneself more or less severely; (8) introversion-extraversion; (9) previous mode of adjustment to stress, that is, types of adjustive mechanisms employed, and at what level of integration; (10) accessibility of motivations, attitudes, emotions to consciousness; (11) degree of insight into adjustive techniques; (12) level of energy; (13) complexity of personality organization; (14) level of neurophysiological irritability as influenced by fatigue, emotion, hormonal balance, etc.; (15) level of resistance to stress situations in terms of reacting with somatic dysfunction (adrenocortical sufficiency); (16) anatomical and physiological integrity of the nervous system; (17) tolerance for anxiety, guilt, ambiguity, and inconsistency; (18) adaptive resources (intelligence; aptitudes, creativity; flexibility).

The reason why ego development is the central organizing variable in the etiology of behavior disorder (as has been shown in the preceding chapters) is because it crucially affects so many of the other important etiological variables, for example, level of prestige aspiration, self-critical faculty, introversion-extraversion, frustration tolerance, tolerance for anxiety and guilt, etc.

The Ego in Psychopathology

The ego is of such crucial importance in psychopathology because it is the central organizing value in personality structure. Our relationship to the environment is ordered on a hierarchical gradient of ego involvement. Most motivations bear some relationships to ego needs (e.g., security, adequacy, prestige, status, power). What we wish to derive from life in terms of work, interpersonal relationships, love, position, etc., usually bears some relation to our self-concept, that is, how great our ego aspirations are, how compelling the need for ego enhancement is, how important we think we are or ought to become. The ego is the one value in personality that people are most concerned about. As Gardner Murphy (1947) puts it, "whatever else we love, we love our ego best". It elicits greater efforts toward defense and enhancement than any other value.

The causes of frustration and conflict in human beings must also be largely formulated in terms of ego needs. When these are thwarted by delay, denial, or conflict, when ego status is debased or threatened, frustration ensues. More important than actual deprivation in determining the degree of frustration experienced are the individual's levels of prestige aspiration, of specific ego involvement in a given task, and of frustration tolerance, plus the strength of his or her self-critical faculty. All of these factors are greatly influenced by the course of ego development, which, in addition, helps determine the source from whence status is sought, the degree of volitional and executive dependence desired, the need for hedonistic gratification, the type and degree of security and adequacy feelings possessed, the sense of moral obligation adhered to, as well as tendencies toward introversion-extraversion and egocentrism. In short, ego development forms the core of personality development; hence, it is not at all surprising if the major predispositions toward acquiring behavior disorder are to be found in aberrant varieties of ego development.

Responses to frustration can likewise be categorized as forms of defense, escape, and damage of self. Defense mechanisms are mainly compensatory attempts to enhance self, to make the ego appear powerful, blameless, and more worthwhile—through substitutive or fantasy achievements, rationalization, disowning weaknesses and perceiving them in others (projection), burying ideas that are unfavorable to self (repression), distorting reality, providing excuses for failure in illness, etc. Escape mechanisms, on the other hand, allow for withdrawal of self beyond the reach of environmental threats, for example, insulation, negativism, etc. Various forms of ego damage have already been described. They include loss of self-esteem, anxiety, agitation, depersonalization, fear of death, and depression.

Our objections to this concept of the unconscious are threefold. (1) We have already objected to the dichotomous notion that all acceptable and self-enhancing motives prevail at the conscious level while their unacceptable, self-debasing, anxiety and guilt-producing counterparts influence behavior solely from an unconscious base of operations. (2) Psychoanalytic theories of the unconscious are topographical rather than functional since they imply an all-or-none differentiation between the conscious and the unconscious depending on regional location. (3) We can agree that unconscious motivation not only gives rise to formation of symptoms that are symbolic but also compounds thereby the seriousness and intensity of guilt and anxiety by impeding integrative and constructive solutions. But, as stated above, these consequences of repression are not mainly responsible for the evolution of behavior disorders but merely have the status of complications. Furthermore, it should be pointed out that displacement of expression not only proceeds from "unconscious sexual" content to conscious symptom formation but also in the reverse direction; that is, awareness of current, non-sexual conflicts can be inhibited by identifying them symbolically with repressed sexual material. Because of the widespread prevalence of psychoanalytic theories, many individuals interpret innocent childhood experiences retrospectively (or invent experiences that never occurred) in Freudian terms, which then serve as foci for the symbolic displacement of current conflicts. Since these sexual urges are now considered normal and respectable, it is less traumatic to plead guilty to possessing them than to acknowledge anxiety, weakness, or lack of moral integrity.

Another psychoanalytic concept lacking in clarity and precision, but one that is very important for general psychopathology, is the concept of regression. First, the depth of regression with respect to psychosexual development is supposed to account psychoanalytically for the degree of behavioral disorganization, for example, the etiological distinction between neurosis and psychosis. Unfortunately, however, this concept does not differentiate between genuine retrogression (true regression) and mere lack of maturation. Second, regression is conceived of only in a psychosexual sense rather than in terms of ego development. Third, differences in type and degree of regression are not related to a developmental history of satellization or non-satellization. Most apparent regression in satellizers represents maturational failure, whereas in non-satellizers who rarely fail to undergo maturation, regressive behavior is more indicative of genuine retrogression. Depth of regression is also greater in non-satellizers since the developmental failure to which it relates occurs at an earlier stage of ego development, that is, the ego-devaluation crisis as opposed to the ego-maturation crisis.

Classification is as necessary in psychiatry as in all scientific disciplines to make possible generalization, concept formation, and investigation of relationships between important variables impinging upon the phenomena encompassed within the discipline. Without classification a separate equation would have to be written for every individual reaction, since identity never prevails phenomenologically. General laws could never be formulated, and anarchy would prevail. Classification does not presume identity, but similarity between events subsumed under a given category. The use of a given diagnostic entity in this sense does not in the least interfere with the further description of the unique personal evolution of a case within a more general category. Hence, it is indulging in sophistry to urge the abolition of classification in favor of "just understanding the mechanisms underlying each case without worrying about diagnostic labels."

Table 5
A Classification of Behavior Disorders from the Standpoint of Ego Development

I. Personality Disorders Due to Maturational Failure (in satellizers)
   A. *Inadequate Personality* (Extraversion: hedonistic gratification in reality)
      1. Complete
      2. Partial
   B. *Process Schizophrenia* (Introversion: hedonistic gratification in fantasy)
II. Personality Disorders Due to Failure in Ego Devaluation (in non-satellizers)
   A. *Maturational or Regressive Disorders*
      1. Aggressive antisocial psychopath
      2. Delinquency secondary to unstable conscience formation
      3. Special problems of adolescent emancipation
      4. Alcoholism
   B. *Disorders Due to Ego Hypertrophy: The Anxiety States*
      1. Manifest anxiety states
      2. Latent anxiety states
   C. *Defensive Reactions against Anxiety*
      1. Secondary elaborations of anxiety
      2. Exhaustion states
      3. Hypochondriasis
      4. Hysteria
      5. Phobia
      6. Compulsion
      7. Obsession
      8. Aggression
      9. "Martyrdom"
     10. Placation
     11. Delusional states
     12. Mania
   D. *Complications of Anxiety*
      1. Withdrawal: Reactive Schizophrenia (especially in introverts)
      2. Depressive Reactions (especially in extraverts)
         a. Agitated depression with exaggerated dependency
         b. Retarded depression (cessation of striving)
         c. Manic-depressive cycles

PERSONALITY DISORDERS IN SATELLIZERS: MATURATIONAL FAILURE

The defects in ego organization that result from maturational failure as well as its predisposing causes in parental over and underdomination and in overprotection have already been described. It will be recalled that ego devaluation as well as attenuation (preliminary maturation) of infantile-ego attributes take place normally in satellizers. However, the next step in maturation that usually occurs in preadolescence and adolescence—desatellization and the acquisition of adult-personality status (volitional independence; striving for long-range, adult-ego demands; increased executive independence; societal moral responsibility)—fails to eventuate. Hence, lack of maturation rather than regression is the keynote of this disorder. Because of the presence of intrinsic security and adequacy, neurotic anxiety does not occur and reality accomplishment that is relatively meager can be tolerated with equanimity. Aspirational tenacity (goal-frustration tolerance) is low, while self-esteem and performance-frustration tolerance are high. The type of behavior disorder that finally prevails in this type of aberrant ego development is largely influenced by the factors of introversion-extraversion. In either case, characteristic modes of gratifying the hedonistic goal structure are found. And since satisfaction is neither sought nor can be gained through normal adult goals, there is some compensatory retrogression to even more childish levels of goal striving, especially when the individual is removed from the supervision of parents for whose sake attenuation of hedonistic impulses occurred in the first place.

The Inadequate Personality

The predominantly extraverted, inadequate personality satisfies his hedonsitic needs in reality by finding ways of gratifying his pleasure-seeking and childish goals. Since it is obviously impossible for an adult to adapt to an adult world of reality while retaining the goal structure of a child, successful adjustment at a mature level fails to take place. Because of lack of emotional identification with normal goals, the inadequate psychopath is unable to sustain his motivation in striving for them or to derive any satisfaction from their realization. His attitude toward life is passive and dependent. He demonstrates no desire to persevere in the face of environmental difficulties or to accept responsibilities which he finds painful.

But despite his underlying sense of intrinsic adequacy, the failure to acquire extrinsic status would still be quite traumatic were it not for a protective inhibition of the self-critical faculty that would otherwise "explode the fiction of serene adequacy so vital to his sense of puerile security." Thus, we find a strange paradox: in the personality disorder in which the most inadquate adaptation to life is made, there are no subjective feelings of inadequacy. Thanks to an impaired self-critical faculty, such an individual is able to deny the very existence of his difficulties and problems as well as his obvious inadequacy. By making unwarranted assumptions about his capacity for meeting new situations, he obviates the necessity for painful planning or preparation. By denying his failures and exaggerating the efficacy of his adjustment, he is thereby required to put forth less effort toward a positive solution of his problems. He becomes preoccupied with the search for an easy, effortless, unearned form of pleasure. All of these factors contribute to the resulting instability and nomadism that is characteristic of the group.

From the ranks of the inadequate personalities are recruited vagrants, hobos, drug addicts, petty criminals of all varieties, poolroom hangers-on, carnival operators, confidence men, race track touts, and a multitude of others. Of all these characters, the narcotic drug addict makes the most satisfactory adjustment (from his own point of view). Drug addiction results in positive, immediate, pleasurable sensations that satisfy the quest for effortless, hedonistic satisfaction. It dulls the self-critical faculty to the point where the addict becomes easily contented with his inadequate, hedonistic adjustment to life, and is more easily able to evade and overlook responsibilities; and where in the complete absence of any actual accomplishment, he feels supremely satisfied with himself and his future. By virtue of its analgesic properties and general dulling effect on consciousness, the drug provides a partial escape from the disturbance and distasteful elements of reality. Thus, if he is actually required to work and assume responsibility, the hard, distasteful edge of the task is softened, much in the way a self-indulged child will fulfill his chores as long as he has a lollipop in his mouth.

The inadquate personality who does not discover opiate addiction leads a very unstable, nomadic type of existence characterized by a precarious and marginal vocational adjustment and by frequent, unnecessary changes of employment. He is also predisposed toward alcoholism, addiction to other drugs, and all thrill-seeking forms of vice. He is able to adjust marginally in an optimal environment, that is, one structured in terms of his hedonistic needs, but in no other.

A *partial* type of inadequate personality has already been described as occurring in overdominated children who accept parental domination.

Process Schizophrenia

Clinically, two distinct varieties of schizophrenia are apparent. In the first or classical (process) form of schizophrenia, the psychosis is merely the culmination or end result of the natural evolution of the preschizophrenic personality. It is the almost invariable and insidious outcome of the continued existence of this type of personality makeup—or, at any rate, if a mental disorder occurs in such a personality, no other type of psychotic reaction seems conceivable. Most commonly these cases fall into the simple or hebephrenic varieties.

On the other hand, in an individual not endowed with the preschizophrenic personality, another type of schizophrenic reaction may occur that is, more or less, a paroxysmal abortive attempt at adjustment upon confrontation with overwhelming environmental demands.* Such an individual has previously adopted normal or other abnormal but non-schizophrenic techniques of adjustment and actually and potentially has a better adjustive capacity than the classical type. This second variety of reaction occurs later in life, begins more acutely, is more exogenous in

---

*This second or "reactive" type of schizophrenia occurs in non-satellizers as a complication of neurotic anxiety. It is therefore, discussed fully later under Disorders of Non-satellizers.

origin, and runs a more benign course. There is often a strong affective component present, as in the catatonic variety, or various compensatory paranoid trends. This reaction is not a cumulative or well-nigh inevitable result of a predisposing personality disorder, but a transitory, or sometimes permanent, incident in the adjustment of an essentially non-schizophrenic reaction type to the vicissitudes of life. From this point on, it will be more convenient to refer to the first or classical type of schizophrenia as *process,* and the second as *reactive.''*

Process schizophrenia represents a marked and functionally complete withdrawal type of adjustment in which the ego is removed beyond the reach of an unsatisfactory objective reality, and imbedded in a subjective, autistic reality of its own making. It occurs in the motivationally inadequate individual who fails to undergo adult ego maturation in goal structure. A strong constitutional predisposition toward introversion facilitates the development of the withdrawal reaction. He is too "tender-skinned," egocentric, and inclined toward indirect emotional participation in reality "through the medium of symbols and intellectualization" to venture the alternative of seeking hedonistic gratification in reality against the opposition of parents and cultural agents. Introversion also becomes a compensatory adjustive mechanism since it permits gratification of immature ego demands in fantasy.

Handicapped by this personality makeup—which has no stake in the adult world of reality motivations and has little opportunity for gratification of infantile desires (as long as he is required to adjust according to adult standards)—the individual gradually withdraws whatever emotional energy he has invested in adult goals and in reality. He does this not because of an overwhelming sense of failure following the frustration of normally motivated drives (for he has no such sense of failure) but because he "concludes" that reality is an unsuitable medium for the gratification of his immature ego demands. He forsakes it for the obvious superiority of the world of fantasy with whose enchantments he has been progressively flirting. Some precipitating event eventually occurs, often trifling and insignificant enough in itself, which convinces him that adult motivations and reality living represent losing propositions; and that he would fare better by dropping all pretense of adult reality adjustment, and by frankly expressing his true desires in fantasy.

The relatively rare occurrence of schizophrenia in children supports the hypothesis that the process type is the outcome of maturational failure relative to the preadolescent and adolescent periods. Reactive schizophrenia, on the other hand, tends to be a terminal type of maladjustment in the non-satellizer, not generally appearing before the third or fourth decades of life. It would be a fair inference, however, to expect juvenile schizophrenics and autistic children to conform more to the process type because of the heavy loading of constitutional and predisposing factors that obviously must operate in such cases. Apparently then, the extreme introversion is a consequence of the convergence of potent constitutional and child-rearing factors.

Process schizophrenia is characterized more by amaturation than by regression. In addition to the limited form of compensatory regression mentioned above, there is also the spurious regression that represents the release of immature drives when the repressive influence of reality censorship is removed. The emotional blunting, apathy, and disinterest in surroundings, together with the resulting personality and intellectual deterioration are but the culmination of the process of emotional withdrawal from meager attachments to adult goals and reality. The lack of correlation between emotional expression and mental trend is only to be expected since there is no longer any emotional identification with the ideational content that most normal persons live by.

These are the essential symptoms characterizing the process form of the disease, which for the most part conform to the simple and hebephrenic varieties of the old classification. The silliness characteristic of the latter type merely reflects the bizarreness that must inevitably mark the behavior of an individual who lives in his own reality but is judged by persons sharing a social reality. In some cases it seems to possess a sardonic and contemptuous quality, as if the patient pitied the poor mortals who were bound by the conventionality and limitations of an objective existence. Simple schizophrenics, on the other hand, are able to remain in reasonably good contact with their environment and often succeed in making a partial adjustment to reality as long as they remain within the protected environment of the institution. The hallucinations and delusions that are frequently found in hebephrenics are not comparable to the paranoid type (which are purposeful distortions of reality), but are simple psychological consequences of the greater vividness of conscious data derived from endogenous rather than from exogenous sources. Since the hebephrenic variety are not in the least referable to reality, they need not be at all consistent, systematic, or logical as the paranoid ones are.

With respect to course, prognosis, and responsiveness to therapy, the differentiation between process and reactive types is clear-cut. The former runs a chronic and malignant course, has uniformly a dismal prognosis, and is relatively unresponsive to pharmacotherapy. This last fact is reinforced by the finding that juvenile schizophrenia continues to exhibit a chronic, unremitting course that only rarely is improved by the administration of anti-psychotic drugs. In contrast reactive schizophrenia is more acute in onset, is much more responsive to pharmacotherapy, and has a more favorable prognosis.

PERSONALITY DISORDERS IN NON-SATELLIZERS: FAILURE IN EGO DEVALUATION

Maturational and Regressive Disorders

The causes and consequences of non-satellization and lack of ego devaluation have been fully described in previous chapters. From the standpoint of psychopathological significance, two main types of developmental predispositions toward behavior disorder are attributable to unsuccessful solution of the crisis of ego devaluation: (1) Most important are the characteristics of ego hypertrophy, that is, the high level of prestige aspiration, ideas of volitional omnipotence and independence, the great need for extrinsic status, the lack of intrinsic security and adequacy, and high goal-frustration tolerance. As already pointed out, these personality characteristics are not incompatible with cultural expectations regarding adult personality status, and, in fact, facilitate its acquisition. However, they do predispose toward neurotic anxiety, abnormal defenses against anxiety, and deteriorative complications of it. (2) Another set of predispositions that are also referable to failure in ego devaluation has to do with the attributes of the infantile ego that are customarily attenuated in the course of satellization, namely, needs for immediate gratification and pleasure, desires for executive dependence, and tendencies to moral irresponsibility. In non-satellizers, one sees these ego attributes modified selectively on an expediential basis according to the needs of ego hypertrophy, or abandoned completely if no longer required for ego aggrandizement.

While maturation in general is favored by the requirements of ego hypertrophy, two weaknesses are inherent in this situation. (a) The characteristics of mature personality structure that do not contribute to ego aggrandizement are accepted with difficulty. This applies specifically to moral responsibility. (b) The characteristics of mature personality status that do contribute to ego aggrandizement are stable only as long as the individual remains within the framework of his hypertrophied goal structure. In the event of severe behavioral disorganization or psychosis, full-blown regression to these infantile ego attributes will occur since genuine unconditional attenuation has not taken place, and mature behavior no longer serves the interests of expediency.

Referable to the first of these latter two categories are the maturational disorders in conscience development found in non-satellizers, namely, complete moral agenesis (aggressive, antisocial psychopathy), and delinquency secondary to unstable internalization of moral obligation. Lack of ego maturation with respect to hedonism and executive dependence occurs sometimes in overvalued children who are harshly rejected by parents later in childhood as a form of aggressive retaliation against parents. Regressive manifestations of these same ego attributes are also encountered in psychotic complications of anxiety states (e.g., depression and reactive schizophrenia).

A type of alcoholism is very common in non-satellizers with hypertrophied ego demands who for constitutional or other reasons find it difficult to maintain the degree of personality maturity necessary for the realization of achievement goals. These individuals lack motivational tenacity and frustration tolerance, are unable to tolerate conscious anxiety, or have excessive needs for visceral and hedonistic satisfactions that interfere with the attainment of long-range goals. Alcoholism serves as a crutch to sustain motivation and self-discipline, as a part-time escape from frustration-laden reality, and (by lowering the self-critical faculty) as an anxiety-reducing mechanism. Because of ego hypertrophy, however, the objectives of maturation are not completely abandoned, and complete surrender to hedonism, as occurs in narcotic drug addiction, or process schizophrenia does not take place. Alcoholism, of course, is also very common among satellizers who fail to undergo maturation; but these individals prefer a more complete form of hedonism, as occurs in narcotic drug addiction, or process schizophrenia does not tics.

Personality Disorders Due to Ego Hypertrophy

ANXIETY STATES

Neurotic anxiety has been described as an acquired reaction sensitivity in an individual with impaired self-esteem to overreact with fear to any stimulus that threatens to impair self-esteem further. It is a psychopathological outcome of faulty ego devaluation combined with a history of catastrophic trauma to self-esteem; fundamentally, therefore, it is a disease process, a reflection of ego damage rather than a compensatory mechanism.

Nevertheless, it must be conceded that anxiety does have some adjustive value *per se*. (1) Before it assumes disorganizing proportions, it mobilizes the individual's adaptive efforts and increases his motivational tenacity. By alerting him in advance, it allows him to prepare responses to threatening stimuli that otherwise might precipitate panic if confronting him unawares. Although this interferes with the capacity for improvisation, it does prevent behavioral disorganization in response to threatening situations that the individual either cannot or chooses not to solve by avoidance behavior. (2) It serves as a warning signal to withdraw from certain situations that threaten to bring him defeat and lowered self-esteem. If this entails the loss of gratifications associated with possible success, it also forestalls the painful humiliation that failure evokes. This protective value of anxiety, however, cannot be utilized in the form of outright avoidance, since fear of failure is not an acceptable justification for withdrawal in our culture. Hence, avoidance must be rationalized by some other device such as illness, gross ineptitude, the virtue of asceticism or self-denial for the sake of others, and in extreme cases by the plea of incapacity due to behavioral disorganization (e.g., panic, agitation). (3) Anxiety is sometimes employed as a bid for help, sympathy, deference, or executive dependence. But since this adjustive use of anxiety is socially hazardous and implies a degree of helplessness that is highly threatening to self-esteem, it is not generally utilized except under conditions of panic.

Although many of the defenses against anxiety help considerably to reduce its tensions and distastefulness, simple conscious anxiety is still a more desirable state of affairs from the standpoint of eventually evolving a constructive adjustment. The defensive reactions tend to become fixed, to acquire a canalized adjustive value, and to limit the variability of behavior, which is one of the main hopes of effecting a more wholesome type of adaptation. We must also amend our earlier interpretation of the defenses against and the complications of anxiety to include their role of rationalizing (making more acceptable) the adjustive value of anxiety *per se* as a technique of avoiding situations where loss of self-esteem is feared.

We have held throughout that the main reason for overreacting with fear to an ostensibly inadequate threat (judged in terms of its objective hazardness to persons not suffering from neurotic anxiety) is an inner feeling of inadequacy that reflects an impaired self-esteem. When panic sets in, however, this reason is compounded by the resulting loss of discriminative ability that further prevents the individual from distinguishing between adequate and inadaquate threats.

The rejected type of non-satellizer generally suffers from a manifest anxiety neurosis. Many overvalued individuals, however, do not go on to develop frank anxiety states; in a sizeable number of cases where catastrophic impairment of self-esteem does not occur, the anxiety remains latent. Driven by implacable ambition, however, they become obnoxiously aggressive, ruthless, self-centered, rigid, humorless, and determined to achieve success at any price. Later, after experiencing considerable frustration, a note of bitterness and cynicism creeps in. It is at this stage that they are ready to seek compensation through the exploits of their own children and thus to perpetuate the same vicious cycle of overvaluation of which they themselves were victims.

DEFENSIVE REACTIONS AGAINST ANXIETY

The varied and numerous types of adjustive mechanisms through which these defensive reactions are mediated have been described in Chapter 9. Here we shall only attempt to relate these mechanisms to the formal diagnostic entities employed in clinical psychiatry. Their elaboration is facilitated by the altered state of behavioral reactivity induced by anxiety, and their general function is to bolster self-esteem, to increase security, and to rationalize avoidance of threatening situations. Psychosomatic symptoms, for example, may have a dual function: they may explain failure to attain eminence in areas where tremendous effort is obviously expended to achieve success; or they may be utilized to justify to self and others withdrawal from threatening situations (rather than to face the risk of possible failure.)

The simplest defenses against anxiety utilize the mechanisms of rationalization and displacement in elaborating upon the physiological accompaniments of anxiety states. The *hypochondriac* reduces anxiety by becoming preoccupied with these physiological complaints and believing that they are indicative of organic disease. This conscious attention to normally autonomous physiological functions further impairs their efficiency. Belief in organic illness rationalizes both failure and avoidance of striving, and displaces both the source and object of the threat with more palatable and less traumatic surrogates. The same mechanisms are operative in "fatigue" and "exhaustion" states except that the individual concentrates on the fatiguing consequences of anxiety instead of on other somatic complaints. Actual organic symptoms of illness can also be developed *de novo,* apart from the usual manifestations of anxiety (e.g., hysterical anaesthesias, blindness, paralysis, tremors, seizures, tics) through the convergence of intense need to escape from catastrophic threats, extreme suggestibility, and fortuitous physiological accident. For example, a hypersuggestible soldier with intense combat fear can develop hysterical blindness by interpreting the momentary loss of sight induced by the glare of a nearby exploding shell as proof of permanent organic deficit.

In *phobias,* displacement of the source of the threat from impaired self-esteem to specific avoidable objects and situations occurs. The selection of surrogate objects is not arbitrary but depends upon some symbolical connection with the actual threat. In *obsessive* disorders, the source of the threat is not displaced or made more tangible or specific, but consciousness is monopolized by a relatively innocuous and symbolically related idea that relieves anxiety by creating an all-consuming distraction. *Compulsions* add the element of magic and ritualistic defense and provide a rigid formula for meeting new situations, thus banishing anxiety in relation to the unreasonable need for absolute certainty. Dependence on stereotyped ritualism eliminates the need for improvising new adjustments. Compulsive activity, is also a simple unadjustive consequence of acute behavioral disorganization.

Self-esteem and security can be enhanced by *delusional* distortion of reality in which (1) guilt, responsibility, unacceptable motivations, etc., are disowned and projected onto others, (2) individuals who are rejecting and unappreciative are unjustifiably deprecated, and (3) the status and accomplishments of self are uncritically inflated or perceived to be the objects of systematic victimization. A related technique is to proclaim the wickedness of all earthly aspirations, to renounce them, and to interpret such acts of renunciation as proof of unusual virtue (asceticism), or to believe in one's divinely inspired mission to redeem mankind (religious delusions).

Martyrs assume the role of neglected, self-sacrificing individuals who voluntarily neglect their own interests and aspirations to enhance the welfare or careers of others. This not only explains their own lack of eminence but also bestows upon them a saint's mantle of selflessness and devotion. The latter claim is not un-founded in fact, since martyrs either allow themselves to endure exploitation by others or else to manipulate situations in such a way that they are obliged to suffer martyrdom. They frequently start their careers as rejected eldest children in large families who are deprived of childhood joys and are burdened with the responsibil-ity of caring for younger siblings. The role of martyrdom may be assumed initially as a reaction formation against resulting feelings of hostility and resentment or as a form of expiation for the guilt feelings arising from such feelings. In addition to rationalizing and finding ego-enhancing values in the act of martyrdom, martyrs also achieve secondary ego gratification by identifying themselves with the ac-complishments of those for whom they sacrifice their own lives and fortunes.

Rationalization, projection, and delusional distortion of reality all imply some degree of impairment of the self-critical faculty. In *manic* reactions, how-ever, an unusual degree of such impairment constitutes the main adjustive mechanism involved and is not specifically related to a single belief. Instead, there is a general euphoric alteration of mood, boundless optimism, unlimited belief in one's abilities and prospects, and loss of all inhibition and sense of propriety.

Aggression and hostility are among the simplest and commonest outcomes of frustration, and are sometimes used defensively to allay anxiety. But as pointed out earlier, they are themselves highly productive of anxiety because of the anticipation of retaliation, and because they threaten to disrupt the placatory defensive techniques that are more effective in our society.

COMPLICATIONS OF ANXIETY

When the burden of anxiety exceeds the individual's level of tolerance because of a breakdown in his defenses or because of new and catastrophic environmental threats to his self-esteem, severe psychotic complications of anxi-ety may ensue. These reactions represent such marked disorganization of behavior that normal interpersonal relationships or participation in a shared social reality become impossible. The disorganization is in part a reflection of the deterioration of behavior and personality occurring in extreme or panic levels of altered behavioral reactivity, a form of damage that has no adjustive value *per se*. In part, these psychotic complications represent an attempt at adjustment beyond the established framework of ego organization from which the patient derives his usual sense of personal identity, and beyond the social reality that he shares with significant persons in his psychological field. In this sense, and in the sense that they remove him from the field of impossible adjustive situations exceeding his adaptive capacity, these reactions may be considered to have some adjustive value.

How are such adjustive crises produced? The anxiety neurotic ordinarily learns how to avoid potentially traumatic situations that he feels might end disastrously in terms of his self-esteem (e.g., rejection by a person with whom he wishes to establish a close emotional relationship). Through various rationalizing techniques he manages to justify avoidance of forming such relationships even though this involves self-frustration and loss of possible gratifications that he deeply desires.

Let us carry the adjustive stress one step further. Suppose that our anxiety patient is confronted with accepting a vocational adjustment below his level of aspiration, a situation that is highly traumatic in terms of his hypertrophic goal structure. Neither fear nor protestations of "being too good for such a job" are valid enough reasons to persuade oneself or others that a practical, modestly oriented adjustment is unsatisfactory when no other employment is available. When hard-pressed by the inexorable logic of accepting this situation, anxiety may give way to panic that in turn disorganizes behavior; makes any type of adjustment impossible; and induces blocking, paralysis, and exaggerated self-criticism. The patient can claim complete incapacity as a result of "a nervous breakdown," justify his dependence on others, and enjoy a reprieve from accepting a half-loaf solution that does violence to his needs for prestige, power, and exalted ego status.

While immersed in this agitated state of panic, which is marked by collapse of self-esteem, self-depreciation, and dependence on others, a constructive solution is still possible as long as the patient continues to strive on an adult reality plane. If he can perceive the new adjustment as only a short-term setback that does not irreparably frustrate his needs for ego aggrandizement, he may be persuaded to accept it as a temporary expedient. If, on the other hand, he feels that his ambitions are completely blocked and that reconciliation to a life of acknowledged mediocrity of status is inevitable, he may choose instead a psychotic adjustment removed from normal adult strivings and from participation in a social reality.

REACTIVE SCHIZOPHRENIA

Reactive schizophrenia is a paroxysmal and extreme form of withdrawal adjustment that occurs in ego-hypertrophic individuals in response to catastrophic adjustive stress. The magnitude of such stress must be evaluated in terms of the individual's particular ego aspirations rather than in relation to conventional criteria of deprivation. For example, to a lawyer who aspires to a professorship in constitutional law, the prospect of becoming reconciled to a $20,000-a-year general law practice might represent an unbearable degree of trauma to self-esteem. In contrast to the depressive reactions, reactive schizophrenia is more apt to occur in introverted individuals; but the introversion is seldom as marked as in process schizophrenia and is by no means an indispensable predisposition, since pronounced extraversion is not a rare finding in the reactive form of the disease. The more crucial differential factors with respect to predisposition are failure of ego maturation in the one (process type) and lack of satellization and ego devaluation in the other (reactive type). In the reactive type, there is abrupt rather than gradual withdrawal from an objective and shared social reality, and abrupt regressive dematuration from mature adult goals rather than failure to achieve an adult goal structure in the first place. It tends to run a more acute and benign course than the process type and is much more responsive to pharmacotherapy.

Symptomatically, reactive schizophrenia includes two categories of symptoms not found in the process form: (1) those that are indicative of other not necessarily schizophrenic adjustive techniques (possibly tried before) and are directed more within the framework of reality; and (2) manifestations of undervalued ego aspirations that are expressed on an infantile level and removed from the sphere of adult reality fulfillment. Typical of the first category are hallucinations and delusions that are referable to the paranoid-reaction tendency to negate frustration by distortion of the environment (rationalization and projection). This condition must be differentiated from the relatively rare disorder, *paranoia,* in which adult goals are not abandoned and loss of contact with reality is neither desired nor attained; but the patient's perception of that portion of his psychological field which is most significant for him is so distorted by a self-consistent delusional system that actual participation in a shared social reality impinging upon this field becomes impossible. Outside of this rather extensive field, however, the attitudes, values, and perceptions of patients with paranoia are entirely reasonable and realistic.

The most common examples of the second type of supplementary symptoms are active catatonic negativism and the ideas of rebirth, "eternality," omnipotence, and cosmic identification that recapitulate the corresponding infantile elements of narcissistic solipsism as modified by the greater breadth of adult experience. Catatonic hypersuggestibility, on the other hand, is more indicative of extensive dematuration and symbolic of complete passivity and dependence. An actively negativistic catatonic schizophrenic tries to destroy the objects and persons in his environment responsible for frustrating his aroused hypertrophic ego; whereas the manic patient is seeking to negate frustration by ceaseless activity, the success of which is internally assured by gross impairment of the self-critical faculty.

In catatonics, the severance and disinvolvement of self from reality and mature standards of goal structure are most complete and abrupt. There is no acknowledgment of defeat or cessation of striving; the same intense struggle for ego aggrandizement is merely transferred to the patient's subjective reality and carried on at a lower level of goal maturity. This transition may be accomplished within the space of several days or even several hours and is most apt to occur in proud, vigorous, and volatile individuals capable of intense, uninhibited rage responses.

DEPRESSIVE REACTIONS

Instead of regressing to a less mature goal structure and seeking ego aggrandizement in a subjective reality of his own making, another alternative is open to a severely traumatized anxiety neurotic. He may accept the defeat of his ego aspirations, wallow in the misery of his impaired self-esteem, and renounce all further striving. Soon he is overcome by emotional depression and physical and mental retardation. Suffering and hopelessness are acute, and the individual is so completely overwhelmed by his self-perceived unworthiness that he sees little point in living. The sense of future time in relation to the ego is lost, and there is a strong desire for death. This often leads to refusal to eat and frequently to attempts at suicide. There is no purposeful withdrawal from reality as such; but preoccupation with his own worthlessness, profound physical and mental retardation, extreme depression of mood and abandonment of striving make participation in social reality completely impossible. When this stage is reached, anxiety can no longer occur since self-esteem cannot possibly sink any lower because both ego aspirations and the future cease to have any meaning.

Depressive reactions are closely related to acute stages of anxiety for several reasons. The anxiety neurotic generally has a well-developed self-critical faculty in relation to his own abilities, which tends to become even more severe as anxiety increases. Furthermore, he or she tends to react to frustration with a lowering of self-esteem and a disorganization of performance ability that further increase feelings of worthlessness. If he is using this state of disorganization as a means of frustrating the acceptance of a "half-loaf adjustment" and of justifying his executive and volitional dependence on others, he has reason to exaggerate his incompetence even further and to erect all kinds of irrelevant barriers and impossibly high standards.

Because of the anxiety sufferer's high goal-frustration tolerance, however, defeat is not accepted easily. He continues for some time to maintain his grandiose ego aspirations despite the collapsed state of his self-esteem, to look for some new basis on which to restructure his shattered ambitions. Hence arises the mixture of frantic, aimless activity, acute anxiety, emotional depression, and intense fear of death that is found in *agitated* depression. *Involutional melancholia* is a form of agitated depression occurring in menopausal women, which is precipitated in part by the threat to biosocial status posed by the prospect of sterility and by the emotional instability secondary to hormonal imbalance. In spite of the characteristic self-condemnatory trend found in this condition, ego hypertrophy betrays itself in the patient's assertion that she is the "*greatest* sinner in the world." The state of agitated depression may either continue chronically or at any point assume the retarded form.

Mania and depression occur singly more frequently than alternately. However, the existence of one condition does predispose toward the occurrence of the other. As convalescence from depression begins, the patient realizes how unwarranted and exaggerated his dismal outlook on life was. Thus, in the first intoxication of release from despair, the seeds of mania are sown; for it seems no less miraculous to be delivered from a state in which the reasonable seemed impossible than to pass into a state in which the impossible seems certain. Conversely, when the manic stage collapses and impossible commitments can't be met the "letdown" may precipitate depression on the same basis. A tendency toward reaction formation in relation to the self-critical faculty also predisposes toward violent fluctuations in self-evaluation by interfering with fusion of positive and negative elements.

Yet, even in the depths of depression, there is some attempt to preserve ego grandiosity through displacement of affect. The patient admits worthlessness, but usually for some irrelevantly innocuous reason. Depressions also are sometimes complicated by obsessive perplexity reactions that serve the same defensive functions as ordinary obsessions.

11

Implications of Ego Development for Psychotherapy*

The Overvaluation of Psychotherapy

We are witnessing today a vast but not inexplicable overvaluation of the field of psychotherapy. Exaggerated and unwarranted claims are being made for this relatively new addition to medicine's therapeutic armamentarium. In some quarters it has taken on the status of a panacea that promises to all within its reach a fuller and richer life; greater personality integration and self-realization; and freedom from tension, anxiety, and disabling psychological symptoms of all varieties. This trend, of course, has its cultural supports. In the first place, there is the tremendous prestige of science in general and of medicine in particular to draw upon. It was relatively easy, therefore, for psychotherapy to establish itself as a branch of medicine and to borrow medicine's mantle of scientific prestige and authority. In the process, two weaknesses in the analogy have escaped general detection. First, it was forgotten that clinical medicine is built upon the firm foundations of anatomy, physiology, biochemistry, pathology, pharmacology, etc., whereas psychotherapy enjoys precious little of an empirical scientific substructure. Second, the theoretical structure of clinical medicine is cogent, self-consistent, and in harmony with the concepts of its parent sciences. In psychotherapy, there are innumerable warring factions with completely antagonistic theories and little consensus with respect to fundamental issues; yet each group claims expertness and reputability, while often formulating its system with consummate disregard for established principles of general psychology.

---

*A detailed discussion of psychotherapy would be out of place in this book. We will only discuss a few general issues particularly germane to ego psychology. As pointed out in the Preface, our approach to treatment in psychiatry is eclectic, e.g. it includes pharmacotherapy.

289

A second cultural support that has favored the overvaluation of psychotherapy is the sudden public awakening to the importance, prevalence, and economic cost of mental illness. The high incidence of psychiatric casualties in the Second World War increased official willingness to remedy the shortage of psychotherapists; and economic prosperity created for the first time an actual surplus of demand over supply in terms of ability to pay for needed services. The federal government underwrote training programs in clinical psychology; many new clinical positions opened up; and many general psychologists climbed on the more promising and more remunerative clinical bandwagon. Concurrently, private and institutional practice in psychiatry greatly expanded.

A third cultural support is traceable to the current tendency to over-psychologize all aspects of modern living. We have already noted this trend in relation to moral problems from which a strong attempt is being made to remove all ethical content and to restate issues simply in behavioral terms. A similar situation has arisen in relation to social, political, and economic problems, which some psychologists attempt to explain on a psychological plane alone. Within such a conceptual framework, psychotherapy naturally looms as a logical cure for all of the world's ills.

A fourth cultural support stems from a long-seething overreaction to a core of ideological trends prominent in the first half of the present century which emphasized principles that limit inherently man's capacity for behavioral change. Illustrative of such ideas are Freud's concepts of the id and of a phylogenetically predetermined sequence of psychosexual development; Jung's "racial unconscious"; the concept of "repetition compulsion"; the emphasis upon the prepotent influence of infant experience upon adult personality structure; the notion of a universal Oedipus conflict; Hall's theory of individual psychological growth as a recapitulation of cultural development, etc. The almost inevitable overreaction to this ideology was the assertion of a rather naive *tabula rasa* doctrine that held human nature to be infinitely plastic and malleable. Hence, problems of psychological development were seen to have no universal common denominator but to reflect in every instance only the operation of unique social conditions; genic and constitutional factors were held to be of minor importance since man, who is primarily a creature of his social environment, can be molded into any form his culture wishes him to take.

This new trend was not without its influence on psychotherapy. It led to an unbounded confidence in the patient's capacity to reconstruct his personality on a more wholesome basis regardless of his previous history as long as the stimulus and motivation for such restructuring were endogenously derived. In some quarters, this point of view naturally led to a de-emphasis of developmental diagnosis and to a concentration upon the current adjustive situation. Perhaps both the optimism and the preoccupation with present problems stem from the predominant experience of non-directive therapists with clients having minor adjustive difficulties largely of a situational nature.

This unlimited optimism with respect to an adult's ability to remake his personality is not only unsupported by any empirical evidence but seems highly unlikely in the light of theoretical considerations with respect to the irreversibility of basic personality patterns. A not-to-be ignored consideration also in determining the limits of possible change is the benevolence of an individual's environment and the degree of control he can exercise over it. In the case of children, for example, this latter factor is especially important.

It is obvious, therefore, that the scientific status and role of psychotherapy must be seen in clearer perspective before much progress can be made. Principles of psychotherapy must be related to principles of psychology. Hypotheses regarding the processes of psychotherapy must be empirically validated and related to outcomes. Clinicians must cease demanding exemption from the laws of scientific evidence and must be willing to regard diagnoses as hypotheses to be proven rather than as unchallengeable facts. Clinical hunches and impressions must motivate the search for general psychodynamic principles and for definitive psychological diagnoses rather than be offered per se as the equivalent of empirically established data. And finally psychotherapists must avoid arousing extravagant and unwarranted hopes for cure, hopes which, when frustrated, only augment adjustive stress. Criteria must be established indicating when psychotherapy can be useful; what the objectives are; what limitations exist; and what maximum change can be expected in terms of developmental history, personality structure, age, diagnostic entity, and the environmental situation of the the patient.

The Overvaluation of Unconscious Motivation and Insight

Contributing to the current overvaluation of psychotherapy, but on a conceptual plane rather than as a cultural support, is the psychoanalytic overemphasis upon unconscious motivation as the central etiological mechanism in the production of neurotic symptoms. If behavior disorders can be interpreted accurately as symbolic expressions of or defenses against repressed unconscious motives, then it seems reasonable to expect complete cure as soon as the patient is made to appreciate the motivation underlying his symptoms (insight). Yet, when this fails to happen in all but a few dramatic cases, analysts explain that intellectual understanding is insufficient and that emotional acceptance and practical application of insight to current life situations ("working through") is also necessary. Emotional acceptance, they argue, is facilitated by catharsis of the affect involved in the repressed complex; and since the source of such complexes supposedly resides in childhood psychosexual development, catharsis can be best effected therapeutically by a "transference" relationship in which the therapist plays the role of parent figure to re-elicit the expression of repressed childhood motives and attitudes. These additional techniques, according to this way of thinking, do not invalidate the crucial role of insight but merely implement it.

Non-directive therapists also stress the role of perceptual reorganization through insight, but they decry therapist participation except for purposes of reflection and clarification of the client's feelings. Interpretation and "transference" are taboo, and attention is focused on current conflicts apart from their developmental origins. It is claimed that emotional acceptance of insight is facilitated by the creation of a permissive atmosphere that minimizes resistance to change, by emphasis upon self-discovery of underlying attitudes and motivations, and by emotional relatedness on the part of the therapist to the client.

The authors agree that "working through", catharsis, "transference," optimal permissiveness, self-discovery, and emotional relatedness of therapist to patient are all valuable aids for the implementation of insight. However, acceptance of the therapeutic value of insight does not imply acceptance of the theory that all neurotic symptoms reflect the operation of repression and unconscious motivation. Many neurotic symptoms can occur with complete possession of insight; and lack of conscious accessibility is not necessarily a precondition for lack of insight, since frequently the relation of symptoms to conscious motives is not appreciated. The reason for this relative unimportance of the unconscious, as has already been noted, is that repression is not the primary cause of anxiety, ego immaturity, and other forms of ego damage, but a defense against anxiety which facilitates the development of neurotic defenses and interferes with the evolution of more constructive solutions. Hence, it is unrealistic to expect that the acquisition of insight can by itself repair lack of self-esteem or create feelings of security and adequacy. More constructive relief from anxiety may conceivably be achieved by optimal manipulation of the environment, reorganization of goal structure, alteration of the quality of interpersonal relationships, increase of tolerance for unalterable disabilities, and creation of a new set of environmental expectations.

In this connection it should be recalled that displacement of affect not only occurs from "unconscious" material to symbolic conscious equivalents but also in the opposite direction. Unless the therapist is aware of this possibility, he may easily confound cause-and-effect relationships. It should also be realized that the perceptual reorganization achieved as a result of insight does not represent absolute and unconditional change, but change that is stable in relation to a given amount of adjustive stress. Let the degree of stress increase, and retrogression to the former level of insight may readily occur.

The Place of Diagnosis in Therapy

While it is true (as claimed by non-directive therapists) that present personality structure represents a precipitate of all the relevant developmental influences entering into its formation, mere attention to the current adjustive problem without definitive diagnosis in terms of developmental history is not likely to lead to permanent therapeutic benefit. Meaningful insight into the present adjustive situation cannot be gained by patient or therapist by examining only the end product of development. Neither sequence nor process of growth is deducible from eventual outcome, although the latter necessarily reflects their operation.

The practical clinical significance of this consideration enters into one of the first decisions that the therapist is obliged to make in every case he undertakes. Are the adjustive difficulties of the patient an outcome of current transitional or situational pressures, or are they reflective of serious abnormalities in ego devaluation or maturation? Until this question can be answered, no intelligent decision with respect to prognosis, length, depth, urgency, and type of therapy indicated can be made.

Nevertheless, all therapy must be postponed until a definitive diagnosis is possible. In acute cases, supportive or drug therapy, environmental manipulation, and relief from immediate pressures and frustration are indicated to forestall imminent psychotic breakdown. In less acute cases, concurrently with developmental diagnosis, progress in solving current problems of adjustment must be made if the later acquisition of insight is to have any practical significance; otherwise not only does exploration of the past become an academic pursuit but also anxiety increases and deterioration of the environmental situation occurs (especially in the spheres of vocational adaptation, social relationships, and personal independence) and makes actual implementation of insight all but impossible.

The common psychoanalytic practice of ignoring situational factors until complete insight is secured is partly a reflection of the Hippocratian concept of the finiteness as well as of the single source of drive and affect to which most analysts subscribe. According to this reasoning, as long as affect is bound up in repressed neurotic complexes, the acquisition of more wholesome adjustive mechanisms is impossible since the latter cannot be energized by necessary emotional components; only after insight is attained can this "frozen" affect be liberated for other purposes. However, if we adopt the more plausible assumption that "functionally autonomous" motives can arise as the result of new life experiences, new tehcniques of adjustment can be successfully sustained even though emotional energy is tied up in unsolved conflicts. It is also a common experience that motivation develops retroactively as a result of the interest aroused and the gratification obtained from successful performance of an activity that might have been grudgingly undertaken in the first place.

The Place of Direction in Therapy

The same fetish of permissiveness that we criticized in our chapter on parent-child relationships is gradually capturing the field of psychotherapy. Almost by definition in some quarters, the more permissive a therapist is, the less he structures the therapeutic situation; the fewer his expectations, the less he tends to judge the patient; and the wider his limits of tolerance and the more lax the authority he wields, the more superior he is accounted to be in professional attitudes and equipment.

The non-directive therapist takes the position that change cannot be imposed upon the individual from without but must originate endogenously. He takes issue with the traditional medical approach in which the physician diagnoses the disorder, explains to the patient the genesis and meaning of his symptoms, and prescribes the necessary treatment. Instead, the patient does all of these things by himself; and the therapist by clarifying and reflecting the former's own productions merely helps him to make better use of his own inherent resources for acquiring insight and instigating change.

This insistence upon the fact that in the final analysis it is only the individual himself who can actually effect a reorganization of his own personality structure is plausible enough, providing it is qualified by certain realistic limitations. First, ego maturation takes place under the impact of mature social expectations and within a realistic framework of interpersonal relations that does not ignore relevant moral problems. Because lasting personality change can occur only when there is genuine internal acceptance of the need for a change does not mean that it can or must always be endogenously stimulated. Second, patients cannot assume the major responsibility for self-direction when they are disorganized, panic-stricken or hopelessly caught between the vicious cycle of anxiety and the fixed, perseverative, and maladaptive responses that it tends to engender. The degree of responsibility and self-direction that a patient can assume cannot be fixed dogmatically at the start of therapy and maintained throughout, but must be flexibly modified to meet the requirements of both his original condition and subsequent improvement therein. In many clinical situations, supportive therapy, environmental manipulation, reliance on drugs and physical therapy, and interpretation by the therapist are indicated.

THE NEED FOR REALISTIC EXPECTATIONS

Throughout this volume we have stressed the fact that ego maturation does not occur spontaneously but largely in response to new social expectations. This principle is supported by evidence from the social psychology of attitude formation and attitude change. Goals, ego attributes, and attitudes toward self also change in response to cultural demands and supports, since individuals are dependent upon their social milieu for status, approval, love, acceptance, security, and a sense of belongingness (Auerbach, 1951).

To the patient, the therapist represents the expectations of the social reality to which he has not yet succeeded in adjusting adequately. Much of the stimulus for change in motivation, attitude, and adjustive behavior during the period of treatment will come from the expectations of the therapist in his role of social reality surrogate. However, if the latter takes the position that it is the patient's prerogative to structure the framework of expectancy and set the limits in the relationship, the patient not only feels under no pressure to abandon his unrealistic, autistic, or immature framework of reference but also feels justifiably encouraged to seek adjustment within such a framework with the tacit approval, support, and sanction of the therapist. The latter, for example, must continue to insist on the patient's acceptance of the need for vocational adjustment on a realistic level, rather than remain non-commital when confronted with grandiose and impractical ambitions that blithely ignore insuperable obstacles of ability and job opportunity.

Part of this framework of realistic and mature expectations in which the therapeutic setting is embedded consists of a code of moral values. Most significant human behavior has an ethical aspect that cannot be ignored without sacrificing much of its essence insofar as interpersonal relationships are concerned. If the therapist articulates no moral expectations and fails to express ethical judgments, the patient is justified in assuming that the former either approves of his immoral behavior or else considers that any type of ethical solution he (the patient) is satisfied with is also satisfactory to the therapist. In the latter case, therapy takes place in an amoral setting, and the patient is supported in his belief that he is above the moral law, which is then taken as applying only to ordinary mortals. Silence on the part of the therapist condones immorality and whitewashes guilt feelings. This does not mean, however, that the patient must necessarily accept the therapist's moral values.

Both therapist and patient must face the problem of guilt and moral accountability squarely. If guilt feelings are unfounded, they should be eliminated; if they are warranted they should be acknowledged and dealt with constructively. Proper timing, good rapport, and tact on the part of the therapist are necessary as well as a constructive approach rather than an attitude of final condemnation. However, if in spite of skillful handling, the patient discontinues therapy because of the therapist's expression of moral judgment, it is doubtful whether he could have benefited from it in the first place. The pragmatic approach to ethical problems employed by many non-directive therapists, that is, moral behavior is desirable simply because it makes for more wholesome, stable, and predictable interpersonal relationships, is actually devoid of any moral content and lends support to current philosophies of expediency.

It is equally unrealistic to deny the inherent authority residing in the role of therapist and to set up the dictum that therapeutic benefit is limited in instances where the therapist is in a position of authority in relation to the patient. First, the very fact that one individual appeals for help on the basis of another's expert knowledge inevitably injects an authoritarian aspect into the relationship. Second, if the therapist plays his necessary role of representing cultural expectations and defining limits for the therapeutic relationship, he automatically becomes invested with authority. Whether he wishes to create a "transference" situation or not, the patient inevitably reacts toward him as an authority figure, since the relationship recapitulates so many features of the parent-child relationship. Third and last, the therapist's effectiveness depends upon his being perceived by the patient as an individual of strength, someone to be respected rather than pushed around like an ineffective, underdominating parent. Without authority, he can set no realistic limits; and in the absence of such limits, therapy can only compound existing ego damage.

It does seem reasonable to expect that there will be less resistance to genuine emotional acceptance of insight if such insight is the product of self-discovery rather than of interpretation by the therapist. However, self-discovery is by no means an indispensable condition for acceptance of insight. Satellizers, for example, are more willing to accept the therapist's interpretations than non-satellizers. Interpretation is also necessary in acute phases of anxiety when panic destroys all ability to think clearly, and in cases where the acquisition of insight is persistently blocked by stubborn "blindspots."

Also, in a large number of cases in which the patient is either hostile, withdrawn, suspicious, or diffident, it is necessary for the therapist to take the initiative in the relationship rather than passively to allow the former to explore the situation by himself. As the more mature and independent person in the relationship, he has to be willing to make the advances if any need to be made. Anyone who has had experience in treating hostile children and adolescents also recognizes that "warmth, love, understanding, and acceptance" (maximal permissiveness) is no magic formula that will automatically diminish the latter's aggressive proclivities. Such is only the case in instances of counteraggression induced by environmental deprivation, not where hostility is a deeply ingrained orientation toward life or a fixed form of defense against anxiety.

By structuring the therapeutic situation in this fashion, the therapist does not necessarily make the patient unduly dependent upon him. Real danger of dependence arises only if direction and support are maintained too long or longer than warranted by the patient's adjustive capacity, especially if during this time no progress has been made toward economic independence. The therapist's presence and support then become necessary conditions upon which the patient's security depends. The therapist also becomes reluctant to terminate the situation since he prefers to earn his living in a familiar setting. The risk of dependency is also greater in the case of satellizers, since non-satellizers do not tend to form deep emotional attachments to their therapists, merely accepting their direction on the basis of its objective validity. Since there is no subservience of self in the latter's acceptance of assistance, volitional independence is not essentially surrendered.

INDICATIONS FOR DIRECTIVE THERAPY

Indications for special forms of directive therapy exist (1) in acute (prepsychotic) cases of maladjustment; (2) in cases rendered inaccessible to interpersonal intervention because of psychotic inaccessibility; (3) in the treatment of children and adolescents; and (4) in cases of chronic anxiety and other forms of chronic maladjustment.

The first therapeutic consideration in agitated and panic states of anxiety, when patients are confused, helpless, desperate, and on the verge either of depressive psychosis or of reactive schizophrenia, is symptomatic relief of anxiety and frustration. In terms of psychotherapy, this may involve the extension of immediate emotional support, and the use of reassurance, suggestion, prestige authority, and cautiously advanced interpretation. The patient's environment must be simplified by the elimination of unnecessary pressures and harassments of all kinds; and the therapist must be prepared to intervene actively in the former's personal affairs, and, if necessary, help make swift decisions for him. Anti-anxiety medications may be necessary to keep acute anxiety under control and prevent the patient from seeking relief in psychotic mechanisms. Explanation of how the surrender of adult strivings in a reality setting may lead to psychosis sometimes has a protective effect. The use of non-directive techniques in such situations can only end in disaster.

In psychotic states where the patient is either preoccupied with his own subjective reality or too overwhelmed by his defeat to remain in contact with objective reality, it is first necessary to make him more accessible by means of pharmacotherapy or shock therapy before psychotherapy has much chance of success. However, Rosen (1942) has shown that this difficulty in communication can be greatly reduced in schizophrenia if the therapist is willing to think and feel in terms of the patient's reality in the early stages of treatment. This obviously requires a degree of individual attention that would be impossible without increasing the number of psychiatrists in mental hospitals by several thousand percent. For practical reasons, therefore, drugs and shock methods of treatment are presently indispensable.

The use of physical methods of therapy represent in no sense an abandonment of a psychological theory of behavior disorder. If we are ready to concede that an altered state of behavioral reactivity can be induced by fatigue, hormonal imbalance, brain injury, brain amine deficiency, syphilitic encephalitis, uremia, etc., it is no less logical to grant that favorable modification of behavior can be brought about by manipulation of the anatomical or physiological substrate of behavior and consciousness. The more plausible theories of the action of psychotropic drugs and of shock therapy are quite compatible with psychological approaches to behavior disorder.

Psychiatric treatment of children and adolescents requires considerable reliance on environmental manipulation for two reasons. (1) Independent acquisition of insight is difficult for children because of limitations in their verbal ability; and (2) both children and adolescents are largely under the immediate control of powerful adults who in most cases are largely responsible for the adjustive difficulties involved, and without whose cooperation, improvement in the interpersonal environment and implementation of insight is impossible.

Since the personality of the parents constitutes the most important variable affecting the child's ego development, it can be safely predicted that psychotherapy with the latter can bring little lasting improvement until favorable modification of parental practices and attitudes is obtained (often through family therapy). As a matter of fact, this is what is actually found in child guidance centers. Where the parent-child relationship is essentially wholesome, simple mediation or interpretation of parent and child to each other is often helpful.

Acceptance of these therapeutic principles does not in the least rule out an attempt to secure the child's active participation in the process of change. Through recognition, objectification, and acceptance of his feelings (by means of role-playing and play techniques in a shared reality), the child patient is often enabled to acquire and implement insight and achieve greater security, integration, and maturity of personality structure.

Directed guidance is also necessary in chronic maladjustments such as anxiety disorders if progress is to be made in solving current problems of adjustment, and if fixed and rigid defensive mechanisms that prevent efficient learning and working are to be overcome. The anxiety neurotic who has acquired maladaptive ways of learning, perceiving, and setting goals is not free independently to select and utilize beneficial insights (that might arise in the course of therapy) because of potent reaction sensitivities that predispose his behavior along rigidly channelized lines of a defensive nature. Guidance in restructuring his environment and response repertory is needed, for example, selective ego disinvolvement from untenable situations, lowering of aspirational level, formation of satellizing-like relationships, emphasis upon economic security with creative avocational opportunities, avoidance of excessive advance preparation in new learning situations, increasing tolerance for conscious anxiety, minimizing the tendency to achieve security and forestall defeat through abnormal circumscription of the environment, etc.

However, the chief practical implication that a psychology of ego development holds for the treatment of behavior disorders can be simply stated: prophylaxis is far more effective than therapy. If during the crisis of ego devaluation, a child is accepted and valued for himself or herself, that child will satellize and acquire an intrinsic sense of security and adequacy which will prove highly resistant to environmental vicissitudes and will protect him or her from neurotic anxiety. If during the crisis of ego maturation a child is spared from overprotection, underdomination, and overdomination, and given opportunity to undergo desatellization, he or she is likely to acquire the mature ego attributes of adult personality structure. And, failing the protection of these prophylactic measures, the earlier therapy is instituted, the greater the possibility that damage and distortion are correctible. However, in the light of the paucity of empirical evidence regarding both rationale for and outcome of psychotherapy, it behooves psychiatrists and clinical psychologists to adopt greater caution and humility in appraising the scientific status, the applicability, and the probable success of their therapeutic techniques.

References

Adams, D. K. The development of social behavior. In Y. Brackbill (Ed.), *Infancy and early childhood: A handbook and guide to human development.* New York: The Free Press, 1967. Chap. 7.

Adler, A. *The neurotic constitution.* New York: Moffat, Yard, 1917.

Adler, A. *The individual and his religion.* New York: Harcourt, Brace, 1925.

Ainsworth, M. D. The effects of maternal deprivation: A review of findings and controversy in the context of research strategy. In J. Bowlby (Ed.), *Deprivation and maternal care: A re-assessment of its effects.* New York: Schocken Books, 1966. pp. 289–357.

Alexander, F., & Ross, R. *Dynamic psychiatry.* Chicago: University of Chicago Press, 1952.

Allport, G. W. *Personality: A psychological interpretation.* New York: Holt, 1937.

Allport, G. W. The ego in contemporary psychology. *Psychological Review,* 1943, *50,* 451–78.

Altus, W. D. Birth order and its sequelae. *Science,* 1965, *151,* 44–49.

Ames, L. B. The sense of self of nursery school children as manifested by their verbal behavior. *Journal of Genetic Psychology,* 1952, *81,* 193–232.

Anastasi, A. *Differential psychology.* New York: Macmillian, 1958.

Anastasi, A., & Cordova, F. A. Some effects of bilingualism upon the intelligence test performance of Puerto Rican children in New York City. *Journal of Educational Psychology,* 1953, *44,* 1–19.

Anastasi, A., & de Jesus, C. Language development and non-verbal I.Q. in Puerto-Rican preschool children in New York City. *Journal of Abnormal & Social Psychology,* 1953, *48,* 357–366.

Andry, R. G. *Delinquency and parental pathology.* London: Methuen, 1960.

Andry, R. G. Paternal and maternal roles in delinquency. In J. Bowlby (Ed.), *Deprivation of maternal care: A re-assessment of its effects.* New York: Shocken Books, 1966. pp. 223–36.

Arahamsen, D. Psychiatric aspects of criminal behavior. Abstract. *Digest of Neurology & Psychiatry*, 1950, *19*, 105.

Aronfreed, J. *Conduct and conscience: Socialization of internalized control over behavior.* New York: Academic Press, 1968.

Ashmore, H. S. *The Negro and the schools.* Chapel Hill, N.C.: University of North Carolina Press, 1954.

Atkinson, J. W., & Litwin, G. H. Achievement motive and test anxiety conceived as motive to approach success and motive to avoid failure. *Journal of Abnormal & Social Psychology*, 1960, *60*, 52–63.

Auerbach, J. G. What makes people change? *American Journal of Psychotherapy*, 1951, *5*, 172–86.

Ausubel, D. P. The psychopathology and treatment of drug addiction in relation to the mental hygiene movement. *Psychiatric Quarterly Supplement*, 1948, *22*, *Part II*, 127–44.

Ausubel, D. P. Ego development and the learning process. *Child Development*, 1949, *20*, 173–90.

Ausubel, D. P. Negativism as a phase of ego development. *American Journal of Orthopsychiatry*, 1950, *20*, 796–805.

Ausubel, D. P. Prestige motivation of gifted children. *Genetic Psychology Monographs*, 1951, *43*, 53–117.

Ausubel, D. P. *Ego development and the personality disorders.* New York: Grune & Stratton, 1952.

Ausubel, D. P. Reciprocity and assumed reciprocity of acceptance in an adolescent group. *Sociometry*, 1953, *16*, 339–48.

Ausubel, D. P. *Theory and problems of adolescent development.* New York: Grune & Stratton, 1954.

Ausubel, D. P. Relationship between shame and guilt in the socializing process. *Psychological Review*, 1955, *62*, 378–90.

Ausubel, D. P. The relationship between social variables and ego development and functioning. In M. Sherif and M. O. Wilson (Eds.), *Emerging problems in social psychology*. Norman: University of Oklahoma Book Exchange, 1957. pp. 55–96.

Ausubel, D. P. Acculturative stress in modern Maori adolescence. *Child Development*, 1960, *31*, 617–30.

Ausubel, D. P. Causes and types of drug addiction: a psychosocial view. *Psychiatric Quarterly*, 1961, *35*, 523–31. (a)

Ausubel, D. P. The Maori: A study in resistive acculturation. *Social Forces*, 1961, *39*, 218–27. (b)

Ausubel, D. P. Personality disorder *is* disease. *American Psychologist*, 1961, *15*, 69–74. (c)

Ausubel, D. P. *Maori youth.* New York: Holt, Rinehart, & Winston, 1965.

Ausubel, D. P. *Educational psychology: A cognitive view.* New York: Holt, Rinehart & Winston, 1968.

Ausubel, D. P., & Ausubel P. Research on ego development among segregated Negro children. In A. H. Passow (Ed.), *Education in depressed areas*. New York: Teachers College, Columbia University, 1963.

Ausubel, D. P., Balthazar, E. E., Rosenthal, I., Blackman, L., Schpoont, S. H., &

Welkowitz, J. Perceived parent attitudes as determinants of children's ego structure. *Child Development,* 1954, *25,* 173–84.

Ausubel, D. P., De Wit, F., Golden, B., & Schpoont, S. H. Prestige suggestion in children's art preferences. *Journal of Genetic Psychology,* 1956, *89,* 85–93.

Ausubel, D. P., Schiff, H. M., & Gasser, E. B. A preliminary study of developmental trends in sociempathy: Accuracy of perception of own and others' sociometric status. *Child Development,* 1952, *23,* 111–82.

Ausubel, D. P., Schiff, H. M. & Goldman, M. Qualitative characteristics in the learning process associated with anxiety. *Journal of Abnormal & Social Psychology.* 1953, *48,* 537–47.

Ausubel, D. P., Schiff, H. M., & Zeleny, M. P. "Real-life" measures of level of academic and vocational aspiration: Relation to laboratory measures and to adjustment. *Child Development,* 1953, *24,* 155–68.

Ausubel, D. P., & Sullivan, E. V. *Theory and problems of child development.* 2nd Ed. New York: Grune & Stratton, 1970.

Bach, G. R. Father-fantasies and father-typing in father-separated children. *Child Development,* 1946, *17,* 63–80.

Baldwin, A. L. Socialization and the parent-child relationship. *Child Development,* 1948, *19,* 127–36.

Baldwin, A. L. *Behavior and development in childhood.* New York: Dryden, 1955.

Baldwin, A. L., Kalhorn, J., & Breese, F. H. Patterns of parent behavior. *Psychological Monographs,* 1945, *58,* 3, (Serial No. 268)

Baldwin, A. L., Kalhorn, J., & Breese, F. H. The appraisal of parent behavior. *Psychological Monographs,* 1949, *63* (299).

Bandura, A. Social learning through imitation. In M. R. Jones (Ed.), *Nebraska symposium on motivation.* Lincoln: University of Nebraska Press, 1962.

Bandura, A., & McDonald, F. J. The influence of social reinforcement in the behavior of models in shaping children's moral judgments. *Journal of Abnormal & Social Psychology.* 1963, *67,* 274–81.

Bandura, A., & Mischel, W. Modification of self-imposed delay of reward through exposure to live and symbolic models. *Journal of Personality & Social Psychology,* 1965, *2,* 698–705.

Bandura, A., Ross, D., & Ross, S. A. Transmission of agression through imitation of aggressive models. *Journal of Abnormal & Social Psychology,* 1961, *18,* 575–82.

Bandura, A., & Walters, R. Aggression. In H. W. Stevenson (Ed.), *Child psychology, Sixty-second yearbook, National Society for the Study of Education.* Part I. Chicago: University of Chicago Press, 1963. pp. 364–415.

Banks, W. M. The changing attitude of black students. *Personnel & Guidance Journal,* 1970, *48,* 739–45.

Barnard, J. W. The effects of anxiety on connotative meaning. *Child Development,* 1966, *37,* 461–72.

Bartlett, E. W., & Smith, C. P. Child-rearing practices, birth order and the development of achievement-related motives. *Psychological Reports,* 1966, *19,* 1207–16.

Baumrind, D. Effects of authoritative control on child behavior. *Child Development,* 1966, *37,* 887–907.

Baumrind, D., & Black, A. E. Socialization practices associated with dimensions of competence in preschool boys and girls. *Child Development,* 1967, *38,* 291–327.

Bavelas, A. A method for investigating individual and group ideology. *Sociometry,* 1942, *5*, 371–77.

Bayley, N. Consistency of maternal and child behaviors in the Berkeley Growth Study. *Vita Humana,* 1964, *7*, 73–95.

Bayley, N., & Schaefer, E. S. Maternal behavior and personality development: Data from the Berkeley growth study. *Psychiatric Research Reports,* 1960. *13*, 155–73. (a)

Bayley, N., & Schaefer E. Relationships between socio-economic variables and the behavior of mothers towards young children. *Journal of Genetic Psychology,* 1960, *96*, 61–77. (b)

Becker, W. C. Consequences of different kinds of parental discipline. In H. L. Hoffman & L. W. Hoffman (Eds.), *Review of child development research.* New York: Russell Sage Foundation, 1964.

Becker, W. C., & Krug, R. S. The parent attitude research instrument: A research review. *Child Development,* 1965, *36*, 329–65.

Becker, S. W., Lerner, M. J., & Carroll J. Conformity as a function of birth order and type of group pressure. *Journal of Personality & Social Psychology,* 1966, *3*, 242–44.

Behrens, M. L. Child rearing and the character structure of the mother. *Child Development,* 1954, *25*, 225–38.

Bell, R. Q. The effect on the family of a limitation in coping ability in the child: A research approach and a finding. *Merrill Palmer Quarterly,* 1964, *10*, 129–42.

Bell, R. Q. A reinterpretation of effects in studies of socialization. *Psychological Review,* 1968, *75*, 81–95.

Belves, P. Le portrait d'après nature. *Enfance,* 1950, *3*, 299–301.

Bender, L. Psychopathic behavior disorders in children. In R. M. Lindner (Ed.), *Handbook of correctional psychology.* New York: Philosophical Library, 1947. pp. 360–77.

Bender, L. Anxiety in disturbed children. In P. H. Hoch and J. Zubin (Eds.), *Anxiety.* New York: Grune & Stratton, 1950. pp. 119–39.

Benedict, R. Continuities and discontinuities in cultural conditioning. *Psychiatry,* 1938, *1*, 161–67.

Benedict, R. The *chrysanthemum and the sword.* Boston: Houghton Mifflin, 1946.

Beres, D., & Obers, S. The effects of extreme deprivation in infancy on psychic structure in adolescence. *Psychoanalytic Study of the Child,* 1950, *5*, 121–40.

Bernard, V. W. School desegregation: Some psychiatric implications. *Psychiatry,* 1958, *21*, 149–51.

Bernstein, B. Some sociological determinants of perception: An enquiry in subcultural differences. *British Journal of Sociology,* 1958, *9*, 159–74.

Bleuler, M. The offspring of schizophrenics. *Schizophrenia Bulletin,* 1974, *8*, 93–108.

Block, J. Personality characteristics associated with fathers' attitudes toward child-rearing. *Child Development,* 1955, *26*, 41–48.

Blumer, H. Psychological import of the human group. In M. Sherif & M. O. Wilson (Eds.), *Group relations at the crossroads.* New York: Harper, 1953. pp. 182–202.

Blumer, H., & Hauser, P. H. *Movies, delinquency, and crime.* New York: Macmillan, 1934.

Boehm, L. The development of independence: A comparative study. *Child Development,* 1957, *28*, 85–92.

Boehm, L. The development of conscience: A comparison of American children of different mental and socioeconomic levels. *Child Development*, 1962, *33*, 575–90.

Boehm, L. The development of conscience of preschool children: A cultural and subcultural comparison. *Journal of Social Psychology*, 1963, *59*, 355–60.

Boehm, L. Moral judgment: A cultural and sub-cultural comparison with some of Piaget's research conclusions. *International Journal of Psychology*, 1966, *1*, 143–50.

Boehm, L., & Nass, N. L. Social class differences in conscience development. *Child Development*, 1962, *33*, 565–74.

Borishevsky, M. I. Characteristics of children's attitudes toward rules of conduct in game situations. *Voprosy* Psikhilogii, 1965, *4*, 44–54.

Bossard, J. H., & Boll, E. S. Personality roles in the large family. *Child Development*, 1955, *26*, 71–78.

Botwinick, J. Drives, expectancies and emotions. In J. E. Birren (Ed.), *Handbook of aging and the individual*. Chicago: University of Chicago Press, 1959. pp. 739–68.

Bowlby, J. Forty-four juvenile thieves. *International Journal of Psychoanalysis*, 1944, *25*, 1–57.

Bowlby, J. *Forty-four juvenile thieves: Their characters and home lives*. London: Balliere, Tindall and Cox, 1946.

Bowlby, J. Maternal care and mental health. *World Health Organization Monograph*, 1952 (2).

Bowlby, J. The nature of the child's tie to his mother. *International Journal of Psychoanalysis*, 1958, *39*, 350–73.

Bowlby, J. Ethology and the development of object relations. *International Journal of Psychoanalysis*, 1960, *41*, 313–17.

Bowlby, J., Ainsworth, M., Boston, M., & Rosenblith, D. The effects of mother-child separation: A follow-up study. *British Journal of Medical Psychology*, 1956, *29*, 211–47.

Boyd, G. F. The levels of aspirations of white and Negro children in a non-segregated elementary school. *Journal of Social Psychology*, 1952, *36*, 191–96.

Bray, D. H. A study of children's writing on an admired person. *Educational Review*, 1962, *15*, 44–53.

Breznitz, S., & Kugelmass, S. Intentionality in moral judgment: Developmental stages. *Child Development*, 1967, *38*, 469–79.

Brim, O. G. The parent-child relation as a social system: I. Parent and child roles. *Child Development*, 1957, *28*, 343–64.

Brim, O. G. Personality development as role learning. In I. I. Scol and H. W. Stevenson (Eds.), *Personality development in children*. Austin: University of Texas Press, 1960.

Brim, O. G. Adult socialization. In J. A. Clausen (Ed.), *Socialization and society*. Boston: Little Brown & Co., 1967. Chap. 5.

Brion, O. G. Personality development as role learning. In I. I. Scol & H. W. Stevenson (Eds.), *Personality development in children*. Austin: University of Texas Press, 1963.

Brodbeck, A. J. The mass media as a socializing agency. Paper read at American Psychological Association, San Francisco, 1955.

Brodbeck, A. J. Eminent psychologist challenges TV writers and producers. *National Association for Better Radio & Television Quarterly*, 1962, *2*(3) 1 & 4.

Brodbeck, A. J., Nogee, P., & De Mascio, A. Two kinds of conformity: A study of the Riesman typology applied to standards of parental discipline. *Journal of Psychology* 1956, *41*, 23–45.

Brodie, R. D., & Winterbottom, M. R. Failure in elementary school boys as a function of traumata, secrecy, and derogation. *Child Development*, 1967, *38*, 701–11.

Brody, G. F. Relationship between maternal attitudes and behavior. *Journal of Personality & Social Psychology*, 1965, *2*, 317–23.

Bronfenbrenner, U. Socialization and social class through time and space. In E. Maccoby, T. Newcomb, and E. Hartley (Eds.), *Readings in social psychology*. New York: Henry Holt & Co., 1958. pp. 400–25.

Bronfenbrenner, U. The changing American child: A speculative analysis. *Journal of Social Issues*, 1961, *17*, 6–17.

Bronfenbrenner, U. The role of age, sex, class, and culture in studies of moral development. *Religious Education*, 1962, *57*, 3–17. (a)

Bronfenbrenner, U. Soviet methods of character education: Some implications for research. *American Psychologist*, 1962, *17*, 560–64. (b)

Bronfenbrenner, U. The psychological costs of quality and equality in education. *Child Development*, 1967, *38*, 909–25.

Bronfenbrenner, U. Soviet methods of upbringing and their effects: A social-psychological analysis. Paper read at National Institute of Child Health and Human Development, May, 1968.

Bronfenbrenner, U. On the making of new men: Some extrapolation from research. *Canadian Journal of Behavioral Science*, 1969, *1*, 4–24.

Brown, A. W., Morrison, J., & Couch, G. B. Influence of affectional family relationships on character development. *Journal of Abnormal & Social Psychology*, 1947, *42*, 422–28.

Brown, M., & Martin, V. The university high school study of adolescents: Characteristics of high school students. *University High School Journal*, 1941, 19, 177–219.

Bruner, J. S., & Tajfel, H. Cognitive risk and environmental change. *Journal of Abnormal & Social Psychology*, 1961, *62*, 231–41.

Bühler, C. The social behavior of children. In C. Murchison (Ed.), *A handbook of child psychology*. 2nd ed. Worcester, Mass: Clark University Press, 1933. pp. 374–416.

Bühler, C. The curve of life as studied in biographies. *Journal of Applied Psychology*, 1935, *19*, 405–409.

Bühler, C. Maturation and motivation. *Personality*, 1951 *I*, 184–211.

Bühler, C., & Massarik, F. (Eds.), *The course of human life*. New York: Springer, 1968.

Burton, R. V. Generality of honesty reconsidered. *Psychological Review*, 1963, *70*, 481–99.

Burton, R. V., & Whiting, J. W. The absent father and cross-sex identity. *Merrill-Palmer Quarterly*, 1961, *7*, 85–95.

Caldwell, B. M. The effects of infant care. In M. L. Hoffman & L. W. Hoffman (Eds.), *Review of child development research*. New York: Russell Sage Foundation, 1964. pp. 9–87.

Cameron, N. *The psychology of behavior disorders: A biosocial interpretation*. Boston: Houghton Mifflin, 1947.

Campbell, J. D. Peer relations in childhood. In M. L. Hoffman & L. W. Hoffman (Eds.), *Review of child development research*. New York: Russell Sage Foundation, 1964. pp. 289–322.

Campbell, J. D., & Yarrow, M. R. Personal and situational variables in adaptation to change. *Journal of Social Issues,* 1958, *14,* 27–46.

Cantril, H. The intensity of an attitude. *Journal of Abnormal & Social Psychology,* 1946, *41,* 129–35.

Carlsmith, L. Effect of early father absence upon scholastic aptitude. *Harvard Educational Review,* 1964, *34,* 3–21.

Caron, A. J. Curiosity, achievement, and avoidant motivation as determinants of epistemic behavior. *Journal of Abnormal & Social Psychology,* 1963, *67,* 535–49.

Carpenter, W. T., Bartko, J. J., Langsner, C. A., & Strauss, J. S. Another view of schizophrenic subtypes: A report from the international pilot study of schizophrenia. *Schizophrenia Bulletin* (in press).

Carrigan, W. C., & Julian, J. W. Sex and birth-order differences in conformity as a function of need affiliation arousal. *Journal of Personality & Social Psychology,* 1966, *3,* 479–93.

Casler, L. Maternal deprivation: A critical review of the literature. *Monographs of the Society for Research in Child Development* 1961, *26.*

Castenada, A., McCandless, B. R., & Palermo, D.S. The children's form of the Manifest Anxiety Scale. *Child Development,* 1956, *17,* 317–26.

Cavan, R. S. Negro family disorganization and juvenile delinquency. *Journal of Negro Education,* 1959, *28,* 230–39.

Champney, H. The variables of parent behavior. *Journal of Abnormal & Social Psychology,* 1941, *36,* 525–42.

Child, I. L. Socialization. In G. Lindzey (Ed.), *Handbook of social psychology.* Vol II. *Special fields and applications.* Cambridge, Mass: Addison-Wesley, 1954. pp. 655–92.

Chittenden, E. A., Foan, M. W., Zweill, D. M., & Smith, J. R. School achievement of first and second-born siblings. *Child Development,* 1968, *39,* 1223–28.

Clark, K. B. Color, class, personality, and juvenile delinquency. *Journal of Negro Education,* 1959, *28,* 240–51.

Clark, K. B., & Clark, M. P. Racial identification and preference in Negro children. In T. M. Newcomb & E. L. Hartley (Eds.), *Readings in social psychology.* New York: Holt, 1947. pp. 169–78.

Clausen, J. A. Mental Disorders. In R. K. Merton & R. A. Nesbet (Eds.), *Contemporary social problems.* New York: Harcourt, Brace & World, 1961. pp. 127–80.

Clausen, J. A. Family structure, socialization and personality. In L. W. Hoffman and M. L. Hoffman (Eds.), *Review of child development research.* New York: Russell Sage Foundation, 1966. pp. 1-54.

Clausen, J. A. Perspectives on childhood socialization. In J. A. Clausen (Ed.), *Socialization and Society.* Boston: Little, Brown Co. 1968. Ch. 4.

Clifford, E. Discipline in the home: A controlled observational study of parental practices. *Journal of Genetic Psychology,* 1959, *95,* 45–82.

Cline, V. B., Richards, J. M., & Needham, W. E. A factor analytic study of the father form of the parental attitude research instrument. *Psychological Record,* 1963, *47,* 184–89.

Cobb, H. V. Role-wishes and general wishes of children and adolescents. *Child Development,* 1954, *25,* 161–71.

Cogan, L., Conklin, A., & Hollingworth, H. L. An experimental study of self-analysis. *School and Society,* 1915, *2,* 171–79.

Cohen, I. S. Rigidity and anxiety in a motor response. *Perceptual and Motor Skills*, 1961, *12*, 127–30.

Collard, R. R. Social and play responses of first-born and later-born infants in an unfamiliar situation. *Child Development*, 1968, *39*, 325–34.

Colley, T. The nature and origins of psychological sexual identity. *Psychological Review*, 1959, *66*, 165–77.

Conant, J. B. *Slums and suburbs: A commentary on schools in metropolitan areas*. New York: McGraw-Hill, 1961.

Cooper, J. E., Kendell, R. E., Gierland, B. J., Sharpe, L., Copeland, J., & Simon, R. J. Psychiatric diagnoses in New York and London: A comparative study of mental ·hospital admissions. Maudsley Monograph No. 20. London: Oxford University Press, 1972.

Costello, C. G. (Ed.) *Symptoms of psychopathology: A handbook*. New York: Wiley, 1970.

Cowan, P. A., Langer, J., Hesvenrich, J., & Nathanson, M. Has social learning theory refuted Piaget's theory of moral development? Unpublished paper, University of California, Berkeley, 1968.

Cowen, E. L., Zax, M., Klein, R., Izzo, L. D., & Trost, M. A. The relation of anxiety in school children to school record, achievement, and behavioral measures. *Child Development*, 1965, *36*, 685–95.

Cox, F. N. Some relationships between test anxiety, presence or absence of male persons, and boys' performance on a repetitive motor test. *Journal of Experimental Child Psychology*, 1968, *6*, 1–12.

Crandall, V. Achievement behavior in young children. In W. W. Hartup and N. L. Smothergill (Eds.), *The young child: Review of research*. Washington, D. C.: Publication Department, National Association for the Education of Young Children, 1967.

Crandall, V., Dewey, R., Katkowsky, W., & Preston, A. Parents' attitudes and behaviors and grade school children's academic achievements. *Journal of Genetic Psychology*, 1964, *104*, 53–66.

Crandall, V., & Rabson, A. Children's repetition choices in an intellectual achievement situation following success and failure. *Journal of Genetic Psychology*, 1960, *97*, 161–68.

Crane, A. Symposium. The development of moral values. IV: Preadolescent gangs and moral development of children. *British Journal of Educational Psychology*, 1958, *28*, 201–208.

Crockett, H. J. A study of some factors affecting the decision of Negro high school students to enroll in previously all-white high schools, St. Louis, 1955. *Social Forces*, 1957, *35*, 351–56.

Cronbach, L. J. The two disciplines of scientific psychology. *American Psychologist*, 1957, *12*, 671–84.

Crowley, T. M. Effect of training upon objectivity of moral judgment of grade-school children. *Journal of Personality & Social Psychology*, 1968, *8*, 228–32.

Cruse, D. P. Socially desirable responses in relation to grade level. *Child Development*, 1963, *34*, 777–89.

Curle, A. Incentives to work. An anthropological appraisal. *Human Relations*, 1949, *2*, 41–47.

Curle, A. Incentives to work: An anthropological appraisal. *Human Relations*, 1949, *2*, 41–47.

Dai, B. Some problems of personality development in Negro children. In C. Kluckhon and H. A. Murray (Eds.), *Personality in nature, society and culture*. New York: Knopf, 1949. pp. 437–58.

Davis, A. Socialization and adolescent personality. In *Adolescence, 43rd Yearbook, National Society for Studies in Education*. Chicago: University of Chicago Press, 1944. pp. 198–216.

Davis, A., & Havighurst, R. J. Social class and color differences in child rearing. *American Sociological Review*, 1946, *11*, 698–710.

De Forest, I. Anxiety: as experienced in the creation and in the discarding of neuroses. *Psychoanalytic Review*, 1950, *37*, 172–77.

Dennis, W. *The Hopi child*. New York: Appleton-Century, 1940.

Dennis, W. Infant development under conditions of restricted practice and minimum social stimulation. *Genetic Psychology Monographs*, 1941, *23*, 143–89.

Deutsch, M. Minority group and class status as related to social and personality factors in school achievement. *Sociology & Applied Anthropology Monographs*, 1960, No. 2.

Deutsch, M., Clark, K. B., Lee, R. S., & Pasamanick, B. Some considerations as to the contributions of social, personality, and racial factors to school retardation in minority group children. Paper read at the American Psychological Association Convention. Chicago, Sept. 1956.

Devereux, G. A sociological theory of schizophrenia. *Psychoanalytic Review*, 1934, *26*, 315–42.

De Vos, G., & Miner, H. Algerian culture and personality in changes. *Sociometry*, 1958, *21*, 255–68.

Dickens, S. L., & Hobart, C. Parental dominance and offspring ethnocentrism. *Journal of Social Psychology*, 1957, *49*, 297–303.

Dillon, M. S. Attitudes of children toward their own bodies and those of other children. *Child Development*, 1934, *5*, 165–76.

Dinitz, S., Kay, B. A., & Reckless, W. C. Group gradients in delinquency potential and achievement score of sixth graders. *American Journal of Orthopsychiatry*, 1958, *28*, 598–605.

Dohrewend, B., & Dohrewend, B. *Social status and psychological disorder: A causal inquiry*. New York: Wiley, 1969.

Dolger, L., & Ginandes, J. Children's attitude toward discipline as related to socio-economic status. *Journal of Experimental Education*, 1946, *15*, 161–65.

Douglass, J. H. The extent and characteristics of juvenile delinquency among Negroes in the United States. *Journal of Negro Education*, 1959, *28*, 214–29.

Draguns, J. G., & Multari, G. Recognition of perceptually ambiguous stimuli in grade school children. *Child Development*, 1961, *32*, 521–50.

Dropplemen, L. F., & Schaefer, E. S. Boys' and girls' reports of maternal and paternal behavior. *Journal of Abnormal & Social Psychology*. 1963, *67*, 648–54.

Dubin, E. R., & Dubin, R. The authority inception period in socialization. *Child Development*, 1963, *34*, 885–98.

Dubin, R., & Dubin, E. R. Children's social perceptions: A review of research. 1965, *36*, 809–38.

Du Bois, C. Attitudes toward food and hunger in Alor. In L. Spier, (Ed.), *Language, culture, and personality*. Menasha, Wisc.: Sapir Memorial Publication Fund, 1941.

Duncker, K. Modification of children's food preferences through social suggestion. *Journal of Abnormal & Social Psychology*, 1938, *33*, 487–507.

Durkin, D. Children's concepts of justice: A comparison with the Piaget data. *Child Development*, 1959, *30*, 59–67.

Eagleson, O. W. Students' reactions to their given names. *Journal of Social Psychology*, 1946, *23*, 187–95.

Earle, A. M., & Earle, B. R. Early maternal deprivation and later psychiatric illness. *American Journal of Orthopsychiatry*, 1961, *31*, 181.

Eberhart, J. C. Attitudes toward property: A genetic study by the paired-comparisons rating of offences. *Journal of Genetic Psychology*, 1942, *60*, 3–35.

Eggan, D. The general problem of Hopi adjustment. *American Anthropology*, 1945, *47*, 516–39.

Emmerich, W. Family-role concepts of children ages six to ten. *Child Development*, 1961, *32*, 609–24.

Emmerich, W. Variations in the parent role as a function of the parent's sex and the child's sex and age. *Merrill-Palmer Quarterly*, 1962, *8*, 3–11.

Erikson, E. H. Childhood and tradition in two American Indian tribes. In C. Kluckhohn and H. A. Murray, (Eds.), *Personality in nature, society and culture*. New York: Knopf, 1948.

Erikson, E. H. *Childhood and society*. New York: Norton, 1950.

Erikson, E. H. Identity and the life cycle. *Psychological Issues*, Monograph I. New York: International Universities Press, 1959.

Escalona, S. K. Patterns of infantile experience and the developmental process. *The Psychoanalytic Study of the Child*. New York: International Universities Press, 1963, *18*, 197–244.

Essen-Moller, E. Twin research and psychiatry. *International Journal of Psychiatry*, 1965, *1*, 466–75.

Faris, R. E., & Dunham, H. W. *Mental disorders in urban areas: An ecological study of schizophrenia and other psychoses*. Chicago: University of Chicago Press, 1939.

Faust, O. A., Jackson, K., Cermak, E. G., Burtt, M. M., & Winkley, R. *Reducing emotional trauma in hospitalized children*. Albany, N. Y.: Albany research project, Albany Medical College, 1952.

Feffer, N. H., & Gourevitch, V. Cognitive aspects of role-taking in children. *Journal of Personality*, 1960, *28*, 383–96.

Feffer, N. H., & Suchotliff, L. Decentering implications of social interaction. *Journal of Personality and Social Psychology*, 1966, *4*, 415–22.

Feldhusen, J. F., Denny, T., & Condon, C. F. Anxiety, divergent thinking, and achievement. *Journal of Educational Psychology*, 1965, *56*, 40–45.

Feldhusen, J. F., & Klausmeier, H. J. Anxiety, intelligence, and achievement in children of low, average, and high intelligence. *Child Development*, 1962, *33*, 403–409.

Fenichel, O. *The psychoanalytic theory of neuroses*. New York: Norton, 1945.

Ferenczi, S. Steps in the development of a sense of reality. *In Sex in Psychoanalysis*. Boston: Badger, 1916.

Ferguson, L. R. & Maccoby, E. E. Interpersonal correlates of differential abilities. *Child Development*, 1966, *37*, 549–72.

Finestone, H. Cats, kicks, and color. *Social Problems,* 1957, *5,* 3–13.

Finney, J. C. Some maternal influences on children's personality and character. *Psychological Monographs,* 1961, *63,* 199–278.

Fischer, L. K. Hospitalism in six-month-old infants. *American Journal of Orthopsychiatry,* 1952, *22,* 522–33.

Fisher, D. L. Black studies and the enhancement of self-concept as it relates to achievement level in Negro high school students. Doctoral dissertation, Western Michigan University, 1972. *Dissertation Abstracts International,* 1972–1973, *33,* 5468A–69A.

Fite, M. D. Aggressive behavior in young children and children's attitudes toward aggression. *Genetic Psychology Monographs,* 1940, *22,* 151–319.

Flavell, J. H. Role-taking and communication skills in children. In W. W. Hartrup & N. N. Smothergill (Eds.), *The young child: Reviews of research.* Washington, D.C.: National Association for the Education of Young Children, 1967.

Ford, C. S., & Beach, F. A. *Patterns of sexual behavior.* New York: Harper, Hoeber, 1951.

Forman, H. J. *Our movie-made children.* New York: Macmillan, 1935.

Frank, L. K. The adolescent and the family. In *Adolescence,* 43rd Yearbook, National Society Study Education. Chicago: University of Chicago Press, 1944.

Frankl, V. E. *Man's search for meaning.* Boston: Beacon, 1962.

Frazier, E. F. The Negro middle class and desegregation. *Social Problems,* 1957, *4.* 291–301.

Freedman, A., & Kaplan, H. (Eds.), *Comprehensive textbook of psychiatry.* Baltimore: Williams & Wilkins, 1967.

Frenkel-Brunswik, E., Levinson, D. J., & Sanford N. The anti-democratic personality. In T. Newcomb & E. Hartley (Eds.), *Readings in social psychology.* New York: Holt, 1947.

Freud, A. *The ego and the mechanisms of defence.* New York: International Universities Press, 1966.

Freud, A., & Burlingham, D. *Infants without families,* New York: International Universities Press, 1944.

Freud, S. *A general introduction to psychoanalysis.* New York: Boni & Liveright, 1921.

Freud, S. *Character and anal erotism.* London: Hogarth, 1924.

Freud, S. *The infantile genital organization of the libido.* London: Hogarth, 1924.

Freud, S. *Instincts and their vicissitudes.* London: Hogarth Press, 1925.

Freud, S. *Three contributions to the theory of sex.* New York: Nervous and Mental Disease Publishing Co., 1930.

Freud, S. New introductory lectures in psychoanalysis. New York: Norton, 1933.

Freud, S. *The ego and the id.* London: Hogarth, 1935.

Freud, S. *The problem of anxiety.* New York: Norton, 1936.

Freud, S. Dora: An analysis of a case of hysteria. New York: Collier, 1974.

Freud, S., & Bullitt, W. *Thomas Woodrow Wilson: A psychological study.* Boston: Houghton Mifflin, 1967.

Fromm, E. *Escape from freedom.* New York: Farrar, 1941.

Fromm, E. *Man for himself: An inquiry into the psychology of ethics.* New York: Rinehart, 1947.

Frumkin, R. M. Race, occupation, and social class in New York. *Journal of Negro Education,* 1958, *27,* 62–65.

Gaier, E. L., & Wambach, H. S. Self-evaluation of personality assets and liabilities of Southern white and Negro students. *Journal of Social Psychology*, 1960, *51*, 135–43.

Garai, J. E. Formation of the concept of self and development of sex identification. In A. H. Kidd & J. L. Rivoire (Eds.), *Perceptual development in children*. New York: International Universities Press, 1966.

Gardner, D. B., Hawkes, G. R., & Burchinal, L. G. Non-continuous mothering in infancy and development in later childhood. *Child Development*, 1961, *32*, 225–34.

Gardner, G. A. The mental health of normal adolescents. *Mental Hygiene*, 1947, *31*, 529–40.

Gardner, L. P. An analysis of children's attitudes toward fathers. *Journal of Genetic Psychology*, 1947, *70*, 3–28.

Gesell, A. Maturation and the patterning of behavior. In C. Murchison (Ed.), *A handbook of child psychology*. Worcester, Mass.: Clark University Press, 1933.

Gesell, A. The ontogenesis of individual behavior. In L. Carmichael (Ed.), *Manual of child psychology*. New York: Wiley, 1946.

Gesell, A. The ontogenesis of infant behavior. In L. Carmichael (Ed.), *Manual of child psychology* (2nd ed.). New York: Wiley, 1954, pp. 335–73.

Gesell, A., & Ilg, F. L. *Infant and child in the culture of today*. New York: Harper & Row, 1943.

Gesell, A., & Ilg, F. L. *The child from five to ten*. New York: Harper & Row, 1946.

Gewirtz, H. B., & Gewirtz, J. L. Caretaking settings, background events, and behavior differences in four Israeli child-rearing environments: Some preliminary trends. In B. M. Foss (Ed.), *Determinants of infant behavior*. London: Methuen, 1968.

Ghosh, E. J., & Sinha, D. A study of parental role-perception in siblings. *Journal of Psychological Research*, 1966, *10*, 8–18.

Gift, M. D. Self-concept and social change among black youth. Doctoral dissertation, University of Utah, 1970. *Dissertation Abstracts International*, 1970–71, *31*, 1372A.

Glover, E. The concept of dissociation. In *On the early development of the mind*. New York: International Universities Press, 1956.

Glueck, S., & Glueck, E. Unravelling juvenile delinquency. New York: Commonwealth Fund, 1950.

Goff, R. H. *Problems and emotional difficulties of Negro children*. New York: Teachers College, Columbia University, 1949.

Goldfarb, W. Effects of early institutional care on adolescent personality. *Journal of Experimental Education*, 1943, *12*, 106.

Goldfarb, W. Effects of psychological deprivation in infancy and subsequent stimulation. *American Journal of Psychiatry*. 1945, *102*, 18–33. (a)

Goldfarb, W. Psychological privation in infancy and subsequent adjustment. *American Journal of Orthopsychiatry*, 1945, *15*, 247–55. (b)

Goldhammer, H., & Marshall, A. *Psychosis and civilization*. Glencoe, Ill.: Free Press, 1953.

Goldstein, K. *The Organism*, New York: American Book Co., 1939.

Gollin, E. S. Developmental approach to learning and cognition. In L. P. Lipsitt & C. C. Spiker (Eds.), *Advances in child development and behavior*, Vol. 2. New York: Academic Press, 1965. pp. 159–86.

Goodenough, F. L. Anger in young children. *Institute of Child Welfare Monograph*, 1931 (9).

Goodman, M. E. *Race awareness in young children*. Cambridge, Mass.: Addison-Wesley, 1952.

Gordon, C., & Shea, P. D. Self-conceptions in family structures of disadvantaged youths. Presented to American Sociological Association, San Francisco, August 1967.

Gould, R. Some sociological determinants of goal strivings. *Journal of Social Psychology*, 1941, *13*, 461–73.

Grant, C. A. Black studies materials do make a difference. *Journal of Educational Research*, 1973, *66*, 400–404.

Greenberg, H., Chase, A. L., & Cannon, T. M. Attitudes of white and Negro high school students in a West Texas town toward school integration. *Journal of Applied Psychology*, 1957, *41*, 27–31.

Greenberg, H., & Fane, D. An investigation of several variables as determinants of authoritarianism. *Journal of Social Psychology*, 1959, *49*, 105–111.

Greenberg, P. J. Competition in children: An experimental study. *American Journal of Psychology*, 1932, *44*, 221–48.

Gregory, I. Studies of parental deprivation in psychiatric patients. *American Journal of Psychiatry*, 1958, *115*, 432–42.

Griffiths, W. *Behavior difficulties of children as perceived and judged by parents, teachers, and children themselves*. Minneapolis: University of Minnesota Press, 1952.

Grossack, M. M. Some personality characteristics of Southern Negro students. *Journal of Social Psychology*, 1957, *46*, 125–31.

Gruber, S. The concept of task orientation in the analysis of the play behavior of children entering kindergarten. *American Journal of Orthopsychiatry*, 1954, *24*, 345–54.

Guerney, B., Stover, L., & DeMeritt, S. A measurement of empathy in parent-child interaction. *Journal of Genetic Psychology*, 1968, *112*, 49–55.

Haggerty, A. D. The effects of long-term hospitalization or institutionalization upon language development of children. *Journal of Genetic Psychology*, 1959, *94*, 205–209.

Handel, G. Psychological study of whole families. *Psychological Bulletin*, 1965, *63*, 19–41.

Handlon, B. J., & Gross, P. The development of sharing behavior. *Journal of Abnormal & Social Psychology*, 1959, *59*, 425–28.

Harris, D. B., Clark, K. E., Rose, A. M., & Valasek, F. The measurement of responsibility in children. *Child Development*, 1954, *25*, 21–28. (a)

Harris, D. B., Clark, K. E., Rose, A. M., & Valasek, F. The relationship of children's home duties to an attitude of responsibility. *Child Development*, 1954, *25*, 29–33. (b)

Harrower, N. R. Social status and moral development. *British Journal of Educational Psychology*, 1935, *4*, 75–95.

Hart, I. Maternal child-rearing practices and authoritarian ideology. *Journal of Abnormal & Social Psychology*, 1957, *55*, 232–37.

Hartmann, H. The mutual influences in the development of the ego and the id. *Psychoanalytic Study of the Child*, 1952, *7*, 9–30.

Hartmann, H. *Ego psychology and the problem of adaptation*. New York: International Universities Press, 1958.

Hartogs, R. The clinical investigation and differential measurement of anxiety. *American Journal of Psychiatry*, 1950, *106*, 929–34.

Hartshorne, H., & May, M. A. *Studies in the nature of character*. Vol. III. *Studies in the organization of character*. New York: Macmillan, 1930.

Hartup, W. W. Dependence and independence. In H. W. Stevenson (Ed.), *Child psychology*. 62nd Yearbook, National Society for the Study of Education. Chicago: University of Chicago Press, 1963. pp. 333–63.

Harvey, O. J., Hunt, D. E., & Schroeder, H. M. *Conceptual systems and personality organization*. New York: Wiley, 1961.

Harvey, O. J., & Sherif, M. Level of aspiration as a case of judgmental activity in which ego-involvements operate as factors. *Sociometry*, 1951, *14*, 121–27.

Hatfield, J. S., Ferguson, L. R., & & Alpert, R. Mother-child interaction and the socialization process. *Child Development*, 1967, *38*, 365–414.

Hauser, S. T. Black and white identity development: Aspects and perspectives. *Journal of Youth and Adolescence*, 1972, *1*, 113–30.

Hausmann, M. F. A test to evaluate some personality traits. *Journal of Genetic Psychology*, 1933, *9*, 179–89.

Havighurst, R. J., Robinson, M. Z., & Dorr, M. The development of the ideal self in childhood and adolescence. *Journal of Educational Research*, 1946, *40*, 241–57.

Havighurst, R. J., & Taba, H. *Adolescent character and personality*. New York: Wiley, 1949.

Healey, W., & Bronner, A. F. *New light on delinquency and its treatment*. New Haven: Yale University Press, 1936.

Heathers, G. Emotional dependence and independence in a physical threat situation. *Child Development*, 1953, *24*, 169–79.

Heathers, G. The adjustment of two-year-olds in a novel social situation. *Child Development*, 1954, *25*, 147–48.

Hellman, I. Sudden separation and its effect followed over twenty years. Hampstead Nursery follow-up studies. *Psychoanalytic Study of the Child*, 1962, *17*, 159–74.

Hemming, J. Some aspects of moral development in a changing society. Symposium: The development of children's moral values. *British Journal of Educational Psychology*, 1957, *27*, 77–88.

Hertz, M. R., & Baker, E. Personality patterns in adolescence as portrayed by the Rorschach ink-blot method: II. The color factors. *Journal of General Psychology*, 1943, *28*, 3–61.

Hertzman, M., & Margolies, H. Developmental changes as reflected in Rorschach test responses. *Journal of Genetic Psychology*, 1943, *62*, 189–215.

Hess, R. D., & Torney, J. *The development of political attitudes in children*. Chicago: Aldine Publishing Company, 1967.

Heston, L. L. Psychiatric disorders in foster-home-reared children of schizophrenic mothers. *British Journal of Psychiatry*, 1966, *112*, 819–25.

Hilgard, E. R. *Theories of learning*. New York: Appleton-Century-Crofts, 1948.

Hilgard, E. R. Human motives and the concept of self. *American Psychologist*, 1949, *4*, 374–82.

Hill, K. T., & Sarason, S. B. The relation of test anxiety and defensiveness to test and school performance over the elementary school years. A further longitudinal study. *Monographs of the Society for Research in Child Development*, 1966, *31* (2).

Hill, M. C. Research on the Negro family. *Marriage & Family Living*, 1957, *19*, 25–31.

Hilton, I. Differences in the behavior of mothers toward first- and later-born children. *Journal of Personality & Social Psychology*, 1967, *7*, 282–90.

Hirschberg, G., & Gilliland, A. J. Parent-child relationships in attitude. *Journal of Abnormal & Social Psychology*, 1942, *37*, 125–30.

Hoch, P. H., & Zubin, J., (Eds.), *Current approaches to psychoanalysis*. New York: Grune & Stratton, 1960.

Hoffman, L. W., Lippitt, R. The measurement of family life variables. In P. Mussen (Ed.), *Handbook of research methods in child development*. New York: Wiley, 1960. Ch. 22.

Hoffman, M. L. Power assertion by the parent and its impact on the child. *Child Development*, 1960, *31*, 129–43.

Hoffman, M. L. Child-rearing practices and moral development. Generalizations from empirical research. *Child Development*, 1963, *34*, 295–318.

Hoffman, M. L., & Saltzstein, H. D. Parent practice and the child's moral orientation. Paper read at the American Psychological Association, Chicago, September 1960.

Hoffman, M. L., & Saltzstein, H. D. Parent discipline and the child's moral development. *Journal of Personality & Social Psychology*, 1967, *5*, 45–57.

Hollingshead, A. B., & Redlich, F. C. *Social class and mental illness*. New York: Wiley, 1958.

Hollingworth, L. S. *The psychology of the adolescent*. New York: Appleton-Century, 1928.

Holt, R. R. (Ed.) *New horizons for psychotherapy*. New York: International Universities Press, 1971.

Honzik, M. P. Personality consistency and change: Some comments on papers by Bayley, MacFarland, Moss and Kagan, and Murphy. *Vita Humana*, 1964, *7*, 139–42.

Horney, K. *The neurotic personality of our time*. New York: Norton, 1937.

Horney, K. *New Ways in psychoanalysis*. New York: Norton, 1939.

Horney, K. *Our inner conflicts: A constructive theory of neurosis*. New York: Norton, 1945.

Horney, K. *Neurosis and human growth: The struggle toward self-realization*. New York: Norton, 1950.

Horowitz, E. L. The development of attitude toward the Negro. *Archives of Psychology*, 1936, *28*, (194).

Horowitz, F. D. The relationship of anxiety, self-concept, and sociometric status among fourth, fifth, and sixth-grade children. *Journal of Abnormal & Social Psychology*, 1962, *65*, 212–14.

Horowitz, R. E. A pictorial method for study of self-identification in pre-school children. *Journal of Genetic Psychology*, 1943, *62*, 135–48.

Horowitz, S. G., & Armantrout, J. Discrimination learning, manifest anxiety, and effects of reinforcement. *Child Development*, 1965, *36*, 731–48.

Hoult, T. F. Comic books and juvenile delinquency. *Sociology & Social Research*, 1949, *33*, 279–384.

Howells, J. G., & Layng, J. Separation experiences and mental health. *Lancet*, 1955, *2*, 285–88.

Hunt, D. E. Adolescence: Cultural deprivation, poverty, and the drop-out. *Review of Educational Research*, 1966, *36*, 463–73.

Hunt, D. E., & Hardt, R. H. Developmental stage, delinquency, and differential treatment. *Journal of Research in Crime & Delinquency*, 1965, *2*, 20–31.

Hurley, J. R. Parental acceptance, rejection, and children's intelligence. *Merrill-Palmer Quarterly*, 1965, *11*, 19–31.

Jackson, P. W. Verbal solutions to parent-child problems. *Child Development,* 1956, *17,* 339–49.

Jackson, T. A. Errors of self-judgement. *Journal of Applied Psychology,* 1929, *13,* 372–77.

Jacobs, P. S., Brunton, M., Mellville, M., Brittain, R., & McClemmont, W. Aggressive behavior, mental subnormality, and the XYY male. *Nature,* 1965, *208,* 1351–52.

Jefferson, R. W. Some obstacles to racial integration. *Journal of Negro Education,* 1957, *26,* 145–54.

Jenkins, W. A. An experimental study of the relationship of legitimate and illegitimate birth status to school and personal adjustment of Negro children. *American Journal of Sociology,* 1958, *48,* 305–17.

Jersild, A. T. *Child psychology.* New York: Prentice-Hall, 1947. 3rd ed.

Jersild, A. T. *Child psychology.* New York: Prentice-Hall, 1954. 4th ed.

Jersild, A. T. *In search of self.* New York: Teachers College, Columbia University, 1952.

Jones, E. Anal-erotic character traits. In *Papers on psychoanalysis.* London: Balliere, 1923.

Jones, H. E. School achievement as related to adult achievement. Unpublished Paper, Institute of Child Welfare, University of California, Berkeley, 1959.

Jones, V. *Character and citizenship gaining in the public schools.* Chicago: University of Chicago Press, 1936.

Kagan, J. The child's perception of the parent. *Journal of Abnormal & Social Psychology.* 1956, *53,* 257–58.

Kagan, J. The concept of identification. *Psychological Review,* 1958, *65,* 296–305.

Kagan, J. On the need for relativism. *American Psychologist,* 1967, *22,* 131–42.

Kagan, J., & Henker, B. A. Developmental psychology. *Annual Review of Psychology,* 1966, *17,* 1–50.

Kagan, J., Hosken, B., & Watson, S. Child's symbolic conceptualization of parents. *Child Development.* 1961, *32,* 625–36.

Kagan, J., & Moss, H. A. *Birth to maturity: A study in psychological development.* New York: Wiley, 1962.

Kahn, M. L. Social class and parental values. *American Journal of Sociology,* 1959, *64,* 337–51.

Kalhorn, J. Values and sources of authority among rural children. *University of Iowa Studies in Child Welfare,* 1944, *20,* 99–151.

Kallman, F. J. The genetic theory of schizophrenia. *American Journal of Psychiatry,* 1946, *103,* 309–32.

Kardiner, A. *The individual and his society.* New York: Columbia University Press, 1939.

Kardiner, A. *The psychological frontiers of society.* New York: Columbia University Press, 1945.

Karon, B. P. *The Negro personality.* New York: Springer, 1958.

Karr, C., & Wesley, F. Comparison of German and U. S. child-rearing practices. *Child Development,* 1966, *37,* 715–23.

Kates, S. L. Suggestibility, submission to parents and peers, and extrapunitiveness, intropunitiveness, and impunitiveness in children. *Journal of Psychology,* 1951, *31,* 233–41.

Katkovsky, W., Preston, A., & Crandall, V. J. Parents' attitudes toward their personal achievements and toward the achievement behaviors of their children. *Journal of Genetic Psychology,* 1964, *104,* 67–82. (a)

Katkovsky, W., Preston, A., & Crandall, V. J. Parents' achievement attitudes and their behavior with their children in achievement situations. *Journal of Genetic Psychology*, 1964, *104*, 105–21. (b)

Kernberg, O. F. Early ego integration and object relations. *Annals of the New York Academy of Sciences*, 1972, *193*, 233–47.

Kight, H. R., & Sassenrath, J. M. Relation of achievement motivation and test anxiety to performance in programmed instruction. *Journal of Educational Psychology*, 1966, *57*, 14–17.

Kinsey, A. C., et al. *Sexual behavior in the human male*. Saunders: Philadelphia, 1948.

Kinstler, D. B. Covert and overt maternal rejection in stuttering. *Journal of Speech and Hearing Disorders*, 1961, *26*, 145–55.

Klein, M. *The psychoanalysis of children*. New York: Norton, 1932.

Knight, R. M. Test anxiety and visual discrimination of social scenes. *Child Development*, 1965, *36*, 1083–90.

Kohlberg, L. The development of modes of moral thinking and choice in the years ten to sixteen. Unpublished doctoral dissertation, University of Chicago, 1958.

Kohlberg, L. The development of children's orientation to the moral order: I. Sequence in the development of moral thought. *Vita Humana*, 1963, *6*, 11–33.

Kohlberg, L. Development of moral character and moral ideology. In M. L. Hoffman & L. W. Hoffman (Eds.), *Review of child development research*. New York: Russell Sage Foundation, 1964, pp. 383–431.

Kohlberg, L. Moral and religious education and the public schools: A developmental view. In T. R. Sizer (Ed.), *Religion and public education*. New York: Houghton Mifflin, 1967.

Kohlberg, L. Stage and sequence: The cognitive-developmental approach to socialization. In D. Goslin (Ed.), *Handbook of socialization*. New York: Rand-McNally, 1968.

Kohlberg, L. *Stages in the development of moral thought and action*. New York: Holt, Rinehart, & Winston, 1969.

Kohlberg, L. The developmental approach to moral education. In C. Beck, B. Crittenden, & E. V. Sullivan (Eds.), *Moral education: Interdisciplinary approaches*. Toronto: University of Toronto Press, 1970.

Kohn, M. L. Social class and parent-child relationships: An interpretation. *American Journal of Sociology*, 1963, *68*, 471–80.

Kohut, H. *The analysis of the self*. New York: International Universities Press, 1971.

Krate, R., Leventhal, G., & Silverstein, B. Self-perceived transformation of Negro to black identity. *Psychological Reports*, 1974, *35*, 1071–75.

Krech, D., Crutchfield, R. S., Livson, N., & Wilson, W. A. *Elements of psychology*. 3rd ed. New York: Knopf, 1974.

Kris, E. Ego psychology and interpretation in psychoanalytic therapy. *Psychoanalytic Quarterly*, 1951, *20*, 15–30.

Kuhlen, R. G. *The psychology of adolescent development*. New York: Harper, 1952.

Kuhlen, R. G. Aging and life adjustment. In J. E. Birren (Ed.), *Handbook of aging and the individual*. Chicago: University of Chicago Press, 1959. pp. 852–97.

Lafore, G. G. Practices of parents in dealing with preschool children. *Child Development Monographs*, 1945, *31*.

Landreth, C., & Johnson, B. C. Young children's responses to a picture and inset test designed to reveal reactions to persons of different skin color. *Child Development*, 1953, *24*, 63–79.

Lantz, B. Some dynamic aspects of success and failure. *Psychological Monographs*, 1945, *59(1)*, Whole No. 271.

Lehner, G. F. J., & Gunderson, E. K. Height relationships on the Draw-a-Person Test. *Journal of Personality*. 1953. *21*, 392–99.

Leighton, A. H., Lembo, T. A., Hughes, C. C., Leighton, D. C., Murphy, J. M., & Macklin, D. B. Psychiatric disorder in West Africa. *American Journal of Psychiatry*, 1963, *120*, 520–27. (a)

Leighton, A. H., Lembo, T. A., Hughes, C. C., Leighton, D. C., Murphy, J. M., & Macklin, D. B. Psychiatric disorder among the Yoruba. Ithaca, N.Y.: Cornell University Press, 1963. (b)

Leighton, D., & Kluckhohn, C. *Children of the people: the Navaho Indian and his development*. Cambridge, Mass.: Harvard University Press, 1947.

Lenrow, P. B. Studies of sympathy. In S. S. Tomkins & C. E. Izard (Eds.), *Affect, cognition, and personality: Empirical studies*. New York: Springer, 1965. pp. 264–94.

Lerner, E. The problem of perspective in moral reasoning. *American Journal of Sociology*, 1937, *43*, 249–69.

Lessing, E. E., & Oberlander, M. Developmental study of ordinal position and personality adjustment of the child as evaluated by the California Test of Personality. *Journal of Personality*, 1967, *35*, 487–97.

Lessing, E. E., & Zagorin, S. W. Black power ideology and college students' attitudes toward their own and other racial groups. *Journal of Personality & Social Psychology*, 1972, *21*, 61–73.

Leuba, C. An experimental study of rivalry in young children. *Journal of Comparative Psychology*, 1933, *16*, 367–78.

Levy, D. M. Fingersucking and accessory movements in early infancy. *American Journal of Psychiatry*, 1928, *7*, 881–918.

Levy, D. M. *Maternal overprotection*. New York: Columbia University Press, 1943.

Lewin, K. Behavior and development as a function of the total situation. In L. Carmichael (Ed.), *Manual of child psychology*, New York: Wiley, 1946.

Lewin, K., Dembo, T., Festinger, L., & Sears, P. S. Level of aspiration. In J. McV. Hunt, (Ed.), *Personality and the behavior disorders*. New York: Ronald, 1944.

Lidson, N. Parental behavior and children's involvement with their parents. *Journal of Genetic Psychology*, 1966, *109*, 173–94.

Lipset, S. M. Democracy and working class authoritarianism. *American Sociological Review*, 1959, *24*, 482–501.

Little, S. W., & Cohen, L. D. Goal setting behavior of asthmatic children and of their mothers for them. *Journal of Personality*, 1951, *19*, 376–89.

Lockhard, E. G. The attitude of children toward certain laws. *Religious Education*, 1930, *25*, 144–49.

Loevinger, J. The meaning and measurement of ego development. *American Psychologist*, 1966, *21*, 190–206.

Lorand, S. Character formation and psychoanalysis. In S. Lorand (Ed.), *Psychoanalysis today*. New York: Covici, 1933.

Lorge, I. Learning, motivation, and education. In J. E. Anderson (Ed.), *Psychological aspects of aging*. Washington, D. C.: American Psychological Association, 1956. pp. 207–10.

Lorimer, R. M. Change in developmental level of moral judgment of adolescents: the influence of an exposition of basic ethical concepts versus social imitation. Unpublished doctoral dissertation, University of Toronto, 1968.

Lorimer, R. M., & Sullivan, E. V. A psychological interpretation of the structure of moral judgment. Paper presented to Moral Development Conference, Ontario Institute for Studies in Education, June 1968.

Lovaas, D. I. Effect of exposure to symbolic aggression on aggressive behavior. *Child Development,* 1961, *32,* 37–44.

Lowenbach, H., & Suitt, R. B. Alterations of anxiety subsequent to physical treatment of psychiatric disorders. In P. H. Hoch & J. Zubin (Eds.), *Anxiety.* New York: Grune & Stratton, 1950. pp. 218–42.

Lunneborg, P. W. Relations among social desirability, achievement, and anxiety measures in children. *Child Development,* 1964, *35,* 169–82.

Luria, Z., Goldwasser, M., & Goldwasser, A. Response to transgression in stories by Israeli children. *Child Development,* 1963, *34,* 271–80.

Lynn, D., & Sawrey, W. L. The effects of father-absence on Norwegian boys and girls. *Journal of Abnormal & Social Psychology,* 1959, *59,* 258–62.

McClelland, D. C., Atkinson, J. W., Clark, R. A., & Lowell, E. L. *The achievement motive.* New York: Appleton-Century-Crofts, 1953.

McCord, J., McCord, W., & Thurber, E. Some effects of paternal absence on male children. *Journal of Abnormal & Social Psychology,* 1962, *62,* 361–69.

McCullough, G. The role of developmental stages in reasoning in the counselling process. Unpublished doctoral dissertation, University of Toronto, 1969.

McGuigan, F. J., Calvin, A. D., & Richardson, E. C. Manifest anxiety, palmar perspiration index, and stylus maze learning. *American Journal of Psychology,* 1959, *72,* 434–38.

McGuire, W. J. The nature of attitudes and attitude change. In G. Lindzey and E. Aronson (Eds.), *The handbook of social psychology* (2nd ed.), Reading, Mass.: Addison Wesley, 1969, Vol III. ch. 21.

McKee, J. P., & Leader, F. B. The relationships of socioeconomic status and aggression to the competitive behavior of preschool children. *Child Development,* 1955, *26,* 135–42.

Maas, H. Some social class differences in the family systems and group relations of pre- and early adolescents. *Child Development,* 1951, *22,* 145–52.

Maas, H. Long-term effects of early childhood separation and group care. *Vita Humana,* 1963, *6,* 34–56.

Maccoby, E. E. Effects of the mass media. In M. L. Hoffman & L. W. Hoffman (Eds.), *Review of child development research.* New York: Russell Sage Foundation, 1964. pp. 323–48.

Maccoby, E., Gibbs, P. K., et al. Methods of child rearing in two social classes. In W. E. Martin & C. B. Stendler (Eds.), *Readings in child development.* New York: Harcourt, Brace, 1954. pp. 380–96.

MacRae, D. A test of Piaget's theories of moral development. *Journal of Abnormal & Social Psychology,* 1954, *49,* 14–18.

MacRae, D. A test of Piaget's theories of mental development. *Journal of Abnormal & Social Psychology,* 1955, *87,* 111–19.

Mahler, M. S. On child psychosis and schizophrenia: Autistic and symbiotic infantile psychosis. *Psychoanalytic Study of the Child.* New York: International Universities Press, 1951, *7,* 286–305.

Mahler, M. S. Autism and symbiosis, two extreme disturbances of identity. *International Journal of Psychoanalysis,* 1958, *39,* 77–83.

Mahler, M. S. *On human symbiosis and the vicissitudes of individuation.* New York: International Universities Press, 1968.

Malinowski, B. *Sex and repression in savage society.* New York: Harcourt, Brace, 1927.

Maller, J. B. *Cooperation and competition: An experimental study in motivation.* New York: Teachers College, Columbia University, 1929.

Markley, E. R. Social class differences in mothers' attitudes toward child rearing. *Dissertation Abstracts,* 1958, *19,* 355–56.

Marks, P. R., & Yestre, N. Relative effects of drive level and irrelevant responses on performance of a complex task. *Psychological Record,* 1961, *11,* 177–80.

Maslow, A. H. Deprivation, threat, and frustration. *Psychological Review,* 1941, *48,* 364–66.

Maslow, A. H. *Motivation and personality.* New York: Harper, 1954.

Maslow, A. H., & Diaz-Guerrerro, R. Delinquency as value disturbance. In J. G. Peatman & E. L. Hartley (Eds.), *Festschrift for Gardner Murphy.* New York: Harper, 1960. pp. 228–40.

Mason, E. P. Some correlates of self-judgments of the aged. *Journal of Gerontology,* 1954, *9,* 324, 327.

Masserman, J. *Principles of dynamic psychiatry.* Philadelphia: W. B. Saunders, 1946.

Matsumoto, M., & Smith, H. T. Japanese and American children's perception of parents. *Journal of Genetic Psychology,* 1961, *98,* 83–88.

Mauco, G., & Rambaud, P. Le rang de l'enfant dans la famille. *Revue Française du Psychanalyse,* 1951, *15,* 253–60.

May, R. *The meaning of anxiety.* New York: Ronald, 1950.

Mead, M. *From the south seas.* New York: Morrow, 1939.

Mead, M. Social change and cultural surrogates. *Journal of Educational Sociology,* 1940, *14,* 92–110.

Mead, M. Age patterning in personality development. *American Journal of Orthopsychiatry,* 1947, *17,* 231–40.

Mead, M. Some anthropological considerations concerning guilt. In M. L. Reymert (Ed.), *Feelings and emotions.* New York: McGraw-Hill, 1950.

Mead, M. A cultural anthropologist's approach to maternal deprivation. *In deprivation of maternal care.* Public Health Paper No. 14. Geneva: World Health Organization, 1962. pp. 45–62.

Medinnus, G. R. Delinquents' perceptions of their parents. *Journal of Consulting Psychology,* 1965, *29,* 592–93.

Medinnus, G. R. *Readings in the psychology of parent-child relations.* New York: Wiley, 1967.

Medinnus, G. R., & Curtis, F. J. The relation between maternal self-acceptance and child acceptance. *Journal of Consulting Psychology,* 1963, *27,* 542–44.

Mednicks, S. A., & Schaffer, J. B. Mothers' retrospective reports in child-rearing research. *American Journal of Orthopsychiatry,* 1963, *33,* 457–61.

Mendel, G. Children's preferences for differing degrees of novelty. *Child Development,* 1965, *36,* 453–65.

Merrill, B. A measure of mother-child interaction. *Journal of Abnormal & Social Psychology,* 1946, *41,* 37–49.

Messerschmidt, R. The suggestibility of boys and girls between the ages of six and sixteen years. *Journal of Genetic Psychology,* 1933, *43,* 422–37.

Meyers, C. E. The effect of conflicting authority on the child. *University of Iowa Studies on Child Welfare,* 1944, *20,* 31–98.

Meyers, C. E. Emancipation of adolescents from parental control. *Nervous child,* 1946, *5,* 251–62.

Miller, D. R., & Swanson, G. E. *The changing American parent.* New York: Wiley, 1958.

Mischel, W. Preference for delayed reinforcement and social responsibility. *Journal of Abnormal Psychology,* 1961, *62,* 1–7.

Mischel, W. Delay of gratification and deviant behavior. Paper read at the Society for Research in Child Development, Berkeley, California, April 1963.

Mischel, W. A social learning review of sex differences and behavior. In E. E. Maccoby (Ed.), *The development of sex differences.* Stanford: Stanford University Press, 1966.

Morland, J. K. Racial recognition by nursery school children in Lynchburg, Virginia. *Social Forces,* 1958, *37,* 132–37.

Morris, D. P., Soroker, E., & Buruss, G. Follow-up studies of shy, withdrawn children. *American Journal of Orthopsychiatry,* 1954, *24,* 743–54.

Mott, S. M. Mother-father preference. *Character & Personality,* 1937, *5,* 302–304.

Mott, S. M. Concept of a mother: A study of four and five-year-old children. *Child Development,* 1954, *25,* 99–106.

Mowrer, O. H. *Learning theory and personality dynamics.* New York: Ronald, 1950.

Mowrer, O. H. "Sin," the lesser of two evils. *American Psychologist,* 1960, *15,* 301–304.

Mowrer, O. H., & Kluckhohn, C. Dynamic theory of personality. In J. McV. Hunt (Ed.), *Personality and the behavior disorders.* New York: Ronald Press, 1944, 69–135.

Moynihan, D. P. *The Negro family: A case for national action.* Washington, D. C.: United States Department of Labor, Office of Policy Planning and Research, 1965.

Murdock, G. P., & Whiting, J. W. Cultural determination of parental attitudes: The relationship between the social structure, particularly family structure, and parental behavior. In M. J. Senn (Ed.), *Problems of infancy and childhood.* New York: Josiah Macy, Jr. Foundation, 1951.

Murphy, G. *Personality: A biosocial approach to its origins and structure.* New York: Harper, 1947.

Murphy, G., Murphy, L. B., & Newcomb, T. *Experimental social psychology.* New York: Harper, 1937.

Murphy, L. B. Childhood experience in relation to personality development. In J. McV. Hunt (Ed.), *Personality and the behavior disorders.* New York: Ronald, 1944.

Murphy, L. B. Social factors in child development. In T. Newcomb & E. Hartley (Eds.), *Readings in social psychology.* New York: Holt, 1947.

Murphy, L. B. Factors in continuity and change in the development of adaptational style in children. *Vita Humana,* 1964, *7,* 96–114.

Murray, H. A. *Explorations in personality.* New York: Oxford University Press, 1938.

Mussen, P. H., & Rutherford, E. Effects of aggressive cartoons on children's aggressive play. *Journal of Abnormal & Social Psychology,* 1961, *62,* 461–64.

Najarian-Svavjian, P. H. The idea of immanent justice among Lebanese children and adults. *Journal of Genetic Psychology,* 1966, *109,* 57–66.

Nash, J. The father in contemporary culture and current psychological literature. *Child Development*, 1965, *36*, 261–97.

Neugarten, B. L. Personality changes during the adult years. In R. G. Kuhlen (Ed.), *Psychological backgrounds of adult education*. Chicago: Center for the Study of Liberal Education for Adults, 1963. pp. 43–76.

Nichols, R. C. A factor analysis of parental attitudes of fathers. *Child Development*, 1962, *33*, 791–802.

Nisbett, R. E. Birth order and participation in dangerous sports. *Journal of Personality & Social Psychology*, 1968, *8*, 351–53.

Nunally, J. C., Duchnowski, A. J., & Parker, R. K. Association of neutral objects with reward: Effects on verbal evaluation, reward expectancy, and selective attention. *Journal of Personality & Social Psychology*, 1965, *1*, 270–74.

Orlansky, J. Infant care and personality, *Psychological Bulletin*, 1949, *46*, 1–48.

Omari, T. B. Changing attitudes of students in West African society toward marriage and family relationships. *British Journal of Sociology*, 1960, *11*, 197–210.

Ostrovsky, E. S. *Father to the child: Case studies of the experience of a male teacher*. New York: Putnam, 1959.

Palermo, D. S. Racial comparisons and additional normative data on the Children's Manifest Anxiety Scale. *Child Development*, 1959, *30*, 53–57.

Palermo, D. S., Castenada, A., & McCandless, B. R. The relationship of anxiety in children to performance in a complex learning task. *Child Development*, 1956, *27*, 333–37.

Palmer, R. D. Birth order and identification. *Journal of Consulting Psychology*, 1966, *30*, 129–35.

Papalia, D. E., & Olds, S. W. *A child's world: Infancy through adolescence*. New York: McGraw-Hill, 1975.

Parsons, T. Age and sex in the culture of the United States. *American Sociological Review*, 1942, *7*, 604–16.

Parsons, T., & Bales, R. F. *Family socialization and interaction process*. Glencoe, Illinois: Free Press, 1955.

Parten, M. B. Leadership among preschool children. *Journal of Abnormal & Social Psychology*, 1933, *28*, 430–40.

Patel, A. S., & Gordon, J. E. Some personal and situational determinants of yielding to influence. *Journal of Abnormal Psychology*, 1960, *61*, 411–18.

Pawl, J. L. H. Some ego skills and their relation to the differences in intelligence between the middle and lower classes. *Dissertation Abstracts*, 1960, *21*, 368.

Penney, R. K. Reactive curiosity and manifest anxiety in children. *Child Development*, 1965, *36*, 697–702.

Perry, J. D. The reliability of high-school averages computed from students' estimates of their high school grades. *School & Society*, 1940, *41*, 437–48.

Phillips, W. B. Counseling Negro students: An educational dilemma. *California Journal of Educational Research*, 1959, *10*, 185–88.

Piaget, J. *The child's conception of the world*. New York: Harcourt, Brace, 1929.

Piaget, J. *Moral judgment of the child*. New York: Harcourt, Brace, 1932.

Piaget, J. *Play, dreams, and imitation in childhood*. New York: Norton, 1951.

Piaget, J. *The origins of intelligence in children*. New York: International Universities Press, 1952.

Piaget, J. *The construction of reality in the child.* New York: Basic Books, 1954.

Pickrel, E. W. The differential effect of manifest anxiety on test performance. *Monographs of the Society for Research in Child Development,* 1963, *28*(2), 185–96.

Pierce-Jones, J. Socio-economic status and adolescents' interests. *Psychological Reports,* 1959, *5,* 683. (a)

Pierce-Jones, J. Vocational interest correlates of socio-economic status in adolescence. *Educational & Psychological Measurement.* 1959, *19,* 65–71. (b)

Plant, J. S. *Personality and the cultural pattern.* New York: Commonwealth Fund, 1937.

Pohlman, E. Mothers' perceptions of relative advantages and disadvantages of children at different ages and of various characteristics. *Perceptual & Motor Skills,* 1967, *24,* 1311–14.

Polite, C. K., Cockrane, R., & Silverman, B. I. Ethnic group identification and differentiation. *Journal of Social Psychology,* 1974, *92,* 149–50.

Porter, B. M. The relationship between marital adjustment and parental acceptance of children. *Journal of Home Economics,* 1955, *47,* 157–64.

Pressey, S. L., & Robinson, F. P. *Psychology and the new education.* New York: Harper, 1944.

Pringle, M. L., & Bosio, V. A. A study of deprived children. I. Intellectual, emotional, and social development. *Vita Humana,* 1958, *1,* 65–92.

Pringle, M. L., & Bosio, V. A. Early prolonged separation and emotional maladjustment. *Journal of Child Psychology & Psychiatry,* 1960, *1,* 37–48.

Proshansky, H. M. The development of intergroup attitudes. In M. L. Hoffman & L. W. Hoffman (Eds.), *Review of child development research.* Vol. 2. New York: Russell Sage Foundation, 1966. pp. 311–72.

Provence, S., & Lipton, R. C. *Infants in institutions.* New York: International Universities Press, 1962.

Prugh, D. G., & Harlow, R. G. "Masked deprivation" in infants and young children. In J. Bowlby (Ed.), *Deprivation and maternal care: A re-assessment of the effects.* New York: Schocken Books, 1966. pp. 201–22.

Prugh, D. G., Staub, E., Sands, H., Kirschbaum, R., & Lenihan, E. A study of the emotional reactions of children and families to hospitalization and illness. *American Journal of Orthopsychiatry,* 1953, *23,* 70–106.

Rabin, A. I. Some psycho-sexual differences between kibbutz and non-kibbutz Israeli boys. *Journal of Projective Techniques,* 1958, *22,* 328–32.

Rabin, A. I. Attitudes of kibbutz children to family and parents. *American Journal of Orthopsychiatry,* 1959, *29,* 172–79.

Rachman, S. *Critical essays on psychoanalysis.* New York: Macmillan, 1963.

Radke, M. J. The relation of parental authority to children's behavior and attitudes. *University of Minnesota Institute of Child Welfare Monographs,* 1946, No. 22.

Radke-Yarrow, M., Trager, H. G., & Miller, J. The role of parents in the development of children's ethnic attitudes. *Child Development,* 1952, *23,* 13–53.

Rank, O. *The trauma of birth.* New York: Harcourt, Brace, 1929.

Rank, O. *Truth and reality.* New York: Knopf, 1936.

Rapaport, D. Behavior research in collective settlements in Israel: A study of kibbutz education and its bearing on the theory of development. *American Journal of Orthopsychiatry,* 1958, *28,* 587–97.

Rapp, D. W. Child-rearing attitudes of mothers in Germany and the United States. *Child Development*, 1961, *32*, 669–78.

Record, W. Social stratification and intellectual roles in the Negro community. *British Journal of Sociology*, 1957, *8*, 235–55.

Redl, F. The phenomenon of contagion and shock effect in group therapy. In K. R. Eissler (Ed.), *Searchlight on delinquency*. New York: International Universities Press, 1949.

Reese, H. W. Manifest anxiety and achievement test performance. *Journal of Educational Psychology*, 1961, *52*, 132–35.

Reymert, M. L., & Kohns, H. A. An objective investigation of suggestibility. *Character & Personality*, 1940, *9*, 44–48.

Reynolds, M. M. *Negativism of preschool children*. New York: Teachers College, Columbia University, 1928.

Riley, M. W., & Foner. *Aging and society*. New York: Russell Sage Foundation, 1968.

Ringness, T. A. Self-concept of children of low, average, and high intelligence. *American Journal of Mental Deficiency*. 1961, *65*, 453–61.

Robertson, J. *Young children in hospitals*. New York: Basic Books, 1958.

Robins, L. N. *Deviant Children Grown up: A sociological and psychiatric study of sociopathic personality*. Baltimore: Williams & Wilkins, 1966.

Roen, S. R. Personality and Negro-white intelligence. *Journal of Abnormal & Social Psychology*, 1960, *61*, 148–50.

Roff, M. A factorial study of the Fels Parent Behavior Scales. *Child Development*, 1949, *20*, 29–45.

Rogers, C. R. *Counseling and psychotherapy*. Boston: Houghton Mifflin, 1942.

Rogg, S. G. Time of decision. *Psychiatric Quarterly*, 1950, *24*, 437–47.

Rogier, A. Psychological viewpoints with reference to father-son relationship. *Gawein*, 1967, *15*, 137–48.

Rosen, B. C. Race, ethnicity, and the achievement syndrome. *American Sociological Review*, 1959, *24*, 47–60.

Rosen, B. C., & D'Andrade, R. The psychosocial origins of achievement motivation. *Sociometry*, 1959, *22*, 185–218.

Rosen, D. C. Family structure and value transmission. *Merrill-Palmer Quarterly*, 1964, *10*, 59–76.

Rosen, J. N. The treatment of schizophrenic psychoses by direct analytic therapy. *Psychiatric Quarterly*, 1947, *21*, 3–38.

Rosenberg, B. G., & Sutton-Smith, B. Sibling association, family size, and cognitive abilities. *Journal of Genetic Psychology*, 1966, *109*, 271–79.

Rosenthal, D., Wender, P. H., Kety, S. S., Schulsinger, F., Welner, J., & Reiber, R. D. Parent-child relationships and psychopathological disorders in the child. *Archives of General Psychiatry*, 1975, *32*, 466–76.

Rosenzweig, S. Preferences in the repetition of successful and unsuccessful activities as a function of age and personality. *Journal of Genetic Psychology*, 1933, *42*: 423–41.

Rosenzweig, S. Need persistent and ego defensive reactions to frustration as demonstrated by an experiment on regression. *Psychological Review*, 1941, *48*, 347–49.

Rosner, J. When white children are in the minority. *Journal of Educational Sociology*, 1954, *28*, 69–72.

Rowdinesco, J. Severe maternal deprivation and personality development in early childhood. *Understanding the child*, 1952, *21*, 104–108.

Ruebush, B. K. Anxiety, In H. W. Stevenson (Ed.), *Child psychology, Sixty-second Yearbook of the National Society for the study of education.* Chicago: University of Chicago Press, 1963. pp. 460–516.

Ruma, D. H., & Mosher, D. L. General relationship between moral judgment and guilt in delinquent boys. *Journal of Abnormal Psychology*, 1967, *72*, 122–27.

Russell, D. G., & Sarason, I. G. Test anxiety, sex, and experimental conditions in relation to anagram solution. *Journal of Personality & Social Psychology*, 1965, *1*, 493–96.

Russell, R. W. Studies in animism. II. The development of animism. *Journal of Genetic Psychology*, 1940, *56*, 353–66.

Rutherford, E., & Mussen, P. Generosity in nursery school boys. *Child Development*, 1968, *30*, 755–65.

Sanford, R., Adkins, M. M., Miller, R. B., Cobb, E. A., Aub, J. C., Burke, B. S., Nathanson, I. T., Stuart, H. C., & Towne, L. Physique, personality, and scholarship: A cooperative study of school children. *Monographs Society for Research in Child Development*, 1943, *8* (1).

Sarason, I. G. Test anxiety and the intellectual performance of college students. *Journal of Educational Psychology*, 1961, *52*, 201–206.

Sarason, I. G. Test anxiety and intellectual performance. *Journal of Abnormal & Social Psychology*, 1963, *66*, 73–75.

Sarason, S. B., Davidson, K. S., Lighthall, F. F., Waite, R. R., & Ruebush, B. K. *Anxiety in elementary school children.* New York: Wiley, 1960.

Sarason, S. B., Hill, K. T., & Zimbardo, P. G. A longitudinal study of the relation of test anxiety to performance on intelligence and achievement tests. *Monographs of the Society for Research in Child Development*, 1964, *29*, (Whole No. 98).

Schachter, S. *The psychology of affiliation.* Stanford: Stanford University Press, 1959.

Schacter, S. Birth order, eminence, and higher education. *American Sociological Review*, 1963, *28*, 757–67.

Schaefer, E. S. Converging conceptual models for maternal behavior and for child behavior. In J. C. Glidewell (Ed.), *Parental attitudes and child behavior.* Springfield, Ill.: Charles C Thomas, 1961. pp. 124–46.

Schaefer, E. S. A configurational analysis of children's reports of parent behavior. *Journal of Consulting Psychology*, 1965, *29*, 552–57.

Schaefer, E. S., & Bayley, N. Consistency of maternal behavior from infancy to preadolescence. *Journal of Abnormal & Social Psychology*, 1960, *61*, 1–6.

Schaefer, E. S., & Bayley, N. Maternal behavior, child behavior, and their intercorrelations from infancy through adolescence. *Monographs Society for Research in Child Development*, 1963, *28* (3) (Whole No. 87).

Schaefer, E. S., & Bell, R. Q. Development of a parental attitude research instrument. *Child Development*, 1958, *29*, 339–61.

Schaeffer, H. R., & Callender, W. N. Psychologic effects of hospitalization in infancy. *Pediatrics*, 1959, *24*, 528–39.

Schaeffer, H. R., & Emerson, P. E. The development of social attachments in infancy. *Monographs of the Society for Research in Child Development*, 1964, *29*, No. 94.

Schaie, K. W. A test of behavioral rigidity. *Journal of Abnormal & Social Psychology*, 1955, *51*, 604–10.

Schildkraut, J. The catecholamine hypothesis of affective disorders: A review of supporting evidence. *American Journal of Psychiatry*, 1965, *122*, 509–22.

Schneider, L., & Lysgaard, S. The deferred gratification pattern: A preliminary study. *American Sociological Review*, 1953, *18*, 142–49.

Schofield, W., & Ballan, L. A. A comparative study of the personal histories of schizophrenic and non-psychiatric patients. *Journal of Abnormal & Social Psychology*, 1959, *59*, 216–25.

Schpoont, S. H. Some relationships between task-attractiveness, self-evaluated motivation, and success, and failure. Unpublished doctoral dissertation, University of Illinois, 1955.

Scott, J. P. Implications of infra-human social behavior for problems of human relations. In M. Sherif & M. O. Wilson (Eds.), *Group relations at the cross-roads*. New York: Harper, 1953. pp. 33–73.

Sears, P. S. Levels of aspiration in academically successful and unsuccessful children. *Journal of Abnormal & Social Psychology*, 1940, *35*, 498–536.

Sears, P. S. Level of aspiration in relation to some variables of personality: Clinical studies. *Journal of Social Psychology*, 1941, *14*, 311–36.

Sears, P. S. Correlates of need achievement, need affiliation and classroom management, self-concept, and creativity. Unpublished manuscript, Laboratory of Human Development, Stanford University, 1962.

Sears, R. R. Ordinal position in the family as a psychological variable. *American Sociological Review*, 1950, *15*, 397–401.

Sears, R. R. A theoretical framework for personality and social behavior. *American Psychologist*, 1951, *6*, 476–83.

Sears, R. R., Maccoby, E., & Levin, H. *Patterns of child rearing*. Evanston, Ill.: Row Peterson & Co., 1957.

Sears, R. R., Pintler, M., & Sears, P. S. Effect of father separation on preschool children's doll play aggression. *Child Development*, 1946, *17*, 219–43.

Sears, R. R., Whiting, J. W. M., Nowlis, V., & Sears, P. S. Some child-rearing antecedents of aggression and dependency in young children. *Genetic Psychology Monographs*, 1953, *47*, 135–254.

Selye, H. *The general adaptation syndrome in the biology of mental health and disease*. New York: Harper, Hoeber, 1952.

Sewall, M. Two studies in sibling rivalry. I. Some causes of jealousy in young children. Smith College Studies in Social Work, 1930, *1*, 6–22.

Sewell, W., & Haller, A. O. Factors in the relationship between social status and the personality adjustment of the child. *American Sociological Review*, 1959, *24*, 511–20.

Sewell, W., & Strauss, M. A. Social status and educational and occupational aspiration. *American Sociological Review*, 1957, *22*, 67–73.

Sewell, W. H., Mussen, P. H., & Harris, C. W. Relationships among child-training practices. *American Sociological Review*, 1955, *20*, 137–48.

Shafer, R. *Aspects of internalization*. New York: International Universities Press, 1968.

Shaffer, J. P. Social and personality correlates of children's estimates of height. *Genetic Psychology Monographs*, 1964, *70*, 97–134.

Shaffer, L. F. *The psychology of adjustment*. Boston: Houghton Mifflin, 1939.

Sheerer, E. T. An analysis of the relationship between acceptance of and respect for self and acceptance of and respect for others in ten counseling cases. *Journal of Consulting Psychology*, 1949, *13*, 169–75.

Sherif, M. The concept of reference groups in human relations. In M. Sherif & M. O. Wilson (Eds.), *Group relations at the crossroads*. New York: Harper, 1953.

Sherif, M. Self-concept. Paper prepared for the *New International Encyclopedia of the Social Sciences*, 1965.

Sherif, M., & Cantril, H. *The psychology of ego-involvements*. New York: Wiley, 1947.

Shirley, M. M. *The first two years*. Vol II: *personality manifestations*. Minneapolis: University of Minnesota Press, 1933.

Shirley, M. M. Impact of mother's personality on the young child. *Smith College Studies in Social Work*, 1941, *12*, 15–64.

Shirley, M. M. Children's adjustments to a strange situation. *Journal of Abnormal and Social Psychology*, 1942, *37*, 201–17.

Shopsin, B., Wilk, S., & Sathananthan, G., et al. Catecholamines and affective disorders: A critical assessment. *Journal of Nervous & Mental Disease*, 1974, *158*, 369–83.

Short, J. F. Juvenile delinquency: The socio-cultural context. In M. L. Hoffman & L. W. Hoffman (Eds.), *Review of child development research*, Vol. 2. New York: Russell Sage Foundation, 1966. pp. 423–68.

Siegel, A. I., & Federman, P. *Employment experiences of Negro Philadelphians: A descriptive study of the employment experiences, perceptions, and aspirations of selected Philadelphia whites and non-whites*. Wayne, Pa: Applied Psychological Services, 1959.

Siegelman, M. Loving and punishing parental behavior and introversion tendencies in sons. *Child Development*. 1966, *37*, 985–92.

Siegman, A. W. Father absence during early childhood and anti-social behavior. *Journal of Abnormal Psychology*. 1966, *71*, 71–74.

Silverman, S. S. *Clothing and appearance: Their psychological implications for teen-age girls*. New York: Teachers College, Columbia University, 1945.

Simpson, M. S. *Parent preferences of young children*. New York: Teachers College, Columbia University, 1935.

Singer, S. L., & Stafflre, B. A note on racial differences in job values and desires. *Journal of Social Psychology*, 1956, *43*, 333–37.

Slaght, W. E. Untruthfulness in children: Its conditioning factors and its setting in child nature. *University of Iowa Studies in Character*, 1928, *1* (4).

Slovic, T. Risk-taking in children: Age and sex differences. *Child Development*, 1966, *37*, 169–76.

Smith, C. U., & Prothro, J. W. Ethnic differences in authoritarian personality. *Social Forces*, 1957, *35*, 334–38.

Smith, M. G. Education and occupational choice in rural Jamaica. *Social & Economic Studies*, 1960, *9*, 332–54.

Smuts, R. W. The Negro community and the development of Negro potential. *Journal of Negro Education*, 1957, *26*, 456–65.

Smock, C. D. Perceptual rigidity and closure phenomenon as a function of manifest anxiety in children. *Child Development*, 1958, *29*, 237–47.

Spiro, M. E. Education in a communal village in Israel. *American Journal of Orthopsychiatry*, 1955, *25*, 283.

Spitz, R. A. Hospitalization: An inquiry into the genesis of psychiatric conditions in early childhood. *Psychoanalytic Study of the Child*, 1945, *1*, 53–74.

Spitz, R. A. The role of ecological factors in emotional development in infancy. *Child Development*, 1949, *20*, 145–54.

Spitz, R. A. Environment versus race: Environment as an etiological factor in psychiatric disturbances in infancy. In G. B. Wilbur and W. Muensterberger (Eds.), *Psychoanalysis and culture*. New York: International Universities Press, 1951. (a)

Spitz, R. A. The psychogenic diseases in infancy. *Psychoanalytic Study of the Child*, 1951, *6*, 255–75. (b)

Spitz, R. A. *A genetic field theory of ego formation*. New York: International Universities Press, 1962.

Spitz, R. A., & Wolf, K. M. The smiling response: A contribution to the ontogenesis of social relations. *Genetic Psychology Monographs*, 1946, *34*, 57–125.

Srole, L., Langer, T. S., Michael, S. T., Opler, M. K., & Rennie, T. A. C. *Mental health in the metropolis: The midtown Manhattan study*. New York: McGraw-Hill, 1962.

Staffire, B. Concurrent validity of the vocational values inventory. *Journal of Educational Research*, 1959, *52*, 339–41.

Staver, N. The child's learning difficulty as related to the emotional problems of the mother. *American Journal of Orthopsychiatry*, 1953, *23*, 131–41.

Steckler, G. A. Authoritarian ideology in Negro college students. *Journal of Abnormal & Social Psychology*, 1957, *54*, 396–99.

Stendler, C. B. *Children of Brasstown*. Urbana, Ill.: University of Illinois Press, 1949.

Stendler, C. B. Possible causes of overdependency in children. *Child Development*, 1954, *25*, 125–46.

Stendler, C. B., & Young, N. The impact of beginning first grade upon socialization as reported by mothers. *Child Development*, 1950, *21*, 241–60.

Stevenson, H. W., & Odom, R. D. The relation of anxiety to children's performance on learning and problem-solving tasks. *Child Development*, 1965, *36*, 1003–12.

Stevenson, H. W., & Stevenson, N. G. Social interaction in an interracial nursery school. *Genetic Psychology Monographs*, 1960, *61*, 37–75.

Stevenson, H. W., & Stewart, E. C. A developmental study of racial awareness in young children. *Child Development*, 1958, *29*, 399–409.

Stolz, H. R., & Stolz, L. M. Adolescent problems related to somatic variations. In *Adolescence*, 43rd Yearbook, National Society for the Study of Education. Chicago: University of Chicago Press, 1944.

Stolz, L. M., et al. *Father-relations of war-born children*. Stanford: Stanford University Press, 1954.

Stone, C. P., & Barker, R. G. The attitudes and interests of pre-menarcheal and post-menarcheal girls. *Journal of Psychology*, 1939, *54*, 27–71.

Strauss, A. The development of conceptions of rules in children. *Child Development*, 1954, *25*, 193–204.

Strodtbeck, F. L. Family interaction, values, and achievement. In D. C. McClelland (Ed.), *Talent and society*. Princeton: Van Nostrand, 1958. pp. 135–94.

Suinn, R. M. A factor modifying the concept of anxiety as an interfering drive. *Journal of Genetic Psychology*, 1965, *73*, 43–46.

Sullivan, C., Grant, M. Q., & Grant, J. A. Development of interpersonal maturity: Applications to delinquency. *Psychiatry*, 1957, *20*, 373–85.

Sullivan, E. V., & Hunt, D. E. Interpersonal and objective decentering as a function of age and social class. *Journal of Genetic Psychology*, 1967, *110*, 199–210.

Sullivan, H. S. Conceptions of modern psychiatry. *Psychiatry*, 1940, *3*, 1–117.

Sutton-Smith, B., & Rosenberg, B. G. Age changes in the effects of the ordinal position on sex-role identification. *Journal of Genetic Psychology*, 1965, *107*, 61–73.

Sutton-Smith, B., Rosenberg, B. G., & Landy, F. Father absence effects in families of different sibling compositions. *Child Development*, 1968, *39*, 1213–21.

Symonds, P. M. *The psychology of parent-child relationships*. New York: Appleton-Century, 1939.

Symonds, P. M. *The dynamics of parent-child relationships*. New York: Teachers College, Columbia University, 1949.

Szasz, T. S. The myth of mental illness. *American Psychologist*, 1960, *15*, 113–18.

Tagiuri, R. Person perception. In G. Lindzey and E. Aronson (Eds.), *The handbook of social psychology*, 2nd Ed. Reading, Mass.: Addison Wesley, 1969, *3*, 395–449.

Tajfel, H., Richardson, A., & Everstein, L. Individual consistencies in categorizing: A study of judgment behavior. *Journal of Personality*, 1964, *32*, 19–108.

Tasch, R. J. The role of the father in the family. *Journal of Experimental Education*, 1952, *20*, 319–61.

Terman, L. M., et al. *Genetic studies of genius*. Vol 1. *Mental and physical traits of a thousand gifted children*. Stanford: Stanford University Press, 1925.

Thetford, W. N., Molish, H. B., & Beck, S. J. Developmental aspects of personality structure in normal children. *Journal of Projective Techniques*, 1951, *15*, 58–78.

Thompson, G. G. *Child psychology* (2nd ed.). Boston: Houghton Mifflin, 1962.

Thurstone, L. L. Influence of motion pictures on children's attitudes. *Journal of Social Psychology*, 1931, *2*, 291–305.

Tiller, P. O. Father absence and personality development of children in sailor families. A preliminary research report. In N. Anderson (Ed.), *Studies of the family*. Göttingen, Germany: Vanderhoeck and Ruprecht, 1957.

Tompkins, S. S. An experimental study of anxiety. *Journal of Psychology*, 1943, *15*, 307–313.

Trassler, G. *In place of parents*. London: Routledge and Kegan, Paul, 1960.

Traweek, M. W. The relationship between certain personality variables and achievement through programmed instruction. *California Journal of Educational Research*, 1964, *15*, 215–20.

Trent, R. D. An analysis of expressed self-acceptance among Negro children. Unpublished doctoral dissertation, Teachers College, Columbia University, 1954.

Turiel, E. Developmental processes in the child's moral thinking. In P. Mussen, J. Langer, & N. Covington (Eds.), *New directions in developmental psychology*. New York: Holt, Rinehart, & Winston, 1968.

Turner, R. H. Negro job status and education. *Social Forces*, 1953, *32*, 45–52.

Turner, R. H. Occupational patterns of inequality. *American Journal of Sociology*, 1954, *59*, 437–47.

Tyler, F. T., Rafferty, J., & Tyler, B. B. Relationships among motivations of parents and their children. *Journal of Genetic Psychology*, 1962, *101*, 69–81.

Ugurel-Semin, R. Moral behavior and moral judgment of children. *Journal of Abnormal & Social Psychology*, 1952, *47*, 463–74.

Van Buskirk, C. Performance on complex reasoning tasks as a function of anxiety. *Journal of Abnormal & Social Psychology*. 1961, *62*, 200–209.

Van den Daele, L. A developmental study of the ego-ideal. Unpublished paper, Child Development Laboratory, University of Illinois, 1967.

Vaughan, W. F. *Social psychology*. New York: Odyssey, 1948.

Walsh, R. P. Parental rejecting attitudes and control in children. *Journal of Clinical Psychology*, 1968, *24*, 185–86.

Walter, D., Denzler, L. S., & Sarason, I. G. Anxiety and the intellectual performance of high-school students. *Child Development*, 1964, *35*, 917–26.

Walter, L. H., & Marzolf, S. S. The relation of sex, age, and school achievement to levels of aspiration. *Journal of Educational Psychology*, 1951, *42*, 285–92.

Walters, J., Connor, R., & Zunich, M. Interaction of mothers and children from lower-class families. *Child Development*, 1964, *35*, 433–40.

Walters, R. H., & Parke, R. D. Progress in experimental personality research. In B. A. Maher (Ed.), *The influence of punishment and related disciplinary techniques on the social behavior of children: Theory and empirical findings*. Vol. 3. New York: Academic Press, 1966.

Ward, S. H., & Braun, J. Self-esteem and racial preference in black children. *American Journal of Orthopsychiatry*, 1972, *42*, 644–47.

Warren, J. R. Birth order and social behavior. *Psychological Bulletin*, 1966, *65*, 38–49.

Washburne, J. N. The impulsions of adolescents as revealed by their written wishes. *Journal of Juvenile Research*, 1932, *16*, 193–212.

Watson, R. *Psychology of the child* (2nd ed.). New York: Wiley, 1965.

Wedge, B. M. Occurrence of psychosis among Okinawans in Hawaii. *Journal of Psychiatry*, 1952, *109*, 255–258.

Weingarten, E. M. A study of selective perception in clinical judgement. *Journal of Personality*, 1949, *17*, 369–406.

Weir, A. J. A developmental measure of fact-value differentiation. *Vita Humana*, 1960, *3*, 65–82.

Wenar, C. The effects of a motor handicap on personality. I. The effects on level of aspiration. *Child Development*, 1953, *24*, 123–30.

Wenar, C., & Coulter, J. B. A reliability study of developmental histories. *Child Development*, 1962, *33*, 453–62.

Wender, P. H., Rosenthal, D., & Katz, S. S. A psychiatric assessment of the adoptive parents of schizophrenics. In D. Rosenthal & S. S. Katz (Eds.), *The transmission of schizophrenia*. London: Pergamon, 1968.

Werner, H., & Kaplan, B. The developmental approach to cognition: Its relevance to the psychological interpretation of anthropological and ethno-linguistic data. *American Anthropologist, 1956, 58*, 866–80.

Wertham, F. Psychological effects of school segregation. *American Journal of Psychotherapy*, 1952, *6*, 94–103.

White House Commission Report: *The report of the National Advisory Committee on Civil Disorders*. New York: Bantam Books, March 1968.

White, R. W. Ego and reality in psychoanalytic theory. *Psychological Issues*, 1963, *3*, 182–96.

Whiteman, T. H., & Kosier, K. P. Development of children's moralistic judgments: Age, sex, I.Q., and certain personal experiential variables. *Child Development*, 1964, *35*, 843–50.

Whiting, J. W. M. Resource mediation in learning by identification. In I. Iscoe & H. W. Stevenson (Eds.), *Personality development in children*. Austin: University of Texas Press, 1960. pp. 112–26.

Whiting, J. W. M., & Child, I. L. *Child training and personality: A cross-cultural study*. New Haven: Yale University Press, 1953.

Wile, I. S., & Davis, R. The relation of birth to behavior. *American Journal of Orthopsychiatry*, 1941, *11*, 320–34.

Willenson, D. Relationship of adult personality characteristics to perceived parental behavior: A partial validation of Ausubel's theory of ego development. Unpublished doctoral dissertation, University of Houston, 1959.

Wilson, D. C., & Lantz, E. M. The effect of culture change on the Negro race in Virginia as indicated by a study of state hospital admissions. *American Journal of Psychiatry*, 1957, *114*, 25–32.

Wilson, J., Williams, N., & Sugarman, B. *Introduction to moral education*. Harmondsworth, Middlesex: Penguin Books, 1967.

Winterbottom, M. M. The relation of need for achievement to learning experiences in independence and mastery. In J. W. Atkinson (Ed.), *Motives in fantasy, actions, and society*. Princeton: Van Nostrand, 1958. pp. 453–78.

Winterbottom, M. R. The relation of childhood training in independence to achievement motivation. Unpublished doctor's dissertation, University of Michigan, 1953.

Witkin, H. A., et al. *A psychological differentiation: Studies of development*. New York: Wiley, 1962.

Witryol, S. L. Age trends in children's evaluation of teacher-approved and teacher-disapproved behavior. *Genetic Psychology Monographs*, 1950, *41*, 271–326.

Wittrock, M. C., & Husek, T. R. Effects of anxiety upon retention of verbal learning. *Psychological Reports*, 1962, *10*, 78.

Wohlwill, J. F. The development of "over constancy" in space perception. In L. P. Lipsitt & C. L. Spiker (Eds.), *Advances in child development and behavior*. New York: Academic Press, 1963. *1*, 265–312.

Wright, B. A. Altruism in children and the perceived conduct of others. *Journal of Abnormal & Social Psychology*, 1942, *37*, 218–33.

Wright, H. F. The influence of barriers upon strength of motivation. *Duke University Series, Contributions to Psychological Theories*, 1937, *1* (3).

Yarrow, L. Maternal deprivation: Toward an empirical and conceptual reevaluation. *Psychological Bulletin*, 1961, *58*, 459–90.

Yarrow, L. Research in dimensions of early maternal care. *Merrill-Palmer Quarterly*, 1963, *9*, 101–14.

Yarrow, L. Separation from parents during early childhood. In L. Hoffman and M. Hoffman (Eds.), *Review of child development research*, Vol. I New York: Russell Sage Foundation, 1964, pp. 89–136.

Yarrow, M. R. Problems of methods in parent-child research. *Child Development*, 1963, *34*, 215–26.

Zachry, C. B. Preparing youth to be adults. In *Adolescence*, 43rd Yearbook, National Society Study Education. Chicago: University of Chicago Press. 1944.

Zander, A. A study of experimental frustration. *Psychological Monographs*. 1944, *56*, No. 3. Whole No. 256.

Zeligs, R. Children's wishes. *Journal of Applied Psychology,* 1942, *26,* 231–40.

Zigler, E., & Child, I. L. Socialization. In G. Lindzey and E. Aronson (Eds.), *The handbook of social psychology.* 2nd ed. Reading, Mass.: Addison Wesley, 1969, *3,* 450–89.

Zubin, J. Vulnerability: A new view of schizophrenia. Paper presented to American Psychological Association, Chicago, 1975.

Zucker, H. J. Affectional identification and delinquency. *Archives of Psychology,* 1943, (286).

Zucker, R. A., Manosevitz, M., & Lanyon, R. L. Birth order, anxiety, and affiliation during a crisis. *Journal of Personality & Social Psychology,* 1968, *8,* 354–59.

Zunich, M. Development of responsibility in perceptions of lower and middle-class children. *Journal of Educational Research,* 1963, *66,* 497–99.

Reference Notes

CHAPTER 1

[1] A frequently raised criticism directed against *all* biological theories of mental disorder (e.g., adrenal cortex insufficiency; functional deficiency or excess of neuro-transmittor brain amines at central synaptic junctions) is that the research design in question typically does not permit one to infer unequivocally whether the symptoms of behavior disorder are the causes or the effects of the purported biological variables in question. It is also possible that the alleged etiological biological factors merely *mediate* the effect of psychogenic factors on behavioral symptoms.

[2] A formidable difficulty faced by the neuro-transmittor brain amine hypothesis is the fact that in the bipolar depressive syndrome depression and mania alternate (in various ratios of frequency to each other) in the same patient. Typically a patient suffering from a metabolic disorder attributable to functional excesses or deficiencies of particular biocatalysts manifests only one form of the disorder (i.e., excess or deficiency, rather than both extremes alternately (e.g., He manifests hypo-or hyperinsulinism, hypo- or hyperthyroidism—not both ends of the biocatalytic spectrum in cyclical fashion.). From the standpoint of what we know of the biocatalytic effects of genic mechanisms (single-gene or polygenic), such alternation is highly implausible in biocatalytically-determined metabolic diseases and mental disorders.

[3] Although Kallman's original concordance rates found in the United States were substantially confirmed shortly afterwards by E. Slater (Genetic investigations in twins, *Journal of Nervous and Mental Diseases,* 1953, *99,* 44–52), more recent findings, particularly in Scandinavian countries, indicate significantly lower rates of concordance in monozygotic twins as compared to dizygotic twins (see D. Rosenthal, *Genetics of psychopathology,* New York: McGraw-Hill, 1971).

Such discrepancies could, of course, be explained by differences in the number of the index cases studied, differences in the type and severity of the schizophrenia involved, etc. Similar discrepancies in the adoptive studies discussed below may be attributed to the same factors, plus age differences in the time of adoption. (See S. S. Kety, D. Rosenthal, & P. H. Schulzinger, The types and prevalence of mental illness in the biological and adoptive families of schizophrenics, in D. Rosenthal & S. S. Kety (Eds.), *The transmission of schizophrenia,* London: Pergamon Press, 1971, pp. 345–362; P. H. Wender, D. Rosenthal, & S. S. Kety (1968); D. Rosenthal, Some factors associated with concordance with respect to schizophrenia in monozygotic twins, *Journal of Nervous & Mental Diseases,* 1959, *129,* 1–10; D. Rosenthal, The offspring of schizophrenic couples, *Journal of Psychiatric Research,* 1966, *4,* 1969–188; J. Shields & I. I. Gottesman (Eds.), *Man, mind, and heredity,* Baltimore: Johns Hopkins Press, 1971; I. I. Gottesman & J. Shields, *Schizophrenia and genetics; A twin study vantage,* New York: Academic Press, 1972; N. Garmezy, Process and reactive schizophrenia, in *The role and methodology of classification* in *psychiatry and psychopathology,* Washington, D.C.: United States Department of Health, Education and Welfare, 1965, pp. 419–466). Critics of the twin studies also point out that monozygotic twins are treated more similarly by parents, siblings, relatives, and peers than are dizygotic twins, and also exert more influence on each other.

Also supporting the genic hypothesis are the facts that more severe cases of schizophrenia generally have an earlier onset; that the incidence of schizophrenia in children is identical, irrespective of which parent (mother or father) is schizophrenic, even though mothers presumably have closer contact, and more intimate interpersonal relationships, with young children than fathers do (See D. Rosenthal, 1971, ibid); that genic factors contribute more to the variance in incidence of a wide variety of personality disorders than do child-*rearing* behavior (although these latter variables may very well be less crucial in their impact on personality development than significant parent *attitudes* (See Chapter 3).

[4]For a review of both twin and adoptive studies in the genetics of schizophrenia, see D. Rosenthal, 1971, ibid, and Wender, Rosenthal, & Kety (1968).

[5]For more recent studies in this area that do not confirm the earlier findings of Jacobs et al., see J. Beckwith & J. King, The XYY Syndrome: A dangerous myth, *New Scientist,* 1974, *14,* 474–476, and D. Borgaonkar & S. Shah, The XYY chromosome male—or syndrome, In *Progress in genetics,* 1975, *10,* 135. The medical and social ethics of applying such findings to the actual treatment of aggressive, antisocial personalities ("sociopathic" personalities) is discussed by F. Ausubel, J. Beckwith, & K. Janssen, The politics of genetic engineering: Who decides who is defective? *Psychology Today,* June 1974, *8,* 30–44. It is generally agreed, however, that definitive evidence is currently not available to substantiate either position unequivocally.

[6]The genic hypothesis is also seriously qualified by the facts that concordance rates in monozygotic twins average only about 50 per cent (even though monozygotic twins possess virtually identical genotypes), and that children are more likely to develop schizophrenia if one or both parents are schizophrenics than parents of schizophrenic children are likely to manifest this disorder themselves if their children are schizophrenic. Both facts suggest that environment factors play some role in the etiology of schizophrenia; in the latter instance it is evident that children are also subjected to a family climate of schizophrenia, in addition to

being genically predisposed to the disorder. It should be further emphasized that approximately 90 per cent of all schizophrenics do not have a schizophrenic parent (See D. Rosenthal, 1971, ibid).

It should be also pointed out that knowing that a given mental disorder is, in part, genically determined accounts only for its higher intra-familial incidence as compared to that found in the general population. It does *not* explain how genic factors *actually* contribute to its etiology. There is obviously a formidable leap between the initial biocatalytic effects of genes on fetal development, on the one hand, and the phenotypic appearance of behavioral dysfunction twenty or more years later, on the other. The *mediating* mechanisms or intervening variables (whether operating through hormones, enzymes, neurotransmittor brain amines; through such temperamental traits as introversion or extraversion, asociality or gregariousness; or through preferred coping mechanisms (e.g., withdrawal, projection of denial) are completely unknown at present, except in such relatively rare disorders as Huntington's Chorea and phenyl-pyruvic amentia. The fact that a monozygotic index case of schizophrenia never has a co-twin who manifests manic-depressive illness, and that the concordance rate in schizophrenia for monozygotic twins averages only 50 per cent (taking all twin studies into account), suggests that the genic mechanism involved in both major types of mental disorder (schizophrenia and manic depressive illness) is specific, rather than general, and that its penetrance is relatively low (thus suggesting a polygenic as opposed to a single-gene or Mendelian model).

Modern genetics also holds that genes do not determine traits or diseases but rather predispose individuals to develop them. Only at the moment of conception are genic factors singly determinative. After that point, extra-genic protoplasm, the larger tissue and fetal environment, substances in the maternal circulation transmitted through the placenta to the fetal circulation, bio-electric fields, proprioceptive and vestibular stimulation arising from fetal movement, differential concentrations of neurotransmittors in neural tissue, etc., all play a role in modifying the initial biocatalytic effects of genes. Later, the physical, social, inter-personal and cultural worlds further modify these genic factors and contribute to the determination of the trait or disease in question.

Finally, it is necessary to appreciate that knowledge about the genic contribution to the etiology of a particular mental disorder, as manifested by increased intrafamilial incidence makes no practical difference whatsoever, in the actual management of the disorder in question. Apart from relatively rare spontaneously occurring mutations, or exposure of the gonads to massive doses of radiation, an individual's genotype, for all practical purposes, is immutable (i.e., fixed at the moment of conception) and cannot be altered by *direct* manipulation. It is the *effects* of genes, rather than genes per se, that are susceptible to normal environmental intervention. Thus, human genes cannot be changed currently by means of direct manipulation as is possible in bacteria or viruses. It is only possible to compensate for the negative effects of unfavorable genes indirectly, (e.g., by giving insulin to diabetics or by surgically repairing a cleft palate or hare lip or, in the case of mental disorder, by providing a sheltered environment to persons who have low tolerance for stress).

The possibility of direct genic engineering in the mental disorders is presently in the realm of the distant future according to most molecular biologists (e.g., F. Ausubel, et al., 1974, ibid). This is the case because not only are the genic mechanisms involved polygenic, rather than single-gene or Mendelian, for the most part, but also even the specific genes predisposing a person to a particular mental disorder, and their chromosomal sites are completely unknown (except in certain rare cases of amentia and dementia). Thus, current revivals of the eugenics movement in the mental health field (parading under the banner of "genic engineering" are not only scientifically misleading but also, in the authors' opinion, professionally unethical when applied to the actual management of behavioral dysfunction (For a more complete discussion of the ethical issues involved, see F. Ausubel, et al., 1974, ibid.).

[7]Family studies of schizophrenia (e.g., R. W. Lidz & T. Lidz, Therapeutic considerations arising from the intense symbiotic needs of schizophrenia patients, in E. B. Brody & F. C. Redlich (Eds.), *Psychotherapy with schizophrenics,* New York: International Universities Press, 1952, pp. 168–178; Mahler (1952); S. Reichard & C. Tillman, Patterns of parent-child relationships in schizophrenia, *Psychiatry,* 1950, 247–257; N. Ackerman, Interlocking pathology in family relationships, In S. Rado & G. Daniels (Eds.), *Changing concepts in psychoanalytic medicine,* New York: Grune & Stratton, 1956; pp. 135–150; D. Jackson, Family interaction, family homeostasis, and some implications for conjoint family therapy. Paper presented at Academy of Psychoanalysis, May, 1956; T. Lidz, A. Cornelison, S. Fleck & D. Terry, The intrafamilial environment of schizophrenic patients, II. Marital schism and marital skew, *American* Journal of Psychiatry, 1957, *114,* 241–248; L. C. Wynne, I. Rychoff, J. Day, and S. H. Hersh. Pseudomutuality in the family relations of schizophrenics, *Psychiatry,* 1958, *21,* 205–208; E. B. Brody & F. C. Redlich (Eds.), 1952, ibid M. T. Singer & L. C. Wynne, Differentiating criteria of childhood schizophrenics, childhood neurotics, and young adult schizophrenics, *American Journal of Psychiatry,* 1963, *120,* 234–243; M. T. Singer & L. C. Wynne, Thought disorder and family relations of schizophrenics, *Archives of General Psychiatry,* 1965, *12,* 187–212; M. T. Singer, Family transactions and schizophrenia, I. Recent research, In The origins of schizophrenia Excepta Medica, International Congress Series, No. 151) have been severely criticized on methodological grounds, i.e., absence of matched control groups, impressionistic analyses of the data, unrepresentativeness of the samples studied in terms of type and severity of the disorder; no tests of statistical significance; very small samples; lack of a "double blind" technique, etc. (See D. Rosenthal & S. S. Kety (Eds.), *Family interaction in schizophrenia* especially paper by editors (Critique of family theories), *Science,* 1976, *192,* 879; and S. R. Hirsch and J. P. Leff, *Abnormalities in parents of schizophrenics: A review of the literature and an investigation of communication defects and deviances,* New York: Oxford University Press, 1975. The latter authors, after reviewing the methodological shortcomings of these studies, conclude that it is unwarranted to infer causality from simple correlation, and that longitudinal investigation of parental communication difficulties and abnormalities (with evidence demonstrating that such deviances antedate behavioral dysfunction in the child) is required to substantiate the family communication hypothesis advanced by the above-mentioned family theorists and researchers, and by such "family system" communication theorists as Bateson, D. Jackson, J. Haley, & J. Weakland (Toward a theory of schizophrenia, *Behavioral Science,* 1956, *1,* 251–264). The essence of the latter theory is that "double messages," vagueness, irrelevancy, and "lack of closure" in parents' communication with their children predisposes them to schizophrenia. It is just as plausible however, to conclude from the reported evidence that the child's preschizophrenic personality generates communication difficulties. In the empirical part of their study, Hirsch and Leff fail to confirm the parental communication hypothesis of Singer and Wynne which was tested mainly by projective (Rorschach and T.A.T.) techniques.

It may be concluded, therefore, that although there is much inferential evidence for the various family hypotheses of the etiology of schizophrenia, and that although many of these hypotheses are both plausible, and even compelling, in their logical cogency and credibility, *direct* confirmatory evidence is still lacking, largely because of vagueness and imprecision of formulation, and because of methodological inadequacies.

[8] Girls perceived their parents as more accepting and intrinsically valuing than boys did and satellized much more with their parents than the latter did. Non-satellizers scored higher than satellizers on test of self-perceived omnipotenence (referrable to both present and future) and were rated more highly by teachers than satellizers on such traits of ego maturity as executive independence and frustration tolerance. On tests of perceived similarity between own and parents' opinions, non-satellizers made lower scores than satellizers (Ausubel, et al, 1954).

[9] There is a pervasive tendency among American psychiatrists to over-diagnose schizophrenia in order to protect themselves from colleagues' criticism, since there is more opprobrium attached to not making the diagnosis of schizophrenia where it is warranted than failing to make this diagnosis where it is appropriate (D. F. Klein & J. M. Davis, *Diagnosis and drug treatment of psychiatric disorders,* Baltimore: Williams & Wilkins, 1969, p. 34). In fact, there is also a tendency in American psychiatry to diagnose *all* cases of bizarre behavior as schizophrenia, even if they do not meet any of the well-known phenomenological pathognomonic criteria [(e.g., K. Schneider's first-rank symptoms (*Die Schizophrenen Symptomverbande,* Berlin: Springer, 1942) and E. Bleuler's well-known primary and secondary criteria (Primary and secondary symptoms in schizophrenia, *Zeitschrift Geselschaft der Neurologie und der Psychiatrie,* 1930, *124,* 607)]. This tendency to overdiagnose schizophrenia is demonstrated by the fact that it is diagnosed twice as frequently by American than by British psychiatrists, even when the same case data are used (Cooper, et al, 1972). The operation of culturally-induced diagnostic biases in this discrepancy between American and British psychiatrists is emphasized by the fact that the reverse situation prevails in regard to manic-depressive illness. A comparable tendency among American psychiatrists is to label as "paranoid" all persecutory ideation, without first investigating whether it has a basis in reality, despite the fact that persecution in marital, parent-child, vocational, academic and inter-racial relationships is ubiquitous in our culture. The relative frequency of such serious forms of persecution as "child abuse" should be sufficient to confirm the reality of this fact to persons who even find it difficult to accept the proposition that parents are capable of emotionally rejecting their own children.

[10] Kinsey et al, (1948) also found very few cases of absent or low sex outlet among his adolescent population that could not be accounted for by serious physical or mental disorder.

[11] Direct evidence on this point by Kinsey, et al, (1948), L. A. Kirkendall (*Sex adjustments of young men,* New York: Harper, 1940), and W. S. Taylor (A critique of sublimation in males: A study of forty superior single men, *Genetic Psychology Monographs,* 1933, *13,* No. 1) indicates that once the sex drive is actually generated it is much too insistent to be successfully repressed. If it is not expressed in sexual intercourse, it is channeled into other direct *sexual* outlets (e.g., masturbation, petting) rather than into non-sexual compensatory (e.g., artistic, athletic, intellectual, peer-group) activities.

[12]More recently various psychoanalytic ego psychologists [(e.g., Ericson (1959); Mahler (1951, 1958, 1968)] and family therapists (e.g., Bowen, ibid; Lidz & Lidz, ibid; Ackerman, ibid.)] have placed considerable emphasis on such concepts as individuation and the achievement of ego identity as the basic task of ego development (in fact, as the only major task, thus ignoring all of the other aspects of ego maturity delineated in Chapter 4 of this book. Thus, they regard the perpetuation of the original symbiotic mother-child relationship as the principal cause of schizophrenia. They also tend to perceive the process of individuation proceeding in a straight line (i.e., from lesser to greater individuation) throughout the life cycle, instead of manifestating various fluctuations, and even reversals, in direction from infancy to childhood, adolescence, adult life, and senescence (see Chapter 4).

CHAPTER 2

[1]G. Allport, J. S. Bruner, & E. H. Jansdorff, (Personality under social catastrophe: Ninety life histories of the Nazi revolution, *Character and Personality,* 1941, *10,* 1–22) for example, found striking continuity in major personality traits and coping mechanisms between the pre-concentration camp personalities of anti-Nazis and their personality traits during and after incarceration in concentration camps during the Nazi era.

[2]Recent evidence indicates that there is a self-consistent tendency, generalized across different subject matters, for individuals to fall on a continuum between extreme "generalizers" and extreme "particularizers." This aspect of cognitive style has significant implications for ways of perceiving details or wholes in Rorschach cards and for learning potentially meaningful material (D. P. Ausubel & F. G. Schwartz, The effects of a generalizing-particularizing dimension of cognitive style on the retention of prose material, *Journal of General Psychology,* 1972, *87,* 55–58; F. G. Schwartz, Validation of the generalizing-particularizing dimension of cognitive style and its implications for meaningful learning, Unpublished Ph.D. thesis, City University of New York, 1972).

[3]See D. P. Ausubel, et al, (1954) for an elaboration of the thesis that *perceived* parent attitudes, rather than *actual* parent attitudes or behavior, influence ego development. In this study a perceived parent attitude rating scale, measuring parental acceptance-rejection and intrinsic versus extrinsic valuation by parents (with children rating their parents on real-life behaviors illustrating such attitudes) proved to be the only reliable (internally self-consistent) instrument. Projective exhibited techniques (e.g., Rorschach, T.A.T.) exhibited generality over different situations (test items).

[4]For a more complete presentation of the thesis that drives are summated, multiply-determined *states* of lowered thresholds of behavioral or perceptual responsiveness to particular drive-reducing behaviors, rather than instinctually derived libidinal or aggressive manifestations of "psychic energy" or actual stimuli (e.g., gonadal hormones, pain) that are innate and necessarily inevitable, see D. P. Ausubel, Introduction to a threshold concept of primary drives, *Journal of General Psychology,* 1956, 56, 209–229.

[5]As noted above the data of Kinsey, et al (1948), Kirkendall (1940) and Taylor (1933)

indicate that sex drives, once generated typically cannot be repressed. Kinsey's data also cast doubt on Freud's 'latency' period hypotheses (between the "genital" phase of psychosexual development at ages 5 to 6 and adolescence). These data convincingly demonstrate that children between ages 6 and puberty manifest much sexual interest, curiosity, and clandestine sexual experimentation (including attempted sexual intercourse). See also Ford & Beach (1951) and Malenowski (1927) for cross-cultural evidence.

[6]Sandor Rado was probably the first psychiatrist trained in psychoanalysis to challenge seriously this basic tenet of Freudian psychodynamics (See S. Rado, *Adaptational Psychodynamics,* New York: Science House, Chapter 3).

[7]Childen experiencing chronic failure in school tend to have unrealistically high or low levels of aspiration in laboratory tasks as compared to normally achieving children (P. S. Sears, Levels of aspiration in academically successful and unsuccessful children, *Journal of Abnormal & Social Psychology,* 1940, *35*: 498–536.

[8]Both laboratory and "real-life" levels of aspiration, as well as "goal tenacity" in hypothetical vocational situations, (in which frustration is encountered) unrealistic vocational choices (i.e., choices incompatible with interests demonstrated by vocational interest), unrealistic needs for high-prestige types of occupations, and high levels of anxiety are found in school children who score high on paper-and-pencil inventories of anxiety and on Rorshach signs of anxiety (See D. P. Ausubel, H. M. Schiff, & M. Goldman, Qualitative characteristics in the learning process associated with anxiety, *Journal of Abnormal & Social Psychology,* 1953, *48*, 537–547; D. P. Ausubel, et al, Perceived parent attitudes as determinants of children's ego structure, *Child Development,* 1954, *25*, 173–183; D. P. Ausubel & H. M. Schiff, A level of aspiration approach to the measurement of goal tenacity, *Journal of General Psychology,* 1955, *52*, 97–110; and D. P. Ausubel & M. P. Zeleny, "Real-life" measures of academic and vocational aspirations in adolescents: Relation laboratory measures. *Child Development,* 1953, *24*, 155–168.

[9]Children also typically identify wrong-doing in others long before they are capable of acknowledging comparable wrong-doing in themselves (See Chapter 7).

[10]These disturbances in the self-critical faculty may be considered the proximate variable in the etiology of manic and depressive states. These states are typically found as a "last-ditch" defence against, and complication, of long-standing neurotic anxiety respectively, in which the individual lacks intrinsic self-esteem and is dependent on compensatorily and unrealistically high needs for achievement as a basis for all of his self-esteem (a condition commonly existing in non-satellizers) (See Chapters 9 and 10).

CHAPTER 6

[1]This chapter is based on the research conducted by investigators working in the segregated black slums of Northern cities of the United States, and on the senior author's eight years of clinical experience with black adolescent drug addicts in East Harlem, New York City. It is highly probable that these findings do not apply, at least in part, to the ego

development of black children growing up in segregated Southern areas of the United States or in the Union of South Africa where different family structures (e.g., non-matriarchal or extended family groupings) and parental and cultural pressures and expectations may prevail.

I am indebted to my colleague Dr. Henry McCurtis of the Bronx Psychiatric Center for suggesting the need for the above qualification.

[2]This practice not only retards the acquisition of an appropriate social sex and gender role among black adolescents, but may also facilitate the development of a homosexual sex orientation.

Index